Early Social Cognition
Understanding Others in the First Months of Life

Early Social Cognition
Understanding Others in the First Months of Life

•⁂•

Edited by
Philippe Rochat
Emory University

LEA LAWRENCE ERLBAUM ASSOCIATES, PUBLISHERS
1999 Mahwah, New Jersey London

Lawrence Erlbaum Associates, Inc., Publishers
10 Industrial Avenue
Mahwah, NJ 07430

Cover design by Kathryn Houghtaling Lacey

Library of Congress Cataloging-in-Publication Data

Early social cognition : understanding others in the first months of life / edited by Philippe Rochat.
p. cm.
Includes bibliographical references and indexes.
ISBN 0-8058-2829-X (cloth : alk. paper)
1. Social interaction in infants. 2. I. Rochat, Philippe, 1950-
BF720.S63E37 1998
155.42'23—dc21 98-24653
CIP

Books published by Lawrence Erlbaum Associates are printed on acid-free paper, and their bindings are chosen for strength and durability.

Printed in the United States of America

10 9 8 7 6 5 4 3 2 1

Contents

Preface vii

Part I: Origins of Social Cognition

1 Social–Cognitive Development in the First Year 3
Philippe Rochat and Tricia Striano

2 The Ontogeny of Human Infant Face Recognition: Orogustatory, Visual, and Social Influences 35
Elliott M. Blass

3 Vitality Contours: The Temporal Contour of Feelings as a Basic Unit for Constructing the Infant's Social Experience 67
Daniel N. Stern

4 Social Cognition and the Self 81
Michael Lewis

Part II: Early Sensitivity to Social Contingencies

5 Early Socio–Emotional Development: Contingency Perception and the Social-Biofeedback Model 101
György Gergely and John S. Watson

6 Infants' Sensitivity to Imperfect Contingency in Social Interaction 137
Ann E. Bigelow

7 Young Infants' Perception of Adult Intentionality: Adult Contingency and Eye Direction — 155
Darwin Muir and Sylvia Hains

8 Early Perception of Social Contingencies and Interpersonal Intentionality: Dyadic and Triadic Paradigms — 189
Jacqueline Nadel and Hélène Tremblay-Leveau

Part III: Early Monitoring of Others

9 Action Analysis: A Gateway to Intentional Inference — 215
Dare A. Baldwin and Jodie A. Baird

10 Gaze Following and the Control of Attention — 241
Chris Moore

11 Infants' Distinction Between Animate and Inanimate Objects: The Origins of Naive Psychology — 257
Diane Poulin-Dubois

12 Emotion Regulation and the Emergence of Joint Attention — 281
Lauren B. Adamson and Connie L. Russell

Part IV: Commentary

13 Social Cognition Before the Revolution — 301
Michael Tomasello

Author Index — 315

Subject Index — 327

Preface

In recent years, an abundance of clever experiments have provided novel information on perception, action, and representation of physical objects at the onset of development. This new wave of findings supports theories that revise traditional views on the origins of physical knowledge. In comparison, the origins of social knowledge did not receive the same attention from basic researchers. This is paradoxical considering that people are obviously more vital entities for infants than midsize physical objects.

The first systematic observations of young infants' visual scanning of the environment made in the 1960s demonstrated the robust preference for facelike displays. These kinds of pioneer observations did not stir basic research in infancy from focusing mainly on the origins of physical cognition. Considering that Piaget has been a major target of theoretical revision, his focus on the physical aspect of reality constructed by infants and children might be his most pervasive legacy in the realm of contemporary research in infancy. But faces and people are primary attractors for neonates and certainly the primary reality they perceive and act on. Animated, self-propelled, planful, intentional, moody, reciprocal, talkative, caring: People are more than physical things. They call for special knowledge.

In recent years, much stimulating research has emerged in relation to children's theories of mind, construed as the understanding of others' intentions, beliefs, and desires. Within this context, there is a renewed interest in the developmental origins of social cognition. This book is an expression of this new interest, assembling current conceptualizations and research on the precursors of joint engagement, language, and explicit theories of mind. The focus is on what announces such remarkable development.

From the first signs of social attunement to the adoption of an intentional stance (understanding of others as intentional, planful agents), there is a 12-month developmental period. This is a giant step over a relatively short period of developmental time, and many questions remain regarding the determinants of such development and what changes over the first year of social cognitive development. As it stands, developmental research on early social cognition has focused mainly on changes occurring by the end of the first year to the beginning of the second year, with the emergence of new communicative and symbolic skills such as joint engagement, social referencing, gestural, and verbal communication. Furthermore, much research effort has been devoted to the investigation of the onset of theories of mind at around 4 to 5 years of age. The recent surge of research on young children's theories of mind has paralleled the wave of research on physical knowledge in infancy. Aside from their historical coincidence, these two research waves also share the common feature of leaving open questions regarding the early development of social cognition. What development precedes and announces the social cognitive changes occurring by the end of the first year? The goal of this book is to address these questions with new ideas, experimental paradigms, and fresh data. Contributors were chosen for the originality of their research and theoretical conceptualization, providing a relatively broad spectrum of current basic research on early social cognition. The contributions are testimonies of up and coming research in infancy with a focus on the origins of social knowledge.

There are four parts to the book. The first part groups four chapters dealing with the nature and development of social cognition in infancy. Each contribution provides a different view on the important features of social cognition in the first months of life. Rochat and Striano (chap. 1) provide a survey of social cognitive development in the first year. The main idea conveyed in their chapter is that intersubjectivity or sense of shared experience is the foundational aspect of social cognition developing between 2 and 9 months of age. Using infant facial recognition as a paradigm, Blass (chap. 2) provides a psychobiological perspective on changes in the determinants of social cognition by neonates and young infants. Stern (chap. 3) proposes that infants develop important knowledge regarding the subjective life of others by detecting invariant temporal features in their action, what he describes as *vitality contours*. Finally, Lewis (chap. 4) puts forth the idea that the origins of social cognition cannot be considered independently of the development of self-knowledge.

The second part of the book consists of four chapters, all providing recent empirical findings on the developing ability by young infants to detect whether caretakers and social partners are attentive and responsive to their own behavior in social exchanges. They all discuss the issue of an early sensitivity to social contingencies as an important determinant of early social cognition. Gergely and Watson (chap. 5) propose a model in which contingency detection and production (i.e., adult mirroring) in early face-to-face social exchanges form the cornerstone of early social–emotional development. Bigelow (chap 6), Muir and Hains (chap. 7), and Nadel and Tremblay-Leveau (chap. 8) provide numerous new data on the early development of social contingency detection. In all, these contributions demonstrate the rich development of social attunement in the first year in which the early sensitivity to social contingencies is viewed as a central mechanism.

The third part of the book assembles four chapters on the early development of infants' ability to monitor others in their action (Baldwin & Baird, chap. 9), their gazing (Moore, chap. 10), their animacy (Poulin-Dubois, chap. 11), and their emotion (Adamson & Russell, chap. 12). All these chapters have in common the assumption that it is based on the fine perceptual analysis of other people's behavior that young infants develop social understanding. It is based on such complex analysis that infants prepare themselves to take the intentional stance by the second year, when they start to show evidence of monitoring attention, emotion, and inferring intentions in others. The final chapter (Tomasello, chap. 13) offers a commentary on the contributions as a whole, discussing the basic theoretical assumptions guiding current research on early social cognition. Tomasello identifies the conceptual strength and weaknesses of the work presented, suggesting interesting avenues for future research. At a personal level, I take the opportunity to thank Mike Tomasello for his friendship and for opening my eyes to the importance of considering the social determinants of cognitive development. I would not have edited this volume without his social influence. This is for you, Mike!

—*Philippe Rochat*

Part I

ORIGINS OF SOCIAL COGNITION

Chapter **1**

Social-Cognitive Development in the First Year

Philippe Rochat
Tricia Striano
Emory University

Recent progress in infancy research demonstrates that early on, infants perceive physical objects and expect them to behave according to core principles. These principles include the fact that objects are substantial, occupy space, and cannot be in two places at the same time (Spelke, 1991). Because infants appear to apply these physical principles at an age when they cannot yet have much hands-on experience with objects (2 to 4 months), and unless we assume that these principles are prewired in the neonate, it is likely that they are acquired via active contemplation of things behaving around them (see the description of the "astronomer infant" by Lécuyer, 1989; or the " 'couch potato' infant" by Willatts, 1997). The numerous studies demonstrating precocious physical knowledge using preferential looking, habituation, or violation of expectation paradigms suggest that this knowledge does not develop primarily from active causation whereby infants learn about objects by analyzing the consequences of their own actions on them. Is this also the case for the development of early social cognition? In this chapter, we suggest that the developing understanding of people in infancy cannot be reduced to what we know regarding the precocious development of physical knowledge. People are more complex than objects, and the development of social knowledge is based on specific processes that reflect this greater complexity.

Intimate, one-to-one relationships are the craddle of social understanding. Although much can be learned from watching people at a distance and not being directly engaged in a social exchange, such learning cannot replace the learning opportunity provided by shared social experiences. This is particularly evident when considering the developmental origins of social cognition. Infants do not develop a social understanding by merely engaging in social "voyeurism," observing and actively monitoring people behaving around them. Rather than as voyeurs, they learn by engaging in reciprocal exchanges with others. Some 50 years ago, René Spitz made this point clear with tragic footage of infants from crowded orphanages. Deprived of one-to-one contacts with caretakers, these infants showed pervasive behavioral stereotypes, rocking their head back and forth as if negating any contact with the outside world. These infants fell back within themselves rather than opening up to the world of people. Unresponsive to social solicitations, they lost the little social learning opportunity left to them.

In general, social cognition can be construed as *the process by which individuals develop the ability to monitor, control, and predict the behavior of others.* This ability entails various degrees of understanding, from the perceptual discrimination of feature characteristics and emotional expressions, to the complex represention of intentions and beliefs as determinants of behavior (theories of mind). In this chapter, we present our view on the early ontogeny of social cognition. This view tries to capture important transitions in the development of social cognitive abilities between birth and 12 months of age. Three developmental periods are described with a particular emphasis on two key transitions by 2 and 9 months postnatal age. We review recent empirical findings supporting our contention that these transitions correspond to radical changes or revolutions in the way infants interact with and understand others (for a summary, see Table 1.1 in the conclusion of the chapter). At birth and in the course of the first 6 weeks, infants manifest an essentially innate sensitivity to social stimuli. During this period (the newborn period), neonates display social attunement. We qualify their stance towards people as *attentional*, with no signs of intersubjectivity. By the second month, infants are presented as manifesting the first signs of shared experience (primary intersubjectivity). This manifestation coincides with the emergence of a novel sense of self as agent in the environment. This represents a first key transition in early social cognitive development (*2-month revolution*), marked by the emergence of a sense of shared experience (intersubjectivity) and reciprocity with others, as part of a new general stance taken by the infant, *the contemplative stance.* Based on recent empirical findings, we try to demonstrate that the early intersubjectivity manifested by young infants in a dyadic context (primary intersubjectivity), and social cognition in general, changes in significant ways between 2 and 6 months, announcing the well-documented social cognitive abilities that emerge by the end of the first year in a triadic context (*9-month revolution*) and the emergence of secondary intersubjectivity. Overall, we discuss social cognitive development in the first year as the transition from a tight coupling between perception and organized action systems at birth to the sense of self and others as differentiated and reciprocal agents by 2 months that leads to the sense of self and others as differentiated and reciprocal agents who can reciprocate as well as *cooperate* by the end of the first year. At this point in development, infants are starting to take an *intentional stance* in addition to the contemplative stance they develop by 2 months of age. In a final discussion, we speculate on the possible mechanisms underlying this development. But first, we set the stage by presenting some general considerations regarding the specificity of social knowledge in comparison to physical knowledge and the specific processes underlying social cognition, namely intersubjective mechanisms.

SPECIFICITY OF SOCIAL KNOWLEDGE

The understanding of people determines special knowledge and entails much more than physical knowledge. Although people have bodies, and physical knowledge can account for part of their behavior (e.g., the fact that they can move on their own, can hide or fall, are subject to the forces of gravity, and cannot be at two different locations at the same time), monitoring people and predicting what they are going to do next entails skills that go far beyond physical understanding. Understanding people also defines special processes. Social cognition entails the reading of affects, emotions, intentions, and subtle reciprocities: all the things that make people fundamentally different from objects. In other words, it entails the understanding of a private or *dispositional* world, what people feel and what characterizes their individual inclinations. But how do we get access to such understanding?

To a large extent, people reveal themselves in the way they reciprocate to us and how, via reciprocity, they convey a sense of shared experience. The same is true for animals and pets. Understanding an animal of a particular species observed in the wild or at a zoo, even for extended periods of time, is different from the understanding of the same animal raised as a pet and with whom we share our life. A sense of shared experience adds to social understanding and gives deeper access to the dispositional characteristics of individuals, whether they are humans or nonhumans. The sense of shared experience that emerges from reciprocity is captured by the term *intersubjectivity*. We will use this term extensively in this chapter, because we believe that the emerging sense of shared experience determines the early development of social cognition.

Intersubjectivity entails a basic differentiation between the self and others as well as a capacity to compare and project one's own private experience onto another (e.g., the "like me" stance). Pet owners obviously understand the nonequivalence between themselves and their animal. In the meantime, there is a projection of shared experience (empathic feelings) that bridges the difference between them. Such projective ability is at the core of social understanding. It is instrumental to the understanding of others. Interestingly, the subjective projection appears to be a recent development in primate evolution. Primate species with closer evolutionary links to humans display more frequent and varied empathic behavior to either conspecific or individuals of other species (de Waal, 1996). There is a possible link in phylogeny between the capacity for intersubjective projection and levels of social cognition. We will see that evidence concurs in suggesting such a link exists in early ontogeny.

In reviewing the recent flow of experimental research on infancy, we learn much about the nature of physical knowledge at the origins of development (Baillargeon, 1995; Spelke, Breinlinger, Macomber, & Jacobson, 1992) and comparatively little about the nature of social knowledge. Based on clever experiments, we know about the early onset of object permanence, counting ability, adaptive actions toward objects, and the early understanding of how things move in the world. In comparison, we know little regarding what infants understand about people at the origins of development, what makes people attractive, recognizable and predictable for the infant. This is somehow ironical considering the commonsensical view that infants develop social skills from an early age (Stern, 1977) and that people are what babies seem to care the most about from birth. Infants' proclivity toward people is obviously adaptive, their survival depending on them directly.

Aside from the fact that people are the main source of nurturance for infants, early behavior and the distribution of attention in newborns also reflect the fact that people provide richer perceptual encounters compared to any other objects in the environment. Neonates display a particular attraction toward people, in particular to the sounds, movements, and features of the human face (Johnson & Morton, 1991; Maurer, 1985). Social cognition probably originates from this innate propensity to devote particular attention to faces. But attending to people is different from attending to physical things. They are more complex entities to learn about and to predict. So how do infants manage to know people? We suggest that they do so primarily by building a sense of reciprocity and developing a sense of shared experiences.

INTERSUBJECTIVITY AS SOCIAL COGNITION

The royal way to crack the surface of people's dispositional world, hence to access crucial information from which their behavior can be monitored, predicted, and controlled, is to *reciprocate* with them. We propose here that the foundation of social cognition is a sense of shared experience or intersubjectivity developing in infancy in the context of intimate, face-to-face interaction. Before we discuss the importance and function of intersubjectivity in early social cognition, we define three basic categories of subjective experiences that are too often confused in the literature and that form the affective determinants of social exchanges from birth. These basic categories of subjective experiences correspond to *feelings*, *affects*, and *emotions*.

- *Feelings* are construed here as the perception of specific private experiences such as pain, hunger, or frustration. In comparison to affects (see next), this category of subjective experiences is in general shorter in duration and terminates following particular actions such as feeding for hunger, comfort for pain, or fulfilling a goal for frustration.
- *Affects* qualify the perception of a general mood or perceived private tone that exists as a background to both feelings and emotions (see next). Affects are diffused and protracted in comparison to feelings. They fluctuate along a continuum from low, general tone (depression) to high tone (inflation). To use a weather metaphor, affects correspond to the perception of the global pressure system at a particular point in time and as it fluctuates from high to low pressure, and vice versa, over protracted time sequences.
- *Emotions* are the actual observable (public) expressions of feelings and affects by invariant movement dynamics, postures, postural changes, and facial displays as in the behavioral expressions of pain, joy, disgust, sadness, surprise, and anger. Emotions have specific, identifiable features (Darwin, 1872/1965) that serve a communicative function and give public access to what is experienced privately, namely feelings and affects.

Feelings, affects, and emotions are three kinds of basic subjective experience that are part of infants' private sense of self, from birth and long before they can talk and theorize about them. Neonates clearly have feelings and affects that they express via specific emotional displays such as pain, hunger, or disgust (Hopkins & van Palthe, 1987; Steiner, 1974; Wolff, 1987). In addition to these private experiences, they also demonstrate early on long lasting temperamental traits and particular affective baselines (Kagan & Snidman, 1991). A central question regarding early social cognition is, How do infants start to relate their own private experience to the private experience of others? In our view, this question is central as we propose that intersubjectivity is the cradle of social cognition. If infants from birth have a subjective life, what they primarily develop in their first social relationships is intersubjectivity or the sense of shared feelings, affects, and emotions.

Intimate interaction with people is the ultimate probing ground of how infants feel and what they experience from within. It is the way by which the sense of shared experience or intersubjectivity develops. Reciprocal exchanges are associated with the coregulation of affects, feelings, and behavior (emotions). In such exchanges, the affects, feelings, and emotions of one person *echo* the affects, feelings, and emotions of the other, either by mirroring, contagion, or merely contingent reactions within a short-time window. This is what characterizes, for example, the mother–infant system while engaging in playful interactions and the emotional coregulation scaffolded by games such as peekaboo or "I'm gonna get you" plays.

The echoing of affects, feelings, and emotions that takes place in reciprocal interaction between young infants and their caretakers is at the origin of intersubjectivity, a necessary element to the development of more advanced social cognition, including theory of mind. Such echoing offers infants the opportunity to match their own private world of experience with the world of others, whether it is a diffuse feeling of well being, sadness, or the intense realization of a precise thought. Before language and the emergence of conventional symbolic systems that enable children to become increasingly explicit about their own experience and to match their private experiences with those of others, dyadic face-to-face interactions and nonverbal play games are the primary source of intersubjectivity. From birth, parents and caretakers nurture the opportunity for infants to match their own experience with theirs. Parents' initiations of face-to-face play interactions with repetitive gestures, particular vocal intonation, and exaggerated facial expressions are the main course of the social regimen imposed probably to all infants, and at least to all the Western middle-class infants who are overwhelmingly represented in our research. These interactions are typically a running commentary by the parent of how the infant should feel.

Here is a casual observation we made that illustrates the kind of emotional scaffolding young infants are typically provided with in a dyadic context: a father lowers his 2-month-old daughter toward the water surface of a swimming pool. He holds her in a way that he can have a clear view of her face and that she can see his face in full view. While staring at her intensely, the father gently lets one of her bare feet touch the water and briskly removes it while commenting with a loud, high-pitched voice, "Oootch it's cold!" In the meantime, he displays a greatly exaggerated expression of pain. This routine is repeated many times in a row, with appropriate pause allowing the infant to regain her calm.

In this observation, the parent creates an emotionally charged context in anticipation of particular feelings in his infant (fear, pleasure, surprise, etc.). He monitors the child to capture the expression of the anticipated feeling in order to echo its expression in an easily discriminable (exaggerated) and contingent manner. It is as if the father is interviewing his daughter to check on her feelings and to create a situation in which he can show empathy and demonstrate his sheer pleasure in being with her. It is doubtful that the father wants to give his daughter her first swimming lesson or to teach her about temperature, liquid, or the dangers of water. Note that this demonstration of empathy requires intimate, one-to-one contacts. It mobilizes the full attention of the adult and requires a great sense of timing and monitoring. What is remarkable is that the vast majority of parents demonstrate a natural talent for highly sophisticated interactional skills with their infant, sometimes referred to as *intuitive parenting* (Papousek & Papousek, 1995). The propensity to express empathy through the echoing of affects and feelings in highly scaffolded ways is part of normal parenting and, we propose, the primary source of intersubjectivity, which itself is at the origin of much social cognitive development.

But what is gained from shared experience? Why do young infants bother trying to match their own experience of feelings with that of other people? Feelings and affects are unquestionably major determinants of behavior and are crucial for the monitoring, prediction, and control of others' behavior, whether we please them or not, whether they are attentive to our actions or not. This can mean much for young infants who depend on others to survive. Because of the prolonged immaturity characterizing human infancy (Bruner, 1972), there is a pronounced necessity in human infants to relate to caretakers and to maintain proximity with them. Developing intersubjectivity allows infants to monitor and predict more accurately the behavior of those they depend on. Furthermore, the development of intersubjectivity is probably linked to the emergence of an understanding of intentions and beliefs underlying people's actions. Taking the perspective of others and predicting how another person would feel in a given situation is indeed a prerequisite to most theory of mind tasks children start to succeed in by the third year (Perner, 1991).

We propose that intersubjectivity is the foundational aspect of social cognition and that the early development of a sense of shared experience is a prerequisite for understanding what drives other people's behavior. Social cognition is based on the matching of self and others' experience within the context of dyadic reciprocal exchanges that infants can grasp the dispositional characteristics of others, and ultimately their intentions and beliefs. It is based on the early development of intersubjectivity that infants can eventually take into consideration the perspective of others, in addition to, or in coordination with their own. This ability is indexed by social cognitive skills emerging by the end of the first year, such as joint attention and symbolic gestures (Bakeman & Adamson, 1984; Bates, Benigni, Bretherton, Camaioni, & Volterra, 1979). The mindblindness of autistic children (Baron-Cohen, 1995; Hobson, 1993) and its devastating interpersonal consequences is linked to a lack or hindered development of intersubjectivity. The absence of intersubjectivity deprives individuals of the opportunity to develop prosocial behaviors, empathy, and moral judgments that are obviously important by-products of developing social cognition. But how do infants develop such ability? When does intersubjectivity start to develop as the foundation of infants' monitoring, control, and prediction of other people's behavior? We turn to these questions now, starting with the status of social cognition at birth and through the course of the first 6 weeks of postnatal development.

NEWBORN STAGE

In the past, newborns were often described as undifferentiated in their action (Mahler, Pine, & Bergman, 1975) and in a state of fusion with the environment (Wallon, 1942/1970; Piaget, 1952). Within the psychoanalytical tradition, Mahler et al. (1975) described newborns as in an initial stage of *normal autism*: ". . . the reaction to any stimulus that surpasses the threshold of reception in the weeks of normal autism (first two months) is global, diffuse, syncretic—reminiscent of fetal life. This means that there is only a minimal degree of differentiation, and that various organismic functions are interchangeable" (p. 43). This view is now seriously challenged in light of recent evidence suggesting that newborns do express some rudiments of a differentiation between themselves, people, and objects.

In a recent study (Rochat & Hespos, 1997), we found that newborns tend to respond differentially to either external or self-administered tactile stimulation. We recorded infants rooting responses following either self-stimulation of the perioral region via spontaneous hand–mouth coordination or following a stimulation of the same region by the experimenter's rubbing her index finger on the baby's cheek. We found that newborns tend to root more frequently to external tactile stimulation than to tactile self-stimulation. These results are the product of multiple analyses, most of them failing to show the phenomenon. However weak the phenomenon is, it suggests that infants at birth express rudiments of a differential responding to self versus externally caused tactile stimulation. Self-stimulation corresponded to a double touch experience (hand touching the cheek and cheek touching the hand) whereas the stimulation from the experimenter entailed a single touch experience (cheek stimulation only). Newborns appear to discriminate between these two experiences, hence suggesting rudiments of a differentiation between what originates from the self and from the environment.

In relation to people, the numerous studies reporting imitation in the newborn demonstrate that from birth, infants are capable of visually perceiving others as differentiated from the self, the behavior of others being used by the infant as a model for self-generated action (Meltzoff & Moore, 1977). The fact that newborns are capable of matching proprioceptively actions they see performed by others (e.g., tongue protrusion) does not fair well with the idea of an initial state of fusion and undifferentiation. In relation to objects, although newborns' ability to interact with them is drastically hindered by early postural, motor, and visual immaturity, recent research suggests that they do manifest visual discrimination and selective attention to certain object configurations. Facelike line drawings are tracked significantly more by newborns than is a scrambled drawing of a face or a blank display (Goren, Sarty, & Wu, 1975; Johnson & Morton, 1991). Newborns are shown to discriminate facelike patterns, and this discrimination provides evidence that they are capable of attending selectively to particular stimulus configurations, despite their poor visual acuity (Slater, 1997). This selective attention further suggests that from birth, infants behave as differentiated entities orienting and attending to meaningful features of their environment. Although a differentiation between self and environment is manifest at birth, it is still fragile, very limited, and linked to basic, probably prewired functional propensities to respond in particular ways to specific stimulus configurations.

The initial differentiation between infants and the environment is tightly linked to the general attunement infants bring with them at birth to tap into fundamental environmental resources, and in particular to people who provide food, care, and the comfort they need to survive (see also Blass, chap. 2, this volume). From a functional or ecological point of view, the behavioral repertoire of the newborn does include action systems that are goal oriented toward specific features of the environment affording particular acts. For example, the rooting response of newborns following a perioral tactile stimulation includes coordinated mouth opening and tongue protrusion, in addition to head orientation in the direction of the stimulation. This response is more than an automatic reflex arc. It is a complex act that is part of the feeding system, considering that the rooting response is hunger dependent and brought to completion when the mouth comes in contact with the nipple or something to suck on (Koupernik & Dailly, 1968; Rochat, 1993; Rochat & Hespos, 1997). There are functional goals underlying infant behavior at birth: calming as in the case of hand-mouth coordination (Blass, Fillion, Rochat, Hoffmeyer, & Metzger, 1989; Butterworth & Hopkins, 1988); communicating as in the case of imitation (Maratos, 1982; Meltzoff & Moore, 1977); exploring as in the case of visual, olfactory, taste, and oral-haptic discrimination (Crook & Lipsitt, 1976; MacFarlane, 1975; Rochat, 1983; Slater, 1997), and feeding functions as in the case of sucking and rooting (Crook & Lipsitt, 1976). Although newborns do not behave randomly but rather act in relation to meaningful environmental resources, their apparent goal orientation corresponds to tight perception–action couplings within a limited repertoire of action (sucking, looking, grasping) and in relation to few objects (things to suck on, feed on, and get comfort from). These action systems are functional at birth and probably even before birth when considering fetuses' sucking behavior, hand-to-mouth ontacts, and sensitivity to particular features of the human voice (De Casper & Fifer, 1980; De Casper, Lecanuet, Busnel, Granier-Deferre, & Maugeais, 1994; De Casper & Spence, 1986; de Vries, Visser, & Prechtl, 1982; Rochat, 1993).

If there is goal orientation at birth, hence an initial infant-environment (including people) differentiation, it is prescribed by the codesign of action systems that are functional at birth (or before birth) and specific features of the environment that exist independently of the infant as goals or affordances for action. The prescribed goal orientation of newborn action means that at this initial stage of development, infant perception and action are essentially directly or tightly linked, in the sense that infants do not yet show any clear signs of an explicit awareness or decoupling between behavior and the goal that guides it. In other words, there is no strong evidence of planning and deliberate acts in neonates. They appear, on the contrary, to respond directly and selectively to particular stimulus configurations (e.g., facelike displays, self-stimulation, people, things in motion) with no clear signs of a differentiation between their behavior and the goal it is geared to, such as probing, coregulating, or anticipating the behavior of things and people in the environment.

At this initial stage of development, we propose that there is no evidence of an explicit awareness of self and others. Newborns might be sensitive and attuned to others, responding to others in a differentiated way, but they do not show many signs of genuine reciprocity and deliberate probing of the social environment. Their stance toward people and things in the environment is essentially *attentional.* The attentional stance is brought by the infant at birth. We will consider now how, at around 6 weeks of age, the attentional stance is complemented with a radically new stance: the contemplative stance that emerges—with a smile.

TWO MONTH REVOLUTION: CONTEMPLATIVE STANCE

We propose that up to approximately 6 weeks, the behavior of healthy term infants is analogous to the behavior of healthy fetuses in the last 2 months of pregnancy. The recent use of ultrasonic techniques for the study of fetal behavior revealed a striking continuity between pre- and postnatal behavior (de Vries et al., 1982; Prechtl, 1984). In a nutshell, the behavior displayed by the newborn infant during the first 6 weeks of life resembles late fetal behavior and seems to be controlled by similar mechanisms. It appears that newborns up to approximately 6 weeks behave in many ways as externalized fetuses. Their wake and sleep cycle is comparable, and many of the sensory-motor coordinations expressed by neonates are remarkably similar to what they expressed in the womb: sucking, orienting, hand–mouth coordination, stepping movements, eye movements, and so forth (Prechtl, 1984). At the level of experience and information processing, studies have shown that fetuses learn and are capable of complex perceptual discrimination (De Casper & Fifer, 1980). There is not only a continuity between prenatal and postnatal development at the level of action but also at the level of experience. In their research, De Casper and Fifer provided evidence that what fetuses learn in utero probably transfers ex utero, reporting that few hour-old infants tend to prefer their mother's voice over the voice of a female stanger reading the same story.

There are no clear signs of a discontinuity in pre- and postnatal development until the beginning of the second month. By 6 weeks, some important behavioral transformations occur, the emergence of externally elicited smiling (as opposed to the "reflex" or automatic smile of newborns) being certainly among the most welcomed and evident index of a major transformation (Spitz, 1965; Wolf, 1987). To parents and attentive observers, the emergence of smiling as a positive emotional display that is oriented *outward*, toward a person or in response to an external event, this new behavior indexes a dramatic change. Parents commonly report that they discover a person in their infant. It is experienced by caretakers as a sort of psychological birth of their infant, the emergence of a new awareness and opening up to the outside world—a dramatic transition from a primarily inward to a newly outward control of behavior. Much converging empirical evidence supports the intimate impression of parents and caretakers regarding the transition indexed by externally elicited smiling.

By 6 weeks, infants demonstrate a sudden shift in state regulation and in particular a dramatic increase in the amount of time they spend in an alert-awake state (Wolff, 1987). Note that it is in this state that infants are shown to attend to and process much information regarding the outside world (Wolff, 1987). Interestingly, by 6 weeks infants also demonstrate a marked peak in crying and fussing duration (Barr, Bakeman, Konner, & Adamson, 1987; Brazelton, 1962; Rebelsky & Black, 1972; St. James-Roberts & Halil, 1991). This peak is another index of a change in state regulation and possibly a change in the communicative function of crying, which becomes more instrumental, newly modulated by environmental and social factors. Although much interindividual variability exists, the crying peak by 6 weeks postnatal age, the coemergence of externally elicited smiling, and an increased alert-awake state are remarkably robust overall and across very different caregiving practices (Barr, Bakeman, Konner, & Adamson, 1987).

The sudden increase in awake alertness by 6-week-old infants does not merely mark a change in state regulation but also a cognitive change. They attend more to the world around them and, more important, attend to the world differently. Infant visual inspection of facelike displays illustrates this point. Over 20 years ago, Maurer and Salapatek (1976) documented a marked change in the way newborn and 2-month-olds scanned visually a two-dimensional schematic representation of a face. Newborns scan principally the outer boundary of the display, as 2-month-olds start to explore systematically the internal features of the face. This transition corresponds to changes in the externality effect reported by Bushnell (1979) at around the same age. In particular, Bushnell reported that before 2 months of age, infants detect only external changes in compound stimuli such as a shape enclosed in another, larger one. They discriminated changes in the larger (external) shape but not in the enclosed (internal) one. In contrast, by 2 months infants start noticing both external and internal changes. In the context of face perception, the new focus of attention to internal features of a configuration allows the infant to pick up important perceptual cues from which people and their emotions, hence their affects and feelings, can eventually be recognized. We view this attentional shift as the variable controlling for the emergence and development of primary intersubjectivity, or the sense of shared experience developing in a dyadic context. We propose that this shift indexes the true origin of social cognition.

Newborn infants have been shown to turn their heads and eyes significantly more to track a two-dimensional facelike schematic display than a display with the same features but scrambled (Goren, Sarty, & Wu, 1975). These intriguing findings that suggest an early propensity for discrimination and enhanced tracking of faces have been replicated in more controlled conditions by Johnson, Dziurawiec, Ellis, and Morton (1991). Johnson & Morton (1991) proposed that what underlies the newborn discrimination of facelike display is an orienting subcortical mechanism (labeled *conspec* mechanisms, in reference to *conspecifics*). Accordingly, it is a discrimination expressed within a prewired subcortically mediated orienting mechanism toward faces. This mechanism and the apparent perceptual discrimination it underlies does not entail any detection of similarities or differences among faces. This latter function is assumed by another cortically mediated mechanism (*conlern*) that does not appear before the second month (Johnson & Morton, 1991). Again, this empirically based account of the early ontogeny of face perception and recognition is articulated around a key transition at around 2 months of age, consistent with our view of a 2-month revolution.

The 2-month revolution is also evident when considering the development of imitiative responses of young infants between birth and 6 weeks of age. In their classic research that was followed by a host of related studies from different laboratories, Meltzoff and Moore (1977) demonstrated that newborn infants are capable of imitating facial movements performed by an adult experimenter, in particular tongue protrusion gestures. These authors proposed that early imitation is mediated by an active intermodal matching, in particular a matching between visual information (perception of the model) and proprioceptive motor information (reproduction and execution of the imitative response.) An alternative explanation of neonatal imitation is that this response is mediated by innate releasing mechanisms. According to this latter interpretation, rather than active matching by the infant, certain facial displays of the adult trigger a preorganized fixed-action pattern in the infant (Abravanel & Sigafoos, 1984; Bjorklund, 1987; Jacobson, 1979.) Contrary to Meltzoff & Moore's account, infants are not actively engaged in molding their response to the visual target. It does not call for any awareness on the part of the infant or the mediation of any higher cognitive and perceptual processes involved but rather an automatic release of prewired responses, without the involvement of any active matching for equivalence. As suggested by Meltzoff and Moore (1994), the crucial test in deciding which interpretation is correct is twofold. First, if the fixed-action pattern is correct, the stimulus–response system that underlies it should be time locked. In other words, the automaticity of the imitative response should correspond to a small time window between stimulus and response, enough to allow the triggering of the response. Evidence of delayed imitation and recall of a model beyond few seconds does not fair well with the fixed-action pattern theory. Second, active matching between model and response supports the idea that higher perceptual and cognitive mechanisms mediate the imitative response of the infant and that it is not automatic but rather involves some active probing and molding by the infant. Evidence of active probing indeed suggests that infants are somehow aware of the difference between themselves and the model to be imitated and are actively engaged in trying to match the two.

In one of their follow-up studies on early imitation, Meltzoff & Moore (1994) tested their own interpretation against the fixed-action-pattern view on 6-week-old infants presented with different models of mouth opening and tongue protrusions (to the side or at midline). Infants were tested for immediate and 24-hour delayed imitation. Meltzoff & Moore reported that 6-week-olds do show delayed imitation after 24 hours and do demonstrate active matching of their motor response. In the course of the immediate or delayed response period following the model of the facial gesture, infants tended to engage in a progressive motor approximation of the model. When presented with the model of a tongue protrusion to the side of the mouth, they first pulled their tongue at midline and in the course of repetive protrusions shifted their tongue to the side. This active matching is clearly incompatible with the idea of a fixed-action-pattern account. However, if 6-week-olds unambiguously demonstrate higher perceptual and cognitive engagement in their imitative responses, to our knowledge this has not been demonstrated with newborns. We turn now to recent findings we collected in our laboratory suggesting that, indeed, by the second month infants do attend and respond in fundamentally different ways to the consequences of their own action compared to newborns. These findings strongly support the idea that the active, differentiated engagement of the infant Meltzoff and Moore observed with 6-week-olds in the context of imitation develops around this time and is probably not present at birth.

In a first experiment (Rochat & Striano, submitted), we recorded the successive positive pressures 2-month-old infants applied on a pacifier introduced in their mouth for nonnutritive exploratory sucking. Infants sat in between two audio speakers that fed back to the infants trills of discrete synthesized sounds contingent on the infants' sucking on a pacifier. A computer recorded the oral pressure applied on the pacifier by the infant, and when it was above a fixed (low) threshold, it generated successive discrete sounds varying in pitch frequency only. In other words, following a 90-second baseline period with no sound, each time infants sucked on a pacifier above threshold, they heard a perfectly contingent sound. Now, here comes the crucial manipulation. Infants were tested in two conditions. In one condition, each time they sucked above threshold, they heard a contingent sound that was analog or commensurate to the amount of pressure or effort they applied on the pacifier (Contingent + Analog condition). In this condition, the infant was presented with an auditory spatial and temporal equivalent of the action they performed on the pacifier. In another condition, each time infants sucked above threshold, they heard a contingent sound that was *not* analog or commensurate to the amount of pressure (effort) they applied on the pacifier (Contingent + Nonanalog condition). In this second condition, the infant was presented with an auditory temporal *only* (contingent only) equivalent of the action they performed on the pacifier.

The question guiding this experiment was whether infants would generate differential patterns of oral activity depending on the temporal only or temporal and spatial equivalence of the auditory consequences of their own action. The rationale was that such differential responding would indicate that infants are sensitive to and systematically exploring the consequences of their own agency. It would index their ability to take a *contemplative stance* in the exploration of themselves, in particular, the exploration of themselves as agent. We view this contemplative stance as analogous to the ability of imitative matching demonstrated by Meltzoff and Moore (1994) with 6-week-old infants. They both suggest that infants are capable of stepping back from the tight link between perception and action and engaging in the active exploration of what they perceive in relation to what they are capable of self-producing: their own effectivity in the world whether it is the world of the self, people, or physical objects.

We found that 2-month-olds generate significantly different patterns of oral actions depending on the two experimental conditions. Overall, infants tended to generate more frequent pressures on the pacifier that were just at theshold in the Contingent + Analog condition compared to the Contingent only condition. Furthermore, they manifested significantly lower average pressure amplitude in the former than in the latter condition. These results suggest that (a) infants are sensitive to the auditory consequences of their own action, (b) they actively explore these consequences if the consequences are both temporally contingent and spatially congruent with their own action, (c) when the auditory consequences are both temporally contingent and spatially congruent with the effort they exert on the pacifier, infants tend to manifest more control and exploraton of their own agency. This last point is inferred from the fact that by exploring the proprioceptive and auditory threshold, infants show more controlled exploration of self-agency, which in turn depends on the condition. Whether the auditory consequences of sucking are both contingent and congruent or only contingent, infants appear to engage in a differential exploration of the threshold, hence of self-agency. Following our rationale, this is an index of their ability to take a contemplative stance.

This interpretation is particularly valid when we compare these results, found with 2-month-old infants, and those we found in a second experiment with newborn infants. In this second experiment, we replicated the research with a population of healthy less-than-48-hour-old infants. Although infants accepted the pacifier we introduced into their mouths and generated a good amount of oral pressures, we found absolutely no evidence of a differential pattern of sucking depending on conditions. In contrast to 2-month-olds, newborns did not show any differential oral responding whether it was followed by Contingent only or Contingent + Analog auditory consequences. Following the rationale of the study and our interpretation, newborns do not show any signs of a systematic exploration of the auditory consequences of their own sucking, hence no signs of systematic and controlled exploration of self-agency. This is important, particularly in light of the fact that newborns' auditory system is well developed at birth and they are capable of operant learning via sucking in the context of speech-sound discrimination tasks (De Casper & Fifer, 1980; Eimas, 1982; Juscyk, 1985).

Based on this research, we conclude that 2-month-olds but not newborns show signs of a contemplative stance or the stepping back from the tight link between perception and action couplings (learning the mere association between sucking and auditory events) to engage in the active exploration of self-agency. In our view, this stance is revolutionary, opening up new ways of interacting with and understanding the world. In particular, we suggest that from the emergence of the contemplative stance that implies a first distanciation of the infant in relation to the environment (including the self), infants will develop a new range of expectations regarding people around them. These expectations are less direct, essentially more reflective (in the sense of reflexion, or reflective awareness) compared to the prospective control newborns might express, for example, in learning and conditioning in the context of their transactions with the human environment (Blass, chap. 2, this volume). By 2 months, infants begin to develop specific expectations about how people behave, who they are, and what they should do when interacting with them. They learn to systematically anticipate, control, and develop likes as well as dislikes of people. Such development requires the stepping back or decoupling that starts to be manifested by 2 months, a key transition that we like to equate to a revolution for its radical departure from what is expressed during the newborn stage. Again, this transition is validated by the remarkably robust experience reported by parents witnessing their infant smiling back at them at around this age. It is most likely that this experience often described by parents as the discorvery of a person in their infant, modifies in radical ways their attitudes toward their progeny. From there, we propose, develops a radically new sense of shared experience (primary intersubjectivity) with novel social expectations and scaffolding initiated from both the baby and the parent or caretaker (Kaye, 1982; Papousek & Papousek, 1995). This forms the developmental origins of early social cognition. We turn now to what develops from here up to 9 months, when infants express yet another radical departure or revolution: the adoption of the intentional stance.

DEVELOPMENT OF SOCIAL EXPECTATIONS BETWEEN 2 AND 6 MONTHS OF AGE

Accompanying the emergence of the contemplative stance by the second month, face-to-face and, in particular, eye-to-eye interactions between infants and caretakers become prevalent, at least in Western middle class culture. As we illustrated at the beginning of this chapter with the anecdote of the father dipping his infant in the pool and establishing intersubjectivity regarding the soaking experience, caretakers start compulsively to present themselves in an *en face* posture to the infant. The face becomes a primordial theater, staging emotional and intentional cues that are used in the monitoring, control, and prediction of others. Caretakers read the infant's facial display of emotions obviously from birth, but when by 2 months infants start to show signs of reciprocity in this reading, there is a dramatic shift in the dynamic of the interaction between caretakers and infants.

The socially elicited facial displays of the infant and in particular smiling, change the social scaffolding offered to the infant. From essentially comforting, calming, and accompanying infants in their fluctuating behavioral states, caregivers' interventions become more playful due to the reciprocity emerging by the second month. There is now a new implicit goal in the interaction, the establishment of shared, pleasurable, and playful experiences. Aside from feeding and calming, cares now include the necessity to check on the infant's well being and emotional attunement via games and routines that have in the past triggered smiling and other emotional displays of positive affects and feelings in the infant. It is as if there is a shift from essentially physical care provided to the infant to both physical and emotional cares. The diapers of babies continue to be checked, together with their emotional state, through tickling, perhaps, and some exagerated verbal commentaries. As their infant's ability to reciprocate becomes unambiguous, parents develop a new sense of their infant as a psychological entity in need of emotional attunement in the context of positive social exchanges. This sense is an addition to the comfort and physical cares they dispensed from birth. It is from this point that intersubjectivity can develop as a coconstruction between the infant and social partners. We view this coconstruction as the true (psychological) beginning of early social cognition. We turn now to the question of what develops from there.

We can assume that infants gain much knowledge about others in the dyadic, face-to-face context they are compulsively placed in by caretakers. It is in this context that caretakers scaffold the infant in routine games and particular patterns of interaction (Gergely & Watson, this volume; Kaye, 1982; Stern, 1977). But starting in the second month, what social knowledge develops in this context? In general, what develops is a primary sense of shared experience, or primary intersubjectivity (Trevarthen, 1979). We mentioned already that in engaging in routine face-to-face interactions, infants are provided with the opportunity to match their own feelings and affects of those of the social partner. By the second month, when infants start taking a contemplative stance with social, reciprocating partners, they probably also start to take a "like me" stance. We propose that the general contemplative stance infants start to adopt by the second month, taken in a dyadic face-to-face context, leads the infant to recognize herself in this object ("like me" stance). This happens because the object of contemplation is reciprocating with appropriate (invariant) timing and emotional displays. Contrary to Meltzoff & Gopnick (1993), who proposed that even newborns take the "like me" stance in their propensity to imitate, we suggest that this stance is a special case of the general stance shift (contemplative stance) emerging during the second month and taken in the dyadic social context.

From the general context of emerging intersubjectivity, infants develop expectations regarding others and the way they should respond in face-to-face interactions. Routine games, mirroring, and parental frames form a dynamic field of contemplation for the infant from which invariants can be picked up and social anticipation can develop. People can be identified in addition to and beyond their physical attibutes in the way they relate to the infant: the timing of their reciprocity, the dynamic of their vitality (see Stern, this volume), the overall tone of their posture. These invariants specify the dispositional world of others in relation to the self. An infant might start to expect to be picked up in a certain way when engaging in a joyful, playful interaction with a particular person. Mom might be in general gentler, softer, and less systematically contingent in the way she reciprocates and handles her infant. Dad might be more forceful, vocal, and marking with excess his contingent mirroring when interacting with the same infant. Infants certainly pick up these invariant characteristics that specify persons in the way they relate to them. For example, the research of Ann Bigelow (this volume) suggests that by 4 months, infants have developed an attunement to their own mother's timing and relative contingency in interacting with them (e.g., frequency of contingent, reciprocal smiles), generalizing this attunement to stanger females who display more or less contingency.

Murray and Trevarthen (1985) reported that infants as young as 2 months of age interacting with their mother via a closed-circuit video system did manifest a differential responding to their mother when she was presented live or in a replay (See also Muir & Hains, this volume; Nadel & Trembley-Leveau, this volume). Infants were reported to display marked decrease in gazing and smiling as well as significant increase in negative affects in the replay compared to the live condition. This suggests that infants, by 2 months, start to be sensitive to their mother's relative emotional attunement to them. In other words, infants somehow appeared to discriminate between true (live) and false (replay) reciprocity of the mother. In the replay condition, the mother was noncontingent in the sense that although displaying much positive, hence engaging, positive feelings and affects, this display was supposedly detected by the infant as being *nonreciprocal*, violating the timing of response that specifies reciprocity, hence the sense of shared experience and intersubjectivity.

In a recent study (Rochat, Neisser, and Marian, in press), we tried to replicate Murray & Trevarthen's (1985) findings, controlling for possible order effect that might have accounted for the phenomenon they reported. In two different experiments, one of them testing 2- as well as 4-month-old infants, we were unable to replicate the basic phenomenon. We proposed that the nonecological validity of the closed-circuit video system that removes important cues of reciprocity, such as distance regulation and touch, might account for the lack of evidence of young infants' sensitivity to social reciprocity and contingency within this experimental context (but see Nadel & Tremblay-Leveau, this volume). In Rochat, et al., and as a control, infants did react to the sudden still face we asked mothers to adopt in their live TV interaction. This suggests that infants, within this experimental set up, were sensitive to some aspects of the ongoing interaction with their mother but not the kind of subtle reciprocity cues that the findings reported by Murray and Trevarthen in their original experiment implied.

In order to capture what is detected by young infants in a more natural dyadic context than the closed-circuit video system set up, we explored in a recent study (Rochat, Querido, & Striano, submitted) the sensitivity of 2- to 6-month-old infants to the relative structure of the interactive frame offered by an adult stranger. The rationale for this study was to capture how infants from 2 months on refine their ability to detect regularities in ongoing social interaction and to develop specific expectations based on a sensitivity to the structure of the interaction. Based on our failed attempt to replicate Murray and Trevarthen's phenomenon, we hypothesized that by 2 months, although infants start to show signs of reciprocity, their sense of the other as reciprocal partner is yet diffused and undifferentiated. At this early age, the social skills and achievement of the infant might be merely the global monitoring of a social presence or absence of an attentive social partner, not yet the degree to which this partner is reciprocating. We hypothesized that from a global sense of a social presence, by way of intimate and animated tracking of eye-to-eye contact accompanied by particular speech sounds in the form of "motherese," infants beyond 2 months of age develop specific expectations in the dyadic context based on cues specifying the *quality* of the interaction (e.g., whether it is organized or disorganized, contingent or noncontingent, predictable or not). This development leads infants to differentiate people in the subtle ways people relate to them.

In our study, we videotaped 2-, 4-, and 6-month-old infants interacting with a female stanger in a face-to-face situation that did not include any touching. Aside from baseline periods, in two different experimental conditions, the experimenter introduced the infant with peekaboo routine that was either structured or unstructured. In the structured condition, the peekaboo routine was strictly organized into three phases articulating a total of eight subroutines: (a) an *approach* phase in which the experimenter leaned foward toward the infant while saying "Look, look, look," and maintaining eye contact; (b) an *arousal* phase in which once the experimenter was close to the infant she covered her face with her hands and then dropped her hand down while saying, "Peekaboo!"; (c) a final *release* phase in which the experimener leaned back to the original posture while saying a long, calming, "Yeaaah" while nodding her head and smiling. In the unstructured condition, the experimenter was wearing an ear piece conntected to a tape recorder playing instructions of subroutines to be performed in a random, disorganized way. In other words, in the unstructured condition, the experimenter engaged in a scrambled peekaboo game, with unrelated subroutines that did not coalesce to form the crescendo–decrescendo or tension building and release script (Stern, 1985). Note that the stuctured and unstructured peekaboo conditions were equated in duration and number of events (subroutines), varying only in their narrative power, that is, power to provide the infant with a simple script of tension building and release. Also, note that in either conditions the experimenter displayed the same attention to the infant, with eye-to-eye contact and the display of exagerated positive affects. In each condition, the peekaboo routine was repeated eight times in successsion over approximately a 1-minute period. Then the normal interaction resumed. Each 1-minute condition was repeated twice in a counterbalanced order among infants of each age group.

In scoring the infant's smiling and gazing at the experimenter, we found that 2-month-olds looked toward the experimenter and smiled equally in both the structured and unstructured conditions. They appeared equally attentive in both conditions and displayed no evidence of differential responding. In sharp contrast, both 4- and 6-month-olds showed marked differential responding in gazing. Both groups of older infants demonstrated a significant increase in gazing in the unstructured compared to the stuctured condition. They stared longer and in higher proportion, particularly relative to the subroutines of the last, release, phase. In the structured condition only, infants tended to look away and smile during the three subroutines of the last release phase. Four- and 6-month-olds smiled significantly more frequently during the subroutines of the last release phase in the structured compared to the unstructured condition. Finally, we found that the average duration of smiling was significantly longer in the organized compared to the unorganized condition for the 6-month-olds only.

Overall, the results of this study demonstrate that from 4 months of age, infants start to be attuned and sensitive to the narrative envelope of the routines provided by social partners. They detect regularities and organized patterns in the dyadic interaction and respond to them in synchrony. From this developing sensitivity to organized patterns of interaction, infants develop more precise expectations about people and the way they should behave in relation to the self. This, in turn, provides new grounds for the social understanding of who people are and what can be expected from them in particular.

Another recent study we performed in our laboratory (Rochat, Blatt, & Striano, submitted) further captures the development of social expectations between 2 and 6 months. We studied infants response to the sudden still face adopted by an experimenter in a dyadic, face-to-face social exchange (Muir & Hains, this volume; Tronick, Als, Adamson, Wise, & Brazelton, 1978). In successive 1-minute still-face conditions, interspersed with 1 minute of normal interaction, the experimenter adopted either a *neutral* still face (typical of studies using a still-face paradigm); a *happy* still face, with mouth open and fixed smile; or a *sad* still face, with wrinkled forehead, frown eyebrows, and inverted U-shaped mouth. We scored the infants' relative smiling and gazing toward the experimenter in these various still-face conditions that provided different static emotional cues (neutral, happy, or sad). In particular, we compared the infants' responses to the still face in comparison to the preceding normal, affectively positive interaction (still-face effect) and the infants' responses to the still face in comparison to the following normal, affectively positive interaction (recovery effect).

In relation to gazing, we found an overall still-face effect (decrease in gazing duration toward the experimenter) in all conditions for the groups of 4- and 6-month-olds but not for the 2-month-olds. In other words, 2-month-olds did not show signs of averting gaze during the still face, regardless of conditions. In relation to smiling, all groups of infants showed decreased smiling in all still-face conditions. Regarding the recovery effect, 4- and 6-month-olds showed more recovery in gazing following the happy still face than either the neutral or sad still face. Two-month-olds showed equally low recovery in all conditions. In relation to smiling, 6-month-olds showed a markedly reduced recovery of smiling when the normal interaction resumed, independent of still-face conditions. In contrast to the groups of 2- and 4-month-olds, 6-month-olds appeared to resist positive reengagement and reciprocity following any of the still-face episodes. This again suggests that they are building different expectations about the social partner based on past, unusual experience (still-face episodes). In general, these observations indicate that by 4 to 6 months, infants are more sensitive to dispositional cues displayed by people and that these cues are the foundations for particular expectations regarding the way they should behave. Depending on age, the still-face effect changes, and the recovery from it appears more dependent on static emotional cues provided by the social partner during the still-face episode. It is as if infants develop an ability to consider the behavior of people beyond the here and now, progressively able to relate current behavior to past interaction.

In summary, what we are suggesting here is that between 2 and 6 months, infants develop social expectations in a dyadic, face-to-face context. This development finds its origins in the contemplative stance infants start to take by the middle of the second month. From this key developmental transition that marks the end of the newborn phase, and can be considered the psychological birth (as opposed to the biological birth) of babies, infants develop new understanding of themselves, objects, and people. In relation to people, 2-month-olds start to reciprocate in an undifferentiated way, sensitive mainly to the overall presence and positive solicitations of caretakers. At this early stage, others are differentiated from the self but yet unspecified. In their transactions with others, 2-month-olds are mainly engaged in monitoring a presence, not who this presence is, what her dispositions are, and what can be expected from her. In contrast, we have seen that 4- and 6-month-old infants start to show signs of a growing sensitivity to subtle social cues, such as the organization of the social scaffolding or relative structure of the narrative offered in routine games by the adult as well as the dispositional (emotional) cues expressed by the adult in these games. It appears that by 6 months, infants are capable of relating present face-to-face interactions with the quality and characters of previous ones. This new "historical" perspective on people and the way people relate to them leads infants to develop rich social expectations based on increasingly subtle emotional and dispositional cues. This development accompanies the emergence of a new sense of shared experience in a dyadic context (primary intersubjectivity). It is from here that infants prepare themselves for their next major developmental step in understanding others—the adoption of the intentional stance or the understanding of others as *intentional agents*.

NINE-MONTH REVOLUTION: THE INTENTIONAL STANCE

By the end of the first year and starting approximately 9 months of age, infants demonstrate marked progress in social cognition, developing triadic social competencies and secondary intersubjectivity (Baldwin & Baird, this volume; Moore, this volume). Triadic competencies correspond to the emerging ability of the infant to monitor others in relation to objects. Infants start to manifest a sense shared attention to the physical world, *coordinating* their own perspective and attentional focus on things with the perspective and attentional focus of others. Gestural communication, in particular pointing, joint attention, gaze following, and social referencing are all indexes of secondary intersubjectivity emerging by 9 months (Bates, Benigni, Bretherton, Camaioni, & Volterra, 1979; Campos & Sternberg, 1981; Carpenter, Nagell, & Tomasello, in press; Trevarthen, 1979).

This inclusion of others' perspective in dealing with them and the world around radically changes the realm of communication: from the coregulation of feelings, affects, emotions and the establishment of basic expectations in routine plays during dyadic, face-to-face interaction to the possibility of learning through teaching and cooperation on things outside the dyadic relationship. Infants' awareness that they can attend jointly, and that others' facial expression and communicative efforts can inform them about the environment, makes teaching and learning with others possible. Cooperating on objects and on others radically enlarges the realm of social cognition in infancy, changing the way infants understand others: from interactive and emotional entities to intentional agents.

But how do infants get to this point? We believe that part of this developmental process is based on the early propensity young infants have in detecting invariant information specifying movement dynamic associated with intentional actions. The sense of their own planning and own intentionality probably develop from the perceptual analysis 2-month-olds start to engage in when showing first signs of a systematic exploration of their own actions' consequences (see previous and Rochat & Striano, submitted). Our contention is that the perceptual analysis of self-agency is at the origin of an understanding of self-intention. Likewise, we propose that at the origin of an understanding of intentions in others there is the perceptual analysis young infants engage in when exploring the consequences of actions originating from entities independent of the self: how animated things, including people, move and act in relation to objects and in relation to one another.

The research we present now suggests that starting at 3 months of age, infants engage in the systematic exploration and detection of movement information that specifies intentionality in animated entities that are moving independently of the self. The research illustrates that beyond 7 months of age, and not before, infants show signs of an intentional stance that goes beyond a mere perceptual discrimination of movement dynamic. We show that if a sophisticated perceptual analysis is evident in young infants, it is yet mysterious how they develop an intentional stance from this perceptual analysis. In relation to this question, we recently conducted an investigation that suggests some developmental links by the end of the first year between social-cognitive competencies developing in dyadic and triadic contexts (Striano & Rochat, submitted).

In adults, there is a robust, almost compulsive inclination to perceive meaningful physical and social causality in the motion of abstract objects, such as two-dimensional geometric figures moving on a screen. The seminal works of Heider and Simmel (1944), Michotte (1963), and more recently Basili (1976), and Dittrich and Lea (1994) documented that physical causality, dispositional qualities, and intentions were systematically perceived in the context of particular sequential movements of two or more geometric figures. Depending on particular patterns of dynamic interactions between these abstract entities is associtated with the phenomenal perception of causal and social events: for example, that one entity caused the other to move by entrainment or by launching; that one is chasing the other with the intend to get it. These impressions are systematic and depend on precise dynamic information specifying the relative movement of the figures on the display. This phenomenon rests on the basic perception of relational movement characteristics (i.e., how one entity moves in relation to the other) that is eventually dressed with the meaning of physical or social causality, including the attribution of intentions and dispositional qualities (e.g., the red square "pushed" the blue circle, or the "nervous" yellow triangle is "trying to catch" the black circle that is swiftly "fleeing away").

In one study (Rochat, Morgan, & Carpenter, 1997), we attempted to capture the developmental origins of a sensitivity to relational movement characteristics that, for adults, specify social causality.The rationale of these studies was that in order for the infant to take the intentional stance, they first had to develop a particular sensitivity and attunement to dynamic perceptual information that specifies social and intentional events for adults. We tested 3- to 6-month-old infants (as well as a control group of adults) for their visual preference for two different dynamic displays showing abstract objects that adults perceive as interacting either intentionally or randomly. Both displays were presented to the infant simultaneously on two computer monitors placed side by side. Each display consisted of a pair of colored discs moving either independently (*independent display*) or in systematic interaction with one another (*chase display*), never actually contacting one another.

The chase display was meant to specify an intentional social event. In the independent display, the movements of the discs were random. In the chase display, one disc (the chaser) systematically approached the other (the chasee) at a constant velocity. When the chaser came close to the chasee, the latter accelerated away from it until it reached a relaxed distance, at which point it returned to normal speed. Except for the relative spatio-temporal dependence of the discs' movements, all dynamic parameters on the two displays were controlled and maintained equal (see Rochat, et al., 1997, for details).

Results show that adults as well as 6-month-old attentive infants (as opposed to infants who did not pay much attention to the displays) tended to look significantly longer at the independent display than the chase display. In contrast, the group of 3-month-old attentive infants tended to look significantly more at the chase display. When ordering infants according to age in days and plotting the ratio of preference to the chase or the independent display as a function of age, there was a significant linear trend from chase to independent preference. Interestingly, posttest interviews of the adults indicated that they spent more time looking at the independent display, trying to pick up invariant dynamic features. Such invariant features were reportedly quickly picked up as specifying a chase in the other display. This would explain their pattern of preferential looking for the independent display. We did not assume that the analogous pattern of preferential looking found with the group of 6-month-olds rested on a similar account. However, the results obtained with infants point to two facts: from 3 months of age, infants demonstrate a sensitivity to movement information specifying social causality for adults (i.e., chase vs. random movements), and this sensitivity is expressed differently and appears to develop between 3 and 6 months of age.

In order to test at what age infants might take an intentional stance in perceiving the chase display, we recently tested groups of 3-, 5-, 7- and 9-month-old infants using the following habituation procedure (Morgan & Rochat, 1997). Infants were habituated in looking at a red and a blue disc chasing one another on one computer display. Except for their color, the discs were identical. For half the infants of each age group, the blue disc was the chaser and the red disc was the chasee. For the other half, the colors were reversed. Once they reached a predetermined habituation criterion, infants were tested in successive posthabituation trials with either the same event or *a role-reversal event.* In the role-reversal event, the chaser became the chasee, and vice versa, through a color switch of the discs. In other words, in the role reversal event trials, the color label of each protagonist (chaser and chasee) was reversed. Remember that except for color, the discs were identical in forms and dimensions.

Results of this study yielded an interesting developmental trend. Infants younger than 7 months of age did not show any signs of dishabituation (i.e., significant regain of visual attention) when comparing trials with the role-reversal event and the habituated event. The group of 7-month-olds started to show signs of increase looking at the novel, role-reversal event, but looking time did not quite reach significance. However, by 9 months of age, infants show unambiguous (massive) increase of looking at the role-reversal event trials. When ordering all the tested infants according to their age in days, and plotting against their age the relative ratio of their dishabituation, there is a sudden change in this dishabituation ratio starting at around 7 months and jumping up by 9 months.

Considering that only the color labeled the role of each abstract protagonist on the computer display and that the protagonists were specified by the way they moved in relation to one another, we propose that the dishabituation starting to be expressed by 7-month-old infants and clearly expressed by 9-month-olds corresponds to the emergence of an intentional stance taken by the infant. This dishabituation is based, as for the previous experiment, on a discrimination of the pattern of relational movements of the two discs on the display, but also a discrimination of a change in *identity* of the protagonists (e.g., blue disc = chasee and red disc = chaser).

The discrimination of the identity change required the infant to take an extra step beyond the mere discrimination of movement dynamic that the first study showed is evident starting at 3 months of age. It required that the infant somehow construe the chase event on display in relation to the question of *who is doing what to whom.* This identification process is the extra step required by the intentional stance that 9-month-olds appear to take. It means that infants start to construe social events as transactions between planning and motivated entities *beyond* the fact that they are merely animated and move in different ways relative to one another (see first study previously described).

But what are the mechanisms underlying this developmental revolution in social cognition? What determines the transition from perceiving animated things in the environment as moving in particular ways based on the detection of particular dynamic invariants (i.e, self-propulsion, action at a distance, crescendo–decrescendo of velocity, etc.) to the understanding of animated things in the environment as planning and self-motivated entities? One possibility is that by 9 months of age, infants bring what they learn in the dyadic context of face-to-face interactions into the context of tryadic interactions. Accordingly, early on infants learn about their caretakers' affects, feelings, and emotions as well as their own in the dyadic context (see previous). When starting to take an intentional stance, infants transfer the understanding of others they develop in a dyadic context into the triadic context, attributing motivations, planning, and intentions to animated entities they perceive and understand beyond a direct, face-to-face interaction. Such interpretations imply a developmental link between social cognition developing in the dyadic and triadic context.

To test this interpretation, Striano and Rochat (submitted) recently compared 7- to 10-month-old infants' responses to a still-face situation in the dyadic context of a face-to-face interaction with an adult stranger to their responses to different triadic situations of shared attention, gestural communication (pointing), blocking and teasing, as well as gaze following with another adult stranger. Overall, we found some evidence of a correlation between the level of infants' responses in the dyadic and triadic situations at both ages. For example, more developed response to the still face, such as the infant's attempt to reengaged the still-faced social partner by poking her or calling her for attention (social probing), was linked to more advanced triadic responding. These results suggest that dyadic and triadic competencies do not develop in independence but rather in interaction. More research is needed to specify the nature of this interaction and to capture mechanisms underlying the emergence of the intentional stance in both dyadic and triadic contexts of social cognition. Because social cognition develops first in a dyadic (face-to-face) context, emerging triadic competencies by the end of the first year certainly depends on this early development. The nature of this dependence is yet unclear. It is, however, an important consideration even when studying later development and, in particular, the emergence of theories of mind by 4 years of age (Perner, 1991). Emerging theories of mind and success in false-belief tasks imply not only the inference of rational thoughts and intentions in others but also the inference of motivations and dispositional qualities. The consideration by children of the affective determinants of people's behavior in a given situation (e.g., a false-belief task) rests in part on the original intersubjectivity children have developed in the dyadic context of early social cognition, starting at 2 months of age and, of course, also on the emergence of the secondary intersubjectivity an the intentional stance manifested by 9 months.

SUMMARY AND CONCLUSIONS

What we tried to convey in this chapter is that the developing sense of shared experience between infants and their caretakers is the craddle of social cognition. It is in the early development of an affective matching between self and others that infants lay the foundations of their social knowledge. Table 1.1 summarizes the basic developmental progression we have proposed. Accordingly, primary intersubjectivity emerges around 2 months postnatal age, when infants demonstrate an emerging capacity to step back and explore the consequences of their own actions on objects and people (contemplative stance). The emergence of social cognition is linked to the emergence of self-agency and the contemplative stance infants start to manifest by the second month. The amplified reciprocity offered by caretakers, reinforced by socially elicited smiles expressed by the infant, scaffold the rapid development of social-cognitive competencies, in particular, the development of basic social expectancies within the dyadic, face-to-face context of early social exchanges. By 9 months of age, infants appear to adopt a new stance, the intentional stance, engaging in coop-

TABLE 1.1
Proposed Developmental Progression of
Social-Cognitive Development in the First Year

Age	*Intersubjectivity Level*	*Social-Cognitive Stance*
0 to 1 month	Sensorimotor attunement	Attentional
2 to 7 months	Primary intersubjectivity: smiling, affective attunement, social expectations	Contemplative
8 to 12 months	Secondary intersubjectivity: joint engagement, social referencing, attention following, gestural communication	Intentional

eration with others in relation to larger functional goals. In the development of primary intersubjectivity that takes place between 2 and 9 months, infants learn about the dispositional world of others. By 9 months, this learning expands beyond the dyadic context to incorporate not only the affectivity of others in relation to the self but also their intentions in relation to the object world that surrounds one-to-one relationships. At this stage of social cognitive development, infants reach new operative levels in matching their own private experience with others'. Now, intersubjectivity serves not only the purpose of being affectively attuned and sensitive to others for the sake of maintaining social relationships but also becomes instrumental in the cooperation of the infant with others in relation to third entities or goals. This development is linked to much cognitive progress including symbolic functioning, communication, and emerging theories of mind.

Beyond the newborn stage and by the second month, infants develop their first knowledge about people and, in particular, what to expect from them and how they reciprocate. Caretakers are particularly attuned to young infants' contingent responding in the context of amplified and repeated interactive frames. They scaffold the infant by engaging in systematic mirroring and exaggeration of their emotional expressions, reflecting back to the infants their own behavior through compulsive running commentaries and exaggerated mimicking of their actions within face-to-face presentations. It is within this highly structured framework that infants start developing a sense of shared experience that, we proposed, is the developing core of social cognition. It is from this intersubjective core that infants develop skills to monitor people and anticipate their behavior.

Dyadic competencies developing first, they lay the foundation for the development of triadic competencies and prepare the infant to take the intentional stance at around 9 months of age. However, the mechanisms underlying the transition from the contemplative stance young infants adopt in a dyadic context of social interaction to the intentional stance they take by 9 months in a triadic context need to be further specified in future research. Beyond 9 months of age, dyadic social competencies continue to develop in interaction with triadic competencies. If infants start to understand people as intentional, their dispositional qualities will continue to be primarily specified in dyadic contexts. Theories of mind, the monitoring, control, and prediction of people behavior, are not merely based on cold, rational inferences. They are also based on social knowledge that develops first in the context of intimate, one-to-one relationships and pertains to the affective determinants of people's behavior. This knowledge is primitive and is based on the way private experience of feelings and affects match the experience of others. Intersubjectivity is indeed the cradle of social cognition.

ACKNOWLEDGMENTS

Part of the research presented in this chapter is supported by a grant from the National Science Foundation to the first author (SBR–9507773).

REFERENCES

Abravanel, E., & Sigafoos, A. D. (1984). Exploring the presence of imitation during early infancy. *Child Development, 55*, 381–392.

Baillargeon, R. (1995). Physical reasoning in infancy. In M. S. Gazzaniga (Ed.), *The cognitive neurosciences* (pp. 181–204). Cambridge, MA: MIT Press.

Bakeman, R., & Adamson, L. (1984). Coordinating attention to people and objects in mother-infant and peer-infant interactions. *Child Development, 55*, 1278–1289.

Baron-Cohen, S. (1995). *Mindblindness: An essay on autism and theory of mind.* Cambridge, MA: MIT Press.

Barr, R., Bakeman, R., Konner, M., & Adamson, L. (1987). Crying in !Kung infants: A test of the cultural specificity hypothesis. *Pediatrics Research, 21*, 178A.

Basili, J. N. (1976). Temporal and spatial contingencies in the perception of social events. *Journal of Personality and Social Psychology, 33*(6), 680–685.

Bates, E., Benigni, L., Bretherton, I., Camaioni, L., & Volterra, V. (1979). *The emergence of symbols: Cognition and communication in infancy.* New York: Academic Press.

Bjorklund, D. F. (1987). A note on neonatal imitation. *Developmental Review, 7*, 86–92.

Blass, E. M., Fillion, T. J., Rochat, P., Hoffmeyer, L. B., & Metzger, M. A. (1989). Sensorimotor and motivational determinants of hand-mouth coordination in 1–3 day old human infants. *Developmental Psychology, 25*, 963–975.

Brazelton, T. B. (1962). Crying in infancy. *Pediatrics, 29*, 579–588.

Bruner, J. S. (1972, August). Nature and uses of immaturity. *American Psychologist*, 687–708.

Bushnell, I. W. (1979). Modification of the externality effect in young infants. *Journal of Experimental Child Psychology, 28*(2), 211–229.

Butterworth, G., & Hopkins, B. (1988). Hand-mouth coordination in the new-born baby. *British Journal of Developmental Psychology, 6*, 303–314.

Campos, J., & Sternberg, C. (1981). Perception, appraisal, and emotion: The onset of social referencing. In M. Lamb & L. Sherrod (Eds.), *Infant social cognition: Empirical and theoretical considerations* (pp. 273–314). Hillsdale, NJ: Lawrence Erlbaum Associates.

Carpenter, M., Nagell, K., & Tomasello, M. (in press). Social cognition, joint attention, and communicative competence from 9 to 15 months of age. *Monograph of the Society for Research in Child Development.*

Crook, C. K., & Lipsitt, L. P. (1976). Neonatal nutritive sucking: Effects of taste stimulation upon sucking rhythm and heart rate. *Child Development, 47*, 518–532.

Darwin, C. B. (1965). *The expression of the emotions in man and animals.* Chicago: University of Chicago Press. (Original work published 1872)

De Casper, A. J., & Fifer, W. P. (1980). Of human bonding: Newborns prefer their mother's voice. *Science, 208*, 1174–1176.

De Casper, A. J., Lecanuet, J. P., Busnel, M. C., Granier-Deferre, C., & Maugeais, R. (1994). Fetal reactions to recurrent maternal speech. *Infant Behavior and Development, 17*, 159–164.

De Casper, A. J., & Spence, M. J. (1986). Prenatal maternal speech influences newborns' perception of speech sounds. *Infant Behavior and Development, 9*, 133–150.

Dittrich, W. H., & Lea, S. T. G. (1994). Visual perception of intentional motion. *Perception, 23*, 253–268.

Eimas, P. D. (1982). Speech perception: A view of the initial state and perceptual mechanisms. In J. Mehler, M. Garrett, & E. Walker (Eds.), *Perspectives on mental representation: Experimental and theoretical studies of cognitive processes and capacities.* Hillsdale, NJ: Lawrence Erlbaum Associates.

Goren, C. C., Sarty, M., & Wu, P. Y. K. (1975). Visual following and pattern discrimination of face-like stimuli by newborn infants. *Pediatrics, 56,* 544–549.

Heider, F., & Simmel, S. (1944). An experimental study of apparent behavior. *American Journal of Psychology, 57,* 243–259.

Hobson, P. (1993). *Autism and the development of mind.* Hillsdale, NJ: Lawrence Erlbaum Associates.

Hopkins, B., & van Palthe, W. (1987). The development of the crying state during early infancy. *Developmental Psychobiology, 20,* 165–175.

Jacobson, S. W. (1979). Matching behavior in the young infant. *Child Development, 50,* 425–430.

Johnson, M. H., Dziurawiec, S., Ellis, H. D., & Morton, J. (1991). Newborns' preferential tracking of face-like stimuli and its subsequent decline. *Cognition, 40,* 1–19.

Johnson, M. H., & Morton, J. (1991). *Biology and cognitive development: The case of face recognition.* Oxford: Basil Blackwell.

Juscyk, P. W. (1985). The high amplitude sucking technique as a methodological tool in speech perception research. In G. Gottlieb & N. A. Krasnegor (Eds.), *Measurement of audition and vision in the first year of postnatal life: A methodological overview* (pp. 195–222). Norwood, NJ: Ablex.

Kagan, J., & Snidman, N. (1991). Temperamental factors in human development. *American Psychologist, 46,* 856–862.

Kaye, K. (1982). *The mental and social life of babies.* Chicago: University of Chicago Press.

Koupernik, C., & Dailly, R. (1968). *Development neuro-pychique du nourrisson: Semiologie normale and pathologique* [Neuropsychological development in infancy: Normal and pathological semiology]. Paris: Presses Universitaires de France.

Lécuyer, R. (1989). *Bébés astronomes, bébés psychologues: L'intelligence de la première année* [Infants as astronomers, infants as psychologists: Intelligence in the first year of life]. Liège: Mardaga.

MacFarlane, A. (1975). Olfaction in the development of social preferences in the human neonate. In R. Porter & M. O'Connor (Eds.), *Parent-infant interaction* (pp. 103–117). Ciba Foundation Symposium 33. Amsterdam: Elsevier/Excerpta Medica/North-Holland.

Mahler, M. S., Pine, F., & Bergman, A. (1975). *The psychological birth of the human infant: Symbiosis and individuation.* New York: Basic Books.

Maratos, O. (1982). Trends in the develoment of imitation in early infnaty. In T. G. Bever (Ed.), *Regression in mental development: Basic phenomena and theories* (pp. 81–101). Hillsdale, NJ: Lawrence Erlbaum Associates.

Maurer, D. (1985). Infants' perception of faceness. In T. N. Field & N. Fox (Eds.), *Social perception in infants* (pp. 37–66). Hillsdale, NJ: Lawrence Erlbaum Associates.

Maurer, K., & Salapatek, P. (1976). Developmental change in the scanning of faces by young infants. *Child Development, 47,* 523–527.

Meltzoff, A. N., & Gopnik, A. (1993). The role of imitation in understanding persons and developing theory of mind. In S. Baron-Cohen, H. Tager-Flusberg, & D. J. Cohen (Eds.), *Understanding other minds: Perspectives from autism* (pp. 335–366). New York: Oxford University Press.

Meltzoff, A. N., & Moore, M. K. (1977). Imitation of facial and manual gestures by human neonates. *Science, 198,* 75–78.

Meltzoff, A. N., & Moore, M. K. (1994). Imitation, memory, and the representation of persons. *Infant Behavior and Development, 17,* 83–99.

Michotte, A. (1963). *The perception of causality.* London: Methuen.

Morgan, R., & Rochat, P. (1997). Intermodal calibration of the body in early infancy. *Ecological Psychology, 9*(1), 1–24.

Morgan, R., & Rochat, P. (1997, April). The perception of social causality by 3- to 9-month-old infants. Poster presentation at the *Conference on Developmental Processes in Early Social Understanding,* University of Michigan, Ann Arbor.

Murray, L., & Trevarthen, C. (1985). Emotional regulation of interactions between two-month-olds and their mothers. In T. M. Field & N. A. Fox (Eds.), *Social perception in infants* (pp. 177–197). Norwood, NJ: Ablex.

Papousek, H., & Papousek, M. (1995). Intuitive parenting. In M. H. Bornstein (Ed.), *Handbook of parenting, Vol. 2: Biology and ecology of parenting* (pp. 117–136). Mahwah, NJ: Lawrence Erlbaum Associates.

Perner, J. (1991). On representing that: The asymmetry between belief and desire in children's theory of mind. In D. Frye & C. Moore (Eds.), *Children's theories of mind* (pp. 139–156). Hillsdale, NJ: Lawrence Erlbaum Associates.

Piaget, J. (1952). *The origins of intelligence in children.* New York: International Universities Press.

Prechltl, H. F. R. (1984). Continuity of neural functions: From prenatal to postnatal life. *Spastics International Medical Publications.* Oxford: Blackwell.

Rebelsky, F., & Black, R. (1972). Crying in infancy. *Journal of Genetic Psychology, 121,* 49–57.

Rochat, P. (1983). Oral touch in young infants: Responses to variations of nipple characteristics in the first months of life. *International Journal of Behavioral Development, 6,* 123–133.

Rochat, P. (1993). Hand-mouth coordination in the newborn: Morphology, determinants, and early development of a basic act. In G. Savelsbergh (Ed.), *The development of coordination in infancy* (pp. 265–288). Advances in Psychology Series. Amsterdam: Elsevier.

Rochat, P., & Hespos, S. J. (1997). Differential rooting response by neonates: Evidence for an early sense of self. *Early Development and Parenting, 6*(2), 105–112.

Rochat, P., Morgan, R., & Carpenter, M. (1997). Young infants' sensitivity to movement information specifying social causality. *Cognitive Development, 12,* 441–465.

Rochat, P., Neisser, U., & Marian, V. (in press). Are young infants sensitive to interpersonal contingency? *Infant Behavior and Development.*

St. James-Roberts, I., & Halil, T. (1991). Infant crying patterns in the first year: Normal community and clinical findings. *Journal of Child Psychology and Psychiatry, 32*(6), 951–968.

Slater, A. (1997). Visual perception and its organisation in early infancy. In G. Bremner, A. Slater, & G. Butterworth (Eds.), *Infant development: Recent advances* (pp. 31–53). London: Psychology Press/Lawrence Erlbaum Associates.

Spelke, E. S. (1991). Physical knowledge in infancy: Reflection on Piaget's theory. In S. Carey & R. Gelman (Eds.), *The epigenesis of mind: essays on biology and cognition* (pp. 133–169). Hillsdale, NJ: Lawrence Erlbaum Associates.

Spelke, E. S., Breinlinger, K., Macomber, J., & Jacobson, K. (1992). Origins of knowledge. *Psychological Review, 99,* 605–632.

Spitz, R. A. (1965). *The first year of life: A psychoanalytic study of normal and deviant development of object relations.* New York: Basic Books.

Steiner, J. E. (1974). Innate discriminative human facial expressions to taste and smell stimuli. *Annals of the New York Academy of Science, 237,* 229–233.

Stern, D. (1977). *The first relationship: Infant and mother.* Cambridge, MA: Harvard University Press.

Stern, D. (1985). *The interpersonal world of the infant.* New York: Basic Books.

Trevarthen, C. (1979). Communication and cooperation in early infancy: A description of primary intersubjectivity. In M. M. Bullowa (Ed.), *Before speech: The beginning of interpersonal communication* (pp. 321–347). New York: Cambridge University Press.

Tronick, E. Z., Als, H., Adamson, L., Wise, S., & Brazelton, T. B. (1978). The infant's response to entrapment between contradictory messages in face-to-face interaction. *Journal of the American Academy of Child Psychiatry, 17,* 1–13.

Vries, J. I. P., de, Visser, G. H. A., & Prechtl, H. F. R. (1982). The emergence of fetal behavior: I. Qualitative aspects. *Early Human Development, 7,* 301–322.

Waal, F., de. (1996). *Good natured: The origins of right and wrong in humans and other animals.* Cambridge, MA: Harvard University Press.

Wallon, H. (1970). *De l'acte à la pensée: Essai de psychologie comparée* [From acting to thinking: Essay of comparative psychology]. Paris: Collection Champs Flammarion. (Originally published 1942).

Willatts, P. (1997). Beyond the "couch potato" infant: How infants use their knowledge to regulate action, solve problems, and achieve goals. In G. Bremner, A. Slater, & G. Butterworth (Eds.), *Infant development: Recent advances* (pp. 109–135). London: Psychology Press/Lawrence Erlbaum Associates.

Wolff, P. H. (1987). *The development of behavioral states and the expression of emotions in early infancy.* Chicago: University of Chicago Press.

Chapter **2**

The Ontogeny of Human Infant Face Recognition: Orogustatory, Visual, and Social Influences

Elliott M. Blass
University of Massachusetts, Amherst, and The Boston Medical Center

This chapter concerns the biology of individual recognition by mammalian infants; in particular, the ontogeny of human face recognition and its underlying mechanisms. In it, I identify an avenue of research in face recognition by infants that is currently in its formative stages. Different models for the development of face recognition are offered for newborns and 1- and 3-month-olds that reflect the different processes through which infants may make new faces familiar at each age. When a new face is presented to infants from 1 month of age onward, lack of familiarity gains control of behavioral systems that actively and purposively seek the information necessary for a face and its bearer to be judged safe and, therefore, familiar.

The views expressed in this chapter take root in the perspective that the face recognition system, like other biologically vital social systems (a) has both narrowly and broadly defined components, some of which are available at birth and are not experience dependent for their organization; (b) has mechanisms underlying learning about the features of individual faces that are specific and available at birth; and (c) is continuously enriched so that at each point in developmental time, infants will greet a new face with behaviors to align that face with the parameters that satisfy facial familiarity at that particular age. This view provides definable interfaces among motivational, cognitive, and neural ontogenies that can be studied with precision.

BIOLOGY OF INDIVIDUAL RECOGNITION

Although the press of biological demands for maternal face recognition in modern societies is surely not as great at the turn of the 21st century as in the recent past or during the course of our evolutionary history, an understanding of the mechanisms underlying individual recognition in human neonates, and their more general mammalian import, is a necessary prelude to understanding the ontogeny of infant–mother affectional systems. These systems are of general import. They promote and maintain the child's close proximity with the mother, who protects her young from actual or anticipated threat. Early recognition of mother and siblings also allows infants to learn from them in the safety of the natal setting. Thus, when weanlings leave the nest independently, they go forearmed with vital ecological information about the safety of particular places, individuals, and objects of which they do not have to learn on their own, on a trial-and-error basis at considerable peril (Blass, 1995; Holmes, 1988).

Mammalian infants are born prepared to learn about the defining idiosyncratic qualities of their mother (Hogan, 1988). Newborn mammals, among others, solve the seemingly daunting task of extracting her unique qualities against the bombardment of competing internal and external stimulation in a new medium through different prenatal and postnatal strategies (De Casper & Spence, 1986). Interestingly, all mammalian postnatal strategies have in common the feature of learning about the mother through her inducing state changes of either marked excitation (Woo & Leon, 1995) or calm (Blass, 1995; Shide & Blass, 1989, 1991) during the course of nursing and suckling exchanges. Newborn rats, for example, learn about their own mother's unique olfactory imprint during the first 4 to 5 postnatal days when she vigorously licks her infants anogenital region before nursing while holding her infants in close proximity to her odor-dense nipple region. This activation is followed by extensive contact, suckling, and milk letdown, each of which is calming and has been demonstrated to support learning about some maternal features (Alberts & May, 1984; MacFarlane, 1975; Porter, Makin, Davis, & Christensen, 1992; Schaal, 1988; Shide & Blass, 1991; Weller, Blass, Gibbs, & Smith, 1995). Indeed, rats get a head start on the problem by learning prenatally about their mothers' olfactory features by sampling amniotic fluid (Pedersen & Blass, 1982) and postnatally through the confluence of olfactory and tactile stimulation by the mother (Pedersen, Williams, & Blass, 1982).

Rats are not the only early learners. Human fetuses discover the prosodic qualities of their mothers voice, evidently through bone transduction (De Casper & Spence, 1986). Thus, human and rat fetuses have sufficiently well-developed neural capacity to learn something about their own mothers' vocal and olfactory characteristics via passive exposure and to match postnatal information with that obtained in a different medium, sometimes through different neural pathways, to provide continuity during the transition from aquatic to air environments. Newborns, therefore, can immediately establish representations of the mother along particular dimensions. These individual representations may be enriched over time and may combine with other sensory information to form appropriately complex intermodal representations of the mother. This may occur by integrating the simultaneous presentation of different maternal qualities, sights and sounds, for example (Spelke, 1979). That infants can match intermodal temporal patterning of vision and audition, or visual and tactile patterns (Streri & Pecheux, 1986), outside the felicitous suckling-contact setting suggests that under propitious natural settings provided by nursing, the task of forming complex intermodal maternal representations should be rather easy.

FUNCTION OF EARLY RECOGNITION SYSTEMS

Two general questions arise, How is this information used? What is it function? I believe that information concerning maternal identification is obtained and used in parallel and serial three-stage processes that inform infants about safe individuals and resources in their immediate niche (Alberts & Cramer, 1988). Initially, infants learn about some set of idiosyncratic maternal features through brain changes directly caused by nursing. Second, under ideal circumstances, a representation of these features becomes the object of infant affectional systems. Third, infants seek and are comforted by these features, and, therefore, by the dam and from other sources (relatives) that, by definition, have proven safe. The mother lives; she has established a nest, is raising her young, and is performing various particular nurturing acts. These acts and the objects and individuals toward which they are directed have not incapacitated her. She and her immediate siblings are a repository of information that provides a safe interface through which her infants can learn about the pitfalls of the larger world from the relative safety of the nest (Galef & Heiber, 1976). For many mammals, the rewarding, charged, yet gentle environment of the nest, therefore, provides sensory information concerning mother and litter mates that influence the infants' social and ingestive behavior in the present and in the immediate and long-term future. By the time of weaning, infants can learn about the features of new individuals in the safe setting without the intimacy and charged ambiance of nursing (Galef & Beck, 1990).

FOOD SELECTION AS A CASE STUDY

Mothers determine food selection of their weanlings. They do not teach the infants how to eat or how to regulate. Hall's important studies (1975, 1990, for review) clearly demonstrated that rats of weaning age (19 days) do not have to suckle the dam or interact with her or siblings in order to eat normally and to adjust their food and water intake to physiological challenges. Either the integrated feeding system is available intact without any suckling experience at all, or only a minimal amount of experience is necessary for normal ingestion, growth, and adjustments to physiological challenges and body weight regulation to occur. The physiological, motoric, and motivational systems that *narrowly define* physiologically determined ingestive behavior are fully integrated prefunctionally and await direction as to which objects in the environment should be categorized as food and which foods and food sources should be selected (Epstein, 1986; Hogan, 1988). It is the selection of safe foods by omnivores that *broadly defines* the ingestive system in the terms of this chapter. The broadly defined system of recognition builds on and incorporates the more specific system to select safe foods from the entire spectrum of substances in the environment that can be classified as edible and from the places that contain food. How does selection occur? How does the broadly defined system that determines food safety and selection take its shape for a particular animal? We later link this with mechanisms underlying human infant face recognition.

Studies from a number of laboratories during the late 1970s and 1980s remain pertinent today. They demonstrated that newborn rats can be classically conditioned and that this information could eventually be brought to the service of food and sibling recognition. Infants' initial suckling episodes are dependent on the presence of amniotic fluid on the nipple (Pedersen & Blass, 1982; Teicher & Blass, 1977). Because amniotic fluid is a blood filtrate, it provides the flavors (odors) of maternal diet during gestation. Information from plasma filtrates concerning food safety is further obtained through mother's milk (Galef & Clark, 1972; Galef & Sherry, 1973). This may be conveyed in two forms: infant's own saliva as it perfuses the mouth, and direct olfactory and gustatory sampling of milk flavor during suckling to inform the young about local food safety at weaning. By delivering milk that contains extracts of new safe foods, and by encouraging the weanlings first bites in her presence, the mother is also preparing their gastrointestinal tract for local flora that will be ingested at weaning. This cascade of events without any penalty to the weanlings directs them toward new foods, tastes, and flavors that are safe. In short, the broadly defined system of food safety and selection is founded on (a) infants quickly learning about the mother very early; (b) their following her; (c) their learning about the things that she eats; and (to a lesser extent) (d) their learning about the places in which she eats.

Human infants can also become familiar with certain foods through mother's milk and can be influenced by these familiar tastes, according to Manilla and Beauchamp (1996). Human and other primate infants also gain information at a distance by watching mother and other relatives select food and eat. It may be the act of a familiar animal eating that categorizes objects either as food or, more likely, as safe food. The same logic follows for human infants watching a familiar (and therefore safe) individual eating food that has proven to be nondetrimental (Birch, 1990; Birch, Marlin, & Rotter, 1984; Birch, Zimmerman, & Hind, 1980). This is a vital area of research about which remarkably little is known.

Selection of safe foods is of such fundamental import that additional features are available to help make safe the transition from sterile milk to eating without the mother as intermediary. Mammalian mothers help smooth this transition both behaviorally and physiologically. Large carnivore mothers, cats and wolves, for example, return to their lair with prey, eat some of it, and then regurgitate the food in front of the young (Martins, 1949; Rheingold, 1963). This causes great excitement, and the infants partake of this newfound meal. It is more than likely that the mother has initiated the digestive process and may be passing along her intestinal flora in the partially digested food to help the infants during their gastrointestinal (GI) transition from a lactose-based milk diet to a heavy, carnivorous protein diet. In this regard, the mother later hunts with her young, stunning prey and allowing the weanlings to attack further before the prey is finally killed, either by mother or young, at which time they all eat simultaneously amid great excitement. It seems very unlikely to me that the young are learning how to hunt; it seems highly likely that they are discovering what to hunt. They may be refining their hunting skills, of course. It is of interest in this regard that mothers extensively chew select morsals before passing the partially digested tidbits to their infants. The contribution of this process to dietary canalization is not known.

Rat mothers use a different strategy to help their infants during the transition. They secrete *caecotrophe*, a gelatinous, olfactory rich substance that is exuded analy and is dense in the bacteria necessary for digesting the mother's current diet. Infants are attracted to this maternal odor (Leon, 1974) and ingest her caecotrophe (Galef & Heiber, 1976), which fortifies the intestine to facilitate the omnivores transition from specialist feeder of mother's milk to generalist feeder of her diet at weaning. In addition, the rat dam when weaning her young, allows them to investigate her mouth while she feeds, and it is the mix of the familiar and presumably attractive salivary odors and food that help direct the infants to the mother's most recent diet (Galef, Mason, Preti, & Bean, 1988). I am not aware of reports on how herbivore mothers help their infants with the transition from a milk-based to a herbivore diet. Domestic cattle, at least, always eat next to their calves, and the weanlings invariably initiate feeding within moments of the mother (Blass, personal observations, August, 1997).

Food safety is not the only lesson taught in the nest. Infants also learn about their kin. In an important series of studies, Holmes and colleagues (review by Holmes, 1988) have presented considerable evidence that a number of squirrel species learn the identity of their sisters in the nest and then, as adults, selectively enter into alliances with them in the face of attack, especially to the young. It is clear that "sisterhood" is conferred through the familiarity of the nest as opposed to "familiality." Thus, the information derived in the nest setting defines defensive alliances during adulthood even though the information was obtained in a completely different context.

NEUROLOGICAL CONSIDERATIONS

The excitement in rat pups generated by vigorous maternal anogenital licking before nursing causes specific changes in brain catecholamines, norepinephrine (NE) especially, that are sufficient to reorganize olfactory bulb microarchitecture underlying olfactory learning. The massive noradrenergic projection to the olfactory bulb in infant rats incorporates about 40 percent of all noradrenergic fibers that arise from the locus coeruleus (LC), the exclusive source of brain NE. This exuberant NE projection to the preferred sensory apparatus is not unique to rats. Comparative studies have demonstrated that LC projections are substantial in all mammals and largely terminate in the dominant sensory region. Thus, in general, primate NE projection is visual, with relatively few olfactory projections—quite the opposite pattern of rodents and lagomorphs, which are more olfactory dependent (Whitehead, 1994). The insight here is that under natural circumstances mammalian mothers, during their periods of contact with their infants, especially those surrounding the nursing setting, incorporate various arousing activities into the prenursing routine that activate the noradrenergic projection system, which terminates selectively in the major central sensory area. This activation and consequent NE release to the target area changes the neural architecture of the target area to register the mother's particular sensory qualities. These changes are ultimately incorporated into the neurology underlying preferences for those very attributes (Shide & Blass, 1991). As we discuss later, the critical event in the cascade appears to be NE change and not necessarily the mode that causes the change; calming also appears to gain access to NE projections in rats. The human newborn data are consistent with this general description.

PARALLELS BETWEEN COOPERATIVE AND INGESTIVE BEHAVIORS

There are strong parallels between the cooperative behavior of squirrels in the face of danger, various social behaviors in primates reflecting their place in the matriarchal social hierarchy of the troop, and the ingestive behavior of weaning rats. Rats do not have to learn either how to eat or how to regulate their caloric intake (narrow constancy). They learn what to eat. Likewise, squirrels do not learn how to fight; these patterns are available (narrow constancy), although they may be finely tuned. The squirrels learn in the nest who their sisters are, that is, with whom to form alliances (broad constancy). In this vein, monkeys do not learn appeasement or threat gestures. They seem to learn to whom the "appropriate" gesture should or should not be directed. Establishing these distinctions between narrow and broad constancies has a number of important features to help unstick us from the bog of the nature–nurture controversy. First, it speaks of integrated multifaceted systems, the components of which inform each other. Second, it emphasizes the control of broadly defined systems in seeking information to fulfill their parameters. Third, the systems are dedicated neurologically. Fourth, they also control behavior when complete, in terms of performing alliance acts, for example.

In short, mammalian mothers and their infants have evolved behavioral and physiological synchronies that facilitate the transition from the early, highly specialized (suckling) and digestive (lactose-based) systems to the diverse feeding strategies and differently specialized gastrointestinal tracts that define the animals from weaning and beyond. A cornerstone of food safety lies in the infant's identifying its mother, maintaining close contact with her to discover safe foods through her, and to ingesting her intestinal flora to facilitate early digestion of these foods.

In a broader sense, the issue of food selection is a classic problem in biological and behavioral development. It is the selection of a restricted range from a potentially unlimited one. Four aspects of the solution to the food selection problem, I believe, are representative of how other "restriction" problems are solved. First, integrated motoric, regulatory, and motivational systems are available at birth, in certain ways at adult levels (Blass, 1995; Hall, 1990, for reviews). Second, cognitive and affective mechanisms guarantee infant recognition of and proximity with the mother. Third, it is through this proximity that she informs the infants about food safety. Fourth, common to all aspects of maternal recognition and education concerning food safety are maternally induced infant state changes of extreme excitation and extreme calming. Both involve noradrenergic engagement; the latter, in certain instances, the engagement of opioid mechanisms. Finally, although accurately capturing the general issue of narrow selection from a potentially broad choice, the aforementioned does not imply that all these facets necessarily contribute to restriction in other domains, language for example (Kuhl, 1985). One challenge that this view presents is to discover the different classes of experiential events that gain control over the available systems in question and the underlying mechanisms.

EXTENSIONS TO HUMAN INFANTS

Does any of this pertain to acquisition of knowledge of parents and siblings by human infants? I believe that it does. Newborns are more attracted to (i.e., look longer at) faces (or, to be more exact, cartoons of faces) than to other equally complex displays. This attraction to a face caricature is manifest even before newborns have ever seen a face. In a famous study by Goren, Sarty, and Wu (1975), newborns followed a facial cartoon by turning eyes and head to track it over considerable distances relative to equally complex control stimuli. This finding has been replicated in all its particulars (Johnson, Dziurawiec, Ellis, & Morton, 1991; Johnson, Dziurawiec, Bartrip, & Morton, 1992). In my view, the preference for facial displays and the tracking system meet the criteria of a narrowly defined component of the broadly defined face recognition system. The narrow capacity is functional at birth: It is immediately pressed into the service of the face-recognition system through preferentially looking at oval objects whose internal features have a facelike configuration.

Visual preferences for the mother can be established within 4 hours postnatally (Walton, Bower, & Bower, 1992), certainly within 24 hours (Bushnell, Sai, & Mullin, 1983; Field, Cohen, Garcia, & Greenberg, 1984). This is remarkable given how little waking time is actually spent with her during this period, how little of that time the infant's eyes are actually open and the many distractions that compete for the newborn's attention. In fact, in Walton, Bower, & Bower (1992), infants sucked a pacifier in order for a static picture of the mother to appear on a television monitor. The virtual mother, bare of scent, movement, and sound and of two dimensions was sufficient to maintain selected levels of the operant more so than images of strangers matched to mothers on basic facial appearance. I am impressed with these findings obtained in infants as young as 4 hours of age; their implications have yet to be explored.

The circumstances of forming, remembering, and preferring a representation of the mother are worthy of experimental attention. Understanding how infants learn about and are attracted to particular faces may allow us to solve the problem of how the infants' potential of directing their affection toward any individual is narrowed to their own mother (caretaker). The following may help direct our inquiries:

1. Processing of faces comes under the domain of a dedicated neural system.
2. Access to this system is provided through the narrowly defined face-attraction system identified by Goren et al. (1975).
3. The endpoint of making a new face familiar is reached in different ways at different ontogenetic time points.

From at least 1 month of age, infants actively seek information when meeting new people and, as indicated (3), the classes of information change over time.

A BASIS FOR MATERNAL IDENTIFICATION AND PREFERENCE

The rapidity of preference formation and the ability to influence the circumstances of preference induction make tractable the origins of human infant facial recognition and preference. Human newborns quickly make their selection through limited contact and suckling experiences with their mother. This early selection may be accounted for by the processes of classical conditioning.

Two studies make this possibility worth considering. First, Blass, Ganchrow, and Steiner (1984) reported that newborns quickly orient to touch on the forehead that predicted sucrose delivery. This was more than abstracting the relationship between two events; there were affective consequences. When sucrose was withheld after conditioning, infants started to cry. They were distressed by the touch that had previously predicted sucrose delivery and had elicited orientation to the locus of delivery. Furthermore, Sullivan et al. (1991) showed that, as in rats, human infants can readily be conditioned to an odor that is paired with gentle tactile stimulation (Field et al., 1975). It follows, therefore, that if classical conditioning can be so easily obtained in newborns in a single experimental session, in which only one rewarding dimension such as taste or touch was engaged, then the unique maternal facial features also should be readily linked with the rich features of the suckling and contact systems that are engaged during repeated intimate mother-infant contacts. In principal, this linkage confers positive affective value to the tactile, olfactory, visual, and auditory features (Walker-Andrews & Lennon, 1991) of the mother that infants perceive during contact, suckling, and milk delivery.

Figure 2.1 provides a schematic that is consistent with the looking and preference data and with the ideas of narrow and broad stabilties in facial recognition and preference. Motivational and assosciation systems that are available at birth to participate in the process of face recognition are presented as ovals and include:

1. the facial detection system described by Goren et al. (1975).
2. the affective component triggered by contact and different facets of nursing (see Blass, 1995, 1997a, 1997b, 1997c, 1997d).
3. a mechanism that induces eye opening, at least for part of the time.

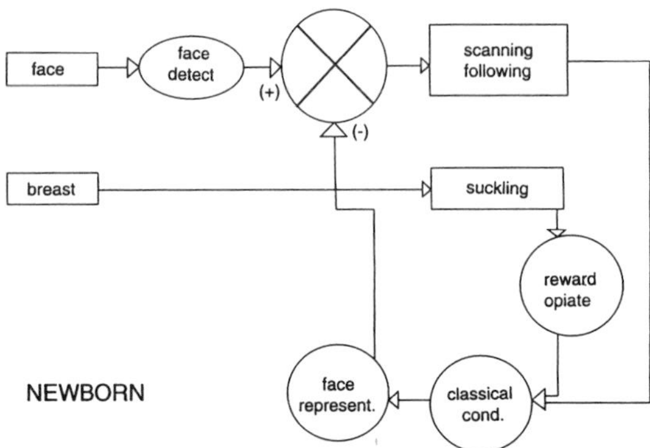

FIG. 2.1. Model to account for and direct future research on calming and the development of face recognition in newborn humans. See text for details.

4. The neurologies that underlie facial representation and classical conditioning.

Three systems (1,3,4) are dedicated to obtaining knowledge about faces. Classical conditioning is available to newborns to discover other facets of the mother (Blass, Ganchrow, & Steiner, 1984; Sullivan et al., 1991), including her olfactory properties (Schaal, 1988).

According to Fig. 2.1, suckling immediately and profoundly influences newborns. Physiologically rewarding changes in state are caused by whole body contact, the suckling act, orotactile stimulation by breast and nipple, and orogustatory stimulation by milk flavor. Suckling-induced calm, changes in the neurochemistry of reward pathways, and lasting preferences for odors and faces associated with these individual nursing components suggest that these events are pleasant to infants. Concomitant with these changes, the infant opens his or her eyes and discerns a face, as defined by both external and internal configuration (Goren et al., 1975; Johnson et al., 1991; Johnson et al., 1992). This engages the search mechanism, and the infant looks at the face for a period of time. These two classes of events, affective change and face scanning, appear to be sufficient to restructure the facial representation system to sculpt a memory and a preference for that face.

Information concerning the new face influences the comparator in at least two ways. To the extent that the face has now become familiar within the suckling context, then the search signal may be inhibited and the infant's eyes may close. There is also a positive feedback system (not shown), when infants are presented with two faces, one of which is familiar. Now the scanning system focuses on the face that has become familiar within the context of nursing. There is an interesting implication to the feedforward system. In addition to triggering the expectancy of suckling and obtaining milk, the conditioned stimulus, face, sound, or odor may also actually induce the state itself.

A report by Shide and Blass (1991) on rats supports this view. Shide and Blass induced a preference in 10-day-old rat pups for a normally avoided orange odor by pairing it with oral infusions of sucrose or fat, substances that calm isolated rats and protect them against pain through endogenous opioid mechanisms (Blass & Fitzgerald, 1988; Blass, Fitzgerald, & Kehoe, 1987; Shide & Blass, 1989). Shide and Blass (1991) demonstrated that injecting rats with naltrexone, a potent opioid blocker, at the time of conditioning prevented preference formation. In additional groups of rats, naltrexone was first injected just before preference testing, well after conditioning. Naltrexone also blocked the expression of olfactory preference. Thus, for rat infants at least, the endogenous systems that were active during conditioning had to be engaged for the preference to be expressed. Rat infants, according to Shide and Blass were attracted to the odor not necessarily in anticipation of milk delivery or the changes that delivery will cause but because the odor itself released endogenous opioids and continued to do so for the duration of time that the infants remained in its proximity. Similar mechanisms may be at play in human newborn affectional development toward the mother in which the broader stability gains control over preference expression, possibly because of endogenous opioid release caused by a conditioned aspect(s) of the mother. A more traditional interpretation of these findings argues that the conditioned opioid release sustains the infant's behavior until maternal contact is established, that is, an incentive interpretation (Mark, Smith, Rada, & Hoebel, 1994). The two views are not incompatible; the emphasis differs, however.

INFANT FACE PROCESSING

Although newborns readily prefer the mother's face to the stranger's, newborn face processing differs importantly from that of adults, indeed, even older children. First, according to de Schonen, Mathivet, & Deruelle (1989) and Pascalis, de Schonen, Morton, Deruelle, & Fabre-Grenet (1995), representations of familiar faces are through their external features, because until about 4 months of age, infants do not prefer mother to stranger when the adult heads are wrapped in scarves, thereby making external facial features unavailable for discrimination. This is of interest because internal features provided the basis for face following in newborns (Morton & Johnson, 1991). Internal features appear not to be available, however, to that part of the system that discriminates among different faces.

Early face representation also differs in its neural mediation. Whereas familiar faces are processed primarily in the right hemisphere in adults (Ellis, 1992), newborn processing is primarily left hemisphere based. According to Pascalis et al. (1995), the mother's face is represented in the right hemisphere by 4 months of age, based on tachistoscopic presentation to right or left hemispheres and recording of evoked potentials. This has been confirmed by de Haan and Nelson (1997) in 6-month-old infants using the ERP (evoked-response potentials) method. ERP distinguished between 500 millisecond presentations of photographs of mothers versus similar- and dissimilar-looking women. The major differences were in the right cortex.

MECHANISMS UNDERLYING FAMILIARITY INDUCTION

Whereas a new face readily becomes familiar to adults through exposure alone, more intimate contact appears to be necessary in infants. We do not know what aspects of the nursing-suckling exchanges induce familiarity, if there is a gradient among components and how the components interact. Recent animal studies in the calming effects of different stimulus combinations suggest idiosyncratic facilititory combinations, at least for pain and distress systems. There are a number of candidates for rewarding stimulation. The contact and nursing system soothes through opioid and other mechanisms. They relieve discomfort (Smith, Fillion, & Blass, 1990) and pain (Blass, 1997c). They conserve energy (Rao, Blass, Brignol, Marino, & Glass, 1997). We do not know which aspects of these maternally induced changes get linked to the mother's external features. Our studies and others have demonstrated that in newborn rats and humans, orogustatory, orotactile, and contact systems that are normally engaged during suckling readily support conditioning. Indeed, tactile or olfactory conditioning and preference are readily obtainable with various tastes and contact paradigms in rats and humans as has been discussed above (see Blass, 1992, 1995, 1996, for further discussion of the details).

Recent preliminary evidence in rats by Matthew Ennis and Barry Davis has shed new light on the neurological consequences of orosensory-orotactile stimulation. Through the use of immunocytochemical techniques that reveal the activity of immediate early genes, and therefore, the pathways of differential activity caused by a behavioral or physiological event, Ennis and Davis obtained heightened activity in the locus coeruleus, the source of brain NE, during suckling with sucrose delivery. This unexpected finding demonstrates that NE systems can be engaged by calming as well as excitatory stimuli that support olfactory classical conditioning. This is consonant with the role of NE in attention (Cooper, Bloom, & Roth, 1991). Thus, both excitatory and calming systems can gain access to the NE transmitter system to cause long-term changes in affect and memory. For orogustatory, but not orotactile, stimulation the mechanisms appear to involve endogenous opioid systems for both preference acquisition and expression. Again, we are dealing with multiple affective and conditioning pathways that contribute to infant representations of their mothers and to the emotions recruited by these representations. Recall that in humans the NE projections are primarily to visual systems. To extend the parallel, on anatomical grounds alone, we would expect very rapid visual conditioning during nursing in human newborns.

FACE DISCRIMINATION IN NEWBORNS

Although rather little is known about the mechanisms that underlie face recognition and preference formation, recent findings provide interesting points of departure. There is a face-discriminating system, probably subcortical (Morton & Johnson, 1991) that causes infants to look at and preferentially track facelike cartoons and presumably real faces as well. The tracking decision appears to be determined by both external and internal facial features. Second, the mechanisms underlying classical conditioning are sufficient to account for the infant's learning about the mother's external features, to represent them and to seek them out through the operants of looking, choosing, and working for a face to appear on a television screen. That is, stability in the broadly defined system of specific facial representation is sufficient to gain control over motivational and motor systems that ensure visual contact with the familiar face even in newborns. Third, and this has not been documented for newborns, we do not know the extent of control exerted over newborn behavior when the broad system is not fully specified for a particular face. I have provisionally indicated in Fig. 2.1 that the system remains open until the face has become familiar, although we do not have an operational definition for the latter. We do not know at this point if eye opening and looking at the face of the nursing caretaker is under the control of a search system or is elicited by the sucking act. This can be resolved empirically.

A SHIFT IN CONTROL OVER CRYING: IMPLICATIONS FOR THE ONTOGENY OF FACE RECOGNITION

Recent studies from my laboratory are relevant here. Recall that crying newborn humans can readily be quieted by tasting microlitter volumes of sucrose, glucose, or fructose (Blass & Smith, 1992), the noncaloric sweetener aspartame (Barr, Pantel, Wright, Gravel, & Young, 1995), or milk (Blass, 1997b). Moreover, these substances also protect the infant against pain (Barr, Quek, Oberlander, Brian, & Young, 1994; Blass & Hoffmeyer,

1991; Blass & Shah, 1996). Sucrose is not effective when delivered to infants whose mothers were maintained on methadone during pregnancy (Blass & Ciarimatero, 1994), which may reduce the availability of the infants endogenous opioids (Finnegan, 1986).

Things change, however. Sucrose remains a potent quieting agent in 2-week-old humans, but not in 4-week-olds (Zeifman et al., 1996). The older infants, as shown in Fig. 2.2 did not quiet to sucrose; their crying was reduced by only about 40 percent, and variability was substantial. This stood in marked contrast to newborns and 2-week-old infants whose crying was reduced essentially to naught with minimal variability and remained suppressed for up to 5 minutes after sucrose delivery terminated. We were struck by the effect's modesty and variability in 4-week-olds. On reviewing the videotapes, we discovered that some infants had engaged the experimenter visually, and it was these infants who quieted to sucrose. Interestingly, the experimenter was not aware of this engagement at the time, an important point to which I will return. In a follow-up experiment, Zeifman et al. (1996) delivered sucrose or water again, only now one-half the infants who received sucrose were deliberately engaged visually by the experimenter, a stranger, and the other half received the same volumes of sucrose on the same schedule, but the experimenter focused her gaze on the infants' foreheads and maintained this position even though the infants repeatedly attempted to establish eye contact. Infants who received water did so with visual contact.

As shown in Fig. 2.3, sucrose delivery during eye engagement essentially caused the same effect as did sucrose alone in newborns. Crying stopped

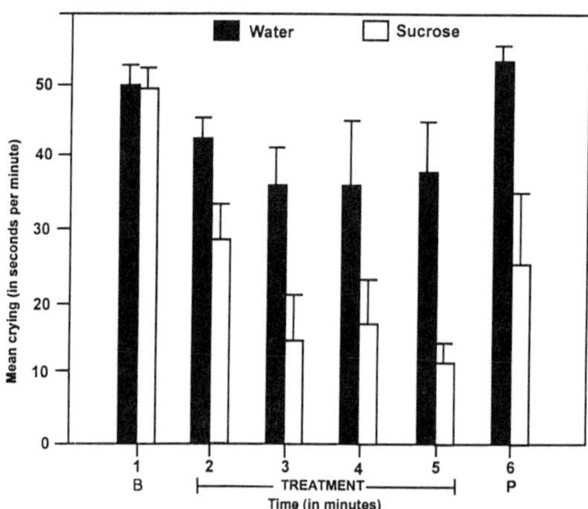

FIG. 2.2 The effects of sucrose on crying in 4-week-old infants who were not in eye contact with the experimenter. (From Zeifman, et al., 1996. Copyright © 1996 by the American Psychological Association. Reprinted with permission.

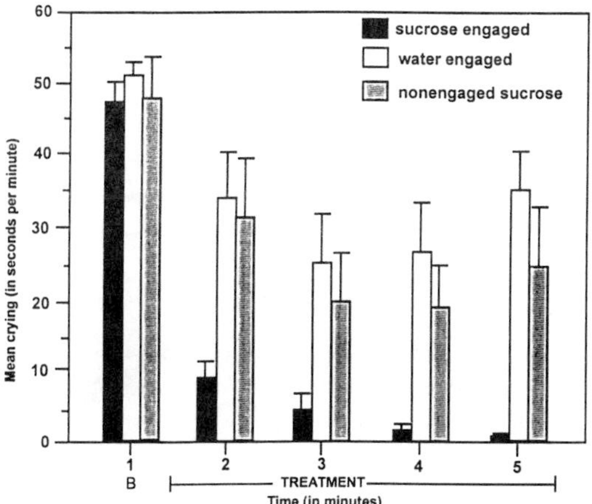

FIG. 2.3. The effects of eye contact and sucrose on crying in 4-week-old infants. Notice that the combination treatment is effective during the first minute, a time that neither treatments alone was. (From Zeifman, et al., 1996. Copyright © 1996 by the American Psychological Association. Reprinted with permission.

and remained at very low levels even after sucrose termination. Moreover (not shown), heart rate was markedly reduced. These changes reflect the emergent property of the combination of particular visual and orogustatory afferents. It is not simply a matter of additivity of two influential events. Visual engagement was ineffective when water was delivered. Likewise, sucrose alone, in the absence of visual engagement, had a very modest effect. The point of an emergent property or a potentiation of two subthreshold stimuli is emphasized by Fig. 2.3, which demonstrates that sucrose-engagement markedly reduced crying during the first treatment minute, whereas neither component alone diminished crying. Thus, circumstances that start to approximate the natural situation, in which a powerful orogustatory stimulus is presented with visual engagement, quiet crying infants. This underestimates the impact of nursing, because normally the infant is held by his or her mother, is engaged in the motor activity of suckling, and has the additional stimulation of nipple and breast in mouth. Thus, under minimal natural conditions, it is the emergent property that causes crying reduction and normalizes heart rate, presumably, in part through opioid mediation. The system is integrative because subthreshold levels of sucrose and visual engagement combine to arrest crying, demonstrating a very early intermodal integration. The interactions among all the natural afferents are currently under investigation in an effort to identify the domains of maternal influences and their interactions.

The 4-week-old infant data are of considerable interest, because within the context of a sweet taste, the eyes take on the properties of unconditioned stimuli. Indeed, among the most striking aspects of this study are the infants' persistent efforts to maintain visual contact with experimenters who maintained their gaze on the infant's forehead. This is especially impressive because of the infants unobstructed view of the experimenter's entire face, including the eyes. By focusing on the mother's eyes, infants may start to learn about the internal features of her face, possibly even it's configuration. My assumption is that when a representation, either featural or configural, of the internal facial features has been achieved, the face is classified as familiar and, by 4 months of age, if not sooner, is processed in the brain's right hemisphere. In the presence of an unfamiliar face, the neurological system underlying face recognition drives search behavior to seek the critical features that satisfy the criteria of familiarity and by definition, safety.

By the sixth week and continuing into at least 9 weeks of age, a second transition has taken place. Sucrose and eye contact with a stranger continue to quiet during sucrose administration, but infants revert to their baseline levels of crying when sucrose delivery terminates. Thus, the protracted effects of sucrose in our paradigm are lost by 6 weeks of age, as shown in Fig. 2.4 (Blass, 1997d). By 12 weeks, sucrose-visual engagement no longer arrests crying. Understanding the basis of this failure will enhance our understanding of the representational and social determinants of the mother–infant bond and of the qualitative changes in the relationship, because they will lead us to discover the additional social and physical features that must be added to baseline characteristics for crying to stop.

Heart rate is disassociated from crying by 6 weeks of age. Although crying was reduced by sucrose-visual engagement, heart rate was not affected. Mechanisms governing heart rate, which are separable anatomically from the more rostral portions of the brain that control affective systems, are also separable functionally by 6 weeks, probably sooner. This is consistent with the anatomical organization of the gustatory system. According to Murphy, Ennis, Shipley, & Behbehani (1994), taste afferents diverge after their initial synapse in the nucleus of the solitary tract (NST). One set of afferents traverses rostrally to the forebrain to engage neural mechanisms governing affect while other neural systems move caudally from the NST to deeper brain stem nuclei that manage cardiovascular systems. Still others synapse directly with midbrain structures that ultimately inhibit pain transmission at the level of the spinal cord (Ren, Blass, Zhou, & Dubner, 1997).

It may be instructive at this point to place these findings in broader biological and developmental contexts. There are parallel physiological and behavioral findings. In newborns, who have the highest surface to mass ratios and who, by definition, are most vulnerable to heat loss, sucrose and milk arrest crying, thereby saving metabolic energy and enhancing its

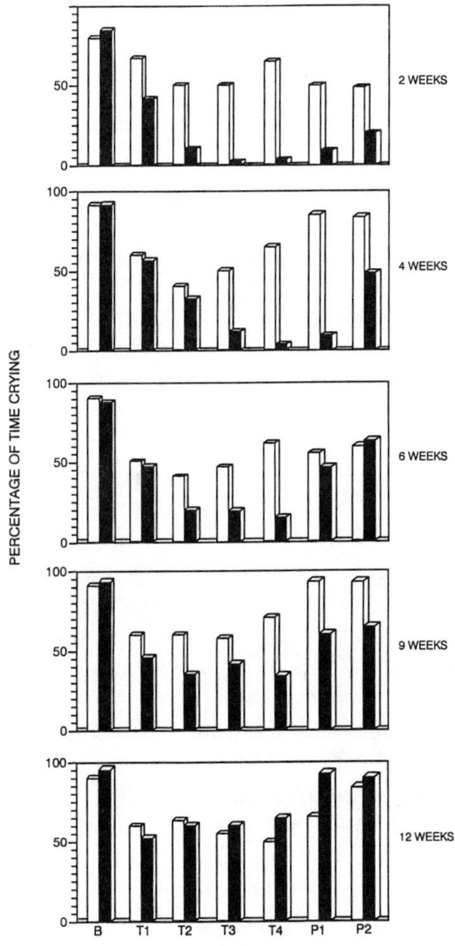

FIG. 2.4. The effects of sucrose or water and eye contact on crying in 2–4-week old infants. (From Blass, 1997d. Reprinted with permission).

utilization, presumably toward somatic and especially brain growth (Rao et al., 1997). Importantly, behavioral and physiological systems are not intrinsically differentiated so that sweet taste affects all systems that conserve energy. From a behavioral perspective, although we do not know why infants were crying, it was not to obtain sucrose, given that sucrose had never been previously tasted. A more likely possibility is that crying stopped because sucrose taste released central opioids, thereby overwhelming the particular circumstances that gave rise to spontaneous crying. Thus, a central mechanism may weigh the sum of its afferents to either increase or terminate crying. There may not necessarily be a recognition of the particular source, only its valance. This changes developmentally when both source and valance are taken into account.

By 4 weeks of age, with rapid growth reducing the surface to mass ratio, the system that allows sucrose to calm has expanded to require conjoint social engagement, in particular eye-to-eye contact. The broader social context builds on and is integrated with energy repletion and conservation provided by suckling; a more complex intermodal stimulus array that involves infant and adult eye contact is required to arrest crying. Eye contact is actively sought by 4-week-olds, thereby providing them an opportunity to learn about the internal features of adult faces.

An important fact for the perspective expressed here is that 4-week-olds are not passive in this test situation. When visual contact was thwarted, they raised their heads in a sustained and clearly purposive effort to capture the experimenter's eyes, despite the fact that they had a full view of her face, including her eyes. It is surely more than coincidence that Wolff (1963, 1987) observed the same pattern during his classic ethological studies. Suddenly, at 4 weeks, there was a substantial increase in eye contact between mothers and infants. The mothers simply were not aware of the change. They regularly commented though that they felt that the baby was more human and that it cared about her. According to Lavelli and Poli (1998), 4-week-old infants spend up to 10 percent of their nursing bouts looking into their mothers eyes, a finding that accords with Berger and Cunningham's (1981) earlier studies. This represents a considerable increase over the 1 percent to 2 percent of the time spent in mutual gaze by 10-day-old human infants and their mothers. Although I am suggesting the primacy of eye contact as a vehicle for learning about the mother's face and establishing the mother–infant bond, it is important to note that increased eye contact may not necessarily have anything to do with facial recognition from a phylogenetic perspective. It may have been selected for enhancing maternal milk yield and for sustaining maternal caretaking.

Parallel findings have also been obtained in an experimental paradigm (Haith, Bergman, & Moore, 1977) in which infants lay on their back and looked at their mothers or strangers through a periscopelike arrangement that allowed the experimenters to precisely measure eye movement through an infrared device. They, too, found that when looking at the mother's face, 4-week-old infants spent about 30 percent of the time looking at her eyes. This increased markedly so that by 8 weeks of age, almost 60 percent of the "face time" was directed toward the eyes. Taken together, the naturalistic observational findings, the perceptual studies, and the quieting data presented by Zeifman et al. (1996) point to an active and purposive role for the infant in choosing where and at what it looks. The eyes, even of a stranger, have now taken on affective value to the infant. This demands a more active and purposive role for the infant in attending to, integrating, and remembering the features of the increasingly greater number of individuals who enter the infant's intimate space.

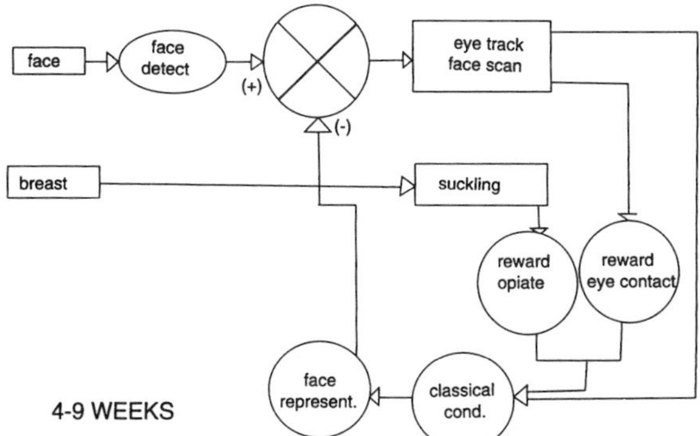

FIG. 2.5. Model to account for and provide future direction to identify calming and face-recognition mechanisms in 4–9-week-old human infants. Note how this model builds on and incorporates the model presented in Fig. 2.1.

Figure 2.5 builds on the earlier schema for newborns to specify 4- to 9-week-old infant calming and, possibly, face identification. There are three additional features. First, the initial, narrowly defined calming system has expanded and thereby helps identify adults through social as well as physiological means, with the physiological controls receding. Second, the asymmetry of unfamiliarity causes active search for eye engagement; the strangers' eyes are sought until contact is established. Stated explicitly, the asymmetry (i.e., error signal) between a strange face and the potential for familiarity engages the search system to reduce the error signal. We are now in a position to define strangeness, familiarity, and the underlying memory. The third additional feature is the emergent intermodal quality of visual contact and taste (flavor) that quiets the infant and presumably induces a preference.

The broadly defined system is seen as homeostatic; it seeks balance. It has terminal frames of reference—facial familiarity and eye contact—that control the effector mechanisms—eye scanning and gross body movements—to achieve these endpoints. In this regard, it is like other, more familiar homeostatic systems that maintain internal constancies through behavior—body fluid balance, for example (Blass & Hall, 1976). It differs importantly, however, because the face-recognition system is engaged through the particular external event of viewing an unfamiliar face. The idea of behavioral endpoints during development may be of heuristic value in a number of ways. It is amenable to formal specification and hypothesis testing. It makes the infant an active seeker of information that is under the influence of control systems that can be specified behaviorally, neurologically, and, ultimately, genetically. These forms of specification are within our grasp and depend squarely on the precision with which we delineate behavior and its underlying processes.

Ideas of control systems and predetermined endpoints in social development lend themselves to interpreting social phenomena that have been well established in the developmental literature. Imitation and play have the same properties as the systems that I have been referring to. They are externally driven. They are under the control of feedback mechanisms. They are information gathering. They have narrowly defined motor features, for example, tongue thrusting, that are determined by more broadly defined endpoints. They participate in the expression of normal social behavior. This is dramatically seen in Meltzoff and Moore's (1989, 1992) reports of infants greeting an adult with the facial pattern that the adult had presented to the infant during their previous and only meeting.

I believe that it is worth extending this notion to other classes of social and cognitive development and to evaluate whether other systems obey these organizational rules. If they do, they may provide a richer, modality-driven view of developmental organization of different and dedicated neural circuits that are organized to seek specific classes of information for completion of their selected function. This view asserts that as infants mature, different, more elaborate criteria come into place to define the broad systems and that these new criteria gain control over infant information gathering. The behavior of 12-week-old infants regarding calming and possibly face recognition speak to this point.

Twelve-week old infants may not have been quieted by the stranger because the experimental situation was sufficiently removed from the context of everyday events to prove distressing. In our studies, infants were tested in the familiarity of their own homes but by strangers; ingested a novel solution, sucrose, from a novel delivery source, a syringe, and did not have contact with their mothers. We know that infants are exquisitely sensitive to contextual cues as shown, for example, by Rovee-Collier. Merely changing the print on the bolster lining the infant's crib markedly disrupted performance in an operant task, leg kicking, that had no experimental relationship with the bolster (Rovee-Collier & Hayne, 1987). Change from normal, well-established routines may exceed the boundaries in which infants can be comforted by strangers, who must overcome their own "strangeness" and that of the context in which they appear.

There are two additional points concerning 12-week-olds. First, they may want their mothers. No longer will any pair of eyes do; they may have to be "her" eyes. This may be part of the contextual issue. More may be involved, however. By this time, infants may have developed their primary bond with the mother so that only she can provide comfort in tense situations. Relaxed infants may be more open to different sources of interaction and better able to learn in familiar supportive contexts. This can be readily evaluated.

The second point speaks to the expanding social skills of 12-week-olds and their expectations of adult behavior. They wanted more from the experimenter than eye engagement and some sugar. I think that they wanted to play. Twelve-week-old and occasionally 9-week-old infants made social overtures to the stranger, extending their tongue, smiling, and turning their shoulders in a seemingly coy manner. According to our protocol, we ignored these gestures and continued to deliver the sucrose with a smiling relaxed face. The overtures stopped and the infants continued crying despite eye engagement and sucrose delivery. Thus, within 3 months after birth, infants moved from a phase of orosensory dominance to one of necessary complex social interactions that seemed to overcome orosensory and visual stimulation. The more complex interactions might be in the service of maintaining a strong social bond with their current caretakers and might also expand the range of acceptable caretakers. Ultimately, these early, intense social interactions may be what defines familiarity (familiality) and may have prepared us phylogenetically to share resources and to enter into defensive alliances.

Figure 2.6 elaborates on the previous control systems. It continues to feature both facial search and visual engagement facets and extends the system to incorporate the persistent social activities of the infant. The driving forces here are eye-engagement, social-engagement, and face familiarity. Achieving the two former goals in the absence of the latter will curtail or modify the particular search activities; having the face become familiar will not necessarily halt social and visual engagements but will modify them considerably. Thus, search stops when the criteria for facial familiarity have been met. This may occur immediately when the face is already familiar, as expressed in the connection between face search and

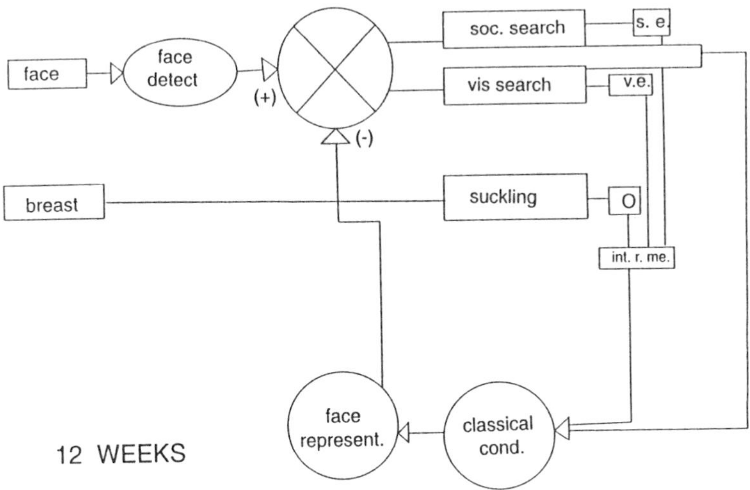

FIG. 2.6. Model for the development of face recognition in 12-week-old infants.

already familiar, as expressed in the connection between face search and the representation of the familiar face. In the absence of this immediate match, search continues until familiarity is obtained through facial and social engagement systems. This may be facilitated by reward systems triggered by contact, taste, or suckling. Although the criteria for familiarity can not be specified at present for infants, I do not see establishing them as daunting, because both behavioral and neural criteria can be specified. Finally, although not emphasized in Fig. 2.6, it is reasonable to assume that the role of classical conditioning is diminished because of the complexity of the interactions that are involved in play and other social interactions. Different forms of mechanisms and their underlying neurology have to be sought for the development of representations in older infants.

It is important to emphasize again that we have isolated and manipulated on a one-time basis only two elements of the rich physical, physiological, and behavioral tapestry presented to infants by their mothers during the normal range of mother–infant interactions. The sparseness of our presentation and our limited understanding of the infant social motivational system(s) can be appreciated from the studies of Muir (this volume, for review) in which the stress caused 16-week-old infants by the mother suddenly assuming a "still-face" (Cohen & Tronick, 1987) was readily overcome by simply touching the baby (Stack & Muir, 1990). Like all motivational systems, affectional ones are under multiple determinants. In the Muir studies, crying was induced by a change in social interactions between mother and infant. Touch calmed. What did the touch represent? Was it touch per se or did the infant treat this as a sign of normal responsivity on the mother's part? (See also Rochat & Striano, this volume, on developing social expectations.)

A PROPOSED SHIFT TO INTERNAL FACE RECOGNITION

The evidence that 3- to 4-month-old infants use internal facial features is indirect, hence the promissory character of this chapter. A number of available facts however, speak to the possibility that if internal representations are used by these infants, they differ from adult usage. According to Carey and Diamond (1977; Diamond & Carey, 1977; reviewed by Carey, 1992), 5- to 6-year-old children are not disturbed in identifying inverted faces. Adults have considerable difficulty with the inverted presentation, however. Yet 5- to 6-year olds are able to use internal facial features for identification (when familiar adults heads are wrapped with scarves) and matching but do not recognize classmates, with whom they had spent 4 months, when internal facial features were presented alone from photographs of faces with no external features. That is, when no information was offered concerning external contours, so that internal features of the face were presented with no context whatsoever, 5- to 6-year-old children failed to recognize or identify very familiar classmates. In contrast, adults recognize familiar people primarily on the bases of internal facial configurations. These identifications, of course, withstand changes in facial expression, and a face border is not necessary for recognition or identification. The children do not appear to have this flexibility. Carey has suggested that adults use configurational representations of internal facial features, whereas children until about 10 years of age use featural information. Thus, if some aspects of the internal face are used by 3- to 4-month-olds to identify very familiar people, their nature is most likely to be featural rather than configurational.

Processing of internal facial features, although differing from adult processing, appears to be available by at least 4 months of age. As indicated, 4-month-old infants process familiar faces in the right side of the brain and unfamiliar faces on the left (Pascalis et al., 1995). To my knowledge, a behavioral study has not been conducted to determine when the infant's preference for the mother would withstand the "transformation" of wrapping the head in a scarf. Thus, a puzzle: If the face-recognition system is so available at birth and capable of quickly forming a representation of the mother, why does the system shift both anatomically and functionally? And, to the extent that it does shift, how does the shift occur? How do infants learn about internal facial features and use them to represent familiar adults? The problem is highlighted by the fact that newborns discriminate among internal configurations in cartoons of faces and differentially follow the most "facial" configuration. Yet external features are used by newborns and infants up to 2 months of age in representing particular individuals; choice breaks down between mother and stranger when external features are masked. A phylogenetic basis for the shift for familiar-face processing is the stability of internal features across transformations of facial expression, external garb and hair style, and angle of regard that provides a foundation for establishing a catalogue of familiar faces in infants whose range of interactive individuals was being radically extended from the exclusivity of the mother to other caretakers in their mobile community. Stability for familiar faces and a basis for differentiating among a larger number of faces may not be provided by shifting external features. According to the view presented here, infants utilize two new strategies in perceiving a new face, then perceiving it as familiar, and treating the person as familiar on future occasions. First, they seem to establish particular criteria as to what will later be considered familiar. This may at first involve eye-to-eye contact and, later, more elaborate social interactions. Second, they both process and store the information differently. Processing appears to be of internal facial features and occurs in the right hemisphere of the brain. The significance of this transition awaits empirical documentation.

As discussed in greater detail earlier, the confluence of (a) field evidence in which infant–mother visual engagement appears to be strongly initiated by about 1 month of age (Wolff, 1963, 1987; Laveli & Poli, 1998; Berger & Cunningham, 1981); (b) experimental perceptual studies demonstrating 4-week-old preferential looking into the adult's eyes (Carpenter, 1973; Hainline, 1978; Haith et al., 1977; see Bloom's, 1974, 1975, interesting interpretation of eye-to-eye contact), and (c) our own studies in which visual engagement took on the properties of an unconditioned stimulus suggest that starting at 4 weeks, infants may learn about and represent the internal characteristics of the face from the eyes out, at least in settings in which they are moving from a state of agitation and distress to one of calm. They actively track the eyes. Regarding the full face in the absence of direct eye-to-eye contact does not halt the search for eye contact. Once eye contact is established, however, it serves as a base for brief forays to the areas surrounding the eyes and also to the face outline. Very little time was spent in Haith's studies looking at nose or mouth in experimental settings in which mouth position remained stable. If this view is valid, then 4-week-olds should be more influenced by changes in facial characteristics, for instance, a large birthmark, that is close to the eyes than ones that border the periphery. This should also hold for 6- and 9-week-old infants, who were calmed by sucrose-eye engagement but for whom the calm did not persist in sucrose absence.

I feel considerably less confident in predictions concerning 12-week-olds, because we have not yet calmed them. The paradigm that we have used to study orogustatory and visual calming effects that was successful in newborns and up to 9 weeks of age is no longer appropriate for 3-month-old crying infants. More social complexity is needed. In the future, calm-alert infants will have to be studied for whom critical social contexts or expectancies are not violated, or more effective means will have to be devised for calming. One lead is provided by Muir's success in overcoming by maternal touch the distress caused by mothers who assumed still faces. Thus, the rapidly developing richness of the infant's social world and strategies in which to navigate that world must be taken into account for enhancing our understanding of the ontogeny of face recognition, the rules of social discourse that infants follow at different ages, and the rapidity with which these rules may change (Rochat & Striano, this volume).

The presence of two face-processing regions, one for familiar, the other for unfamiliar, is worthy of attention and may be better appreciated within the context of developmental ecology. I suggest that the basis for facial familiarity is proven safety. Faces rapidly become familiar to adults, at least, during contemporary communication through inconsequential repeated exposure at the distance of TV, movies, magazines, and newspapers. My assumption is that modern communication at a distance of many repeated exposures with no consequence to the individual mimics the more phylogenetically relevant circumstances of familiarity, that is, safety, being conferred on a person who has not caused harm to the individual over the course of actual repeated exposures. It would be of considerable interest in this regard to present adults with faces of strangers, pairing some faces with positive events, others with neutral ones, and still others with negative, innocuous events. The subjects will surely learn about all three classes of faces. My guess is that the representation of the familiar negative face, at some level of the cortex, will differ from those of the positive and neutral faces.

It is worth pursuing this idea further concerning infants. After exposure to a face or other objects for a few trials, infants turn away or seek other forms of stimulation. They have habituated to the face. This does not appear to be the case for the mother's face, which is preferred to the strangers, certainly in the short run. This presents two issues. First, what is learned about the new face that serves as the basis for habituation? Second, what causes the affective change such that the face associated with some facet of maternal largesse becomes preferred and the infant does not habituate to it? There are other issues. Is the face processing the same in both instances? Are the memories the same or does the infant learn about the two faces anew on future exposures? The fact that 4-week-olds prefer the face of a stranger who delivered sucrose while visually engaging the infant, according to our preliminary data, and being indifferent to faces that were not linked with sucrose delivery or other pleasant changes, may present a salient to identify the circumstances under which a face becomes familiar (safe) to infants at different ages. This may help predict when the shift to the right hemisphere for processing may occur starting at 3 to 4 months of age and to evaluate the content of those memories. To the extent that right and left hemispheric functions differ and become distinctive by at least 4 months of age, we are presented with a unique opportunity to use development to help explore the bases of face recognition, social behavior, and their neurological mediation. The extensive research on learned safety, both of individuals (e.g., Holmes, 1988) and foods (Sclafani, 1997) can provide usseful conceptual and paradigmatic directions in this quest.

SUMMARY AND DISCUSSION

This chapter addressed a number of issues concerning infant motivation, changes induced by the mother through nursing and, in particular, the contribution of these changes toward learning about and preferring the mother's face to a stranger's. Within this context, the chapter has started to address the control exerted by the infant in seeking information about faces and their bearers at different points in development. The view is put forward that familiarity is the equivalent of safety at 3 months of age and that this is accompanied by two shifts in face processing.

Within a psychobiological framework, I have provided a homeostatic model for learning about faces that emphasizes active seeking of information by the infant. The model, as presented, is consonant with the available data; identifies areas for further specification at behavioral, cognitive, and neural levels; and provides further hypotheses for evaluation. The model rests on a number of assumptions that are accepted in various fields of biological and behavioral inquiry. First, it proposes that face-recognition systems are modular and encapsulated. They have a dedicated neurology and a particular cognitive structure that utilizes different forms of specific information at particular developmental time points. The information and its means of being obtained differs across time points; different behavioral strategies are employed to meet the demands of different cognitive structures.

Second, I propose that motivational and cognitive systems have both narrowly and broadly defined components. In this instance, the narrowly defined components are available at birth to define what constitutes a face, based especially on its internal configuration, and to focus attention on faces from birth. The broadly defined components including learning and motivational systems that allow particular faces and the affective changes that accompany them to be learned, represented, and remembered.

Third, when the system has been engaged by an unfamiliar face, a discrepancy is produced that sustains particular behavioral patterns until the discrepancy is reduced below threshold. The infant actively seeks particular age-specific classes of information through different, age-related behavioral strategies. The information sought, at least during the initial 3 months, becomes increasingly complex. In this regard, the system is homeostatic, because error signals (e.g., not recognizing a face or not achieving eye contact) trigger specific behavioral patterns. The proposed system is more complex than traditional homeostatic systems, because it is engaged by external not internal events (e.g., deficits in body fluid balance). The constancies and error signals will prove more difficult to identify.

Finally, on a more personal scientific note, all of these findings in 1- to 3-month-old infants were unexpected. I have been impressed by the precision, persistence, apparent goal directedness, and regular time of onset of these ontogenetic changes. Given the underlying neurology, in terms of dedicated pathways, neurochemical distribution, and the persistence of the behaviors, their functional import is probably equally impressive. Finally, the arguments presented here and the data on which they are founded speak to behavioral strategies that, at this point, seem rather constrained; for 4-week-old infants, it is engaging the adults eyes and not simply seeing them. This is followed by seeking social reciprocity with the adult. Any model for the acquisition of biologically vital information concerning affect and safety will have to take these restrictions into consideration.

REFERENCES

Alberts, J. R., & Cramer, C. P. (1988). Ecology and experience: Sources of means and meaning of developmental change. In E. M. Blass (Ed.), *Handbook of behavioral neurobiology, 9, Devlopmental psychobiology and behavioral ecology.* New York: Plenum Press.

Alberts, J. R., & May, B. (1984). Nonnutritive thermotactile induction of fillial huddling in rat pups. *Developmental Psychobiology, 17,* 161–181.

Barr, R. G., Pantel, M. S., Wright, J. H., Gravel, R. G., & Young, S. N. (1995). *The "sucrose effect" is a sweetness effect.* Program of Society for Research in Child Development, Indianapolis, IA. (Abstract O. 284).

Barr, R. G., Quek, V., Oberlander, T. F., Brian, J. A., & Young, S. N. (1994). Effects of intraoral sucrose on crying, mouthing and hand-mouth contact in newborn and six-week old infants. *Developmental Medicine Child Neurology, 36,* 608–618.

Berger, J., & Cunningham, C. C. (1981). The development of eye contact between mothers and normal versus Down's Syndrome infants. *Developmental Psychology, 17,* 678–689.

Birch, L. L. (1990). Development of food acceptance patterns. *Developmental Psychology, 26,* 515–519.

Birch, L. L., Marlin, D. W., & Rotter, J. (1984). Eating as the "means" activity in a contingency: Effects on young children's food preference. *Child Development, 55,* 431–439.

Birch, L. L., Zimmerman, S. I., & Hind, H. (1980). The influence of social-affective context on the formation of children's food preferences. *Child Development, 51,* 856–861.

Blass, E. M. (1992). The ontogeny of motivation: Opioid bases of energy conservation and lasting affective change in rat and human infants. *Current Directions in Psychological Science, 1,* 116–120.

Blass, E. M. (1995). The ontogeny of ingestive behavior. In A. Morrison & S. Fluharty (Eds.), *Progress in psychobiology and physiological psychology.* New York: Academic Press.

Blass, E. M. (1996). Mothers and their infants: Peptide-mediated physiological, behavioral and affective changes during suckling. *Regulatory Peptides, 66,* 109–112.

Blass, E. M. (1997a). Milk-induced hypoalgesia in human newborns. *Pediatrics, 99,* 825–829.

Blass, E. M. (1997b). Infant formula quiets crying human newborns. *Journal of Developmental and Behavioral Pediatrics, 18,* 162–168.

Blass, E. M. (1997c). Interactions between contact and chemosensory mechanisms in pain modulation in 10-day-old rats. *Behavioral Neuroscience, 111,* 147–154.

Blass, E. M. (1997d). Changing influences of sucrose and visual engagement in 2–12-week-old human infants: Implications for maternal face recognition. *Infant Behavior and Development, 20,* 423–434.

Blass, E. M., & Ciaramitaro, V. (1994). Oral determinants of state, affect, and action in newborn humans. *Monographs of the Society for Research in Child Development, 59,* 1–96.

Blass, E. M., & Fitzgerald, E. (1988). Milk-induced analgesia and comforting in 10-day-old rats: Opioid mediation. *Pharmacology, Biochemistry and Behavior, 29,* 9–13.

Blass, E. M., Fitzgerald, E., & Kehoe, P. (1987). Interactions between sucrose, pain and isolation distress. *Pharmacology, Biochemistry and Behavior, 26,* 483–489.

Blass, E. M., Ganchrow, J. R., & Steiner, J. E. (1984). Classical conditioning in newborn humans 2–48 hours of age. *Infant Behavior and Development, 7,* 223–235.

Blass, E. M., & Hall, W. G. (1976). Drinking termination: Interactions among hydrational, orogastric, and behavioral controls in rats. *Psychological Review, 83*, 356–374.

Blass, E. M., & Hoffmeyer, L. B. (1991). Sucrose as an analgesic in newborn humans. *Pediatrics, 87*, 215–218.

Blass, E. M., & Shah, A. (1996). Pain-reducing properties of sucrose in human newborns. *Chemical Senses, 20*(1), 29–35.

Blass, E. M., & Smith, B. A. (1992). Differential effects of sucrose, fructose, glucose and lactose on crying in 1–3-day-old human infants. *Developmental Psychology, 28*, 804–810.

Bloom, K. (1974). Eye contact as a setting event for infant learning. *Journal of Experimental Child Psychology, 17*, 250–263.

Bloom, K. (1975). Social elicitation of infant vocal behavior. *Journal of Experimental Child Psychology, 20*, 51–58.

Bushnell, I. W. R., Sai, F., & Mullin, J. T. (1983). Neonatal recognition of mother's faces. *British Journal of Developmental Psychology, 7*, 3–15.

Carey, S. (1992). Becoming a face expert. In V. Bruce, A. Cowey, A. W. Ellis, & D. I. Perrett (Eds.), *Processing the facial image: Proceedings of a Royal Society discussion meeting* (pp. 95–103). Oxford: Clarendon Press.

Carey, S., & Diamond, R. (1977). From piecemeal to configurational representation of faces. *Science, 195*, 312–314.

Carpenter, G. C. (1973). Visual regard of moving and stationary faces in early infancy. *Merrill-Palmer Quarterly, 19*, 181–194.

Cohen, J. A., & Tronick, E. Z. (1987). Mother-infant face-to-face interaction: The sequence of dyadic states at 3, 6, and 9 months. *Developmental Psychology, 23*, 68–77.

Cooper, J. R., Bloom, F. E., & Roth, R. H. (1991). *The Biochemical Basis of Neuropharmacology*. Oxford University Press.

De Casper, A. J., & Spence, M. J. (1986). Prenatal maternal speech influences newborns' perception of speech sounds. *Infant Behavior and Development, 6*, 19–25.

Diamond, R., & Carey, S. (1977). Developmental changes in the representation of faces. *Journal of Experimental Child Psychology, 23*, 1–22.

Ellis, H. D. (1992). The development of face processing skills. In V. Bruce, A. Cowey, A. W. Ellis, & D. I. Perrett (Eds.), *Processing the facial image: Proceedings of a Royal Society discussion meeting* (pp. 105–110). Oxford: Clarendon Press.

Epstein, A. N. (1986). The ontogeny of ingestive behaviors: Control of milk intake by suckling rats and the emergence of feeding and drinking at weaning. In R. Ritter, S. Ritter, & C. D. Barnes (Eds.), *Neural and humoral controls of food intake* (pp. 1–25). New York: Academic Press.

Field, T. M., Cohen, D., Garcia, R., & Greenberg, R. (1984). Mother-stranger face discrimination by the newborn. *Infant Behavior and Development, 7*, 19–25.

Finnegan, L. P. (1986). Neonatal abstinence syndrome: Assessment and pharmacotherapy. In F. F. Rubaltelli & B. Granati (Eds.), *Neonatal therapy: An update* (pp. 122–146). New York: Excerpta Medica.

Galef, B. G., Jr., & Beck, M. (1990). Diet selection and poison avoidance by mammals individually and in social groups. In E. M. Stricker (Ed.), *Handbook of behavioral neurobiology*, Vol. 10 (pp. 329–352). New York: Plenum Press.

Galef, B. G., Jr., & Clark, M. M. (1972). Mother's milk and adult presence: Two factors determining initial dietary selection by weanling rats. *Journal of Comparative and Physiological Psychology, 78*, 220–225.

Galef, B. G., Jr., & Heiber, L. (1976). The role of residual olfactory cues in the determination of feeding site selection and exploration patterns of domestic rats. *Journal of Comparative and Physiological Psychology, 90*, 727–739.

Galef, B. G., Jr., Mason, J. R., Preti, G., & Bean, N. J. (1988). Carbon disulfide can mediate socially induced attenuation of taste-aversion learning in rats. *Physiology and Behavior, 42*, 119–124.

Galef, B. G., Jr., & Sherry, D. F. (1973). Mother's milk: A medium for the transmission of cues reflecting the flavor of mother's diet. *Journal of Comparative and Physiological Psychology, 83,* 374–378.

Goren, C. C., Sarty, M., & Wu, P. Y. K. (1975). Visual following and pattern discrimination of face-like stimuli by newborn infants. *Pediatrics, 56,* 544–549.

de Haan, M., & Nelson, C. A. (1997). Recognition of the mother's face by six-month-old infants: A neurobehavioral study. *Child Development, 68,* 187–210.

Hainline, L. (1978). Developmental changes in visual scanning of face and nonface patterns by infants. *Journal of Experimental Child Psychology, 25,* 90–115.

Haith, M. M., Bergman, T., & Moore, M. K. (1977). Eye contact and face scanning in early infancy. *Science, 198,* 853–855.

Hall, W. G. (1975). Weaning and growth of artificially reared rats. *Science, 190,* 1313–1314.

Hall, W. G. (1990). The ontogeny of ingestive behavior: Changing control of the components in the feeding sequence. In E. M. Stricker (Ed.), *Handbook of Behavioral Neurobiology,* Vol. 10. New York: Plenum Press.

Higley, J. D., & Suomi, S. J. (1986). Parental behaviour in nonhuman primates. In W. Slukin & M. Herbert (Eds.), *Parental behaviour* (pp. 152–207). Oxford: Basil Blackwell.

Hogan, J. A. (1988). Cause and function in the development of behavior systems. In *Handbook of Behavioral Neurobiology,* Vol. 9 (pp. 63–106). New York: Plenum Press.

Holmes, W. G. (1988). Kinship and the development of social preferences. In *Handbook of Behavioral Neurobiology,* Vol. 9 (pp. 389–414). New York: Plenum Press.

Johnson, M. H., Dziurawiec, S., Bartrip, J., & Morton, J. (1992). The effects of movement of internal features on infants' preferences for face-like stimuli. *Infant Behavior and Development, 15,* 129–136.

Johnson, M. J., Dziurawiec, S., Ellis, H., & Morton, J. (1991). Newborns' preferential tracking of face-like stimuli and its subsquent decline. *Cognition, 40,* 1–19.

Kuhl, P. K. (1985). Methods in the study of infant speech perception. In G. Gottlieb & N. A. Krasnegor (Eds.), *Measurement of Audition and Vision in the First Year of Postnatal life.* New York: Academic Press.

Lavelli, M., & Poli, M. (1998). Early mother-infant interaction during breast and bottle feeding. *Infant Behavior and Development.*

Leon, M. (1974). Maternal pheromone. *Physiology and Behavior, 13,* 441–453.

MacFarlane, A. J. (1975). Olfaction in the development of social preferences in the human neonate. *Ciba Foundation Symposium, 33,* 103–117.

Manilla, J. A., & Beauchamp, G. K. (1996). The human infants' response to vanilla flavors in mother's milk and formula. *Infant Behavior and Development, 19,* 13–19.

Mark, G. P., Smith, S. E., Rada, P. V., & Hoebel, B. G. (1994). An appetitively conditioned taste elicits a preferential increase in mesolimbic dopamine release. *Pharmacology, Biochemistry and Behavior, 48,* 651–660.

Martins, T. (1949). Disgorging of food to the puppies by the lactating dog. *Physiological Zoology, 22,* 169–172.

Meltzoff, A. N., & Moore, M. K. (1989). Imitation in newborn infants: Exploring the range of gestures imitated and the underlying mechanisms. *Child Development, 25,* 954–962.

Meltzoff, A. N., & Moore, M. K. (1992). Early imitation within a functional framework: The importance of person identity, movement and development. *Infant Behavior and Development, 15,* 479–505.

Morton, J., & Johnson, M. H. (1991). CONSPEC and CONLERN: A two-process theory of infant recognition. *Psychological Review, 98,* 164–181.

Muir, D. W., & Hains, S. M. J. (1993). Infant sensitivity to perturbations in adult facial, vocal, tactile, and contingent stimulation during face to face interactions. In B. de Boysson-Bardies, S. de Schonen, P. Jusczyk, P. McNeilage, & J. Morton (Eds.), *Developmental neurocognition: Speech and face processing in the first year.* Dordrecht: Kluwer.

Murphy, A., Ennis, M., Shipley, M. T., & Behbehani, M. M. (1994). Directionally-specific changes in arterial pressure induce differential patterns of FOS expression in discrete areas of the rat brainstem: A double labeling study for FOS and catecholamines. *Journal of Comparative Neurology, 349,* 36–50.

Pascalis, O., de Schonen, S., Morton, J., Deruelle, C., & Fabre-Grenet, M. (1995). Mother's face recognition by neonates: A replication and an extension. *Infant Behavior and Development, 18,* 79–86.

Pedersen, P. E., & Blass, E. M. (1982). Prenatal and postnatal determinants of the first suckling episode in albino rats. *Developmental Psychobiology, 15,* 349–355.

Pedersen, P. E., Williams, C. L., & Blass, E. M. (1982). Activation and odor conditioning of suckling behavior in three day old albino rats. *Journal of Experimental Psychology, Animal Behavior Processes, 8*(4), 329–341.

Porter, R. H., Makin, J. W., Davis, L. B., & Christensen, K. M. (1992). Breast-fed infants respond to olfactory cues from their own mother and unfamiliar lactating females. *Infant Behavior and Development, 15,* 85–93.

Rao, M., Blass, E. M., Brignol, M. M., Marino, L., & Glass, L. (1997). Reduced heat loss following sucrose ingestion in premature and normal human newborns. *Early Human Development, 48,* 109–116.

Ren, K., Blass, E. M., Zhou, Q., & Dubner, R. (1997). Differential effects of intraoral sucrose and suckling on forepaw and hindpaw inflamatory hyperalgesia and spinal FOS expression in infant rats. *Proceedings of the National Academy of Sciences, 104,* 1471–1475.

Rheingold, H. L. (1963). Maternal behavior in the dog. In H. L. Rheingold (Ed.), *Maternal Behavior in Mammals.* New York: John Wiley & Sons.

Rovee-Collier, C., & Hayne, H. (1987). Reactivation of infant memory: Implications for cognitive development. *Advances in Child Development and Behavior, 20,* 185–238.

Schaal, B. (1988). Olfaction in infants and children: Developmental and functional perspectives. *Chemical Senses, 13,* 145–190.

Sclafani, A. (1997). Learned controls of ingestive behaviour. *Appetite, 29,* 53–158.

Shide, D. J., & Blass, E. M. (1989). Opioid-like effects of intraoral infusions of corn oil and polycose on stress reactions in 10-day-old rats. *Behavioral Neuroscience, 103,* 1168–1175.

Shide, D. J., & Blass, E. M. (1991). Opioid mediation of odor preferences induced by sugar and fat in 6-day-old rats. *Physiology and Behavior, 50,* 961–966.

Smith, B. A., Fillion, T. J., & Blass, E. M. (1990). Orally mediated sources of calming in one to three day-old human infants. *Developmental Psychology, 26,* 731–737.

Spelke, E. S. (1979). Perceiving bimodally specified events in infancy. *Developmental Psychology, 15,* 626–636.

Stack, D. M., & Muir, D. W. (1990). Tactile stimulation as a component of social interchange: New interpretations for the still-face effect. *British Journal of Developmental Psychology, 8,* 131–145.

Streri, A., & Pecheux, M.-G. (1986). Vision-to-touch and touch-to-vision transfer of form in 5-month-old infants. *British Journal of Developmental Psychology, 4,* 161–167.

Sullivan, R. M., Taborsky-Barbar, S., Mendoza, R., Itino, A., Leon, M., Cottman, C., Payne, T., & Lott, I. (1991). Olfactory classical conditioning in neonates. *Pediatrics, 87,* 511–518.

Teicher, M. H., & Blass, E. M. (1977). First suckling response of the newborn albino rat: The roles of olfaction and amniotic fluid. *Science, 198,* 635–636.

Walker-Andrews, A. S., & Lennon, E. (1991). Infants' discrimination of vocal expressions: Contributions of auditory and visual information. *Infant Behavior and Development, 14,* 131–142.

Walton, G. E., Bower, N. J. A., & Bower, T. G. R. (1992). Recognition of familiar faces by newborns. *Infant Behavior and Development, 15,* 265–269.

Weller, A., Blass, E. M., Gibbs, J., & Smith, G. P. (1995). Odor-induced inhibition of intake after pairing of odor and CCK-8 in neonatal rats. *Physiology and Behavior, 57*(1), 181–183.

Whitehead, M. C. (1994). Functional connections of the rostral nucleus of the solitary tract in viscereosensory integration of ingestion reflexes. In R. A. Barraco (Ed.), Nuclei of the Solitary Tract (pp. 105–118). Boca Raton, FL: CRC Press.

Wolff, P. H. (1963). Observations on the early development of smiling. In. B. M. Foss (Ed.), *Determinants of infant behaviour: II* (pp. 113–138). London: Methuen.

Wolff, P. H. (1987). *The development of behavioral states and the expression of emotions in early infancy: New proposals for investigation.* Chicago: University of Chicago Press.

Woo, C. C., & Leon, M. (1995). Distribution and development of beta-adrenergic receptors in the rat. *Journal of Comparative Neurology, 352,* 1–10.

Zeifman, D., Delaney, S., & Blass, E. M. (1996). Sweet taste, looking and calm in two- and four-week-old infants: The eyes have it. *Developmental Psychology, 32,* 1090–1099.

Chapter 3

Vitality Contours: The Temporal Contour of Feelings as a Basic Unit for Constructing the Infant's Social Experience

Daniel N. Stern
University of Geneva

I suggest a global unit of social understanding that is based on an appreciation of the temporal contouring of experience. Feelings as experienced in real time have been relatively unexplored. In spite of this neglect, the nonverbal phenomena of interest to us, such as delayed imitation, inferring intentions and motives, and attuning affects, unfold in real time, usually in a matter of seconds. The actual duration is very important as we will see later. This temporal unfolding, which is key to the concepts that follow, occurs in several domains simultaneously. There are the external, objectifiable movements and sounds, such as head turning, pointing, and facial and vocal expressions, that form and decompose. Synchronous with these behavioral events there are internal subjective events consisting, among other things, of the continual, instant-by-instant shifts in feeling state, resulting in an array of temporal feeling flow patterns that we will call *vitality contours.* This term is defined further on.

This book is devoted to exploring the precursors of social cognition, and this chapter suggests a basic format on which the capacities of greatest interest to us can be based and from which they can develop.

I will concentrate largely on subjective events as a source of information for reading social events. I plan to approach the patterned flux of feelings in terms of the temporal transformations and invariants that it affords. Such an approach is, in part, ecologically inspired (Gibson, 1966, 1979; McCabe & Balzano, 1986) but applied to the temporal feeling flow as a subjective source of information about social interaction.

In searching for the salient features of this subjective field, I examine psychological phenomena in terms of analogic time contours. These feeling flow patterns that we call vitality contours are best captured by dynamic kinetic terms, such as *surging, fading-away, fleeting, explosive, tentative, effortful, accelerating, decelerating, climaxing, bursting,* and *drawn out.*

These vitality contours do not reflect the categorical content of an act but rather the manner in which the act is performed and the feeling that directs the act. It is for this reason that vitality contours underlie the appreciation of most abstract art forms that are formally devoid of "content," such as most music and much dance (see Langer, 1967; Stern, 1985).

Vitality contours are intrinsic to all experience in all modalities and domains. They occur in both the presence and absence of categorical affects. For example, a rush of anger or joy, a sudden flooding of light, an accelerating sequence of thoughts, a wave of feeling evoked by music, a surge of pain, a shot of narcotics can all feel like "rushes." They share a similar distribution of excitation and activation over time, a similar feeling flow pattern. In other words, a similar vitality contour.

This account is a diachronic one that goes beyond the digital time concepts of before and after, or sequence. Rather, it is an analogic notion of events as contoured and lived in real time. We are tempted to call it microdiachronic, because the relevant events and their corresponding vitality contours have short durations, usually around 1 to 3 seconds and rarely over 5 seconds.

Why start there, with the inner subjective environment viewed in terms of vitality contours?

- It concerns phenomena readily accessible to the very young infant as well as adults.
- It brings the relatively neglected dimension of time into our considerations.
- The feeling flow pattern, or vitality contour, as a basic unit would be isomorphic to the phenomena that it specifies, yet it could be generative and apply to various events that evoked similar feeling flows. It would thus not have to be greatly constructed and abstracted from experience. It is closer to a primitive experience.
- It could specify the event as an integral whole, a global event, while at the same time allow for closer analyses of the components of the global pattern.
- It would take into account the subjective aspect of lived events, in particular, feelings, that vague yet necessary category.
- It permits an approach to the problems of acquiring a sense of directionality, intentionality, and motives in human behavior.

- It permits an approach to the problem of acquiring the capacity for the narrative formatting of human events.
- It helps in thinking about mechanisms of cross-modality.
- Finally, it may provide a format or scaffold on which later-developing social cognitions can be built.

We propose these units of experience for their value in helping the infant to construct his or her social world.

WHAT ARE THESE FEELING FLOW PATTERNS THAT WE WILL CALL VITALITY CONTOURS?

During the performance of any physical or mental act, several primary amodal features of the stimulation impinging on the nervous system change: intensity, speed (either or both beat and rhythm) and usually shape (form). This is so regardless of the domain or modality of the act and regardless of whether the act is self-performed or perceived in a social partner. These changes that make up the performance show both invariant temporal features and temporal transformations. Imagine any social act (e.g., a head turn, a tongue protrusion, the formation of a facial expression). Because the act has a duration, the intensity and shape of the act trace a temporal contour of shifts during the performance of the act, sometimes slight, other times dramatic. A gesture can start slowly and then accelerate, or the reverse, or it can crescendo, or fade. Even if the intensity and shape were perfectly unchanged during some portion of the act, that too is a very salient temporal contour, namely, temporal flatness.

So far we have only described a *stimulus flow pattern*, or when digitalized by the nervous system, a sequential pattern of neural firing. How can we jump to the analogic patterns of feeling flow that make up vitality contours?

Any just perceivable shift in stimulus flow pattern will illicit a corresponding perceivable shift in arousal, activation, and hedonic tone, however slight they may be. At this level of phenomena, the nervous system receives analogic information from the internal and external world, processes it, in part by digitalizing it, but also "presents" it so that it may be subjectively experienced in analogic form as vitality contours. The neuronal processes whereby these transformations occur are currently under very active examination. They raise many of the fundamental problems that are currently at the forefront of the cognitive neurosciences, such as: binding; understanding feelings as against affects; examining background feelings arising from the continual input from body and mind; and the conscious and unconscious integration of mental processes that are distributed and cooccurring (see Crick & Koch, 1990; Damasio, 1994; Dennett, 1991;

Eckhorn, et al., 1988; Edelman, 1990; Singer, et al., 1993). We will not attempt to explore the neuroscience basis for the subjective phenomenon of vitality contours. Suffice it to say that such experiences are known to all of us, although they go mostly unnoticed and unnamed.

What we mean, then, by *vitality contours* are the continual shifts in arousal, activation, and hedonics occurring split-second-by-split-second that are evoked by events taking place in the body and mind of the self and others and which are integrated into temporally contoured feelings.

For instance, when a baby sees a tongue being protruded, there is not only the form of the act at its highpoint, as if it were a photograph, there is also the duration, velocity, and shape transformation contour during the act. While the mouth is opening and the tongue is coming out of the mouth, there is an accelerating increase in stimulus strength, both in movement and visual contrast. A large area of the central visual field with high light–dark contrast is growing rapidly, and something is coming toward the infant. These perceptions will be accompanied by corresponding increases in arousal and activation. The reverse occurs when the tongue goes back in, and the mouth is closed. In between, when the protruded tongue is held out, there is a flattening of the contour of stimulation shifts and a holding of the heightened level of arousal and activation and hedonics. The entire act, besides having a gestural form, is a temporally contoured global event with progressive shifts in stimulus strength, rate change, and shape change that elicit corresponding shifts in the feeling flow pattern, which acts on the infant as a sort of subjective microdrama. It is worth recalling that the infant does not yet have a category of events that can be instantly summarized by the words *tongue protrusion* nor an established schema that can be activated to cut short the on-line experience. He must live the entire event as it unfolds in time.

The vitality contour traced is *how* the tongue protrusion was performed. It is the phraseology of the act. In contrast, the separate pieces of action that make up the form of the act are like the notes.

The basic idea of a feeling flow pattern owes much to but is distinct from several previous ideas. Tomkins (1962) associated the contour of stimulation to a density of neural firing and tied specific patterns to specific discrete Darwinian emotions, for example, a rapid rise in stimulus intensity regardless of the modality of stimulation causes fear, a slower rise causes interest, and so on. Clynes (1978) proposed a basically similar idea but tied the temporal shape of stimulation to a different palette of feeling states, for example, love. Werner and Kaplan (1963), and the philosopher S. K. Langer (1967) raised the same issues with similar concepts. I have previously talked of *vitality affects* (Stern, Hofer, Haft, & Dore, 1984; Stern, 1985) but now change the name to vitality contours, which is a larger category of phenomena that includes but is not confined to affects.

In the notion presented here, the feeling flow patterns that make up vitality contours are not conceptualized like categorical affects nor associated with specific ones. They are different in the following ways. Categorical affects concern a quality of feeling (joy, fear, etc.) as the essential ingredient, whereas the subjective intensity or its objective fullness of display can vary widely and can take many different temporal paths of formation and dissolution. (Fear can mount slowly or rapidly, slightly or greatly.) Accordingly, a photograph of a face in a particular Darwinian emotional expression is effective because the category of feeling quality is captured, and usually the expression is assumed to be at its fullest point of intensity or display at that time and at its temporal high point. The intensity-time course can be imagined. (Paradoxically, some exceptional photos may gain their magic because they capture expressions headed, in the very immediate future, to a different level of intensity or temporal resolution. They imply a time path.)

In contradistinction, vitality contours, or feeling flow patterns, concern the pattern of shifting intensity over time. They are more like a musical phrase that cannot be captured or even imagined by taking a single note, that is, a slice of time, or a "sound-photograph," so to speak. Vitality contours are global entities of feeling that are revealed only in time. The essential ingredient of their quality of feeling comes from the sensations of accelerating, growing, fading, climaxing, and so forth, in which the exact quality of feeling, or modality of feeling, that is in motion is nonspecific. This is why vitality contours apply to all activities that have a characteristic intensity-time course: gestures, body movements, facial expressions, and internal phenomena such as affects and thoughts. Each smile, for instance (as a Darwinian emotion), also has a vitality contour. There are smiles that grow slowly and steadily, others that explode, and some that progress slowly and suddenly burst open. For each of these smiles, there is both a qualitative Darwinian emotion (joy or pleasure) and simultaneously a vitality contour (more difficult to summarize in one word). Each adds a different meaning to the experience, as acted or perceived.

Sometimes the Darwinian emotion is experienced as central and the vitality contour as providing a secondary or modifying message. This is the case in most examples of social referencing (Emde & Sorce, 1983; Klinnert, Campos, Emde, & Svejda, 1983), in which the infant wants a rapid categorical sign from the parent so as to know how to act and feel ("Is this okay or not?"). At other times, such as in the examples of affect attunement in which the parent matches the infant's vitality contour to indicate that they have shared the baby's experience (Stern et al., 1984; Stern, 1985), the vitality contour carries the central message, and the Darwinian affect carries a complementary one. In many social interactions, it is the vitality contour that carries the key information. For instance, when a smile is expected during a ritualized response, such as greetings or joke telling, it is the manner of its performance that carries the essential social information.

THE TIME SCALE OF VITALITY CONTOURS

The vast majority of the vitality contours that concern us here have durations of several seconds at the most. This duration is of great importance, because it corresponds to what has been designated as the duration of the psychological (subjective) present moment, or the "sensible present" (James, 1891); or the "perceived present" (Fraisse, 1963). It is also the duration of "working memory" (Baddeley, 1986). As Fraisse (1963) points out, 2 seconds is also the duration of time needed to produce a sentence of 20 to 25 syllables, a long line of poetry, a long bar of music. It is also the duration of most gestures and facial expressions, at least their formation.

All these events occur in the perceived present. Vitality contours, also, are experienced in the perceived present. Accordingly, the unit of time that interests us is the subjective "now," that is, the perceived present. The reason for stressing this phenomenological unit is that the mental processes that occur during the perceived present must organize experience into a whole as it unfurls in that time frame and may have special features including different forms of memory.

CAN INFANTS IDENTIFY, DISCRIMINATE, AND REPRESENT THESE CONTOURS?

There is abundant evidence that considerable timing abilities operate very early in life. Many experimental studies suggest explicitly or implicitly that young infants are sensitive to the temporal features of both speech and nonspeech sounds (Beebe, Jaffe, Feldstein, Mays, & Alson, 1985; Bertonici, Bijeljac-Babic, Blumstein, & Mehler, 1987, 1988; Clarkson, Swain, Clifton, & Cohen, 1991; Jaffe, Feldstein, Beebe, Crown, & Jasnow, 1994; Kaye, 1992; Spence, 1992; Swain, 1992; Zelazo, Brody, & Chaika, 1984).

Papousek and Papousek (1981), suggest that by the age of 3 months, infants can vocally imitate musical elements of what they hear from others. These musical elements may last several notes, consisting of short pitch or rhythm phrases, that is, contours. Simple games played by parents and infants during the first 6 months demand a precise evaluation of short periods of time (roughly 2 seconds) on the infant's part, (Stern, Beebe, Jaffe, & Bennett, 1997; 1985). Lewkowicz (1992) has documented the early abilities of infants to discriminate different features of time, such as duration and rhythm, and even to make cross-modal matches of temporal features.

Not only are infants well endowed in the temporal domain, it would be hard to imagine how they could make sense of facial expressions, gestures, vocalizations, in short the human social world without such abilities.

To help the infant make maximal use of these abilities, parents, while interacting with their infants during the first half-year of life, break the interactive flow into short episodes, usually lasting not more than several seconds. These episodes are well bounded by pauses or marked shifts in the direction of activity (Stern et al., 1977). More recently, Weinberg and Tronick (1994) remarked on similar phrasing (and parsing?) specifically linked to affective communication and have called the separate packages or phrases *affective configurations.* This marking of behavioral phrase boundaries is often highly exaggerated as a normal part of infant-elicited parental behavior.

Repetition is another feature of behavioral phrases and their corresponding vitality contours that render them more recognizable. In the first year of life, so much of the parent–infant social interaction is built around daily psycho-physiological cycles (feeding, putting to sleep, and the like) that repetition of behavioral patterns is the rule. However, exact repetitions rarely occur. No two feedings are quite the same. The basic patterns are infinitely varied, with the variations improvised on the spot each time. This constant variation on established themes is especially marked in behaviors such as play, which by necessity is an improvisation, required to avoid habituation and maintain the level of arousal. For all these patterns and micropatterns that are constantly varied, parents are forced to package their behavioral phrases in a theme and variation format. One of the problems posed by this format is, How does the infant identify the invariant from the variant elements of the variations on a theme? Here too, the vitality contour of a behavioral package may prove helpful in providing an invariant feature that can be created with multiple behavioral possibilities. After all, it is not only the external behaviors of the social partners that are repeated and varied but also the vitality contours that their behavior elicits in the infant.

It requires but a small leap to assume that infants are capable of identifying and discriminating the temporal contours of these behavioral phrases and apprehending them as global events, as well as being sensible to their component parts. For it is these behavioral phrases that are, in our terms, the vitality contours, experienced as the patterned flow of feelings.

In sum, the infant most likely has the capacities and his parents create the optimal interactive opportunities for the infant best to identify, discriminate, and represent those vitality contours that are characteristic of his social experience as acted, perceived, and sensed.

VITALITY CONTOURS AND DIRECTIONALITY

The notion of vitality contours helps to understand better how and why human experience is felt to be directional and teleological. Vitality contours, as global units like musical phrases, have a beginning, a middle course, and end somewhere. By definition these units move toward a potentially recognizable end point. They are inherently end-point oriented.

It is interesting in this light to consider that the ability to predict the ending of a musical phrase that one has heard only part of is suggested to be universal, operating across different cultures. Subjects can predict the endings across different styles of music (e.g., traditional Western and traditional Chinese, which have different tonal systems) regardless of their different levels of musical education (Schellenberg, 1996).

In a similar fashion, most of the vital internal events of living are like predictable musical phrases as far as their end point is concerned. Breathing is a good example. Inspirations have a family of vitality contours with a clear beginning, middle, and end point. So do expirations. Crying makes up another related family of vitality contours, and sobbing yet a third. Urinating, defecating, gastric pains, hunger, and satiation are all experienced with their characteristic families of vitaliy contours. It is no different for physical acts, sucking, reaching, walking, brushing back your hair. And it is no different for the perceived acts of others in direct social contact.

Our experience since birth is composed of temporally bounded sensations from the inside and outside that give rise to an infinitely rich world of vitality contours. When we recall that these vitality contours are feeling flow patterns that intrinsically move to an end point that is usually predictable, it is most natural that an infant from the beginning will experience the human world in terms of temporal directionality toward an end state. It is no surprise that infants discover there is directionality in the animate world. What else could they find?

VITALITY CONTOURS AND INTENTIONALITY

The developmental point at which an infant becomes aware of intentions depends largely on the definition of intentional communication. Bates (1979) provides a helpful definition of true intentional communication where the sender is aware in advance of the effect that the signal will have on the receiver and will continue to act so as to obtain that expected goal. Using this distinction, intentional communication starts to appear around 9 months of age, if not before. By 3 months, however, infants perform instrumental behaviors, such as crying to get fed, vocalizing to receive a vocalization in return, and so forth.

In the previous section we suggested that infants already experience their human world in terms of units, vitality contours, that have directionality in that they move to an end point or an equilibrium point. In this light, the major developmental questions now become, "How specific is the end point in the baby's mind?" What are the clues that will reveal the goal intended by others? And how will the movement toward the goal be conceived? As soon as the end point is anticipated in advance, it becomes a goal. Once the anticipation of a relatively specific goal exists, and the time of arrival of the goal can be estimated, the feeling flow contour toward the goal takes on another aspect, namely, an ongoing appreciation of the continuous temporal approach toward, and the decreasing distance from, the expected end point. This is a form of "count down" that goes on in the background. This temporal movement toward the expected has its own course of shifting intensity over time creating a parallel vitality contour that becomes added to the sensori-motor-affective vitality contour. (Just as with music, several melodic lines can be followed simultaneously.)

The discovery, then, of intentionality in self or others is not a social cognitive event or capacity that arises in a vacuum. It gets grafted onto the directional vitality contours that already make up the infant's world. Or stated differently, a format already exists in which the intention can be inserted. We can now speak of *intentional vitality contours.*

VITALITY CONTOURS AND MOTIVES

Once secondary intersubjectivity is evident in infants after 9 or so months of age (Trevarthen & Hubley, 1978), they can infer goals that they have not seen, because they now grasp the motives behind actions. For example, the recent experiments of Meltzoff (1995) on deferred imitation show that infants, themselves, from grasping someone's motive, can infer and enact their intention although they have never observed the goal state. Similarly, the experiments of Gergely, Nádasdy, Csibra, and Bíró (1996) with animated abstract forms suggest the salience of motives in infants' understanding of teleological actions.

Once the motive is discernible, it becomes an element in the unfolding of the vitality contour. Again, the vitality contour as a global unit provides the format in which the motive operates. The infant does not have to discover the entire structure that makes up a motivated event. He or she already understands the phraseology of directionality, the subjective "pull" of the goal, and now adds the subjective "push" of the motive or desire and has a format in which to place them. We can now speak of *motivated vitality contours.*

VITALITY CONTOURS AND NARRATIVITY

Beginning around 3 or 4 years of age, infants start to tell autobiographical narratives (Peterson & McCabe, 1983). The telling requires more than the ability to use speech, it also requires the psychological formatting of events in the narrative form. It is thought by many that infants start to perceive and experience the human world that they interact with in terms of narrative formats much earlier than their ability to produce (i.e., tell) narratives. This is largely what Bruner (1990) meant when he argued for the primacy of "acts of meaning" in our parsing of human social interactions. The central idea is that infants, very early in life, tend to parse and experience the human world in terms of narrative forms.

What then is a narrative format? In its most minimal form, it is a story, strictly speaking, told to someone, that has a beginning, middle, and end (Labov, 1972). It is thus a global unit that has a coherent flow and directionality.

The two essential aspects of a narrative format are a plot and a line of dramatic tension. The first aspect, the plot, contains several necessary elements: an agent; who performs an action; with a means or instrumentality; to achieve a goal; to satisfy a motive, or belief; all of which takes place in a physical and temporal context (Burke, 1945; Bruner, 1990). The second essential aspect of the narrative form is the line of dramatic tension (Labov, 1972). This is the temporal course of the rise in arousal, activation, and affect as the plot unfolds to reach its high point and then falls to achieve its resolution. The dramatic line of tension is the affective or feeling contour on which the elements of the plot unfold in a time-locked fashion.

Returning now to vitality contours, these contours are, in fact, the lines of dramatic tension of the daily microevents that make up social interactions. In other words, an appreciation of the possible temporal patterns of the narrative format is already in place long before the infant can talk or narrate. In the beginning, the elements of plot can be minimal; however, with the progressive acquisition of the senses of agency, goals, intentions, and motives, the infant has more and more content to hang on the temporal skeleton of the patterned flow of feelings. (In a previous publication, I have called these *proto-narrative envelopes*; see Stern, 1995.)

When a child has finally grasped the idea of a plot as a coherent global entity pulling together its different elements, has inserted those sequenced plot elements into the temporal flow of its vitality contour (which is the same as the story's line of dramatic tension), and can speak, the child will begin to narrate autobiographical stories.

FURTHER NEEDED RESEARCH

Many of the main ideas suggested here lack empirical backing, as yet. However, they are researchable. First, a demonstration that infants can, indeed, identify and represent time-intensity contours, and when, is needed. It will be important to learn if the ability to identify such contours depends on the modality in which the contour is composed, and if it is also task dependent. It may be equally applicable to all modalities and domains because the essential element is time; however, this is an open question.

If infants can identify and remember these vitality contours, we may be forced to reevaluate how time is experienced, processed, and represented. Is a vitality contour to be considered a scriptlike sequence, or elements in working memory, or a global present moment, that is, a perceived present? I am inclined to opt for the latter as is evident in what has gone before. But to do so requires that we develop further what can be meant by a subjective present moment. There is little empirical work to go on here, but some of the major guidelines have long been laid down by phenomenological philosophers, for example, Husserl (1964).

The central problem is this. (Once again, think of a melodic line that occurs phenomenologically in a single present moment of time.) If the present moment has a duration, it will be subjectively broken down into three phases: the immediate past of the present moment, its immediate future, and the present instant—itself, a very thin slice of time that moves from the past horizon of the present moment to the future horizon of the same present moment, eating up the future as it passes and leaving in its wake the past. All this is occurring *now* in a phenomenologic present moment. This view poses some problems. The past of the present moment is still resonating, as Husserl (1964) describes, like the "tail of a comet." He calls this *retention* or *primary memory*. But this is not the same as working memory or traditional memory. What is it? Similarly, the future of the present moment, which is inherent in the past of the present moment, is a very loose expectation, more like an implication that may be realized (what Husserl calls *protention*, which is also an act of primary memory). These processes occurring in the perceived present require further exploration before we can understand the fundamental nature of vitality contours. They may also lead us to consider the temporal axis of experience more seriously, with the possible result of finding new questions and new ways of posing our questions to infants.

We must also examine the temporal and form relationships between stimulation contours, as they occur in natural social interactions, and both the arousal and the activation contours they elicit. It will also be important to know the range of categories of stimulation contours and corresponding vitality contours that naturally prevail in social interactions, as well as their individual and cultural differences. It will be more problematic but not impossible to infer the importance of the vitality contour as the framework that makes the apprehension of intentions, motives, and narrations easier, or even possible.

The greatest problems arise when dealing with these phenomena at the level of an infant's subjective experience. It can only be hoped that advances in the cognitive neurosciences will make these speculations about feelings and subjectivity, and phenomenology in general, more approachable.

SUMMARY

We have conceptualized the vitality contour as a basic subjective feature of infants' experience of their social world. Vitality contours are conceived as temporal units, an experiential phrase during which the subjective sense of arousal, activation, and hedonics changes almost constantly during the stimulation created by a social microevent. This results in a patterned flow of feeling that we call the vitality contour.

This unit of experience is seen as a fundamental format on which developmental advances can be built. We have postulated an initial vitality contour that could also be called a directional vitality contour in that directionality is inherent in the patterned flow of the unit.

The apprehension of intentions is readily acquired developmentally in large part because the vitality contour provides the framework in which the intention can be placed and have a sense. The directional vitality contour then becomes an intentional vitality contour.

The infant's acquisition of a sense of motives also depends on the motive, as a notion, having an intentional temporal framework in which it can be placed to have a sense. The intentional vitality contour then becomes a motivated vitality contour.

And when the child has mastered the elements of plot, and temporally folds them into the flow of the vitality contour, we have narrative vitality contours.

By putting time back into our conception of subjective life in the form of temporal contours, we postulate a unit of experience unique to the self and to animate others that provides a framework and skeleton on which further developments in social understanding can be constructed.

REFERENCES

Baddeley, A. D. (1986). *Working memory.* Oxford: Clarendon Press.

Bates, E. (1979). Intentions, conventions and symbols. In E. Bates (Ed.), *The emergence of symbols: Cognition and communication in infancy.* New York: Academic Press.

Beebe, B., Jaffe, J., Feldstein, S., Mays, K., & Alson, D. (1985). Interpersonal timing: The application of an adult dialogic model to mother–infant vocal and kinesic interaction. In T. Field & N. Fox (Eds.), *Infant social perception.* New York: Ablex.

Bertonici, J., Bijeljac-Babic, R., Blumstein, S., & Mehler, J. (1987). Discrimination in neonates of very short CVs. *Journal of the Acoustical Society of America, 82,* 31–37.

Bruner, J. S. (1990). *Acts of meaning.* Cambridge, MA: Harvard University Press.

Burke, K. (1945). *Grammar of motives.* New York: Prentice-Hall.

Clarkson, M. G., Swain, I. U., Clifton, R. K., & Cohen, K. (1991). Stimulus duration and repetition rate influence newborn's head orientation towards trains of brief sounds. *Journal of the Acoustical Society of America, 89,* 2411–2420.

Clynes, M. (1978). *Sentics: The touch of the emotions.* Garden City, NY: Anchor Press/Doubleday.

Crick, F. H., & Koch, C. (1990). Towards a neurobiological theory of consciousness. *Seminars in the Neurosciences, 2,* 263–275.

Damasio, A. R. (1994). *Descartes' error.* New York: Putnam.

Dennett, D. (1991). *Consciousness explained.* Boston: Little, Brown.

Eckhorn, R., Bauer, R., Jordan, W., Brosch, M., Kruse, W., Munk, M., & Reitboeck, H. J. (1988). Coherent oscillations: A mechanism for featuring linking in the visual cortex. *Biologica Cybernetica, 60,* 121–130.

Edelman, G. M. (1990). *The remembered present: A biological theory of consciousness.* New York: Basic Books.

Emde, R. N., & Sorce, J. E. (1983). The rewards of infancy: Emotional availability and maternal referencing. In J. D. Call, E. Galenson, & R. Tyson (Eds.), *Frontiers of infant psychiatry, Vol. 2* (pp. 17–30). New York: Basic Books.

Fraisse, P. (1963). *La psychologie du temps* [The psychology of time]. (J. Leith, Trans.). London: Eyre & Spottiswoode.

Gergely, G., Nádasdy, Z., Csibra, G., & Bíró, S. (1996). Taking the intentional stance at 12 months of age. (to appear in *Cognition.*)

Gibson, J. J. (1966). The problem of temporal order in stimulation and perception. *The Journal of Psychology, 62,* 141–149.

Gibson, J. J. (1979). *The ecological approach to visual perception.* Boston: Houghton Mifflin.

Husserl, E. (1964). *The phenomenology of internal time-consciousness* (James S. Churchill, Trans.; Calvin O. Schrag, intro.). Bloomington: Indiana University Press.

Jaffe, J., Feldstein, S., Beebe, B., Crown, C., & Jasnow, M. (1994). Interpersonal timing and infant social development. *Monograph of the N.Y. State Psychiatric Institute.*

James, W. (1891). *Principles of Psychology. 2 Vols.* London: Macmillan.

Kaye, K. L. (1992, May). *Nonsense syllable list learning in newborns.* Poster presentation at the Ninth International Conference of Infancy Studies (ICIS), Miami, FL.

Klinnert, M. D., Campos, J. J., Sorce, J. F., Emde, R. N., & Svejda, M. (1983). Emotions as behavior regulators: Social referencing in infancy. In R. Plutchik & Kellerman (Eds.), *Emotion: Theory, research and experience, Vol. 2.* New York: Academic Press.

Labov, W. (1972). *Language in the inner city.* Philadelphia: University of Pennsylvania Press.

Langer, S. K. (1967). *Mind: An essay on human feeling, Vol. 1.* Baltimore, MD: Johns Hopkins University Press.

Lewkowicz, D. J. (1992). The development of temporally based intersensory perception in human infants. In F. Macar et al. (Eds.), *Time Action and Cognition* (pp. 33–43). Netherlands: Kluwer.

McCabe, V., & Balzano, G. J. (1986). *Event cognition: An ecological perspective.* Hillsdale, NJ: Lawrence Erlbaum Associates.

Meltzoff, A. N. (1995). Understanding the intentions of others: Re-enactment of intended acts by 18-month-old children. *Developmental Psychology, 31,* 838–850.

Papousek, M., & Papousek, H. (1981). Musical elements in the infant's vocalization: Their significance for communication, cognition and creativity. In L. P. Lipsett (Ed.), *Advances in infancy research* (pp. 164–225). Norwood, NJ: Ablex.

Peterson, C., & McCabe, A. (1983). *Developmental psycholinguistics: Three ways of looking at a child's narrative.* New York: Plenum Press.

Schellenberg, E. G. (1996). Expectancy in melody: Tests of the implication–realization model. *Cognition, 58,* 75–125.

Singer, W., Artola, A., Engel, A. K., Koenig, P., Kreiter, A. K., Lowel, S., & Schillen, T. B. (1993). Neuronal representations and temporal codes. In T. A. Poggio & D. A. Glaser (Eds.), *Exploring brain functions: Models in neuroscience* (pp. 179–194). Chichester: Wiley.

Spence, M. J. (1992, May). Infants' discrimination of novel and repeatedly experienced speech passages. Poster presented at the Ninth International Conference on Infancy Studies (ICIS), Miami, FL.

Stern, D. N. (1985). *The interpersonal world of the infant.* New York: Basic Books.

Stern, D. N. (1995). *The motherhood constellation: A unifying view of parent–infant psychotherapy.* New York: Basic Books.

Stern, D. N., Beebe, B., Jaffe, J., & Bennett, S. L. (1977). The infant's stimulus world during social interaction: A study of caregivers' behaviors with particular reference to repetition and timing. In H. R. Schaffer (Ed.), *Studies in mother–infant interaction.* London: Academic Press.

Stern, D. N., Hofer, L., Haft, W., & Dore, J. (1984). Affect attunement: The sharing of feeling states between mother and infant by means of inter-modal fluency. In T. Field & N. Fox (Eds.), *Social perception in infancy.* Norwood, NJ: Ablex.

Swain, I. U. (1992, May). *Newborn response to auditory stimulus complexity.* Poster presented at the Ninth International Conference of Infancy Studies (ICIS), Miami, FL.

Tomkins, S. S. (1962). *Affect, imagery and consciousness, Vol. 1, The positive affects. & (1993) Vol. 2, The negative affects.* New York: Springer.

Trevarthen, C., & Hubley, P. (1978). Secondary intersubjectivity: Confidence, confiders, and acts of meaning in the first year. In A. Lock (Ed.), *Action, gesture and symbol.* New York: Academic Press.

Weinberg, K. M., & Tronick, E. Z. (1994). Beyond the face: An empirical study of infant affective configurations of facial, vocal, gestural and regulatory behaviors. *Child Development, 65,* 1495–1507.

Werner, H., & Kaplan, B. (1963). *Symbol formation: An organismic-developmental approach to language and expression of thought.* New York: Wiley.

Zelazo, P. R., Brody, L. B., & Chaika, H. (1984). Neonatal habituation and dishabituation of headturning to rattle sounds. *Infant Behavior and Development, 7,* 311–321.

Chapter 4

Social Cognition and the Self

Michael Lewis
Robert Wood Johnson Medical School

When we use the term *social cognition*, we imply that the *social* part of the phrase somehow differentiates it from other types of cognition. It is this question that we wish to focus on. The position I will take is that the study of cognition—whatever we might mean by this term—involves to a more or less degree the role of the self in knowing. To the degree that the self as knower is part of the process of knowing is the degree to which the cognition is social (Lewis, 1993, 1997). There are several types of examples that involve the self. In the first, I may know about a sunset over the Chianti Hills of Tuscany by watching it, or I may know of it by reading a guidebook. In both cases, I have knowledge, but in one, that knowledge is gained through the self's experience of the phenomenon whereas in the other, it is through the self's knowledge of words.

The second example has to do with knowledge that involves the self. This is best captured by the sentence, "I know that you know that I know your name." Such sentences and their meaning cannot be independent of the self since the self knows something about what another self knows about the self. The meaningfulness of such a sentence is dependent on knowledge of myself and knowledge of another self's knowledge of myself. As we shall see, it is this type of social cognition that represents the unique aspect of the class of cognitions I shall refer to as social.

In this chapter, I wish first to address how varied the use of the phrase *social cognition* is and how we study it. Here, I want to point out one particular problem, namely the studies that ask the question, "Are social events different from nonsocial events?" Next, I address the issue of the role of the self or knower in what is known. This then leads to a discussion of the development of an important and central mental state, namely, the "idea of me." Finally, I suggest a developmental model where the self in connection with other selves leads to higher forms of knowing.

WHAT IS SOCIAL COGNITION?

Implied in *social cognition* is the belief that social cognition is in some way different from nonsocial cognition. When we raise this question, we need to make sure first of all whether reference to cognition here means both content and process or just one of these. For example, social cognition might refer to cognitions about social events or schemas, or it might mean processes of cognition that differ from social events or schemas. Whereas many argue that social schemas are different from nonsocial ones, more argument exists about whether processes are different. Tulving's (1985) distinctions for memory state that both schema differences *and* processes may be different and that this difference might aid us in our understanding of social cognition. Tulving has distinguished between semantic and episodic types of memories. In the former, the self is not involved; in the latter, it is. This distinction between cognitions that involve or do not involve the self goes to the heart of my understanding of social cognition, and in what follows, much will be made for the role of self in social cognition.

Social cognition has been studied by many, including attributional, cognitive, personality, and phenomenological psychologists. It has been studied under the guise of recognition of various emotions exhibited by others, the ability to judge others' emotional states (Bruner & Tagiuri, 1954; Darwin, 1965; Tagiuri, 1969), the reasons why people act as they do, and the perceptions of others' actions, role taking, empathy, and person perception (Hoffman, 1975). Taking a more developmental stance, Shantz (1975) defined social cognition as "a child's intuitive or logical representations of others, that is, how he characterizes others and makes references about their covert, inner psychological experiences" (p. 258). Unfortunately, this definition does not include other important aspects of social cognition, such as self-knowledge of relationships. Youniss (1975) offered a more inclusive definition, adding a sense of self, knowledge of self vis-à-vis society, and a sense of values and principles, as well as knowledge of others and one's relationship to them.

Historically, social cognition, especially in the first year of life, has been explored by looking at the development of social schema. Thus, Fantz (1961) explored whether newborn infants could discriminate human faces from other visual stimuli. Although Fantz's research indicated that they could, it is now recognized that his failure to properly control for complexity rendered his results invalid. Lewis (1969) demonstrated that, controlling for complexity, infants by 3 months of age could discriminate faces from nonfaces *and* preferred facelike stimuli. By 6 months, presumably after the face schema is established, infants now come to prefer nonfacelike to facelike stimuli. Kagan, Henker, Hen-Tov, Levine, and Lewis (1966), using three dimensional masks, also found that infants could discriminate and preferred facelike stimuli.

These early studies of social schema have continued with studies exploring whether moving faces and face–voice, presumably representing more "real" faces, are better discriminated and preferred and whether with these modifications allow for early demonstration of social discrimination and preference. Not only has research on face versus nonface schema been explored but also whether or not nonsocial as well as social stimuli can elicit imitation. Jacobson (1979) and Lewis and Sullivan (1985) were able to show that both tongue protrusion and protrusion of an object through a tube elicit equal amounts of tongue protrusion in very young infants. Lewis (Lewis, Sullivan, & Vasen, 1987; Lewis, Wilson, & Baumel, 1971) looked at face–body schema development. Information obtained from such studies is of some interest, but there are problems that make such studies problematic.

To begin with, when a social versus nonsocial (or an accurate vs. inaccurate) stimulus is presented, it is extremely difficult if not impossible to know what aspect of the stimulus an infant is using to make the discrimination and showing the preference for. For example, we present the infant with two different facial emotional stimuli, fearful and happy. If we find a preference, we can conclude that infants have the ability to discriminate between them. If we find no preference, then we do not know whether or not they are discriminable (Irwin, 1971). More important, if there is a preference, we do not *a priori* know what aspects of the stimuli are discernable; a fear face has a different eyebrow and mouth position than a happy face, and the infant might focus on both, one or the other, or none of these. This same problem exists whether we examine two different emotional faces or an accurate versus an inaccurate representation of a social stimulus. For example, in examining face schema development, do we use photos, masks, or real faces, and how, if we use real faces, can we control for all the other features that covary with a real face, for example, muscle movement or sound?

This latter point brings us directly to the second problem; namely, What are social stimuli? For example, in the studies of imitation, a tongue protrusion with a real tongue in a real face and a stick protruding from a toilet paper cardboard roll both produce equal amounts of tongue protrusion in the infant. What are we to conclude about the social event? Do such findings mean that a social stimulus is not necessary for infant imitation, or does a toilet paper roll with a stick reflect a social stimulus? The development of social schema are likely to be plagued by such problems.

I prefer to think of social cognition and its development from a different perspective, returning to a starting point suggested by others (Shantz, 1975; Youniss, 1975). We prefer to think of social cognition as the relationship among three aspects of knowledge: knowledge of the self; knowledge of others; knowledge of one's relationships to others. We explore these aspects after we consider the role of the self or knower in social cognition.

THE ROLE OF THE KNOWER

The epistemological issue of the relation between the knower and the known has been recognized by modern philosophers and psychologists for over 50 years (Merleau-Ponty, 1964; Piaget, 1960; Polyani, 1958). Nevertheless, knowing involves the interaction of the knower with objects, events, or people, but the mind of the knower, although formed through interactions, is believed to exist independently of the knower. Indeed, the degree to which the knower remains involved in the known is a measure of the immaturity or egocentrism of the knower. We, however, believe that the class of knowing we call social cognition depends on just such a connection. Following the early work of Mead (1934) and Cooley (1912), we believe that knowledge of the self and knowledge of others are dependent on one another: "I cannot know another unless I have knowledge of myself." Furthermore, a child's knowledge of self and others is developed through interactions with these others, social interaction being the basic unit out of which social cognition derives. Many who subscribe to an interactionist position agree that knowledge of others (and the world in general) is derived through interaction: "To understand that a person is . . . involves understanding what sorts of relationships can exist between mere things and between people and things" (Hamlyn, 1974, p. 7).

Because what a child knows of the other through interaction (usually nonsocial "other," characterized by physical properties such as weight, length, etc.) has been the major focus of researchers, the fact that knowledge of other, gained through interaction, must provide information about oneself has been ignored. If I find one object hard and the other soft by holding them, then not only do I know something about objects (in this case, hardness), but I know something about myself (how hard the object feels to me). As Merleau-Ponty (1964) has indicated, "If I am a consciousness turned toward things, I can meet in things the actions of another and find in them a meaning, because they are themes of possible activity for my own body" (p. 113).

Although it may be possible to separate the knower from the known for some forms of knowledge, in even the most abstract knowledge, the known interacts with the knower. For instance, Bower and Gilligan (1979) demonstrated that whom one identifies with in a story will affect and change the person's interpretation of the story. There also is evidence in memory research to indicate that memory is facilitated if what is to be remembered is made relevant to the self (Hyde & Jenkins, 1969; Kuiper & Rogers, 1979; Rogers, Kuiper, & Kirker, 1977). Language acquisition is another area in which the relationship between self and knowing can be demonstrated. Although 2-year-olds can demonstrate "on" or "under" knowledge by manipulating objects, they have far less difficulty when they use their own bodies rather than objects. Moreover, there is evidence to indicate that intentional verbs are applied to the self before being applied to others (Janellen Huttenlocker, personal communication, 1980). These examples indicate that there is a difference in cognitive ability when the self is engaged; this is what I call *social cognition.*

Social cognition has been defined in many different ways; for example, as social perception—the ability to discriminate different faces or to discriminate the face from a nonface stimulus. It has also been defined as the learning of social rules and obligations. In each of these cases, the knowledge is considered social in that it applies to human beings, human attributes, and human products such as rules and obligations. Although this knowledge pertains to the features of human beings in some general sense, there is no reason to think that the process of knowledge formation should differ in any marked way from that explicated by Piaget and others for knowledge that is not social, because these features, perceptions, and rules require little or no knowledge about the self. They do not involve knowledge about the self, so they are not relative, and as such, they can be studied like any other variable; such as, for example, weight or volume.

There should be no difference between studying social perception and studying other features of the environment, such as weight, time, and duration. For example, a child comes to understand the notion of weight by interacting with objects, lifting them, and receiving proprioceptive feedback at the same time as seeing them. Through development the child learns to conserve the concept of weight independently of transformations of the object and, in general, is no longer fooled by experimental manipulations of some of the object's properties. In the classical example of this type of study, a child is given two large balls of clay that are equal in weight. One of these balls is cut into five or so smaller balls, using up all the clay. The child is asked whether the five smaller balls will weigh the same as the one bigger ball. Until a certain point of maturity, the child will say that the five balls weigh more than the single large ball. Having been schooled in gravitational fields, a person may learn that the weight of an object is related to the mass on which it is weighed. Thus, experience forms the knowledge about weight, and when the person thinks about the weight of objects, the self is not involved. The self can, however, be involved in the knowing. I can estimate the weight relative to my idea about heavy or light. When we think of weight in regard to another person, the other can be treated as an object: we can think about the features of another person independently of ourselves or in relation to ourselves.

Social knowledge also has been defined to include communicative competence, inferences about others, role taking, and emotional experiences such as empathy. Years ago, Tagiuri (1969), for example, offered a classification of social knowledge that involves events inside the person, such as intentions, attitudes, perceptions, consciousness, and self-determination, and events between persons, such as friendship and love. These forms of knowledge are not independent of the knower or self, because they pertain to knowledge that requires the use of the self. Role taking and empathy, for example, require that knowers put themselves in the place of another.

Social knowledge involves interpersonal relationships. The process involves the self in at least two ways. When I think about relationships, by definition they involve me; and when I think about relationships, one of the things that I may think about is what the other thinks of me. Recursive cognitions can become quite complex, as, for example, when I think of what others think that I think of them. In his discussion of interpersonal relationships, Asch (1952) makes a similar point: "The paramount fact about human interactions is that they are happenings that are psychologically represented in each of the participants. In our relationship to an object, perceiving, thinking, and feeling take place on one side, whereas in relations between persons, these processes take place on both sides and are dependent upon one another" (p. 93).

Knowledge about self and other are not separate processes but rather a part of the duality of knowledge. For example, Bannister and Agnew (1977) note, "The ways in which we elaborate our construing of self must be essentially those ways in which we elaborate our construing of others. For we have not a concept of self, but a bipolar construct of self-not self, or self-other" (p. 101). The definition of social knowledge involves the relationship between the knower and the known rather than characteristics of people as objects. By utilizing the self in knowing, we can differentiate when we are treating people as objects from when we are treating them as people. If the self is not involved, then the people are being treated as objects; when the self is involved, people are being treated as people.

The role of the self in cognitive processes is illustrated by an experiment by Feldman (1979), who was interested in person perception or, more precisely, the formation of inferences by young children regarding the traits, motivations, and probable behavior of others. Earlier research had indicated that younger children tended to use what we call *featural knowledge*, descriptions of others' physical appearance or possessions, whereas older children described both physical appearance and the inner dimensions of the self, such as traits or stable dispositions. Such descriptions are recursive in nature and relational. In one study of 5- and 6-year-olds and 9- and 10-year-olds, Feldman showed that age was not necessarily the determining factor in the type of cognition used and the knowledge gained. The children observed on videotape four unknown peers who illustrated the traits of generosity, clinginess, physical coordination, and physical clumsiness. In one group, the instructions the experimenter gave were made personally relevant by informing the young subjects that they would meet the children in the videotape after the study. In the other group, this information was omitted. Feldman found that children who expected future interactions exhibited more and different inferences about the actors: "Subjects appeared to be formulating a search in which a criterion of personal relevance mediated a change in proposition of statement types . . . used in descriptions of the actions" (pp. 44, 49).

The relevance of these findings to the notion of involvement between the knower and what or how knowledge is gained is clear. As the engagement of the self becomes more relevant to the task of knowing, social knowledge increases. Descriptions such as *nice*, *friendly*, and *helpful* are used more because they refer to the possible relationship the actor can have with the other. Feldman's study also provides support for the converse: that even with human stimuli, the absence of the usage of the self results in a proportional decrease in the number of featural descriptions. In light of these findings, it seems reasonable to believe that when the self is withdrawn from human stimuli, the interactions with these stimuli appear little different from those not possessing human features. This intrinsically appeals to our notion that people can be referred to and treated as objects and that objects can be referred to and treated as people. The critical factor appears to be the degree of involvement of the self. Social knowledge and social action depend on the role of the knower. This is reflected in Heider's (1958) belief that "social perceptions in general can best be described as a process between the center of one person and the center of another person, from life space to life space. . . . A, through psychological processes in himself, perceives psychological processes in B" (p. 33).

The role of the knower in what is known provides us with the basis for considering social cognition. Social cognition differs from other cognition, in both content and process, to the degree that the cognition involves the self. The self is always involved in knowing, but some forms of knowing involve the self more than others; these I call *social cognition.*

THE DEVELOPMENT OF SELF

Our definition of social cognition rests on three aspects of knowledge—of self, of other, and of the relation of self to other. This being so, we need to consider again the concept of self (see Lewis, 1995a, for a fuller explanation).

The adult self is made up of a variety of different aspects, functions, and structures that occasionally work in harmony (see Wylie, 1961, for a historical review of this idea). For example, I certainly know, as I sit here writing, that I have a plan to write this chapter and an outline, which I have made to help formulate my thoughts. It is clear that I have intentions and desires and presumably the ability to carry out the task of thinking and writing. Yet, the very acts themselves seem to emerge from me almost effortlessly. Indeed, if I focus my attention on them, I find that doing so interrupts the very act that I am performing. It is clear, then, that this self of mine—the body and the mind—that carries out this task does not need and, in fact, may be hindered by my paying attention to myself. A self is necessary to formulate at least sometimes what it is that I wish to think about but does not appear to be involved in the process that actually carries out the task of thinking.

Consider an example: We give a subject the problem of adding a 7 to a sum of 7s that preceded it (e.g., 7 + 7 = 14 + 7 = 21 + 7 = 28, etc.). It is clear that as we carry out this task, we cannot watch ourselves do the arithmetic. It would seem that one aspect of the self has set up the problem and another will solve it; and it is likely that the first will evaluate the result of what the second did. Let us consider self-deception. How is it possible for a self to deceive its self? It appears to be a logical impossibility, but only if we believe that a self is a single thing. A self as a single thing could not deceive its self. If, however, we conceive of a self in the manner that Freud (1959) did, one that consists of several aspects or features, then we are able to argue that one part of the self can deceive another part.

The idea of self-deceptions suggests that the one way to understand the self is to assume the position that there are multiple aspects to the self, which may mean that the self is a modular system, an idea applied to brain structure and process (Gazzaniga, 1988). It is clear that whatever the self may be, it is a complex multiaspect sort of "thing" or "process." This multiaspect self has been considered in many different ways. In early writing, I referred to it in terms of subjective versus objective self-awareness (Lewis & Brooks-Gunn, 1979; see also Duval & Wicklund, 1972) or the machinery of self versus the idea of "me" (Lewis, 1994, 1995a).

Given this idea of a multiaspect adult self, how are we to treat the idea of the development of self? From a developmental perspective, not all these aspects exist at birth or even develop at the same time. If they did, there would be little to develop. Thus, it is essential when studying the development of the self that we first agree to the general principle that the term *self* in and of itself imparts little meaning, since it does not specify particular aspects of a self. If investigators talk about the existence of a self at birth or even at 3 months (Gopnik & Meltzoff, 1994; Watson, 1994), they may mean something very different than what others might mean when they talk about the self as evolving in the middle of the second year of life (Lewis, 1992, 1995b; Lewis & Brooks-Gunn, 1979).

What I should like to do is to make a distinction between different aspects of the self and to argue that the aspect that we, adult humans, refer to as *ourselves*, is, in fact, a rather unique aspect of self, one that we share with few other species (the exceptions being the great apes and, perhaps, porpoises and whales). This aspect of the self develops somewhere toward the middle of the second year of life (Lewis, 1994). It may grow out of other aspects of the self that appear earlier, or it may have little connection to them—being related only as part of a developmental function of emerging skills associated with maturational processes. More important, however, is the need to make clear, both in our conceptions and language, that the functions of this late-maturing aspect of self not be assigned to earlier aspects of the self.

Lewis (1995a) suggested that to understand the self, we need to distinguish between the self as a system in that the self may contain many elements, such as awareness, communication capacities, and perceptual abilities, without necessarily involving any mental states. The self-system eventually does develop mental states and, in particular, the mental state of the idea of "me," which then leads to the idea of others also having a "me like-me," does not mean that the infant from the beginning has such states. The distinction between the machinery of myself (the system properties) and the idea of me (a mental state) needs to be made.

MYSELF AND ME

Making this distinction allows us to consider what I call the *system properties* of the self—something that many, if not all, living organisms possess, including young infants—and the idea of me—a mental state that emerges slowly in the human young, possibly as a function of frontal lobe maturation and which is likely to exist (although not in a human form) in the great apes.

Such an idea allows us to consider diverse properties of thought. Although I may know about some aspects of me, I do not know about all. For example, I have no knowledge of a large number of my motives—organized coherent thoughts and ideas that we sometimes call *unconsciousness*—which control large segments of my life. I have no knowledge of how my thoughts occur or why I feel one way or another. Nevertheless, I know that I think and feel, even without this knowledge.

The claim has been made that it is possible to know of all things related to the self; for example, the yoga's belief in the control of much of our autonomic nervous system functioning. It may be true that I could know more of some parts of myself if I chose to focus my attention on them, but it is nonetheless the case that what is known by myself is greater than what I can state I know. If such facts are true, it is fair to suggest the metaphor of my self. I imagine myself to be a biological machine that is an evolutionarily fit complex set of processes; regulating, growing, feeling, thinking, planning, and learning. One aspect of this machine is the idea of me. An aspect of this machine that knows is that it knows itself and knows it does not know all of itself. The me that recognizes the me in the mirror is part of that machinery, likely located in the frontal lobes (Weiskrantz, 1986).

The self, then, is greater than the me, the me being only a small portion of myself. This idea can be understood best from an epistemological point of view. The idea that I know is not the same as the idea that I know I know. The me aspect of the self that I refer to is that which knows it knows. The failure to make the distinction between these features of self can be blamed for much confusion when studying the issue of development. The distinction between self and me, or between knowing and knowing I know, involves two aspects of me. If we do not confuse knowing with knowing I know, then the argument around the issue of the developmental sequence in self becomes clearer. As I have already suggested, many features of the self exist early and exist as part of the system from birth or soon after. The idea of me—the knower who knows—is not developed until somewhere in the middle of the second year of life (Darwin, 1965; Lewis, 1992).

We have already given some attention to two early features of the self. These are the self–other differentiation and self-regulation. Both features are likely to be part of the machinery of myself and not related to the idea of me. Certainly, by 3 months, and most likely from birth, an infant can differentiate itself from other. Self-and-other differentiation also has associated with it a type of self-awareness. It is the self-awareness of elements of a system in communication with one another. This type of recognition and the self–other differentiation is part of the hardware of any complex system. T cells recognize and differentiate themselves from foreign protein. A rat does not run into the wall but runs around it. A newborn infant recognizes and responds appropriately to intersensory information. Therefore, we should not expect that these aspects of self are the differentiating features when we compare wildly different organisms. All organisms, as systems, should have these capacities.

What may distinguish organisms in regard to their system organization is the complexity of the machinery of these systems. What may differentiate humans from most other living organisms is not the functions of the system but the ability to have mental states and, more specifically, the mental states related to the idea of me.

The ontogenetic and phylogenetic coherences found to date support the idea that in order to understand the concept of self, we need to disentangle the common term, *self,* into at least two aspects. I suggest we call these *the machinery of the self* and *the idea of me.* They have been referred to by other terms, for example, as *objective self-awareness,* which reflects the idea of me, and *subjective self-awareness,* which reflects the machinery of self (Lewis, 1990b, 1991, 1992). The same objective–subjective distinctions have been considered by Duval and Wicklund (1972). In any consideration of the concept of self, especially in regard to adult humans, it is important to keep in mind that both biological aspects exist. There is unbeknownst to us most of the time an elaborate complex of machinery that controls much of our behavior, learns from experience, has states and affects, and affects our bodies, most likely including what and how we think. The processes are, for the most part, unavailable to us. What is available is the idea of me, a mental state.

What is particularly impressive is the recent research on brain function and the findings that point to the possibility that different areas of the brain may be associated with different functioning. Thus, both the machinery of the self and the mental state involving the idea of me appear to be the consequences of different biological processes and locations. For example, the recent work by LeDoux (1990) points to specific brain regions that may be responsible for different kinds of self-processes. Working with rats, LeDoux found that even after the removal of the auditory cortex, the animals were able to learn to associate an auditory signal and shock. After a few trials, the rats showed a negative emotional response to the sound, even though its auditory cortex had been removed. These findings indicate that the production of a fear state is likely to be mediated by subcortical, probably the thalamic-amygdala, sensory pathways. Similar findings have been reported in humans, suggesting that states can exist without one part of the self experiencing them. Weiskrantz (1986), among others, reported on a phenomenon called *blind-sighted.* Patients have been found who lack the visual cortex, at least in one hemisphere. When asked if they could see an object placed in their blind spot, they reported that they could not see it, that is, that they did not have the experience of the visual event. The self, reflecting on its self, my recognition of what I know, the me—the mental state—in fact, does not see. When, however, the patients were asked to reach for it, they showed that they have the ability to reach, at least some of the time, for the object. Thus, they can "see" the event but cannot experience their sight. These findings, as well as Gazzaniga's work (1988) on split brain, suggest that separate brain regions are responsible for the production and maintenance of both the machinery of self-processes and the mental state of the idea of me. A similar analysis involving a memory has been suggested by Tulving (1985).

This idea of the machinery of the self, or subjective awareness, versus the mental state, or the idea of me, an objective awareness, can best be seen in emotional life. I have tried, in the past, to distinguish between emotional state and experiences and have argued that adults can have emotional states and, yet, have no experience of them (Lewis, 1990a; Lewis & Michalson, 1983). This distinction is especially true for the infant, if, by experience, we refer to a mental state about the self. Thus, for example, if I say, "I am happy," I mean by that statement that I am in an emotional state of happiness, and I can experience that state. A young infant can be in a state but may not have an experience of that state. Emotional states, therefore, refer to objective self-awareness, or the machinery of our self-system. This machinery can have goals, can learn and profit from experience, can control functions, and can react to events, including people. The experience of our emotional states refers to objective self-awareness. The idea of different aspects of the self are clearly necessary, given the data of our adult lives. The question is whether such distinctions make sense in considering the development of self (Pribram, 1984).

To summarize the idea of me or mental state of self, let me state some basic principles:

1. All living systems self-regulate. By this we mean that within any living system there needs to be communication between parts of that system. This we can call awareness, but not the mental state of awareness. This can include a unit as small as a cell, a plant or animal, or even more complex organisms. As I write, my systems are regulating my temperature or regulating my blood sugar level. Regulation is a property of living matter. Regulation makes no assumptions about objective self-awareness or intentions, although there is intentionality in the process.

2. In order to act, it is necessary for organisms to be able to distinguish between self and other. Whether this ability is learned as Watson suggests (1994) or, as others have suggested, part of the process of action—including perceiving, feeling, and thinking—is unknown (Butterworth, 1990). What appears to be so is that no organism can act without being able to distinguish between self and other. The ability to regulate or to distinguish self from other is part of the machinery of all living systems (von Bartalanffy, 1967).

3. Even higher-order functions such as perception and complex actions (i.e., driving a car) can be carried out by adult humans without objective self-awareness; that is, without their being able to look in and observe the processes that allow these behaviors to be carried out. I cannot watch myself think, I can only look at the product of my thinking.

4. A unique aspect of some self-systems is objective self-awareness. By objective self-awareness, I mean the capacity of a self to know it knows or to remember it remembers. It is this mental state that we refer to when we say self-awareness. The capacity of objective self-awareness may be uniquely human (although the great apes, porpoises, and whales appear capable of this as well; Lewis, 1994, 1995a).

5. Specific developmental processes of the self follow the general principles of development. Earlier capacities, such as the machinery of the self, *may* give rise to later capacities, like mental states (e.g., the idea of me) but are not transformed. Furthermore, both capacities exist once the latter emerges. Thus, unlike a more classical genetic epistemological approach, I see the retention of earlier structures or functions as not only possible but a necessary aspect of development. In some sense, then, old structures in interaction with the environment or as a function of maturation, or both, give rise to new structures. These new structures do not replace the old ones but coexist with them. Under certain conditions, individuals will utilize the most mature aspect they have achieved. However, this does not mean other aspects are not utilized. In some sense, then, mature adults possess within their repertoire all aspects, whereas younger children possess only those aspects already achieved (Lewis, 1997).

The end result of any developmental trajectory is the existence of all aspects. In fact, the various aspects, once they have emerged, are likely to be elaborated over the entire life course; not only do they not replace one another, but they are likely to continue to develop (Fischer, 1980). Finally, similar types of behavior, which may or may not be related to the same aspect, exist in adults as in infants. For older children—perhaps past 2 to 3 years of age—and adults, both aspects of self exist and are used. The aspect used by adults may be valuable in understanding their development.

We recognize, then, that there are different aspects of self. Objective self-awareness, an occurrence we have marked as taking place in the middle of the second year of life (Lewis & Brooks-Gunn, 1979), joins the subjective self, which either exists at birth or develops soon after. Objective self-awareness does not replace subjective self-awareness but coexists with it. Thus, adults are capable of functions that involve both objective and subjective self-awareness. In fact, the objective self can even think about the subjective self.

If social cognition rests on the emergence of the mental state of me, then social cognition, as distinguished from social perceptions, emerges in the second year of life and, through it gives rise to mental states in regard to others and in the states of the relation between self and other. Darwin's (1965) discussion in regard to mental states necessary for certain emotions suggests such a developmental framework:

> The nature of the mental states of shyness, shame, and modesty have as their emotional element self-attention. It is not the simple act of reflecting on our own appearance, but the thinking what others think of us, which excites a blush . . . and I have received authentic accounts of two little girls blushing at the ages of between 2 and 3 years. . . It appears that the mental powers of infants are not as yet sufficiently developed to allow of their blushing (p. 310).

DEVELOPMENT OF SOCIAL COGNITION

I have argued for a particular definition of social cognition that involves the mental state of the idea of me, a mental state that allows for consideration of the idea of the other as well as the interaction of me with the other. Utilizing this definition, the development of the particular mental state becomes central to any understanding of social cognition. Moreover, as I have argued elsewhere (Lewis, 1992, 1995a, 1997), the emergence of this mental state appears to occur somewhere in the middle of the second year of life. Using self-recognition in mirrors as a measure of this construct, the 15- to 18-month-old period appears to be a reasonable estimate, one supported by the apparent myelinization of the frontal cortex (Barkovich, 1995).

This does not mean that the human infant cannot discriminate between what we call social versus nonsocial events, nor does it not mean that infants cannot behave differently to these same types of events. Certainly, lower-order animals (rats, for example), and even single cells, behave differently to social versus nonsocial events. However, I reserve the term *social cognition* (either schema or process) to mental states and their creation and use. For this argument, the mental states do not exist early, and their emergence is likely due to maturation of particular brain sites.

Given these assumptions, the question of the development of social cognition depends on the emergence of the mental state of me. One way to start our discussion of the developmental aspects is to address what is likely to be part of the end product of this development. For my example I return to what Lang referred to as *Knots* (1970), which in its general form appears as, "I know you know I know." Here self, other, and the relationship between them is given.

In the last few years I have been struggling with this problem (Lewis, 1994), and I would like to suggest a developmental sequence. It involves four levels. Level 1 I call *knowing* (or *I know*). This level prevails from birth until the middle of the second year of life and is likely to be driven by basic processes common to other animals. It is not based on complex mental states, involves little or no language, and is not supported by the particular mental state of me. Many organisms can share in this kind of knowledge. For example, when an object in the visual field rapidly expands, children, as well as adults and animals, show surprise or discomfort. This response is simply built into the machinery of perceptual-motor knowledge. It is what I have called the *machinery of the self.*

Level 2 is *I know I know.* This level involves consciousness and self-referential behavior. It is based on the mental state of me and thus allows for the capacity to reflect on one's self and to reflect, in part, on what one knows. This mental state is a metarepresentation. It is similar to a memory of a memory. Whereas a child at the first level may have a memory, it is at the second level that metamemory is possible. Here the child remembers that he or she remembers. This capacity emerges somewhere in the middle of the second year of life. It can be marked by referencing and mirror behavior (Lewis, 1990a, 1990b).

Level 3 is *I know you know.* This form of knowing takes into account the mental state that not only do I know something, but I believe others know it as well; it is the ability and basis of shared meaning. This representation, that you know what I know, does not need to be accurate. Adults know more than children know; thus the child may not really know what the adult knows. The child is likely to make egocentric errors. At this level children know, they know they know, and they also know you know. What they cannot yet do is to place themselves in opposition to what they know. This level, in combination with the earlier ones, accounts in part for the early ability to deceive. A 2½-year-old child who deceives knows that she knows and she knows that you know; thus deception is possible. It is also the reason why children are likely to make the traditional false belief errors. This level is likely to last until somewhere in the third year of life.

Before going on to the fourth level, it is worth mentioning that this level may not be distinct from the one before it in which the child knows he or she knows. Earlier, we have discussed the possibility that the mental state of me and what I know may emerge at the same time as the mental state of what the other knows. Thus for some, what I know about me supposes that I know the same about the other. If this indeed is the case, then a separate level might not be called for.

Level 4 is the adultlike level. It addresses the interactive and recursive nature of social cognition. It is characterized as *I know you know I know.* At this level not only are there two actors, as at Level 3, but each actor has a perspective. These perspectives can be different. It is when there are two perspectives that one has the ability to recognize false belief. Only when one has reached the level of knowing that "they know I know" that your knowledge about what *they know* can be correct, since you can check their knowledge of what they know about you against what you know. That is, once a child knows that he or she can be the subject and also the object of the knowledge of another, the child is capable of recognizing the difference in perspectives between individuals. It is at this final level of perspective taking that mature metaknowledge can emerge. Here, the mental states of me, other, and the relation of me to other and other to me can be explained.

As these levels of knowing are reached and mastered, there is at the same time an increase in general cognitive competence, in particular language usage. Language ability is laid down on the general cognitive scaffolding that allows the language to reflect increasingly the available cognitive ability. Our problem in studying children's development is that language ability may not precede this general cognitive capacity but may follow it. Thus, children's observed social behavior and cognition may reflect a level higher than their verbal capacities.

The model outlined here is only one example of a number of possible approaches to examining the development of social cognition. Whatever our ultimate explanation of the difference between ways of knowing, social and nonsocial, and ways of processing information, the role of the self in knowing must be considered. Without the introduction of mental states involving self, other, and their interaction, the study of early social cognition will be restricted to perceptual and behavioral differences in response to stimuli labeled social or nonsocial. As we already have suggested, there are inherent difficulties in this procedure. Thus, although such perceptual and behavioral differences may underlie subsequent mental states, I feel we need either to study the relation between these earlier behaviors and later mental states or to study directly the mental states themselves.

REFERENCES

Asch, S. E. (1952). *Social psychology*. Englewood Cliffs, NJ: Prentice-Hall.

Bannister, D., & Agnew, J. (1977). The child's construing of self. In A. W. Landfield (Ed.), *Nebraska Symposium on Motivation* (1976; Vol. 24; pp. 99–125). Lincoln: University of Nebraska Press.

Barkovich, A. J. (1995). *Pediatric neuroimaging* (2nd ed.). New York: Raven Press.

Bower, G. H., & Gilligan, S. G. (1979). Remembering information related to oneself. *Journal of Research on Personality, 113*, 404–419.

Bruner, J. S., & Tagiuri, R. (1954). The perception of people. In G. Lindzey (Ed.), *Handbook of social psychology, Vol. 2* (pp. 161–192). Cambridge, MA: Addison-Wesley.

Butterworth, G. (1990). Origins of self-perception in infancy. In D. Cicchetti & M. Beeghly (Eds.), *The self in transition: Infancy to childhood* (pp. 119–137). Chicago: University of Chicago Press.

Cooley, C. H. (1912). *Human nature and the social order*. New York: Scribner's.

Darwin, C. (1965). *The expression of emotions in man and animals*. Chicago: University of Chicago Press. (Original work published 1872)

Duval, S., & Wicklund, R. A. (1972). *A theory of objective self-awareness*. New York: Academic Press.

Fantz, R. L. (1961). The origin of form perception. *Scientific American, 204*, 66–72.

Feldman, N. S. (1979). *Children's impressions of their peers: Motivational factors and the use of inference.* Unpublished doctoral dissertation, Princeton University, Princeton, NJ.

Fischer, K. W. (1980). A theory of cognitive development: The control and construction of hierarchies and skills. *Psychological Review, 87,* 477–531.

Freud, S. (1959). The ego and the id. In J. Strachey (Ed. and Trans.), *The complete psychological works of Sigmund Freud* (Vol. 19, pp. 3–66). London: Hogarth Press. (Original work published 1923)

Gazzaniga, M. S. (1988). Brain modularity: Towards a philosophy of consciousness experience. In A. J. Marcel & E. Beseach (Eds.), *Consciousness in contemporary science* (pp. 218–256). Oxford, England: Clarendon Press.

Gopnik, A., & Meltzoff, A. N. (1994). Minds, bodies and persons: Young children's understanding of the self and others as reflected in imitation and theory of mind research. In S. T. Parker, R. W. Mitchell, & M. L. Bocchia (Eds.), *Self-awareness in animals and humans: Developmental perspectives* (pp. 166–186). Cambridge, England: Cambridge University Press.

Hamlyn, D. W. (1974). Person-perception and our understanding of others. In T. Mischel (Ed.), *Understanding other persons.* Totowa, NJ: Rowman & Littlefield.

Heider, F. (1958). *The psychology of interpersonal relations.* New York: Wiley.

Hoffman, M. L. (1975). Developmental synthesis of affect and cognition and its implications for altruistic motivation. *Developmental Psychology, 11,* 607–622.

Huttenlocker, J. (1980). Personal communication.

Hyde, T. S., & Jenkins, J. J. (1969). The differential effects of incidental tasks on the organization of recall of a list of highly associated words. *Journal of Experimental Psychology, 82,* 472–481.

Irwin, F. W. (1971). *Intentional behavior and motivation.* New York: Lippincott.

Jacobson, S. W. (1979). Matching behavior in the young infant. *Child Development, 50,* 425–430.

Kagan, J., Henker, B., Hen-Tov, A., Levine, J., & Lewis, M. (1966). Infants' differential reactions to familiar and distorted faces. *Child Development, 37,* 519–532.

Kuiper, N. A., & Rogers, T. B. (1979). Encoding of personal information: Self-other differences. *Journal of Personality and Social Psychology, 37*(4), 499–514.

Lang, R. D. (1970). *Knots.* New York: Pantheon.

LeDoux, J. (1990). Cognitive and emotional interactions in the brain. *Cognition and Emotions, 3*(4), 265–289.

Lewis, M. (1969). Infants' responses to facial stimuli during the first year of life. *Developmental Psychology, 1,* 75–86.

Lewis, M. (1990a). Thinking and feeling—The elephant's tail. In C. A. Maher, M. Schwebel, & N. S. Fagley (Eds.), *Thinking and problem solving in the developmental process: International perspectives (the WORK)* (pp. 89–110). Hillsdale, NJ: Lawrence Erlbaum Associates.

Lewis, M. (1990b). Social knowledge and social development. *Merrill-Palmer Quarterly, 36*(1), 93–116.

Lewis, M. (1991). Ways of knowing: Objective self-awareness or consciousness. *Developmental Review, 11,* 231–243.

Lewis, M. (1992, April). Shame, the exposed self. *Zero to Three, XII*(4), 6–10.

Lewis, M. (1993). Commentary. (Raver, C. C., & Leadbeater, B. J.), The problem of the other in research on theory of mind and social development. *Human Development, 36,* 350–362, 363–367.

Lewis, M. (1994). Myself and me. In S. T. Parker, R. W. Mitchell, & M. L. Boccia (Eds.), *Self-awareness in animals and humans: Developmental perspectives* (pp. 20–34). New York: Cambridge University Press.

Lewis, M. (1995a). Aspects of self: From systems to ideas. In P. Rochat (Ed.), *The self in early infancy: Theory and research* (pp. 95–115). Advances in Psychology Series. Amsterdam, The Netherlands: North Holland, Elsevier Science.

Lewis, M. (1995b). *Shame: The exposed self* (paperback edition). New York: The Free Press.

Lewis, M. (1997). *Altering fate: Why the past does not predict the future.* New York: Guilford.

Lewis, M., & Brooks-Gunn, J. (1979). *Social cognition and the acquisition of self.* New York: Plenum Press.

Lewis, M., & Michalson, L. (1983). *Children's emotions and moods: Developmental theory and measurement.* New York: Plenum Press.

Lewis, M., & Sullivan, M. (1985). Imitation in the first six months of life: Phenomenon in the eye of the beholder. *Merrill-Palmer Quarterly, 31,* 315–333.

Lewis, M., Sullivan, M. W., & Vasen, A. (1987). Making faces: Age and emotion differences in the posing of emotional expressions. *Developmental Psychology, 23*(5), 690–697.

Lewis, M., Wilson, C. D., & Baumel, M. H. (1971). Attention distribution in the 24-month-old: Variations in complexity and incongruity of the human form. *Child Development, 42*(2), 429–438.

Mead, G. H. (1934). *Mind, self and society: From the standpoint of a social behaviorist.* Chicago: University of Chicago Press.

Merleau-Ponty, M. (1964). *The primacy of perception* (J. Eddie, Ed., & W. Cobb, Trans.). Evanston, IL: Northwestern Universities Press.

Piaget, J. (1960). *The psychology of intelligence.* New York: Littlefield Adams.

Polyani, M. (1958). *Personal language: Toward a post-critical philosophy.* London: Routledge & Kegan Paul.

Pribram, K. H. (1984). Emotion: A neurobehavioral analysis. In K. R. Scherer & P. Ekman (Eds.), *Approaches to emotion* (pp. 13–38). Hillsdale, NJ: Lawrence Erlbaum Associates.

Rogers, T. B., Kuiper, N. A., & Kirker, W. S. (1977). Self-reference and the encoding of personal information. *Journal of Personality and Social Psychology, 35,* 677–688.

Shantz, C. U. (1975). *The development of social cognition.* Chicago: University of Chicago Press.

Tagiuri, R. (1969). Person perception. In G. Lands & E. Ironstone (Eds.), *The handbook of social psychology: Vol. 3. The individual in a social context* (pp. 395–449). Reading, MA: Addison-Wesley.

Tulving, E. (1985). How many memory systems are there? *American Psychologist, 40,* 385–398.

von Bartalanffy, L. (1967). *Robots, men, and mind.* New York: Brazilles.

Watson, J. S. (1994). Detection of self: The perfect algorithm. In S. T. Parker, R. W. Mitchell, & M. L. Boccia (Eds.), *Self-awareness in animals and humans: Developmental perspectives* (pp. 131–148). New York: Cambridge University Press.

Weiskrantz, L. (1986). *Blindsight: A case study and implications.* Oxford, England: Oxford University Press.

Wylie, R. C. (1961). *The self concept.* Lincoln: University of Nebraska Press.

Youniss, J. (1975). Another perspective on social cognition. In A. D. Pick (Ed.), *Minnesota Symposium on Child Psychology, Vol. 9.* Minneapolis: University of Minnesota Press.

Part II

EARLY SENSITIVITY TO SOCIAL CONTINGENCIES

Chapter 5

Early Socio-Emotional Development: Contingency Perception and the Social-Biofeedback Model

György Gergely
University College London

John S. Watson
University of California at Berkeley

The past century of theory about human development has placed much responsibility for normal socio-emotional development on the social interactions experienced in infancy (e.g., Bandura, 1992; Bowlby, 1969; Bruner, 1990; Freud, 1949; Skinner, 1948; Stern, 1985; Trevarthen, 1979; Watson, 1930). The reliance on nurture over nature in each of these theories may need to be tempered in light of some recent proposals about a variety of richly structured innate mechanisms to interpret social stimulation [e.g., Leslie's (1987, 1994) theory of mind module; Baron-Cohen's (1995) detectors for perceiving another person's intention and eye direction; Meltzoff's (Meltzoff & Gopnik, 1993; Meltzoff & Moore, 1977, 1989) neonatal imitation mechanism; or Gergely and Csibra's (1996, 1997; Csibra & Gergely, in press) teleological stance for interpreting another's action]. Even if incorporating one or more of these specific interpretive mechanisms, however, these diverse theories will surely continue to rely heavily on an assumption they share, at least implicitly, to the effect that human infants are sensitive to the existence of *contingencies between their behavior and environmental events.*

The capacity to accurately interpret stimulation as contingent or not could well be viewed as the most fundamental of an infant's arsenal of innate modules for interpreting early sensory stimulation. Whether as a means to establish a basis of conditioning (e.g., Bandura, Skinner) or a basis for building representations of social relations (e.g., Bowlby, Bruner, Trevarthen), an infant's capacity to detect contingency is taken for granted.

However, a definition of what constitutes a perceivable contingency is often only vaguely provided.

It has also been a common assumption of most developmental theories (including Freud, Bruner, and Stern) that early experience includes perceptual awareness of one's basic emotional states, at least initially (i.e., before any "repressive" mechanism). For example, even John B. Watson's (1930) extreme empiricism incorporated an assumption that an infant by nature experiences a set of simple emotions such as fear, love, and rage.

This chapter presents and extends a model of human socio-emotional development that we have recently proposed (Gergely & Watson, 1996). Our model gains its uniqueness by the fact that even though it embraces the common assumption that young infants are sensitive to contingency experience, at the same time, it rejects the general view that they are initially perceptually aware of their specific basic emotion states. Indeed, it is our contention that contingency detection is crucially involved in an infant's progressively developing awareness of his or her internal affective states. More specifically, our "social-biofeedback model" holds that the caregiver's contingent reflections of the infant's emotion expressive displays play a central causal role in the development of emotional self-awareness and control that is mediated by the contingency detection module.

We begin by trying to make very clear what we mean by *contingency perception, contingency seeking,* and its special limitation to *perceivable contingencies,* because we shall place considerable theoretical weight on these foundational constructs. We then consider the implications of this view of early contingency perception when conjoined with an assumption that an infant begins life with little or no awareness of his or her dispositional states. That leads us to our social-biofeedback model of how the infant progressively becomes aware of his or her emotional dispositions through the process previously identified as social mirroring. Our model includes an assumption about a change in the target magnitude of contingency seeking that appears to occur at about 3 months of age. The possible relevance of this for the understanding of the deviant developmental pattern in autism is also briefly considered.

THE CONTINGENCY DETECTION MODULE: BASES AND LIMITS OF CONTINGENCY PERCEPTION IN INFANTS

One of us (Watson, 1979, 1985, 1994, in press) has provided evidence for the very early existence of a complex perceptual contingency detection module that analyzes the conditional probability structure of the contingent relations between responses and stimulus events. Briefly, this analytic device applies two independent mechanisms: one (called the *sufficiency index*) is looking forward in time, registering the conditional probability of an upcoming stimulus event as a function of an emitted response, and the other (called the *necessity index*) is testing backward in time, monitoring the relative likelihood that a given stimulus event was preceded by a given response. The two separate indices estimate two aspects of the contingency relation that can vary independently of each other providing a scale of different magnitudes of contingent relatedness. However, whenever the two indices provide different estimates of contingency, it is possible that this difference may signal the fact that the actual contingency is higher than the average of the two estimates. This is so because the device may be monitoring either a too narrow or a too broad class of responses. There is some evidence, however, that the contingency detection mechanism can discover the maximal degree of contingency (contingency maximizing, see Watson, 1979) by either reducing or expanding the sampled set of responses, eventually zeroing in on the correct response set and identifying the actual degree of contingent control (the details of the workings of the module are described in Gergely & Watson, 1996, pp. 1191–1192; see also Watson, 1979).

In a series of experiments, Watson (1979, 1985) examined infants' reactions to different magnitudes of response-stimulus temporal contingencies varying between less than 1 but greater than zero (in terms of conditional probability). He found that between 4 and 6 months of age, infants appear to have great difficulty with contingency magnitudes that are less than .5. Unexpectedly, they also appeared to fail to engage contingencies that approached a magnitude of 1 on both indices (i.e., on both necessity and sufficiency).

Though much of the supporting evidence has come from studies examining temporal contingency relations, a case has been made (Watson, 1984a) for there being at least three separate and independent bases of contingency: temporal, sensory relational, and spatial. In fact, we wish to argue that the contingency detection module can be conceived of as an analytic device that at its input end monitors for and registers all these three parameters of response-stimulus contingencies in parallel and provides as its output a value indicating the estimated degree of *causal relatedness* between responses and stimuli. Evidence of infants' use of these three informational bases in detecting contingency is available. The temporal variable has been investigated most, and the sensory relation variable has received the least amount of attention.

1. Temporal Contingencies

Many studies have shown infants to be sensitive to situations in which their behavior is followed in time by a stimulus event (e.g., a vocalization is followed by an auditory or visual stimulus, Bloom, 1979; Ramey & Ourth,

1971), or a leg movement is followed by movement of a mobile (Rovee-Collier, 1987; Rovee & Rovee, 1969; Watson, 1972). Under such circumstances, infants will rather quickly display a change in their pattern or rate of behavior. Even newborns will alter their sucking when it immediately affects what they see (Walton & Bower, 1993) or hear (De Casper & Prescott, 1984).

An infant's sensitivity to temporal contingency has limits, however. A delay of the contingent stimulus by as little as 3 seconds appears capable of blocking the detection of the contingency, at least for infants younger than 6 months of age (Millar, 1972; Millar & Watson, 1979, Ramey & Ourth, 1971). Whether or not the 3-second delay is an absolute barrier, however, it is clear that temporal delay has a profound affect on how well a contingency will be perceived, and it seems likely that longer delays would eventually make any temporal contingency undetectable (Watson, 1967; 1984b).

2. Sensory Relations

There is a further source of information about the contingent relatedness between events over and above their temporal contingency that is provided by sensory relations. There is no doubt that, as adults, we recognize the relationship between how much energy we put into an instrumental act and the amount of consequence we obtain. For example, we expect that a bell struck softly will produce a muted tone but one struck vigorously will produce a clanging one. In other words, we note the correspondence between the sensory effects of our behavior and the sensory consequences of the ensuing stimulus event that adds sensory relational information to the existing temporal one about their contingent relatedness.

Although sensory relational and temporal information about contingency often appear together, it is important to realize that sensory relations form an independent parameter that may provide information about contingency even in the absence of information regarding the temporal distribution of behavior and stimuli. Suppose that you have limited memory for the events that transpired in a certain situation. Your memory has a diminished quality such as you may have experienced in reflecting on a dream. The individual events are reasonably clear, but their temporal order is not. You recall being in a room watching a person making an impassioned speech. You recal his facial expressions. Among other events that transpired, you recall three instances in which he pounded his fist on the lectern while at the podium. One blow was hard, one soft, and one slightly softer yet. The order in which these occurred is not clear in your memory, however.

Now suppose you recall entering the room again sometime later. The room is empty except for the presence of three flowers. They differ only in size. One is large, one is smaller, and one is yet slightly smaller. Assume that you are moved to ask how they came to exist. You consider the information available. You notice something that, although fantastic, is nonetheless to some degree compelling. The ratio of sizes of the flowers (2, 6, 14 inches) matches perfectly the ratio of sound intensities (10, 30, 70 decibels) you recall the speaker generating when at the podium. Note that even though one cannot compare absolute intensity levels of stimuli across modalities, it is quite possible to order and compare intensities within a modality, and the patterns thus generated can then be compared across modalities. Accordingly, it is the sensory relational correspondence between the ratios within the two modalities that forms the basis of our judgement of causal relatedness between the speaker's podium pounding and the appearance of flowers.

Of course, this example still retains an important reference to temporal sequence in our analysis of cause and effect. We have not wondered whether flowers may cause exuberant podium pounding. Our commitment to efficient causes requires that we distinguish this aspect of sequence in time between those events that may stand as causes from those that may stand as effects. Yet, clearly, in the process of sorting through our memories of the different things that have preceded the events we wish to explain (the appearance of the flowers), the evidence we have turned to is not temporal but sensory relational. For example, we have not worried whether each flower ag each strike to the lectern. Rather, we based our judgement on the correspondence between the ratios of flower sizes, on the one hand, and of the sound intensity of the strikes, on the other.

That infants are also sensitive to sensory relational information about contingency is highlighted, for example, by the work of Rovee-Collier and her colleagues (Fagen & Rovee, 1976; Rovee-Collier, 1987; Rovee & Rovee, 1969). These researchers have been studying the young infant's capacity to learn and remember response-reward contingencies under conditions employing what is termed *conjugate reinforcement*. This procedure involves placing the infant in a crib with a mobile overhead. A ribbon is tied to the infant's foot while its other end is attached to a mobile that is suspended overhead on a flexible rod. As a consequence of this arrangement, whenever the infant moves his or her leg, the mobile moves in a manner that is similar in frequency and intensity to the leg extensions. Thus, Rovee-Collier's subjects are receiving sensory relational contingency along with temporal contingency. Evidence that the infants are attentive to the sensory relational parameter is indicated by the fact that when a change in the magnitude of stimulus consequence is introduced, after an initial adaptation to a specific contingency, infants as young as 3 months of age readily detect the change (Fagen & Rovee, 1976).

3. Spatial Relational Information

To illustrate the role of spatial relational information about contingency, let us return to our fanciful example introduced previously. Suppose, however, that we do not remember the variation in intensity of the speaker's podium pounding, nor do we recall the relative size differences among the flowers. Instead, our limited memory provides us only with images of where things happened. We now note that the flowers reside at three places on the lectern. More than that, there is a flower at each place we recall the speaker hitting the lectern—one at the lower left corner, one in the center, and one midline at the top. We do not know the temporal order of the flowers' appearance nor do we have any evidence of correlated variation in the sensory quality of the flowers. Yet, despite the lack of temporal or sensory pattern information, it is clear that *the pattern of spatial positioning alone* provides a powerful implication for the attribution of causal relatedness between podium pounding and the presence of the flowers.

Recent work by Rochat & Morgan (1995) is the clearest demonstration of infants' sensitivity to spatial contingency. In a variation on a task previously used by Bahrick & Watson (1985), Rochat & Morgan presented 3.5- and 4.5-month-old infants with a choice between two views of a video image of their legs. In three experiments, they varied the choice presented. In one study, the infant was shown a normative view (wherein the image shows the legs projected upward and the right–left distribution of legs is correct in the visual field) versus a rotated image (wherein the legs projected downward and the left–right distribution was reversed). In the other two experiments, the comparison was between the normative view and a view in which only the orientation was reversed (keeping the left–right distribution normative) or only the distribution was reversed (keeping the orientation normative, i.e., projecting upward). Rochat & Morgan measured the degree of preferential looking and the amount of kicking while looking. They found that infants showed a selective preference for the images that presented a left–right inversion of the image. The infants also kicked more vigorously while looking at this image of their legs.

These results imply that the infants were sensitive to the spatial contingency between directional movement of their legs and the movement of the video image. Note that the two images were both perfectly matched in terms of temporal contingency and sensory relational dynamics with the infants' leg movements. It might seem odd that the infants showed a seeming preference for the less perfect contingency. However, this avoidance of the perfectly contingent image is consistent with the prior results of Bahrick & Watson (1985) and is consistent with Watson's (1985, 1994) hypothesis according to which the preferential target setting of the contingency detection device is "switched" around 3 months of age from seeking out perfect respo-stimulus contingencies toward a bias for high but imperfect degrees of response-contingent stimulation (see further on).

Recently, Schmuckler (1996) has replicated Rochat & Morgan's findings in a task involving manual exploration of an object by 4- to 6-months-old infants. In three experiments, infants were given a visual choice between on-line video feedback of their hand movement or an alternative image. Again, in all three experiments the infants looked longer at the alternative image than at the on-line feedback representing the perfect contingency. Significant effects were found for the directionality (left–right inversion) but not for orientation (up–down inversion), paralleling Rochat's pattern of results. Without some comparative measure of the amount of motion the infants in these studies created in the two spatial dimensions, it is not yet clear whether these results indicate an intrinsic difference in the salience of the two dimensions of spatial variation. What is clear is that spatial contingency is detected at least for variation in the left–right dimension.

Meltzoff's work on the infant's sensitivity to being imitated (Meltzoff, 1990) also provides relevant evidence for an infant's use of spatial distribution as a source of information about contingency. (We consider this work again further on in the context of the infant's differential attraction to various levels of contingency.) Meltzoff used a preferential interaction paradigm in which 14-month-old infants were faced with two adult models, one of whom imitated as best as he or she could the child's object-related behaviors, whereas the other always performed a temporally contingent but dissimilar (spatially noncontingent) action. The infants looked and smiled more at the adult who mimicked them than at the one whose actions were only temporally contingent with theirs. As in the case of Rochat's study, the spatial (or *structural* as Meltzoff & Gopnik, 1993, call it) contingency was concurrent with very high temporal contingency. Under this condition, at least, it would seem that infants managed to detect differences in spatial contingency with ease and showed differential responsiveness on that basis.

DEVELOPMENTAL FUNCTIONS OF THE CONTINGENCY DETECTION MODULE

Watson (1972) has provided evidence that 2-month-olds increase their rate of leg kicking over a 2-week period when this response results in a contingent stimulus event (the movement of a mobile above their cribs) but not when they experience a similar but noncontingent event. Furthermore, after 3 to 5 days of contingent control over the mobile's movements, these infants exhibited what appear to be social smiling and cooing when the mobile was presented. These results indicate that very young infants are able to detect contingent relations between their responses and external stimulus events and that the ensuing experience of causal control over an external event is generally positively arousing for them as well as potentially a triggering experience in filial imprinting (Watson, 1981).

Bahrick and Watson (1985; see also Rochat and Morgan, 1995, and Schmuckler, 1996) demonstrated in a preferential looking paradigm that both 3- and 5-month-olds are capable of differentiating between a perfectly contingent image (live video feedback) versus a noncontingent image (delayed feedback) of their own moving legs suggesting that *contingency analysis may be the underlying mechanism for early self-detection.* Interestingly, while 3-month-olds displayed a significant bimodal distribution of preference (i.e., about equally divided between preferring perfect versus preferring imperfect contingency of the image of their moving body), 5-month-olds showed a normal distribution of aversion to exploring such a perfect response-stimulus contingency. Similarly, in other studies (see Watson, 1985) it appears that after 3 months infants are most motivated to explore high but imperfect degrees of response-stimulus contingencies.

Watson (1994) argued that the initial target setting of the contingency detection device is to seek out perfect response-stimulus contingencies so as to identify the range of self-generated (perfectly response-contingent) stimuli. This presumably forms the basis of the *construction of the primary representation of the bodily self.* It is hypothesized that around 3 months the target value of the contingency analyzer in normal infants is "switched" to a preference for high but imperfect response-stimulus contingency. This change presumably serves the function of orienting the infant toward the external environment and thus supports the building of representations on the basis of stimulation provided by a responsive social environment.

THE SOCIAL-BIOFEEDBACK MODEL OF AFFECT-REFLECTIVE MIRRORING INTERACTIONS

We have argued so far that the contingency detection mechanism serves such central functions in development as self–other differentiation and orientation toward the social environment. In what follows we summarize our recent proposal (Gergely & Watson, 1996) concerning a further significant function that we believe is mediated by the contingency detection module; namely, *the development of emotional self-awareness and control* in infancy. Our model is based on two central assumptions: that in its initial state the human organism has no differential awareness of his or her basic categorical emotion states, and that affect-reflective parental *mirroring* interactions play a vital role in the development of perceptual sensitivity to the infant's internal affect states. We argue that this sensitization process (similar to that of adult biofeedback training) is mediated by the mechanism of contingency detection and maximizing. In terms of our model, apart from sensitization, affect mirroring serves three further developmental functions as well:

1. It contributes directly to the infant's state-regulation.
2. It leads to the establishment of secondary representations that become associated with the infant's primary procedural affect states providing the cognitive means for accessing and attributing emotions to the self.
3. It results in the development of a generalized communicative code of "marked" expressions characterized by the representational functions of referential decoupling, anchoring, and suspension of realistic consequences.

INITIAL SENSITIVITY TO INTERNAL VERSUS EXTERNAL STIMULI

It is interesting to note that most classical as well as current approaches to infancy tend to adhere to the basic assumption that infants have conscious access to their internal basic emotion states from the beginning of life. For example, Meltzoff and Gopnik (1993) proposed that there are innate mechanisms that allow the infant to attribute emotions to other minds starting from birth. Based on evidence on neonatal imitation (Meltzoff & Moore, 1977, 1989) on the one hand and on the innate basis for primary emotions (Ekman, 1992; Ekman, Friesen, & Ellsworth, 1972; Izard, 1977, 1978) on the other, they proposed that by imitating the parent's facial emotion expression, the infant activates through prewired connections (see Ekman, Levenson, & Friesen, 1983) the corresponding physiological emotion state in himself or herself. The imitation-generated internal emotion state is then introspectively accessed, and the felt affect is attributed to the other's mind (but see Gergely & Watson, 1996, pp. 1183–1185, for a critical evaluation of this view). Similarly, proponents of differential emotions theory (Izard, 1977; Izard & Malatesta, 1987; Malatesta & Izard, 1984) also hold that "there is an innate expression-to-feeling concordance in the young infant" (Malatesta, Culver, Tesman, & Shepard, 1989, p. 6,). Stern (1985) also enumerates "categorical affects" as belonging to "the basic elements of early subjective experience" (p. 67).

In assuming that the infant's initial state is characterized by direct introspective access to internal emotion states, these modern authors follow the tradition of a long line of developmental theorists. For example, Freud and his followers (e.g., Mahler, Bergman, & Pine, 1975) have long held the view that an infant is initially more sensitive to internal than to external stimuli. Bruner, Olver, and Greenfield (1966) also proposed that the infant moves from an initial reliance on internal, proprioceptive cues to a reliance on exteroceptive cues (see also Birch & Lefford, 1967; Gholson, 1980; for a review, see Rovee-Collier, 1987).

However, as Colombo, Mitchell, Coldren, and Atwater (1990) have pointed out, there are practically no empirical data to directly support this classical view. In contrast, in a series of experiments designed to test this assumption, these authors have demonstrated that 3-month-olds show discrimination learning on the basis of exteroceptive as well as interoceptive cues.[1] Moreover, in 6- and 9-month-olds, they actually found dominance of the *exteroceptive* over the interoceptive cues in learning.

In light of such evidence, we have proposed to explore the consequences of abandoning the classical assumption concerning the presumed dominance of internal stimuli in the initial state of the infant (Gergely & Watson, 1996). In contrast, we hypothesize that at the beginning of life *the perceptual system is set with a bias to attend to and explore the external world and builds representations primarily on the basis of exteroceptive stimuli.* In this view, then, the set of internal (visceral as well as proprioceptive) cues that are activated when being in and expressing an emotion state are, at first, not perceived consciously by the infant, or, at least, are not grouped together categorically in such a manner that they could be perceptually accessed as a distinctive emotion state.[2]

LEVELS OF REPRESENTATIONS OF SELF-STATES: AUTOMATIC VERSUS CONTROLLED PROCESSES

There are a number of dichotomies in cognitive theory such as the procedural–declarative, implicit–explicit, unconscious–conscious, or automatic–

[1]Note furthermore that one cannot rule out the possibility that the position cues in Colombo, et al.'s study, which were based on eye fixation, might have been computed on the basis of the position of the nose, which, in fact, is an *exteroceptive* cue (see Bower, 1974).

[2]As will become apparent, our proposal (although compatible with does not necessarily imply the more radical view that at the beginning of life infants are lacking any kind of awareness of their internal states). It is possible that infants have some awareness of the component stimuli that belong to the groups of internal state cues that are indicative of categorical emotions, but only as part of the "blooming, buzzing confusion" (James, 1890/1950) of internal sense impressions they may experience. Such state cues may also contribute to the overall (positive or negative) hedonic quality of infants' awareness. Our (less radical) suggestion is (a) that the groups of internal state cues that are indicative of dispositional emotion states are initially not perceptually accessible as distinct feeling states (see Lewis & Michaelson, 1983; Lewis & Brooks, 1978; and Kagan, 1992) and (b) that the perceptual system is at the start set with a bias to actively explore and categorize external rather than internal stimuli.

controlled distinctions (e.g., Karmiloff-Smith, 1992; Shiffrin & Schneider, 1977) that refer to qualitatively different levels of information representation in humans. *Automatized processes* refer to prewired or over-learned structures of behavioral organization in which information is represented implicitly, embedded in procedures, and is unavailable to other representational systems of the mind. Such automatisms are inflexible, perceptually driven, and operate outside consciousness. In contrast, *deliberative or controlled processes* refer to voluntary and conscious operations that are flexible and modifiable, can be governed by higher-order cognitive goals, and can override automatisms.

In this framework, infants' primary emotions can be conceived of as prewired, stimulus driven, dynamic behavioral automatisms over which they have no control at first. Affect-regulation is carried out mainly by the caregiver who, reading an infant's automatic emotion expressions, reacts with appropriate affect-modulating interactions. In this view, emotional self-control will become possible only with the establishment of *secondary control structures* that (a) monitor, detect, and evaluate the primary level dynamic affective state changes of the organism and (b) can inhibit or modify the emotional reaction if the anticipated automatic affective response would jeopardize higher-order cognitive plans.

Therefore, a precondition for the voluntary control and self-regulation of primary affective states is that the level of deliberative processes be informed about the on-going dispositional state changes of the organism that take place at the level of automatized processes. Within this framework, consciously felt emotions can be conceived of as *signals* that inform the level of deliberative processes about the automatic affective state changes of the organism.

This leads then to the question, How does an infant develop awareness of and come to represent the sets of internal state cues as indicating categorically distinct emotion states? We propose that the species-specific human propensity for the facial and vocal reflection of the infant's emotion-expressive displays during affect-regulative interactions plays a crucial role in this developmental process.

AFFECT-REFLECTIVE MIRRORING INTERACTIONS IN EARLY SOCIO-EMOTIONAL DEVELOPMENT

Historically, there are two traditions in developmental psychology that emphasize the formative importance of the role of the caretaker's inclination to behaviorally reflect the internal emotional and intentional states that she attributes to her infant. One is the social constructivist tradition, starting with Hegel and continuing with the work of Baldwin, Cooley, G. H.

Mead, and Bruner, which emphasizes the social origins of the development of the self. In this general view, the inferential basis for constructing the representation of the self is provided by the social reflections of the child's states and properties as those are perceived by the infant in the reactions of others. The second tradition is that of psychoanalytic object relations theories that have long identified the maternal mirroring function as an important causal factor in early emotional and personality development (e.g., Bion, 1962, 1967; Fonagy & Target, 1996; Jacobson, 1964; Kernberg, 1984; Kohut, 1971; Mahler et al., 1975; Mahler & McDevitt, 1982; Stern, 1985; Winnicott, 1967).

Recent empirical work on early mother–infant interactions (e.g., Beebe & Lachmann, 1988; Hains & Muir, 1996; Kaye, 1982; Murray & Trevarthen, 1985; Papousek & Papousek, 1987, 1989; Sroufe, 1996; Stern, 1985; Trevarthen, 1979; Tronick, 1989) has in general confirmed the traditional view that *facial and vocal mirroring of affective behavior* may be a central feature of parental affect-regulative interactions during the first year. The currently dominant biosocial view of emotional development holds that mother and infant form an affective communication system from the beginning of life (Beebe, Jaffe, & Lachmann, 1992; Bowlby, 1969; Brazelton, Koslowski, & Main, 1974; Hobson, 1993; Sander, 1970; Stern, 1985; Trevarthen, 1979; Tronick, 1989) in which the mother plays a vital interactive role in modulating the infant's affective states. Young infants do have some rudimentary means of affective self-regulation (such as turning away from over arousing stimuli or thumb sucking) (Demos, 1986; Malatesta et al., 1989), but there is agreement that the quality of maternal interactions exert a strong regulative influence on the infant's affective state changes (Field, 1994; Malatesta & Izard, 1984; Tronick, 1989; Tronick, Ricks, & Cohn, 1982). Mothers are generally rather efficient in reading their infants' emotion displays, and sensitive mothers tend to attune their own affective responses to modulate their infant's emotional states (Malatesta et al., 1989; Tronick, 1989).

Studies using the still-face procedure (Tronick, Als, Adamson, Wise, & Brazelton, 1978) or delayed feedback techniques (Murray & Trevarthen, 1985; see, however, Rochat, Neisser, & Marian, in press) indicate that young infants are sensitive to the contingency structure of face-to-face interaction and are actively searching to reestablish such a pattern of communication when being abruptly deprived of it. By using time-based microanalytic methods (e.g., Gottman & Ringland, 1981), several researchers provided evidence for the early existence of bidirectional influence of behavior and mutual regulation of affective communication between mothers and infants (Beebe & Lachmann, 1988; Beebe, Lachmann, & Jaffe, 1997; Cohn & Tronick, 1988; Tronick, Edward, Als, & Brazelton, 1977; Tronick, 1989). Imitative matching activity has been reported to be frequent during mother–infant interactions (Užgiriš, Benson, Kruper, & Vasek, 1989), and mother–infant pairs have been shown to increase their degree of coordination in terms of matching and synchrony with infant age (Tronick & Cohn, 1989). Maternal imitative behavior was found to evoke more smiling and vocalization in 3½-months old babies than nonimitative responses (Field, Guy, & Umbel, 1985). Mothers react with differential facial attunements to infants' emotion expressions producing contingent imitations more often to their baby's categorical emotion displays than to their more "random" facial movements (such as twitches or half smiles) (Malatesta & Izard, 1984; Malatesta et al., 1989). Infants' expressions of sadness and anger have been observed to produce affective responses of sadness and anger in their mothers (Tronick, 1989), and maternal reactions to negative affect include mock expressions of negative affect (Malatesta & Izard, 1984).

Research on the facial and vocal interaction between depressed mothers and their infants (Bettes, 1988; Cohn, Matias, Tronick, & Connell, 1986; Murray, Fiori-Cowley, Hooper, & Cooper, 1996; Tronick, 1989; Tronick & Field, 1986) have shown that there is a decrease in the amount of contingent affective interactions as well as more intrusiveness and more negative affect expression on the part of the mother. Furthermore, such infants' affective and regulatory reactions as well as their later security of attachment have been found to be related to the affect and behavior of their depressed mothers (Field, 1994; Field et al., 1988; Murray, 1992; Murray et al., 1996; Pickens & Field, 1993; Tronick, 1989; Tronick & Field, 1986).

In sum: It can be said that whereas theoretical, clinical, and empirical approaches all converge on the view that parental affect-reflective interactions play a central role in early emotional and self-development, the exact nature of the causal mechanisms mediating such effects has not yet been identified.

PARENTAL AFFECT-MIRRORING AS A MECHANISM OF EMOTION REGULATION

When we look at the structural relation between the stimulus features of the parent's mirroring expression and those of the infant's state-expressive behavior, it becomes clear that the term "mirroring" is a seriously misleading one. No matter how well attuned a mother is to the baby's state, her facial and vocal mirroring will never match perfectly the temporal, spatial, and sensory intensity parameters of her infant's behavioral expressions. Thus, by necessity, the degree of contingent relatedness between the infant's state expressive behaviors and the caretaker's reflective mirroring displays will be high but only imperfect. Earlier we discussed evidence indicating that the infant's contingency detection module is extremely sensitive to the distinction between perfect versus high but imperfect degrees of response–stimulus contingencies, and a normal infant is preferentially biased to attend to and explore highly but imperfectly response contingent environmental stimuli after about 3 months of age (Bahrick & Watson, 1985; Watson, 1979, 1994). Since affect-reflective displays tend to provide relatively high contingency values on all three stimulus parameters (temporal, spatial, and sensory intensity) that are monitored by the contingency detection mechanism, they can be considered optimal naturalistic social target stimuli for the module, the detection of which will induce a sense of causal control and concomitant positive arousal in the infant.

This may, in fact, help us explain the soothing effect that emotion-reflective interactions seem to have on infants in negative affect. Imagine a helpless, whimpering or fearful baby who perceives his mother repeatedly presenting him with bouts of empathic affect-reflective displays in an attempt to sooth him. The infant's contingency detection device will automatically register the high degree of contingent relatedness between his emotion-expressive behavior and the parent's affect-reflective displays. This will result in an experience of causal efficacy in controlling and bringing about the parental mirroring behavior, which, in turn, will reduce the infant's feeling of helplessness. The high degree of perceived contingent control will also induce positive arousal in the infant (Watson, 1972) that, through reciprocal inhibition, can be expected to further decrease his negative affect state.

Note that an interesting additional feature of this process is that the infant will experience the ensuing emotional state regulation as an *active causal agent.* Apart from experiencing causal efficacy in controlling the adult's emotion-reflective displays, the infant will simultaneously register the ensuing positive modification of his negative affect state as well. Therefore, it can be hypothesized that successful emotion-regulative interactions involving parental affect mirroring may provide the experiential basis for the establishment of a *sense of self as self-regulating agent.* Thus, affect-regulative mirroring interactions may provide the original proto-situation in which infants can learn that by externalizing their internal emotion states, they can achieve successful regulation of their affective impulses (see Gergely & Watson, 1996, p. 1196, for more detailed arguments along these lines).

PARENTAL AFFECT MIRRORING AS A MECHANISM OF EMOTIONAL SENSITIZATION: THE SOCIAL-BIOFEEDBACK HYPOTHESIS

Above we hypothesized that the internal state cues that are activated when being in an emotion state are initially not perceived consciously or, at least, do not form a categorical group that could be perceptually accessed as a distinctive emotion state. We have then proposed that the repetitive presentation of an external reflection of the infant's affect-expressive displays serves a vital teaching function that results in gradual sensitization to the relevant internal state cues as well as to the identification of the correct set of internal stimuli that correspond to the distinctive emotion category that the baby is in. As a result of this process, the infant will eventually come to develop an awareness of the differential internal cues that are indicative of categorical affect states and will become able to detect and represent his particular dispositional emotion states.

One, of course, may ask, In what way would the presentation of an external emotion display that is contingent on the baby's internal affect state lead to sensitization to and recognition of the internal state that was not consciously accessible before? Furthermore, is there any evidence that such externally induced sensitization to internal states is possible?

We believe there is at least one intriguing example of such a process that shows a high degree of family resemblance to the current proposal, namely, *biofeedback training procedures* (e.g., Dicara, 1970; Miller, 1969, 1978). In such studies, continuous measurements are made of the on-going state changes of some internal stimulus state to which the subject has no direct perceptual access initially (such as blood pressure). The internal state changes are mapped onto an *external* stimulus equivalent directly observable to the subject, the state of which covaries with that of the internal stimulus. Repeated exposure to such an externalized representation of the internal state eventually results in *sensitization to*, and in certain cases, subsequent *control over*, the internal state.

We hypothesize that the psychological mechanism involved in affect mirroring is the same process as that demonstrated in biofeedback training procedures. Thus, our proposal is that parental affect mirroring provides a kind of *natural social biofeedback training* for the infant. The internal emotional state cues are at first not consciously accessible to the baby, but the parent, who can read and interpret their automatic behavioral expressions, can provide a highly contingent external stimulus equivalent for them in the form of his or her affect-reflective displays that covary with the baby's internal affect state. We hypothesize that the contingency detection module, which has access to the (nonconscious) internal physiological state changes involved in an affective response as well as to the proprioceptive stimuli generated by their automatic expression, can identify the contingent relatedness between these internal cues on the one hand and the external affect-mirroring display, on the other. This leads to two consequences: (a) the infant will become gradually sensitized to the internal stimulus cues involved in the contingency relation, and (b) he will learn to group together those internal state cues whose combined presence correlates highly with the external affect-reflective display (and, consequently, with the internal emotion sate reflected). As a result, eventually the infant will become sensitive to the set of distinctive internal state cues that indicate the onset of a dispositional emotion state and will be able to attribute such a state to himself or herself even in the absence of the external affect-mirroring biofeedback cue.

Elsewhere we have argued that the underlying information-processing mechanism that mediates the influence of both affect mirroring and biofeedback training is that of *contingency detection and contingency maximizing* (Gergely & Watson, 1996). The explication of the details of this process is beyond the scope of the present chapter (the interested reader can find a detailed account in Gergely & Watson, 1996, pp. 1190–1196). Suffice it to remind the reader here of the fact that the contingency detection module applies two independent mechanisms for analyzing the conditional probability structure of contingent response–stimulus events: The sufficiency index is looking forward in time and registers the conditional probability of stimulus events as a function of the monitored set of responses; the necessity index is testing backward in time, monitoring the relative likelihood that a given stimulus event was preceded by the responses in question. As mentioned previously, the estimated degree of control over the stimulus event, however, may not correspond to the actual degree of control. This is so because the device may be monitoring either a too narrow or a too broad class of responses. The contingency-detection mechanism can, however, discover the maximal degree of contingency (contingency maximizing, see Watson, 1979) by either reducing or expanding the sampled set of responses, eventually zeroing in on the correct response set and identifying the actual degree of contingent control.

THE REPRESENTATIONAL CONSEQUENCES OF PARENTAL AFFECT MIRRORING: THE "MARKEDNESS" HYPOTHESIS

One of the most intriguing and apparently paradoxical aspects of parental affect mirroring during state-regulative interactions is the fact that when a baby is in a negative state, the parent presents a reflection of a negative emotion display to the infant. This raises the potential danger of misattribution: How does the baby know that the affect-reflective emotion expression refers to his or her own state and not to that of the parent? Were the infant to misattribute the expressed negative affect to the parent, his or her own negative emotion state, instead of becoming regulated, would likely to escalate, as the sight of a fearful or angry parent is clearly cause for alarm (and, if occurring systematically, of possible trauma, see Main & Hesse, 1990; Fonagy & Target, 1997).

We have argued (see Gergely, 1995a, 1995b; Gergely & Watson, 1996, pp. 1196–1200) that this attribution problem is solved by a specific perceptual feature of the parent's affect-reflective emotion displays that we refer to as their *markedness.* It is proposed that mothers are instinctually driven to saliently *mark* their affect-mirroring displays to make them perceptually differentiable from their realistic emotion expressions. Marking is typically achieved by producing *an exaggerated version* of the parent's realistic emotion expression (similarly to the marked "as if" manner of emotion displays that is characteristically produced in pretend play). The marked affect display, nevertheless, remains sufficiently similar to the parent's normative emotion expression for the infant to recognize the dispositional content of the emotion. It is assumed that the infant has been adaptively discriminating parental dispositional displays (Watson, 1995). However, it is hypothesized that due to the markedness of the display during affect mirroring, the attribution of the perceived emotion to the parent will be inhibited. We call this process *referential decoupling,*[3] referring to the fact that in the interpretation of the marked affect display, the referential connection between the emotion expression and the corresponding dispositional state of the agent producing the display will be *suspended:* The perceived emotion display will be decoupled from its referent.

Note, however, that due to its markedness, the parental emotion display may become decoupled from its referent, but it still needs to be interpreted by the infant from a referential point of view as expressing *someone's* emotion. We suggest that this process of *referential anchoring* is determined by the *high degree of contingent relation* between the parent's affect-reflecting display and the infant's emotion-expressive behavior that is registered by the contingency detection module. On the basis of the perceived contingent relation, the infant will referentially anchor the marked mirroring stimulus as expressing his or her *own* self-state.

In this view, then, infants tend to experience the emotion displays of caregivers in two different forms over time: in their *realistic* and in their *marked* (affect-reflective) versions. We hypothesize that the infant will come to represent these two forms as qualitatively different variants of the emotion expression not only because of their marked differences in terms of perceptual features but also because of two further distinguishing characteristics.

---

[3]The terms "*referential decoupling*" and "*referential anchoring*" originally were introduced by Alan Leslie (1987, 1994) to characterize the representational properties of communicative expressions produced in pretend play. We apply these terms in the current context to suggest a potential developmental and functional relationship between the markedness of affect-reflective expressions on the one hand and the markedness of expressions in the "pretend" mode of communication, on the other. The detailed exposition of this hypothesis, however, is beyond the scope of this chapter (see Gergely, 1995a, 1995b; Gergely & Watson, 1996).

First, the situational features and behavioral outcomes that will become associated with the realistic emotion expression (e.g., with the sight of an angry mother) will be qualitatively different from those that are characteristic of the corresponding marked display (i.e., the sight of an anger-reflecting mother). In other words, the *dispositional outcomes* associated with the realistic emotion will not hold for the case of the marked expression. Instead of the negative behavioral and emotional consequences typically accompanying a realistic anger expression, when faced with a marked anger-reflecting display, the infant is likely to experience positive outcomes in the form of successful affect regulation.

Second, the realistic and the marked emotion displays of caretakers will also become differentiated in terms of their *different contingency relation* to the infant's on-going behavior. Realistic emotion expressions are typically much less under the infant's contingent control than the marked emotion-reflective displays. A realistic expression of, say, fear on the mother's face, is more likely to be contingent on some external event or to be induced by some intrapsychic stimulus in the mother than to be under the control of the infant. The marked affect-reflective version of the emotion display is, however, under the contingent behavioral control of the baby, because it is produced as a mirroring response to the infant's corresponding emotion expression during affect-regulative interactions.

Furthermore, it can be hypothesized that in normal development, the behavioral transformations of a normative display that correspond to its marked form become established as a *generalized communicative code* associated with (a) referential decoupling of the expressed content from the agent producing the display, (b) with referentially anchoring the expressed content in an agent other than the one displaying the emotion,[4] and (c) with the suspension of the dispositional consequences of the realistic version of the expressed content (Gergely, 1995a, 1995b). Note that these features will become the central characteristics of the *'as if' mode of communication* as it first emerges in the ability to comprehend and to produce pretend play during the second year of life (see Fonagy & Target, 1996, 1997; Gergely, 1995a, 1995b; Gergely & Watson, 1996; Leslie, 1987, 1994).

The markedness of the affect-mirroring display is likely to have a further interesting effect as well. Since the mirroring display is differentiated from the corresponding realistic emotion expression by its perceptual markedness, its differential dispositional consequences, and its high degree of contingency with the baby's affective behavior, we hypothesize that the infant will construct a separate representation for it. Due to its contingent

---

[4]Note that although in affect-regulative interactions the marked emotion is anchored in the infant as a result of the experience of contingent control, later however—for example, in the use of the marked code in pretend play—the expressed content may be anchored in another (possibly imaginary) agent with whom the person producing the marked behavior identifies (see Leslie, 1987, 1994).

association with the infant's automatic affective reactions registered during the affect-regulative interactions, this representation will retain its associative link to the baby's primary level affective states. Therefore, the separately represented marked emotion display will come to function as a *secondary representational structure* that will become activated through associative routes whenever the set of internal state cues corresponding to the given dispositional emotion state are activated in the infant. Henceforth, the onset of an emotion state will result in the automatic activation of this protosymbolic secondary emotion representation in the baby's awareness that will allow him or her to attribute the dispositional emotion state to himself or herself. As we argued earlier, the activation of such secondary representations mediate the signal function of felt affect states that forms the basis of emotional self-awareness and control.

In sum, we have argued that the instinctive inclination of parents to expose their infants to marked affect-reflective behavioral displays during emotion-regulative interactions results in three significant developmental consequences[5]:

1. The infant will come to detect and group together the sets of internal state cues that are indicative of his or her categorically distinct dispositional emotion states.
2. The infant will establish secondary representations associated with his or her primary level procedural affect states providing the cognitive means for accessing and attributing emotion states to the self.
3. The infant will acquire a generalized communicative code of "marked" expressions characterized by the representational functions of referential decoupling, anchoring, and suspension of realistic consequences.

SOME IMPLICATIONS

"Affect Attunement" From the Point of View of the Social-Biofeedback Theory

Stern (1984, 1985; Stern, Hofer, Haft, & Dore, 1985) has also proposed a theory concerning the role of parental affect-reflective behaviors in early social-emotional development. Similarly to our position, Stern believes that interactions involving emotion-reflective parental displays have a significant

---

[5]Our social biofeedback theory of affect mirroring and the markedness hypothesis also provide a new perspective on the potential pathological consequences of deviant mirroring styles or lack of parental mirroring. These implications for developmental psychopathology, however, are beyond the scope of this chapter and are treated elsewhere (see Gergely, 1995a; Gergely & Watson, 1996, pp. 1200–1205).

influence on self-development and affective self-regulation. His views on the developmental functions and mediating mechanisms involved in affect-reflective parental interactions, however, differ from ours in several important respects.

Stern's theory focuses on a specific type of affect-reflective interaction that he calls *affect attunements*, which he demonstrated to occur regularly in normal mother–infant interactions between 9 and 12 months (Stern et al., 1985). He noted that during free play, mothers periodically reflect some aspect of their infant's actions by providing a partial match of the baby's behavior in another modality. For example, he describes an 8½-month-old boy reaching for a toy just beyond reach. As he is stretching his body in an obvious voluntary effort to achieve his goal, "his mother says, 'Uuuuuh . . . uuuuuh!' with a crescendo of vocal effort. . . . The mother's accelerating vocal-respiratory effort matched the infant's accelerating physical effort" (Stern et al., 1985, p. 250).

Stern (1984) makes several interesting points concerning the nature of such acts of behavioral attunements. Among other things, he emphasizes the fact that they are not simple acts of imitation because they involve only a partial match of the amodal (temporal, intensity, and shape) characteristics of the infant's target act rendered in a different modality. He also points out that "during the first half year of life it is our impression (as yet untested) that imitations predominate over attunements (the reverse is true after nine months)" (p. 11).

Stern proposes that the reason why around 9 months the mother (nonconsciously) chooses to "attune" to rather than simply provide an imitative replica of the infant's behavior is that she intends to refer to the internal affect state of the infant rather than to his or her surface behavior. In his view, the matched amodal characteristics correspond to the abstract representational form of affects that accompany the external behavioral act. Thus, the suggested function of such affect attunements is that of "interpersonal communion"—"to share" or "to participate in" the internal affective experience of the infant. Of course, for the infant to interpret affect attunements as indicating parental sharing of his or her internal mental state, he or she (a) must be aware of his or her affect state and (b) must understand that the parent also experiences internal mental states, which (c) can be either shared or different from the particular mental state of the infant. Stern argues for this view by pointing at a purported correlation between the emerging dominance of parental attunements (over imitations) starting at 9 months, on the one hand, and the emergence of the infant's "naive theory of interfaceable minds" (Bretherton & Bates, 1979) during the same period, on the other.

Before contrasting Stern's ideas with ours, let us call attention to some aspects of his proposal that seem to us questionable. First, central to Stern's argument is the contention that around 9 months of age there is a shift in the mother's reflective behaviors from intramodal, faithful imitations to cross-modal attunements of amodal properties rendered in a different modality. However, it should be pointed out that in the technical sense, all imitative behaviors are (at least partially) cross-modal: If a tongue protrusion is faithfully imitated by a tongue protrusion, the infant experiences an intermodal (motor-visual) correspondence between his own behavior and the imitative act of the parent. It is also well known that even newborn infants are able to appreciate cross-modal correspondence as shown by phenomena such as neonatal imitation (Kaye & Bower, 1994; Meltzoff & Borton, 1979; Meltzoff & Moore, 1977, 1989; Stern, 1985). Obviously, then, what Stern has in mind is not so much the question of intra- versus intersensory modality but rather the fact that the attunement behavior, although showing a partial match in terms of amodal properties, is a different act than the target behavior of the infant.

Second, whether Stern's impression about a qualitative shift around 9 months from imitations to attunements can be empirically substantiated remains to be seen. Certainly, mothers do engage in attunement behaviors even much earlier (as in the prototypical theme-variation games proposed by Watson, 1972). However, even if we assume with Stern that there is a statistical tendency to engage in more attunements than imitations after 9 months, there seems to be a more mundane reason for this than Stern's account in terms of the emerging mentalism of the infant. At the end of the first year, infants become more mobile, and the previous dominance of face-to-face interactions are superceded by object-oriented joint activities (Stern, 1985; Trevarthen & Hubley, 1978). This imposes a pragmatic constraint on the mother's choice of behavior when she intends to reflect the infant's target act in a way that is accessible to the infant. For example, if the baby is visually orienting toward a toy that he or she is reaching for rather than toward the parent, the mother may be forced to attune to the baby's motor effort vocally.

Third, while the momentous changes in an infant's competence after 9 months (such as joint attention, pointing and gaze following, or social referencing) have been interpreted by some researchers as indicating the emergence of understanding intentional mind states (Bretherton, 1991; Bretherton & Bates, 1979; Stern, 1985), others have resisted this temptation and proposed nonmentalistic interpretations for the same phenomena (Barresi & Moore, 1996; Gergely, Nádasdy, Csibra, & Bíró, 1995; Gewirtz & Pelaez-Nogueras, 1992; Moore & Corkum, 1994). For example, as one of us has argued in detail elsewhere (Gergely & Csibra, 1997; Csibra & Gergely, in press), the emerging new competencies at the end of the first year can be understood in terms of a "naive theory of rational action" that is an as yet nonmentalistic teleological interpretational system. Furthermore, while the 9-month-old may not have an appreciation of mind states as yet, mothers certainly attribute intentionality and mentalizing to their infant even at a much earlier age (as shown by the work on cognitive scaffolding by Bruner, Stern, and others). In terms of Stern's hypothesis about the function of attunements being that of signaling the sharing of attributed internal affect states, this would predict that caretakers engage in affect attunements even before their infant is 9 months of age.

In our minds, these arguments raise enough doubts concerning Stern's interpretation of the function and nature of affect attunements that it may be worthwhile to explore an alternative approach to this intriguing developmental phenomenon. Such an alternative is provided by our contingency-based social biofeedback model of affect-reflective parental behaviors.

Note first of all that the three amodal features (time, intensity, and shape) identified by Stern as the abstract stimulus properties matched in affect attunements correspond to the three sources of contingency that the contingency-detection module monitors. Therefore, even if an attunement behavior is presented only on a single occasion, the combined value of the three contingency parameters can be sufficient to indicate a highly but imperfectly contingent external stimulus that is controlled by the infant's preceding behavior. In other words, the contingency detection device will categorize the parent's attunement behavior as a causal consequence of the infant's on-going activity, resulting in a momentary sense of causal efficacy and the concomitant induction of positive arousal. The ensuing fleeting sense of causal control and instrumentality will become associated with the particular act that the infant is engaged in while being attuned to. This leads to our first proposal concerning the developmental function of reflective attunements. By momentarily attuning to them, the parent can selectively reinforce those affective, voluntary, or playful acts of the infant's that she would like to see continued or repeated in the future. In other words, reflective attunements are an efficient tool of early nonverbal socialization whereby the parent can selectively reinforce and shape the infant's emerging voluntary, goal-oriented, or playful social activities.

In a somewhat more speculative vein, we also would like to propose that selective attunements may serve an additional sensitizing and representation-building function as well. Recall that, unlike Stern's, our model assumes that the infant initially lacks awareness of his or her internal affective and proprioceptive states that accompany his or her behaviors. By providing a partial rendering of some of the amodal features of the target act in a different behavioral format, the attunement behavior presents the infant with a nonidentical but highly contingent externalized version of his or her procedural behavioral routine. As a result, the infant will form a representation of the reflected amodal features that will become associated, due to their high degree of perceived contingency, with the nonconscious, primary, procedural representation of his or her on-going activity. In this way, reflective attunements result in the establishment of secondary representations of primary procedural states that will be more cognitively accessible and more subject to conscious awareness.

This hypothesized secondary representation building process can be conceived of as a special case of what Annette Karmiloff-Smith (1992) called *representational redescription.* She argued that the human mind has the capacity to access and re-represent in a more explicit and cognitively accessible form the implicitly represented structural information embedded in nonconscious, automatic procedural routines. Although Karmiloff-Smith's theory postulates an innate endogenous epistemic drive that carries out such a process of self-discovery of one's own mind, our social biofeedback model identifies the contingent reflective externalizations provided by social partners as the informational basis for re-representing the amodal internal structure of nonconscious primary representations.

But do affect attunements serve the function of interpersonal communion or internal state sharing as well, as suggested by Stern? Our guess is that initially this may not yet be the case, especially in so far as the infant has not yet been sensitized to his or her internal categorical affect states as a result of the social biofeedback training provided by affect-reflective interactions. We agree, however, that communicating the sharing of internal states may become a secondary function of attunement behaviors later in life. In verbal behavior, paraphrasing often serves the function of informing the other that the underlying meaning of his or her surface utterance has been correctly encoded. Nonverbal reflective attunements are likely to come to serve a similar communicative function as well later in life.

Meltzoff and Gopnik's "Like Me" Hypothesis

Meltzoff and Gopnik (Gopnik & Meltzoff, 1997; Meltzoff, 1990; Meltzoff & Gopnik, 1993) have proposed that imitative interactions between caregivers and infants can provide a basis that could lead babies to pay special attention to fellow human beings. This arises in specific regard to the times that the caregivers imitate their infants as opposed to when the babies imitate the caregivers. Meltzoff and Gopnik propose that an infant may use his or her innate cross-modal capacity to map the caregiver's visual movements onto the proprioceptive feelings of his or her own movements that the parent is imitating. The caregiver's movements become attractive (attention capturing) because they are perceived (via the mapping) to be very much like the baby's own. Meltzoff and Gopnik hypothesize that it is this *"like me" experience* that explains the infants' preferential attention and smiling to the mimicking adult model over the only temporally contingent one in the in Meltzoff's (1990) preferential interaction study described earlier.

Since our contingency-based social biofeedback theory also generates specific predictions for the infant's attraction to parental mirroring acts, we would like to make explicit two important differences between our position and that of Meltzoff and Gopnik. First, Meltzoff and Gopnik (1993) assume that infants have direct introspective access to their internal feeling states from the beginning of life. By contrast, we are assuming that, initially, much of infants' state transitions are outside of their perceptual awareness. We assume this to be so both for the visceral and physiological state cues that accompany basic emotion states and for much of the proprioceptive consequences of facial muscular movement. Indeed, a central aspect of our model is that such internal state cues only become liminal after a period of biofeedback sensitization brought about as a result of parental mirroring interactions. This difference in assumption about what is and what is not felt by an infant is not likely to be resolvable empirically, however. The reason for this pessimism is that we, and very likely Meltzoff and Gopnik as well, are using the term *felt* in the sense of a state of conscious awareness. For example, we do not contend that the infant has no functional use of proprioceptive feedback from facial muscle movement before social mirroring experiences. What we contend is that whereas such feedback exists and is used in various motor control systems, it does not enter conscious awareness. As adults, many motor events are subliminal until we attend to them; for example, eye movement, head rotation, chest diaphragm expansion, and even limb motion. But it is not easy to think of how to measure such a distinction in relation to the subjective experience of an infant.

The second point of difference between our model and Meltzoff and Gopnik's "like me" hypothesis about the attractiveness of social mirroring is far more assessable empirically. The "like me" hypothesis seems to clearly predict that theative mirroring reproduces the infant's behavior, the more attractive it will be for the baby. By contrast, we assume (see Bahrick & Watson, 1985; Watson, 1994) that after about 3 months, the target setting of the contingency detection module of the normal human infant is switched toward seeking out high but imperfect degrees of contingency. This predicts a preference for high but imperfectly contingent mirroring displays over perfectly contingent ones, whereas the opposite prediction follows from the "like me" hypothesis.

Our explanation for the looking pattern in Meltzoff's (1990) study is that the mimicking model provides a high but nevertheless only imperfectly contingent action that is preferred as such over the simply temporally contingent model that produces a much lower degree of contingency. We agree with Meltzoff and Gopnik that the infants appear to use the spatial (or structural) information in differentiating between the two models. Somewhat tautologically, however, we propose that the preference for the temporal plus spatial (the mimicking adult) over the just temporal (the alternative model) contingency simply indicates that the imitating model provided a contingency magnitude that was closer to the target criterion of best (high-but-not-perfect) contingency of the contingency detection module than was the alternative model.

The "Nearly, but Clearly Not, Like Me" Hypothesis

In contrast to Meltzoff and Gopnik's "like me" hypothesis, however, we predict that if given a choice between a perfectly contingent versus the highly but only imperfectly contingent imitative display used by Meltzoff, the infant (after 3 months) would preferentially attend to the latter. In other words, we predict that the infant would be attracted to the "nearly, but clearly not, like me" versus the "like me" display. The infant would do so, because rather than preferentially orienting toward a self-like (perfect) contingency, the infant is committed to engage contingencies that are specifically not self-based (i.e., not perfect).

Judit Magyar, in her Ph.D. research, has specifically contrasted the effect on young children's behavior of the availability of perfect versus imitative feedback of their manual activity (see Magyar & Gergely, 1998). Magyar tested 32 normal subjects (between 18 and 36 months of age) who sat in front of two TV monitors each displaying the moving image of a schematic hand. The subjects moved a small metal bowl (with a computer mouse hidden inside) freely on the surface of the table in front of them. On one of the screens, they saw the perfectly response-contingent movements of the schematic hand generated by a computer program controlled by the subjects' manual manipulation of the bowl. The second screen displayed a highly but imperfectly response-contingent image of the schematic hand that was generated by the imitative efforts of a human experimenter. This person attempted to faithfully copy the subject's manual behavior by moving a mouse under the visual guidance of the subject-generated movements of the schematic hand (the perfect feedback display) viewed on a separate monitor in another room. This procedure was used in an attempt to provide the normal lag and imperfection of a human act of direct imitation. Magyar found (see Fig. 5.1, Panel A) that normal children attended more to the imitation-based (highly but imperfectly) contingent image than to the perfectly contingent one ($p < .05$). This, then, provides support for our hypothesis that normal children are selectively attracted to response-con-

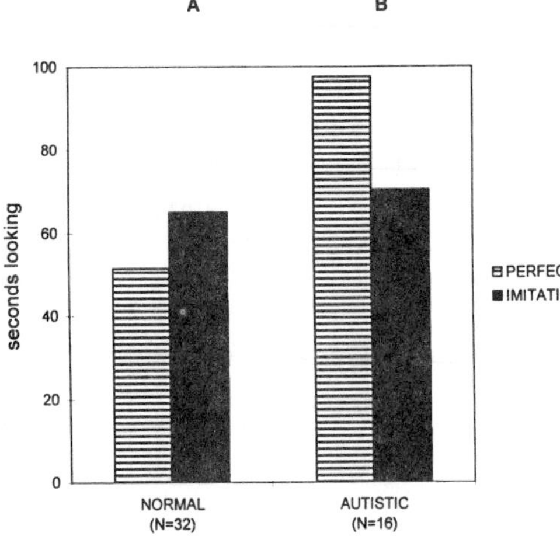

FIG. 5.1. Looking times at video monitors containing "imitative" versus "perfect" computer simulation of image movement contingent on hand movement for 32 normal children (Panel A) and for 16 autistic children (Panel B).

tingent stimuli that are "nearly, but clearly not, like me" rather than being "just like me."

CONTINGENCY DETECTION AND CHILDHOOD AUTISM: A HYPOTHESIS

Finally, we would like to briefly further sketch a hypothesis initially developed by one of us (Watson, 1994) that considers the aetiology of childhood autism to be related to a genetically based dysfunction of the contingency detection module. In recent years, a number of new hypotheses have been offered concerning the primary causes of autism. These have ranged from global deficits such as "a missing drive for global coherence" (Frith, 1989); to specialized modular deficits such as a missing "theory of mind module" (Baron-Cohen, Leslie, & Frith, 1985; Leslie, 1994); a deficient "eye tracking module" (Leekam, Baron-Cohen, Perrett, Milders, & Brown, 1997); a deficient "attention switching mechanism" (Courchesne et al., 1994); an "executive function deficit" (Ozonoff, Pennington, & Rogers, 1991; Russell, 1996); or a deficient "imitation mechanism" (Meltzoff & Gopnik, 1993)—each concentrating on some subset of the complex symptom cluster of this pervasive developmental disorder. This is not the occasion to compare the relative merits of these proposals; neither shall we contrast them in any detail to the alternative view we are offering. Our present aim is simply to add to the list of these intriguing theories a conceptually different approach that we believe sheds new light on a number of the central symptoms that characterize childhood autism.

Earlier in this chapter we argued on the basis of a set of infant learning studies (Watson, 1979, 1985) and a set of studies on preferential looking at visual feedback of body motion (Bahrick & Watson, 1985; Field, 1979; Papousek & Papousek, 1974; Rochat & Morgan, 1995; Schmuckler, 1996) that there is a biologically based transition around 3 months of age in the preferred target setting of the contingency detection module. During the first 2 to 3 months, infants are preferentially engaging perfect response-stimulus contingencies typically provided by cyclic repetitions of body-centered activities (which Piaget, 1936/1952, described as primary circular reactions). We hypothesized that the self-generated perfect contingencies provide an important source of self-calibrating information (Watson, 1994) leading to the progressive differentiation of the self and the construction of the primary representation of the body schema. In the long run, however, selective evolutionary pressure is for adaptation to the external environment. In service of this requirement, infants must shift orientation from self-based perfect contingencies to environment-based contingencies. This shift is accomplished by resetting the target magnitude of the contingency detection module from perfect to something discriminably less than perfect at about 3 months of age. By doing that, an infant's preference shifts from engaging self-stimulation to engaging stimulus consequences of action on the environment that, for a variety of reasons, typically provide less than perfect contingent effects. As a result, in normal infants, after 3 months of age the preferential engagement in primary circular reactions is progressively replaced by producing and attending to secondary circular reactions; that is, by exploring the external stimulus consequences of acts on the environment. We also argued that the infant-induced reactions of responsive social objects, such as affect-reflective mirroring interactions or repetitive gamelike interactions (Watson, 1972), provide optimal, highly but imperfectly response contingent stimulation that approximates best the preferential target value of the contingency detection device after 3 months. This functions as the basis for the infant's emerging orientation toward and exploration of the social environment and forms the basis for the establishment of the representations of object relationships with primary attachment figures.

Our proposal concerning the aetiology of autism is a simple one. We hypothesize that in autistic individuals the normal shift at around 3 month (as triggered by maturation or experience) in the genetically based target value of the contingency detection module does not take place (or not by enough) and, as a result, autistic children continue to invest in perfect contingencies throughout their life. This tragic devotion to life-long perfection seeking can be seen as underlying a wide range of the symptoms characteristic of autism, as we shall try to briefly indicate here.

1. *Stereotypies.* Autistic children often exhibit characteristic behavioral rhythmicities and stereotypic motor activities as well as an intolerance of

variation in routines. These central features of the disorder can be seen as a direct consequence of the fact that the target setting of the contingency detection module remains in its original position of seeking out perfect contingencies. The preference for invariance and the repetitive engagement in primary circular reactions generate close to perfect response-stimulus contingencies, whereas the high but imperfect contingencies provided by responsive social interactions remain too low in contingency value to positively engage the autistic child's attention.

2. *Executive function problems.* Perseveration with habitual routines and a difficulty in inhibiting circular reactions may contribute to the difficulties that autistic children show in carrying out complex, planned, goal-directed activities. They can also be expected to be less motivated and efficient in engaging in planning action outcomes involving conditional (less than perfect) contingencies, especially when competing habitual action alternatives with clearly predictable perfectly contingent outcomes are available.

3. *Aversion to social objects.* To be able to predict the behavior of social objects, one needs to learn about the significance of dispositional behavioral cues, which, however, are displayed in a contingency matrix that is by necessity lower than perfect. By hypothesis, autistic children show a deficit in attending to and processing the facial and gestural dispositional cues produced by their social environment. This will render the behavioral variation of social partners largely unpredictable to autistic children, which will be anxiety provoking and will lead to aversion to and avoidance of social interaction.

4. *Inattention to faces and lack of social responsivity.* Whether or not there exists an innate bias to orient toward faces (see Morton & Johnson, 1991), there is reasonable evidence that the power of faces to attract attention and elicit smiling increases markedly at around 3 to 4 months in the life of a normal infant. Watson (1972, 1981) proposed that the face acquired special ethological potency for eliciting smiling and drawing attention by virtue of its association with high but not perfect contingency as exemplified in repetitive gamelike face-to-face interactions. In this view, the failure of an autistic infant to modify contingency seeking from a target of perfect to high but not perfect undermines the infant's capacity to engage the early interactional games that normally would generate the special social potency of the face to capture attention and elicit smiling.

5. *Lack of social understanding.* Inferring actions of others based on attributed dispositional and intentional mental states implies a sensitivity to the behavioral cues (such as facial expressions or gaze direction) that indicate such internal states in others. Note that such discriminative cues enter into conditional probability relations with consequent actions that are typically less than perfect and, therefore, may be missed by autistic children. This fact, together with the inattention to facial cues discussed

earlier, may help explain the profound difficulties autistic children have in reading other peoples' minds.

6. *Emotional impulsivity and abnormal sensitivity to internal stimuli.* Autistic children have serious problems in impulse control, showing uncontrollable tantrums and irritability. This may be related to the fact that parental affect-reflective mirroring interactions, which as we have argued, play a central causal role in the development of emotional self-awareness and control, are by necessity high but imperfect in contingency. Therefore, due to the setting of the target value of the contingency detection module to seek out only close to perfect contingencies, autistic children may simply not register the less than perfectly contingent relation between the parent's mirroring displays and their own affect-expressive behaviors. As a result, they will not anchor the representations of marked affect-reflective displays to their own internal self states, and so they will not establish secondary representations for their dispositional emotion states. This predicts a consequent deficiency in being perceptually aware of internal affect states as well as an inability to anticipate and control emotional impulses. Furthermore, due to their 'blindness' to lower than perfect contingencies, the hypothesized sensitization to internal state cues that results from the social biofeedback effects of affect mirroring is also likely to be impaired. This may explain the characteristically abnormal thresholds to internal stimuli (such as pain) found in autistic individuals.

7. *Lack of pretense.* If the availability of secondary representations and an understanding of 'markedness' as a generalized communicative code associated with decoupling (see previous and Gergely, 1995a, 1995b; Gergely & Watson, 1996) are cognitive prerequisites for understanding and producing pretense (Leslie, 1987, 1994), the inability to process marked affect-mirroring displays may contribute to an autistic child's deficient ability to comprehend and produce pretend play. This could be so in so far as the repeated encounters with marked forms of emotion displays during affect-regulative mirroring interactions are causally involved in the acquisition of markedness as a cue of decoupling and suspension of dispositional outcomes (Gergely, 1995a, 1995b; Gergely & Watson, 1996). Since marked affect-reflective displays are characterized by less than perfect degrees of contingency, autistic infants, due to their dysfunctional obsession with only perfectly contingent stimulation, are likely to show deficiency in processing and producing marked transforms of behavioral expressions and will lack understanding of the representational implications of such expressions.

This brief account of autism as 'blindness' to less than perfect contingencies is admittedly highly speculative. One obvious reason for caution has to do with the fact that the supporting evidence concerning the contingency switching hypothesis at 3 months comes from studies with normal infants only. Until now, we had no direct evidence to indicate that autistic children remain seekers of perfect contingencies. Judit Magyar's Ph.D. research, however, has changed this situation by providing the first indication that autistic children react to response-stimulus contingencies significantly differently than normals. We have briefly described her study (Magyar & Gergely, 1998) which showed that normal children preferentially orient toward a highly but imperfectly contingent (imitative) feedback of their manual actions when compared to a perfectly contingent computer-generated feedback. Magyar has also tested 16 autistic children on the same task and found the opposite effect. The autistic children spent significantly more time ($p < .02$) looking at the perfectly contingent computer-generated feedback than at the imitative, human-generated feedback display (see Fig. 5.1, Panel B).

CONCLUSION

Our discussion has been primarily a theoretical venture. The theory we have advanced, regardless of its degree of validity, is clearly a product of its time. It is basically a story in the tradition of nurture over nature, but it recruits some basic guidance for nurture in the form of our proposed contingency seeking module. Modules are, of course, a way of patching nurture with nature; and although we hesitated to add another member to the growing modularity family, it was a temptation we could not resist. Our theory of early socio-emotional development is also of its time in that it draws heavily on recent conceptual advances regarding mental representation. The theory also embraces the classic but still current assumption about the important causal role of affect-mirroring in human socio-emotional development. The potential virtue of our theory, as we see it, is that it provides a relatively precise story as to how this uniquely human form of early caregiving behavior might be responsible for an infant's development of emotional awareness and emotional control behavior.

We believe our theory has some unique heuristic value. Magyar's study of contingency preference should at least illustrate the degree to which certain assumptions of the theory are empirically testable. We would note as well that the theory's specific prescription for marked affect reflection introduces the basis for empirical predictions about developmental outcome when this process is deficient or disorganized (see Gergely & Watson, 1996, for some examples). We also are hopeful that this theory may offer some fruitful perspective on patterns of deviant development resulting from specific faults in the contingency-seeking module. Our attempt to consider autism as one such case is a tentative step toward that goal.

REFERENCES

Bahrick, L. R., & Watson, J. S. (1985). Detection of intermodal proprioceptive-visual contingency as a potential basis of self-perception in infancy. *Developmental Psychology, 21,* 963–973.

Bandura, A. (1992). Social cognitive theory of social referencing. In S. Feinman (Ed.), *Social referencing and the social construction of reality in infancy* (pp. 175–208). New York: Plenum Press.

Baron-Cohen, S. (1995). *Mindblindness: An essay on autism and theory of mind.* Cambridge, MA: MIT Press.

Baron-Cohen, S., Leslie, A. M., & Frith, U. (1985). Does the autistic child have a "theory of mind"? *Cognition, 21*(7), 37–46.

Barresi, J., & Moore, C. (1996). Intentional relations and social understanding. *Behavioral and Brain Sciences, 19,* 107–154.

Beebe, B., Jaffe, J., & Lachmann, F. M. (1992). A dyadic systems view of communication. In N. Skolnick & S. Warshaw (Eds.), *Relational perspectives in psychoanalysis* (pp. 61–82). Hillsdale, NJ: Analytic Press.

Beebe, B., & Lachmann, F. M. (1988). The contribution of mother-infant mutual influence to the origins of self- and object representations. *Psychoanalytic Psychology, 5,* 305–337.

Beebe, B., Lachmann, F. M., & Jaffe, J. (1997). Mother-infant interaction structures and presymbolic self- and object representations. *Psychoanalytic Dialogues,* 7(2), 133–182.

Bettes, B. A. (1988). Material depression and motherese: Temporal and intonational features. *Child Development, 59,* 1089–1096.

Bion, W. R. (1962). *Learning from experience.* New York: Basic Books.

Bion, W. R. (1967). A theory of thinking. In *Second thoughts* (pp. 110–119). London: Heinemann.

Birch, H. G., & Lefford, A. (1967). Visual differentiation, intersensory integration, and voluntary control. *Monographs of the Society for Research in Child Development, 32* (Serial No. 110).

Bloom, K. (1979). Evaluation of infant vocal conditioning. *Journal of Experimental Child Psychology, 27,* 60–70.

Bower, T. G. R. (1974). *Development in infancy.* San Francisco: W. H. Freeman.

Bowlby, J. (1969). *Attachment and loss: Vol. 1. Attachment.* New York: Basic Books.

Brazelton, T. B., Koslowski, B., & Main, M. (1974). The origins of reciprocity: The early mother–infant interaction. In M. Lewis & L. Rosenblum (Eds.), *The effect of the infant on its caregiver* (pp. 49–76). New York: Wiley.

Bretherton, I. (1991). Intentional communication and the development of an understanding of mind. In D. Frye & C. Moore (Eds.), *Children's theories of mind: Mental states and social understanding* (pp. 49–75). Hillsdale, NJ: Lawrence Erlbaum Associates.

Bretherton, I., & Bates, E. (1979). The emergence of intentional communication. In I. C. Užgiriš (Ed.), *Social Interaction and Communication during Infancy* (pp. 81–100). San Francisco: Jossey-Bass.

Bruner, J. S. (1990). *Acts of meaning.* Cambridge, MA: Harvard University Press.

Bruner, J. S., Olver, P. R., & Greenfield, P. M. (1966). *Studies on cognitive growth.* New York: Wiley.

Cohn, J. F., Matias, R., Tronick, E. Z., & Connell, D. (1986). Face-to-face interactions of depressed mothers and their infants. *New Directions for Child Development, 34,* 31–45.

Cohn, J. F., & Tronick, E. Z. (1988). Mother-infant face-to-face interaction: Influence is bidirectional and unrelated to periodic cycles in either partner's behavior. *Developmental Psychology, 24,* 386–392.

Colombo, J., Mitchell, D. W., Coldren, J. T., & Atwater, J. D. (1990). Discrimination learning during the first year: Stimulus and positional cues. *Journal of Experimental Psychology: Learning, Memory, and Cognition, 16,* 98–109.

Csibra, G., & Gergely, G. (in press). The teleological origins of causal mentalistic explanations: A developmental hypothesis. *Developmental Science.*

De Casper, A. J., & Prescott, P. A. (1984). Human newborns' perception of male voices: Preference, discrimination, and reinforcing value. *Developmental Psychobiology, 17,* 481–491.

Demos, V. (1986). Crying in early infancy: An illustration of the motivational function of affect. In T. B. Brazelton & M. W. Yogman (Eds.), *Affective development in infancy* (pp. 39–73). Norwood, NJ: Ablex.

Dicara, L. V. (1970). Learning in the autonomic nervous system. *Scientific American, 222,* 30–39.

Ekman, P. (1992). Facial expressions of emotion: New findings, new questions. *Psychological Science, 3,* 34–38.

Ekman, P., Friesen, W. V., & Ellsworth, P. (1972). *Emotion in the human face.* New York: Pergamon Press.

Ekman, P., Levenson, R. W., & Friesen, W. V. (1983). Autonomic nervous system activity distinguishes between emotions. *Science, 221,* 1208–1210.

Fagen, J. W., & Rovee, C. K. (1976). Effects of quantitative shifts in a visual reinforcer on the instrumental response of infants. *Journal of Experimental Child Psychology, 21,* 349–360.

Field, T. (1979). Differential behavioral and cardiac responses of 3-month-old infants to a mirror and peer. *Infant Behavior and Development, 2,* 179–184.

Field, T. (1994). The effects of mother's physical and emotional unavailability on emotion regulation. *Monographs of the Society for Research in Child Development, 59*(23).

Field, T., Guy, L., & Umbel, V. (1985). Infants' responses to mothers' imitative behaviors. *Infant Mental Health Journal, 6,* 40–44.

Field, T., Healy, B., Goldstein, S., Perry, S., Bendell, D., Schanberg, S., Zimmerman, E. A., & Kuhn, C. (1988). Infants of depressed mothers show "depressed" behavior even with nondepressed adults. *Child Development, 59,* 1569–1579.

Fonagy, P., & Target, M. (1996). Playing with reality: I. Theory of mind and the normal development of psychic reality. *International Journal of Psycho-Analysis, 77,* 217–233.

Fonagy, P., & Target, M. (1997). Attachment and reflective function: Their role in self-organization. *Development and Psychopathology, 9,* 677–699.

Freud, S. (1949). *An outline of psycho-analysis* (Rev. ed., J. Strachey, Trans.). New York: Norton. (Original work published 1940)

Frith, U. (1989). *Autism: Explaining the enigma.* Oxford: Basil Blackwell.

Gergely, G. (1995a, March). *The role of parental mirroring of affects in early psychic structuration.* Paper presented at the International Psychoanalytic Association's Fifth Conference on Psychoanalytic Research: "Advances in Our Understanding of Affects: Clinical Implications," London.

Gergely, G. (1995b, March). *The social construction of self-awareness and first-person authority.* Paper presented at the Twelfth SRCD Conference, Indianapolis.

Gergely, G., & Csibra, G. (1996, April). *Understanding rational actions in infancy: Teleological interpretations without mental attribution.* Paper presented at the Symposium on "Early Perception of Social Contingencies" at the Tenth Biennial International Conference on Infant Studies (ICIS), Providence, RI.

Gergely, G., & Csibra, G. (1997). Teleological reasoning in infancy: The infant's naive theory of rational action. A reply to Premack and Premack. *Cognition, 63,* 227–233.

Gergely, G., Nádasdy, Z., Csibra, G., & Bíró, S. (1995). Taking the intentional stance at 12 months of age. *Cognition, 56,* 165–193.

Gergely, G., & Watson, J. S. (1996). The social biofeedback theory of parental affect-mirroring: The development of emotional self-awareness and self-control in infancy. *International Journal of Psycho-Analysis, 77,* 1181–1212.

Gewirtz, J. L., & Pelaez-Nogueras, M. (1992). Social referencing as a learned process. In S. Feinman (Ed.), *Social referencing and the social construction of reality in infancy* (pp. 151–173). New York: Plenum Press.

Gholson, B. (1980). *The Cognitive-Developmental Basis of Human Learning: Studies in Hypothesis Testing.* New York: Academic Press.

Gopnik, A., & Meltzoff, A. (1997). *Words, thoughts, and theories.* Cambridge, MA: MIT Press.

Gottman, J. M., & Ringland, J. T. (1981). The analysis of dominance and bidirectionality in social development. *Child Development, 52,* 393–412.

Hains, S. M. J., & Muir, D. W. (1996). Infant sensitivity to adult eye direction. *Child Development, 67,* 1940–1951.

Hobson, R. P. (1993). *Autism and the development of mind.* Hove, UK: Lawrence Erlbaum Associates.

Izard, C. E. (1977). *Human Emotions.* New York: Plenum Press.

Izard, C. E. (1978). Emotions as motivations: An evolutionary-developmental perspective. In H. E. Howe, Jr. (Ed.), *Nebraska Symposium on Motivation* (Vol. 26, pp. 163–199). Lincoln: University of Nebraska Press.

Izard, C. E., & Malatesta, C. Z. (1987). Perspectives on emotional development. I. Differential emotions theory of early emotional development. In J. D. Osofsky (Ed.), *Handbook of Infant Development* (2nd ed., pp. 494–554). New York: Wiley.

Jacobson, E. (1964). *The self and the object world.* New York: International Universities Press.

James, W. (1950). *The principles of psychology.* New York: Dover. (Originally published 1890)

Kagan, J. (1992). The conceptual analysis of affects. In T. Shapiro & R. N. Emde (Eds.), *Affects: Psychoanalytic perspectives* (pp. 109–129). Madison, WI: International Universities Press.

Karmiloff-Smith, A. (1992). *Beyond modularity: A developmental perspective on cognitive science.* Cambridge, MA: MIT Press.

Kaye, K. L., & Bower, T. G. B. (1994). Learning and intermodal transfer of information in newborns. *Psychological Science, 5*(5), 286–288.

Kaye, S. (1982). Psychoanalytic perspectives on learning disability. *Journal of Contemporary Psychotherapy, 13,* 83–93.

Kernberg, P. F. (1984). Reflections in the mirror: Mother-child interactions, self-awareness, and self-recognition. In J. D. Call, E. Galenson, & R. L. Tyson (Eds.), *Frontiers of infant psychiatry, vol. II* (pp. 101–110). New York: Basic Books.

Kohut, H. (1971). *The analysis of the self.* New York: International Universities Press.

Leekam, S., Baron-Cohen, S., Perrett, D., Milders, M., & Brown, S. (1977). Eye-direction detection: A dissociation between geometric and joint attention skills in autism. *British Journal of Developmental Psychology, 15,* 77–95.

Leslie, A. M. (1987). Pretense and representation: The origins of "theory of mind." *Psychological Review, 94,* 412–426.

Leslie, A. M. (1994). ToMM, ToBy, and Agency: Core architecture and domain specificity. In L. Hirschfeld & S. Gelman (Eds.), *Mapping the mind: Domain specificity in cognition and culture* (pp. 119–148). New York: Cambridge University Press.

Lewis, M., & Brooks, J. (1978). Self-knowledge and emotional development. In M. Lewis & L. A. Rosenblum (Eds.), *The development of affect* (pp. 205–226). New York: Plenum Press.

Lewis, M., & Michaelson, L. (1983). *Children's emotions and moods: Developmental theory and measurement.* New York: Plenum Press.

Magyar, J., & Gergely, G. (1998, April). *The obscure object of desire: "Nearly, but clearly not like me": Perception of self-generated contingencies in normal infants and children with autism.* Poster, ICIS, Atlanta, GA.

Mahler, M., Bergman, A., & Pine, F. (1975). *The psychological birth of the human infant: Symbiosis and individuation.* New York: Basic Books.

Mahler, M., & McDevitt, J. B. (1982). Thoughts on the emergence of the sense of self, with particular emphasis on the body self. *Journal of the American Psychoanalytic Association, 30*, 827–848.

Main, M., & Hesse, E. (1990). Parents' unresolved traumatic experiences are related to infant disorganized attachment status: Is frightened and/or frightening parental behavior the linking mechanism? In M. T. Greenberg, D. Cicchetti, & E. M. Cummings (Eds.), *Attachment in the preschool years: Theory, research, and intervention* (pp. 161–182). The John D. and Catherine T. MacArthur Foundation series on mental health and development. Chicago: University of Chicago Press.

Malatesta, C. Z., & Izard, C. E. (1984). The ontogenesis of human social signals: From biological imperative to symbol utilization. In N. A. Fox & R. J. Davidson (Eds.), *The psychobiology of affective development* (pp. 161–206). Hillsdale, NJ: Lawrence Erlbaum Associates.

Malatesta, C. Z., Culver, C., Tesman, R. J., & Shepard, B. (1989). The development of emotion expression during the first two years of life. *Monographs of the Society for Research in Child Development, 54* (Serial No. 219).

Meltzoff, A. N. (1990). Foundations for developing a concept of self: The role of imitation in relating self to other and the value of social mirroring, social modeling, and self practice in infancy. In D. Cicchetti & M. Beeghly (Eds.), *The self in transition: Infancy to childhood* (pp. 139–164). Chicago: University of Chicago Press.

Meltzoff, A. N., & Borton, R. W. (1979). Intermodal matching by human neonates. *Nature, 282*, 403–404.

Meltzoff, A. N., & Gopnik, A. (1993). The role of imitation in understanding persons and developing a theory of mind. In S. Baron-Cohen, H. Tager-Flusberg, & D. J. Cohen (Eds.), *Understanding other minds: Perspectives from autism* (pp. 335–365). Oxford: Oxford University Press.

Meltzoff, A. N., & Moore, M. K. (1977). Imitation of facial and manual gestures by human neonates. *Science, 198*, 75–78.

Meltzoff, A. N., & Moore, M. K. (1989). Imitation in newborn infants: Exploring the range of gestures imitated and the underlying mechanisms. *Developmental Psychology, 25*, 954–962.

Millar, W. S. (1972). A study of operant conditioning under delayed reinforcement in early infancy. *Monographs for the Society for Research in Child Development*, vol. 37, no. 2, Serial No. 147.

Millar, W. S., & Watson, J. S. (1979). The effect of delayed feedback on infant learning reexamined. *Child Development, 50*, 747–751.

Miller, N. E. (1969). Learning visceral and glandular responses. *Science, 163*, 434–445.

Miller, N. E. (1978). Biofeedback and visceral learning. *Annual Review of Psychology, 29*, 373–404.

Moore, C., & Corkum, V. (1994). Social understanding at the end of the first year of life. *Developmental Review, 14*, 349–372.

Morton, J., & Johnson, M. (1991). The perception of facial structure in infancy. In G. R. Lockhead & J. R. Pomerantz (Eds.), *The perception of structure: Essays in honor of Wendell R. Garner* (pp. 317–325). Washington, DC: American Psychological Association.

Murray, L. (1992). The impact of postnatal depression on infant development. *Journal of Child Psychology and Psychiatry, 33*, 543–561.

Murray, L., Fiori-Cowley, A., Hooper, R., & Cooper, P. (1996). The impact of postnatal depression and associated adversity on early mother–infant interactions and later infant outcomes. *Child Development, 67*, 2512–2526.

Murray, L., & Trevarthen, C. (1985). Emotional regulation of interactions between two-month-olds and their mothers. In T. M. Field & N. A. Fox (Eds.), *Social perception in infants* (pp. 177–198). Norwood, NJ: Ablex.

Ozonoff, S., Pennington, B. F., & Rogers, S. J. (1991). Executive function deficits in high-functioning autistic individuals: Relationship to theory of mind. *Journal of Child Psychology and Psychiatry and Allied Disciplines, 32,* 1081–1105.

Papousek H., & Papousek, M. (1974). Mirror-image and self-recognition in young human infants: A new method of experimental analysis. *Developmental Psychobiology, 7,* 149–157.

Papousek, H., & Papousek, M. (1987). Intuitive parenting: A dialectic counterpart to the infant's integrative competence. In J. D. Osofsky (Ed.), *Handbook of infant development* (pp. 669–720). New York: Wiley.

Papousek, H., & Papousek, M. (1989). Forms and functions of vocal matching in interactions between mothers and their precanonical infants. *First Language, 9,* 137–158.

Piaget, J. (1952). *Origins of Intelligence.* New York: Norton. (Original work published 1936)

Pickens, J., & Field, T. (1993). Facial expressivity in infants of depressed mothers. *Developmental Psychology, 29,* 986–988.

Ramey, C. T., & Ourth, L. L. (1971). Delayed reinforcement and vocalization rates of infants. *Child Development, 42,* 291–297.

Rochat, P., & Morgan, R. (1995). Spatial determinants in the perception of self-produced leg movements in 3- to 5-month-old infants. *Developmental Psychology, 31,* 626–636.

Rochat, P., Neisser, U., & Marian, V. (in press). Are young infants sensitive to interpersonal contingency? *Infant Behavior and Development.*

Rovee, C. K., & Rovee, D. T. (1969). Conjugate reinforcement in infant exploratory behavior. *Journal of Experimental Child Psychology, 8,* 33–39.

Rovee-Collier, C. K. (1987). Learning and memory in infancy. In J. D. Osofsky (Ed.), *Handbook of infant development* (2nd ed., pp. 98–148). New York: Wiley.

Russell, J. (1996). *Agency: Its role in mental development.* Hove: Lawrence Erlbaum Associates.

Sander, L. W. (1970). Regulation and organization of behavior in the early infant-caretaker system. In R. Robinson (Ed.), *Brain and early behavior.* London: Academic Press.

Schmuckler, M. A. (1996). Visual-proprioceptive intermodal perception in infancy. *Infant Behavior and Development, 19,* 221–232.

Shiffrin, R. M., & Schneider, W. (1977). Controlled and automatic human information processing: II. Perceptual learning, automatic attending, and a general theory. *Psychological Review, 84,* 127–190.

Skinner, B. F. (1948). *Walden two.* New York: Macmillan.

Sroufe, L. A. (1996). *Emotional development: The organization of emotional life in the early years.* New York: Cambridge University Press.

Stern, D. N. (1984). Affect attunement. In J. D. Call, E. Galenson, & R. T. Tyson (Eds.), *Frontiers of infant psychiatry, vol. II* (pp. 3–14). New York: Basic Books.

Stern, D. N. (1985). *The interpersonal word of the infant.* New York: Basic Books.

Stern, D. N., Hofer, L., Haft, W., & Dore, J. (1985). Affect attunement: The sharing of feeling states between mother and infant by means of inter-modal fluency. In T. M. Fields & N. A. Fox (Eds.), *Social perception in infants.* Norwood, NJ: Ablex.

Trevarthen, C. (1979). Communication and cooperation in early infancy. A description of primary intersubjectivity. In M. Bullowa (Ed.), *Before speech: The beginning of human communication* (pp. 321–347). Cambridge: Cambridge University Press.

Trevarthen, C., & Hubley, P. (1978). Secondary intersubjectivity: Confidence, confiding and acts of meaning in the second year. In A. Lock (Ed.), *Action, gesture and symbol: The emergence of language* (pp. 183–229). New York: Academic Press.

Tronick, E. Z. (1989). Emotions and emotional communication in infants. *American Psychologist, 44,* 112–119.

Tronick, E. Z., Edward, M., Als, H., & Brazelton, T. B. (1977). Mutuality in mother-infant interaction. *Journal of Communication, 27,* 74–79.

Tronick, E. Z., Als, H., Adamson, L., Wise, S., & Brazelton, T. B. (1978). The infant's responses to entrapment between contradictory messages in face to face interaction. *Journal of the American Academy of Child Psychiatry, 16,* 1–13.

Tronick, E. Z., & Field, T. (1986). *Maternal depression and infant disturbance.* San Francisco: Jossey-Bass.

Tronick, E. Z., & Cohn, J. F. (1989). Infant–mother face-to-face interaction: Age and gender differences in coordination and the occurrence of miscoordination. *Child Development, 60,* 85–92.

Tronick, E. Z., Ricks, M., & Cohn, J. F. (1982). Maternal and infant affective exchange: Patterns of adaptation. In T. Field & A. Fogel (Eds.), *Emotion and early interaction* (pp. 83–100). Hillsdale, NJ: Lawrence Erlbaum Associates.

Užgiriš, I. C., Benson, J. B., Kruper, J. C., & Vasek, M. E. (1989). Contextual influences on imitative interactions between mothers and infants. In J. J. Lockman & N. L. Hazen (Eds.), *Action in Social Context: Perspectives on Early Development* (pp. 103–127). New York: Plenum Press.

Walton, Gail E., Bower, T. G. (1993). Newborns form "prototypes" in less than 1 minute. *Psychological Science, 4,* 203–205.

Watson, J. B. (1930). *Behaviorism* (Rev. ed.). Chicago: University of Chicago Press.

Watson, J. S. (1967). Memory and "contingency analysis" in infant learning. *Merrill-Palmer Quarterly, 13,* 55–76.

Watson, J. S. (1972). Smiling, cooing, and "the game." *Merrill-Palmer Quarterly, 18,* 323–339.

Watson, J. S. (1979). Perception of contingency as a determinant of social responsiveness. In E. Thoman (Ed.), *The origins of social responsiveness* (pp. 33–64). Hillsdale, NJ: Lawrence Erlbaum Associates.

Watson, J. S. (1981). Contingency experience in behavioral development. In K. Immelmann, G. W. Barlow, L. Petrinovich, & M. Main (Eds.), *Behavioral development: The bielefeld interdisciplinary project* (pp. 83–89). New York: Cambridge University Press.

Watson, J. S. (1984a). Bases of causal inference in infancy: Time, space and sensory relations. In L. P. Lipsitt & C. Rovee-Collier (Eds.), *Advances in infancy research, vol. 3* (pp. 152–165). Norwood, NJ: Ablex.

Watson, J. S. (1984b). Memory in learning: Analysis of three momentary reactions of infants. In R. Kail & N. Spear (Eds.), *Comparative perspectives on the development of memory* (pp. 159–179). Hillsdale, NJ: Lawrence Erlbaum Associates.

Watson, J. S. (1985). Contingency perception in early social development. In T. M. Field & N. A. Fox (Eds.), *Social perception in infants* (pp. 157–176). Norwood, NJ: Ablex.

Watson, J. S. (1994). Detection of self: The perfect algorithm. In S. T. Parker, R. W. Mitchell, & M. L. Boccia (Eds.), *Self-awareness in animals and humans: Developmental perspectives* (pp. 131–148). New York: Cambridge University Press.

Watson, J. S. (1995). Mother-infant interaction: Dispositional properties and mutual designs. In N. S. Thompson (Ed.), *Perspectives in ethology, vol. 11* (pp. 189–210). New York: Plenum Press.

Watson, J. S. (in press). Contingency and its two indices within conditional probability analysis. *The Behavior Analyst.*

Winnicott, D. W. (1967). Mirror-role of mother and family in child development. In P. Lomas (Ed.), *The predicament of the family: A psychoanalytical symposium* (pp. 26–33). London: Hogarth Press and the Institute of Psycho-Analysis.

Chapter 6

Infants' Sensitivity to Imperfect Contingency in Social Interaction

Ann E. Bigelow
St. Francis Xavier University

Infants' early self-knowledge emerges with their ability to notice contingency between their own actions and external responses. This self-knowledge is perceptually based and arises before representational thought (Neisser, 1988, 1991, 1993). By perceiving change as a result of their actions, infants develop a sense that they are agents of that change. This sense of self-efficacy underlies infants' social exchanges with others, which are essential to their social and emotional development. This awareness also stimulates curiosity about the environment, which leads to exploration and cognitive development. Thus, infants' self knowledge, generated by their awareness of the contingency between their behavior and external changes, influences their subsequent developmental processes.

Infants' sense of self-efficacy develops readily in interactions with others who respond to infants' behavior in socially contingent ways. People have perceptual characteristics that virtually assure that infants will orient toward them. They have visually contrasting and moving faces. They produce sound, provide touch, and have interesting smells. When in face-to-face interactions with infants, people exaggerate their facial expressions, inflect their voices, and produce a style of speech called *motherese,* which is not the sole domain of mothers, that infants find fascinating. In addition to these interesting perceptual characteristics, people behave responsively toward infants; that is, they vary the pace and level of their actions in response to infant behavior. Consequently, early social interactions provide a context in which infants can easily notice the effect of their actions on the external world.

The social responses that are most effective in facilitating early self-knowledge in infancy are those that reflect infants' own behavior (Rochat, 1995).

Infants may more easily recognize the external effect of their behavior when the actions of others mirror the behavior the infants produce (Gergely & Watson, 1996). It is not surprising that in naturally occurring interactions between parents and young infants, parental responses are primarily imitations of the infants' actions (Stern, 1985). These parental imitations are not exact but match the infants' actions in intensity, affect, and tempo. Infants' early perceptual capacities may allow them to recognize the imperfectly matched behavior as mirroring their own. Studies by Meltzoff and Moore (1977, 1983, 1989, 1994) indicate that from the beginning of life, infants are aware of the matching quality of their behavior and that of others. Older infants have demonstrated that they are particularly sensitive to the imitative quality of the behavior of their responding partner. In a series of studies with 14-month-olds, Meltzoff (1990) showed that the more imitative the adult partners' actions are, the more attentive and interested infants are in the interactions. Perhaps infants learn about their own actions by seeing them reflected in others. Such reflections may affirm and acknowledge to the infants that their behavior has been understood and may give them a sense that their self-reality is shared by others.

Although imitative in nature, parental responses are not perfectly contingent with their infants' behavior. Parents are selective in their responsiveness to infants' actions. Parents respond to behavior they perceive to contain emotional content; the parental responses reflect to infants the emotional content the parents perceive, mirroring the infants' behavior in a marked and selected manner (Gergely & Watson, 1996). Such responses, particularly to infants under 6 months of age, are predominantly modified facial imitations or responsive vocalizations (Stern, Hofer, Haft, & Dore, 1985). These typically occur after infants' vocalizations, gestures, and facial expressions that are perceived to be most vigorous (Trevarthen, 1979). Thus, parental contingent responsiveness to infants' behavior is imperfect, and the level of imperfection varies among parent–infant dyads marking selected infant actions that are salient to the parents (Gergely & Watson, 1996). Individual differences in parents' contingent responsiveness to their infants are reflected in the quality of infants' attachments (Blehar, Lieberman, & Ainsworth, 1977), in their emotional responsiveness (Stern, 1985), and in their coping strategies and cognitive mastery (Dunham & Dunham, 1990; Lamb & Easterbrooks, 1981).

INFANTS' SENSITIVITY TO IMPERFECT SOCIAL CONTINGENCY

The imperfect contingency present in early parental exchanges with infants may be key to infants' interest in these interactions. Almost 2 decades ago, Watson (1979) found that the learning scores of infants controlling an array of lights and sounds by their kicks to a motion-sensitive pillow were higher in conditions of imperfect contingency than in conditions of perfect contingency. This finding was surprising, because it was originally assumed that infants would learn best under conditions of 100 percent reward, that is, perfect contingency between self-action and external response. In further studies, Watson (1985) found that behavioral arousal was reduced when no contingency existed or when contingency was approaching perfection and was maximum at moderate levels of contingency. There is cognitive advantage to the reduction of arousal to perfect contingency. Perfect contingencies are inherent in self-actions, such as sucking on one's own fingers. Infants' sustained investment of attention and energy to such perfect contingencies would be unproductive. Focusing attention on the imperfect contingencies present in the environment or in others' behavior rather than on intrinsic sensations is adaptive. Watson (1985) proposed that the reduction in arousal to perfect contingency begins around 3 months of age, when infants become more focused on the external world and less interested in self-actions on their own bodies. It is noteworthy that within Piagetian theory (Piaget, 1963) it is at approximately this age that infants move from being able to perform only primary circular reactions, which form repeated action schemes having to do with their own bodies, to being able to perform secondary circular reactions, which form repeated action schemes that incorporate other people and objects. Infants' ability to detect differences between perfect and imperfect contingencies is acquired early and may be one of the first ways they distinguish self from other (Watson, 1985).

Infants' contingency preferences in social interactions mirror those Watson (1985) found in nonsocial tasks. Infants are more aroused in conditions of imperfect contingency than in those of noncontingency or perfect contingency.

There has been a series of studies that demonstrate infants' preference for imperfect contingency, present in face-to-face interaction, over noncontingency, present in video replays of social partners whose interactions are unrelated to what the infant viewers are currently doing. Murray and Trevarthen (1985) were the first to present infants with sequential displays of imperfectly contingent and noncontingent social interactions. Their procedure was modeled after the one used to demonstrate the still-face effect. When adults shift from active face-to-face interaction with infants to being silent and expressionless, infants respond with changes in behavior, typically exhibiting reduced attention and less positive affect (Carter, Mayes, & Pajer, 1990; Ellsworth, Muir, & Hains, 1993; Field, 1981; Field, Yega-Lahr, Scafidi, & Goldstein, 1986; Fogel, Diamond, Langhorst, & Demos, 1982; Gusella, Muir, & Tronick, 1988; Mayes & Carter, 1990; Murray & Trevarthen, 1985; Stoller & Field, 1982; Tronick, Als, Adamson, Wise, & Brazelton, 1978).

Such changes in the infants' behavior clearly demonstrate that they have noticed changes in the adults' behavior, yet the still-face effect confounds the adults' changes in contingency with the adults' changes in affectivity. That is, studies of the still-face effect remove the adults' contingent responsiveness to the infants' behavior along with the adults' exaggerated facial expressions and vocal tones characteristic of motherese.

In order to examine more specifically the effect of contingency per se on infants' behavior, Murray and Trevarthen (1985) replaced the still-face episodes with video replays of adults interacting with infants. They had mothers and infants interacting via video so that each partner saw and heard the other on video monitors. Then the mothers' tapes were quickly rewound and played back to the infants. In the replay, the mothers' facial expressions and vocalizations were exactly as they had been moments before, except that the mothers' actions were unrelated to what the infants were currently doing; that is, the contingency was missing. Murray and Trevarthen reported that for the four 2-month-olds tested, the response to the replay was loss of positive affect and attention, much like the still-face effect.

Murray and Trevarthen's (1985) original design of this simple yet clever means of isolating infants' response to social contingency had some methodological problems. Specifically, the order of imperfectly contingent and noncontingent presentations confounded changes in contingency with changes due to time; that is, the infants' behavioral change may have been due to fatigue or declining interest in watching the same person over time rather than the lack of contingency. In recent years, several researchers have attempted to replicate the effect found by Murray and Trevarthen using various methodologies (Bigelow, MacLean, & MacDonald, 1996; Hains & Muir, 1996; Muir & Hains, 1993; Rochat, Neisser, & Marian, 1998). Although the results have been mixed, the issue appears to be when infants begin to show this sensitivity to contingency and not whether they do. Studies have demonstrated that by 4 months of age, infants respond with reduced attention and less positive affect to the noncontingent replay condition than to the live contingent condition (Bigelow, et al., 1996; Hains & Muir, 1996).

Other researchers have sought to examine infants' response to imperfectly contingent versus noncontingent social interaction by presenting infants with simultaneous displays (Bigelow, 1996; Muir, Hains, Cao, & D'Entremont, 1996). In these studies, infants were seated in front of two video monitors; on one monitor an adult stranger responded contingently to them and on the other monitor an adult stranger responded noncontingently. The noncontingent stranger was a tape of an adult interacting with another infant, therefore, both adults displayed infant-directed facial and vocal expressions. Although this context is more unusual for infants, 3- to 5-month-olds were more attentive to the imperfectly contingent adult than to the noncontingent adult, demonstrating that by 3 months of age infants prefer imperfect contingency present in social interaction to noncontingency present in the replay of a social partner.

Infants also demonstrate their preference for imperfect social contingency when it is compared to perfect contingency. Although infants are sensitive to the imitative quality of adults' responses to them, contingency in social interactions is by necessity imperfect. The images that perfectly match the infants' behavior are their mirror reflections. These images exactly match the infants' actions behaviorally as well as in intensity, affect, and tempo.

Most of the literature on infants' reaction to their mirror images focuses on the development of visual self-recognition, which is a late acquired ability emerging at the end of the second year (Amsterdam, 1972; Bigelow, 1981; Schulman & Kaplowitz, 1977). Before visual self-recognition, however, infants show an interest in their own reflections. Initially, they attend to aspects of the reflected environment or to the images of others rather than to the self-image. Then, beginning around 4 months of age, infants' attention is directed toward their self-image (Dixon, 1957). Smiles, vocalizations, touching the image, and even attempts to look behind the mirror become prevalent. Toward the end of the first year, infants specifically test the correspondence between the action of the image and their own behavior (Amsterdam, 1972; Dixon, 1957; Gesell & Ames, 1947; Lewis & Brooks-Gunn, 1979). They study the movements of their reflections while at times systematically varying these movements. Most characteristic is repeated limb activity while observing the mirror image or a repeated bobbing, bowing, or bouncing while attending to the image. This movement-testing behavior increases and peaks just before self-recognition (Bigelow, 1981). Such behavior is evidence that infants explore the uniqueness of their reflected self-image and its perfect match to their behavior. It is possible that it is this realization that is the initial cue to self-recognition. That is, the first recognition of the visual self-image may be the recognition of self-movement (Bigelow, 1981; Meltzoff, 1990).

As mentioned, before the emergence of movement-testing behavior, infants show interest in their reflected self-image. This interest begins around 4 months of age (Dixon, 1957), when they also show sensitivity to contingency in social interactions. There are differences that distinguish the reflected behavior of the self-image and the contingent behavior of a social partner. Although self-images share features in common with social partners, they are not social partners. In addition to perfectly matching the infants' behavior, reflected self-images differ from social partners in that they lack the temporal spacing between self-behavior and the behavior of other; there is no turn taking. The reflected self-image consistently, simultaneously, and perfectly matches the infant's behavior, whereas the social partner selectively and imperfectly matches the infant's behavior, responding in a reciprocal turn-taking manner to the infant's gestures, vocalizations, and facial expressions. Such differences are deemed detectable by young infants. The features of social interaction may be more adaptive to the development of infants' understanding of self and other, which would lead them to be more responsive to the images of a socially responding partner than to their self-images. Infants also may be more sensitive to disruptions in the contingent behavior of a social partner than to disruptions in the matching behavior of self-images. Infants' preference for imperfectly contingent social behavior over behavior that is perfectly matched to self-actions can be examined by comparing infants' reactions to the contingent behavior of a social partner and a replay of the partner's behavior and their reactions to the matched behavior of a self-image and a replay of that behavior.

Bigelow et al. (1996) investigated 4-, 6-, and 8-month-old infants' responses to live and replay interactions with their mothers and with their own images. Infants interacted with their mothers and their own images via videotape under conditions of initial live feedback, replay, and subsequent live feedback, with half the infants interacting with their mothers first and half with their own images first. At all ages, the infants showed more attention and smiling to the socially contingent behavior of their mothers than to the perfectly matched behavior of their self-images. Changes from imperfect contingency to noncontingency in the interactions with mothers resulted in reduced smiling and an immediate drop in attention, which cannot be attributed to prolonged interaction with the same image. However, the infants' responses did not change when the perfectly matched actions of their self-images became noncontingent in replay; in response to the self-images, attention and smiling remained at low levels. The reinstatement of perfectly matched self-actions in the subsequent live feedback condition resulted in no change in smiling and a nonabrupt decline in attention characteristic of infants' response to the continued presentation of the same image over time. When imperfect contingency was reinstated with mothers in the subsequent live feedback condition, attention and smiling increased for the 8-month-olds but not for the 4- and 6-month-olds. Others also have found that for infants under 6 months of age, the loss of attention and positive affect to experimentally induced disruptions of social contingency carries over to the immediately following episodes of contingent interaction (Fogel et al., 1982; Hains & Muir, 1996; Muir & Hains, 1993; Tronick et al., 1978). Although these carryover effects are temporary, they demonstrate that young infants' expectations for contingency are influenced by their previous experience.

The results of the Bigelow et al. (1996) study indicate that the infants found the imperfect contingency of their mothers' actions more arousing and interesting than the perfectly matched behavior of their self-images. Changes in the mothers' interaction from imperfect contingency to noncontingency was noticed immediately and responded to with reduced attention and less positive affect. Although the infants may have noticed the difference between the matched behavior of their self-images in the live feedback conditions and the mismatched behavior of those images in the replay condition, they did not respond to the difference by either changes in attention or smiling. Perhaps more sensitive measures of attention and affect are necessary to detect infants' responses to changes in the matching behavior of their self-images. Comparatively, infants' responses to changes in contingency during social interactions are robust.

Previous research has indicated that infants can discriminate the matched behavior of their self-image and the noncontingent behavior of a peer or a prerecorded video of self. Field (1979) tested 3-month-olds and found that their preference was for the reflected self-image. Yet Papousek and Papousek (1974) tested 5-month-olds and found that it was the noncontingent image that was preferred. These findings suggest that infants shift their preference away from behavior that is perfectly matched to self-action. A confounding artifact of the reflected self-image versus the behavior of a peer or a prerecorded video of self is that, when looking at the reflected self-image, the eyes are immobile whereas the image of the peer or prerecorded self has moving eyes that are seldom fixated on the infant observer. In order to eliminate this artifact, Bahrick and Watson (1985) showed infants images of their legs and feet instead of their faces. The results of their studies confirm that infants perceive differences between perfectly matched self-images and noncontingent images. Like previous findings with facial images (Papousek & Papousek, 1974), infants older than 3 months prefer the noncontingent images to the perfectly matched images. In their pivotal study, Bahrick and Watson found that 3-month-old infants demonstrated a bimodal distribution in attentional preference. Approximately half the infants preferred the matched behavior of the self-image and half preferred the noncontingent image. The experimenters concluded that 3-month-olds are capable of discriminating self from other but are in a transitional phase between focusing attention on self and focusing attention on the behavior of others. Around 3 months of age, the intrinsic perfect contingency inherent in self-actions on the self becomes less arousing than the imperfectly contingent behavior inherent in social interactions.

Mandler (1992) proposed three ways in which contingency might be noticed by infants: one-way contingency, back-and-forth contingency, and simultaneous contingency. In one-way contingency, the infant acts, and there is a resultant external event, which could be social or nonsocial. In back-and-forth contingency, actions or events are responsive to each other, much like the behavior that occurs in face-to-face interactions between infants and social partners. In simultaneous contingency, actions or events are linked together at the same time, like infants' actions and those of their reflected self-images. The awareness of the different types of contingency may not be mutually independent. Before 3 months of age, infants are most aroused by the perfect contingency inherent in self-actions on the self. This focus on their own actions on the self helps them to form their body schema (Rochat & Morgan, 1995) and allows them to differentiate self from nonself. Once this is established, interest in the perfectly contingent self-actions wanes and interest in the imperfect contingency present in the external world becomes paramount. Imperfect contingency occurs in the back-and-forth contingency present in social interactions and in the one-way contingency present in infants' actions on the environment. Watson (1985) proposed that infants become interested in the one-way contingency in nonsocial events because of their experience with back-and-forth contingency in social interactions. It is noteworthy that social interaction with other members of the species may be necessary before self-recognition occurs (Lewis & Brooks-Gunn, 1979). Such speculation is based on findings which show that chimpanzees raised in isolation do not perform self-directed mirror behavior like those raised with other chimpanzees (Gallup & McClure, 1971). Perhaps it is necessary to experience the mutuality of self-action and another's action before it is possible to become aware that the unique simultaneous matching between self and image action is an indication that the image seen is of self.

INFANTS' SENSITIVITY TO PARTICULAR LEVELS OF IMPERFECT SOCIAL CONTINGENCY

The imperfect contingency present in early parent–child interactions may influence infants' subsequent sensitivity to various contingency patterns in the social and nonsocial environment. Bower (1982) proposed that infants become accustomed to the particular imperfect levels of contingency they experience in their family interactions. Parent–child social interactions may create optimal contingency levels through familiarization, which in turn, are reflected in infants' responsiveness to new stimuli both social and nonsocial. Research on year-old infants indicates that parental contingencies to infant behavior are stable within mother–infant pairs but vary across the normal population (Stern et al., 1985). This stability within dyads and variability in the population is believed to be present by the time infants are 3 months old (Watson, 1985). Infants' detection of, and preference for, imperfect contingency undoubtedly helps them orient toward people. Watson (1985) hypothesized that because people are imperfectly contingent to different degrees, infants are oriented toward particular people whose levels of contingency have become familiar.

This hypothesis goes against some of our intuitive thinking about infants and their learning processes, namely, that infants would be increasingly responsive to increased social contingency, albeit social contingency is rarely, if ever, perfect. Research indicates that the more responsive parents are to infants, the more infants are able to rely on their own self-efficacy (Bell & Ainsworth, 1972; Dunham & Dunham, 1990). For example, Dunham and Dunham (1990) found that infants who were high on vocal turn taking with their mothers learned a perfectly contingent nonsocial task more easily than infants who experienced less vocal turn taking with their mothers. In this study, infants participated in face-to-face interaction with their mothers in which vocal turn taking was measured, then infants were seated in front of a visual-auditory display that was activated only when the infants visually fixated on it. The time infants spent in vocal turn taking with their mothers predicted individual differences in their subsequent performance on the nonsocial contingency task. These results are interpreted as indicating that infants, who learned their behavior was effective in vocal turn taking, transferred the expectation that their actions would be effective to the nonsocial task. From the perspective of Watson's hypothesis an explanation for this transfer might be that infants with highly responsive mothers were sensitive to high levels of contingency and, therefore, did well in recognizing and responding to the perfect contingency in the nonsocial task. Would infants with less responsive mothers do better at recognizing and responding to lower levels of contingency? High levels of parental responsiveness may, indeed, facilitate infants' understanding that they are effective agents in the world and, therefore, influence their readiness to seek the effects of their self-actions. Nevertheless, infants may develop sensitivities to particular levels of perceived contingency based on past experience and, as a consequence, they may be most responsive to other external stimulation that has similar levels of contingency.

Bigelow (1998) investigated Watson's hypothesis by having 4- and 5-month-old infants participate in face-to-face interactions with their mothers and with strangers. Half the infants interacted with their mothers first and half with the strangers first. The contingent responsiveness was assessed for each partner (infant and adult) in both the mother–infant and the stranger–infant interactions. Watson's hypothesis predicts that infants would be more responsive to strangers whose level of contingent responsiveness to them was similar to that of their mothers and that they would be less responsive to strangers who were either more contingent or less contingent to them than their mothers. The onset of vocalizations and smiles were scored for each partner. Of specific interest were those vocalizations and smiles that followed, within 1 second, a vocalization or smile by the other partner. Measures of contingent responsiveness (Watson, 1979, 1985) were calculated as the difference between observed conditional probabilities (e.g., probability of smile by Partner A follows smile by Partner B within 1 second) and expected unconditional probabilities (e.g., probability of smile by Partner A). These measures were then converted to z scores. Four different contingent responsiveness scores (z scores) were calculated for each infant for vocalizations and for smiles: mother's contingent responsiveness to infant (*Mi*), infant's contingent responsiveness to mother (*Im*), stranger's contingent responsiveness to infant (*Si*), and infant's contingent responsiveness to stranger (*Is*). To measure how similar the strangers and the mothers were in their contingent responsiveness to the infants, the z scores for the strangers' contingent responsiveness to the infants (*Si*) were subtracted from the z scores for the mothers' contingent responsiveness to the infants (*Mi*). Likewise, to measure how similar the infants were in their contingent responsiveness to the mothers and the strangers, the infants' z scores for contingent responsiveness to the strangers (*Is*) were subtracted from the infants' z scores for contingent responsiveness to the mothers (*Im*).

Watson's hypothesis predicts a U-shaped curve when the infants' contingent responsiveness to mothers minus the infants' contingent responsiveness to strangers (*Im* – *Is*) is plotted against the mothers' contingent responsiveness to infants minus the strangers' contingent responsiveness to infants (*Mi* – *Si*). The quadratic trends depicted both for vocal contingency in Fig. 6.1 and for smiling contingency in Fig. 6.2 support the prediction. When infants interacted with strangers whose contingent responsiveness to them was similar to that of their mothers, the infants' contingent responsiveness to the strangers was much like their contingent responsiveness to their mothers. However, when strangers' contingent responsiveness to the infants was more dissimilar to that of the mothers, the infants were less contingently responsive to the strangers relative to their mothers. Because infants' development of self-efficacy depends on their noticing the contingency between their self-actions and external consequences, one might expect that infants would be more responsive to the adult who demonstrated the higher levels of contingent responsiveness to them. Thus, it is not surprising that infants were more responsive to mothers when mothers were more responsive to the infants than the strangers were. Yet infants were more responsive to the mothers (who were demonstrating the familiar level of contingency) even when the mothers were less responsive to them than were the strangers. The familiarity of the strangers' level of contingent responsiveness was more predictive of the infants' contingent responsiveness to the strangers than was the level of the strangers' contingent responsiveness per se.

Mothers showed individual differences in their contingent responsiveness across vocalizations and smiles, such that their contingent responsive-

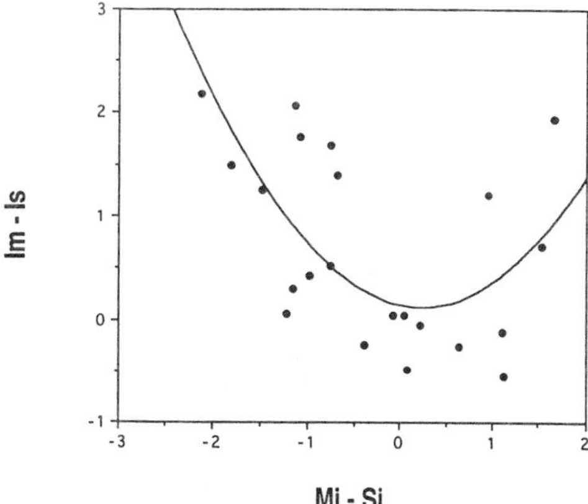

FIG. 6.1. The relational plot of the difference between infants' contingent vocal responsiveness to mothers and strangers (*Im – Is*) and the difference between mothers' and strangers' contingent vocal responsiveness to infants (*Mi – Si*).
Note. From "Infants' sensitivity to familiar imperfect contingencies in social interaction," by A. E. Bigelow, 1998, *Infant Behavior and Development, 21*, p. 155. Copyright by Ablex Publishing Corporation, Greenwich, CT. Reprinted with permission.

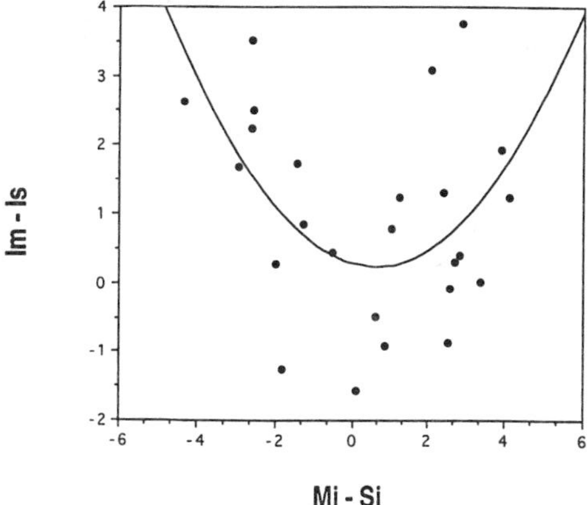

FIG. 6.2. The relational plot of the difference between infants' contingent smiling responsiveness to mothers and strangers (*Im – Is*) and the difference between mothers' and strangers' contingent smiling responsiveness to infants (*Mi – Si*).
Note. From "Infants' sensitivity to familiar imperfect contingencies in social interaction," by A. E. Bigelow, 1998, *Infant Behavior and Development, 21*, p. 156. Copyright by Ablex Publishing Corporation, Greenwich, CT. Reprinted with permission.

ness in one of the behaviors was not predictive of their contingent responsiveness in the other behavior. Stern and colleagues (Stern et al., 1985), who studied maternal responding in mothers of older infants, found individual patterns both in the behavior mothers most frequently used to respond to their infants and in the kind of infant behavior to which they chose most frequently to respond. Kaye (1982) also found individual differences in the behavioral characteristics of mothers' interactions with their infants that persisted over time as well as individual styles in strangers during interactions with different infants that persisted across infants. Thus, mothers do not necessarily respond with similar levels of contingency to different behaviors of their infants; they may be highly vocally contingent to their infants' vocalizations and not highly contingent in their smiling to their infants' smiles or vice versa. Indeed, most of the mothers showed such a pattern. Although one-third the mothers did not have either their vocal or smiling contingency in the top half of the distribution, other modes of contingent responding are possible, for example, tactile responding, which was not measured in the study. Mothers and infants find their own particular modes of exchanging contingency. What is interesting is that the infants were sensitive to the familiar levels of contingency experienced with their mothers in each of the behaviors studied and were most responsive to strangers who demonstrated the familiar levels of contingent smiling and the familiar levels of contingent vocalizations, regardless of what those levels were.

These findings suggest that Watson (1985) was correct in his hypothesis that infants become sensitive to particular levels of contingency in the external world that approximate the levels of contingency most familiar to them. Such sensitivities may influence infants' affiliative and wary behavior toward strangers, although other factors may also be operating, such as the physical resemblance between parents and strangers. Children may more likely show wariness to strangers whose levels of contingent responsiveness to them differ from those of their parents, and they may be more responsive and interactive with others whose levels of contingent responsiveness resemble those of their parents. Because of the variability in parental contingent responsiveness, both who particular infants become wary of and expand their attachments to and the prevalence of their wariness and attachments may be influenced by the contingencies in their early parental interactions. Children whose parents' interactive styles are less common in the population may show more stranger anxiety than other children. Thus, early contingency levels experienced in parental interactions may influence the breadth of infants' social relations.

Infants learn about self and others through their dynamic interactions with others. The imperfect contingency present in their most intimate interactions plays a key role in this learning. Infants as well as parents have some control over their interaction patterns; both infants and parents operate in their interactions to maintain the infants' optimal range of stimulation. Infants avert their gaze to cut out stimulation that has risen above the optimal range and reinstate gaze and positive affect when seeking higher levels of stimulation. Sensitive parents regulate their activity to adjust to the infants' current level of excitement. When in their optimal range of stimulation, infants operate within their zone of proximal development, in which the potential for learning in the social and nonsocial world is at its peak. Because familiar contingency levels are the most engaging for infants, parents' contingency levels may help establish the infants' optimal range of excitement, that is, the range above which stimulation becomes aversive and below which it is uninteresting. Infants' experience with parents as regulators of their stimulation also allows infants to self-regulate their own level of stimulation in the absence of the parents (Stern, 1985). Familiar contingency levels discovered in novel interactions in the social and physical world may be the most arousing and optimally interesting for infants.

The infant behaviors that parents select to respond to are those in which the parents perceive emotion that they, either with or without awareness, wish to reinforce, modify, or share with the infants. Stern (1985) proposed that these emotions will necessarily vary among parents because of the parents' own emotional histories and expectations regarding their infants. Consequently, the range of what parents respond to and what they do not is probably extensive. What is important for infants' sense of self-efficacy is that the presence of contingent responsiveness to them be such that the infants notice the effect of their actions on their parents' behavior. Once such an effect is noticed, infants show evidence of adapting their behavior to maintain it. Experimentally, Cohn and Elmore (1988) had mothers become still faced whenever their 3-month-old infants expressed positive affect. The infants repeatedly engaged their mothers in these bizarre interactions, leading the experimenters to speculate that the potential for infants to learn maladaptive as well as adaptive means of interacting as a function of the contingency pattern presented is high.

In naturally occurring parent–infant interactions, difficulties can develop in parental contingent responsiveness that occur for a wide variety of reasons. There may be disruptions caused by parental illness, grief, or other emotionally distracting circumstances. Although such disruptions may continue for some time, they are most often temporary. The familiar contingency in the parent–child interactions almost inevitably becomes reinstated. Infants are compelling forces for parental attention. Of more concern are difficulties in contingent responsiveness caused by serious parental insensitivities to infant cues, but even these circumstances are not necessarily indicators of damaging outcomes for infants. Clinical followings indicate that many dyads, who have troublesome beginnings, spontaneously resolve their difficulties (Stern, Beebe, Jaffe, & Bennett, 1977). Parents also may have difficulties in establishing contingent responsiveness with their infants because the infants are biologically compromised. But here too the difficulties are typically short term, because the pairs discover adaptive means of responding contingently to each other. Most impressive are reports of how infants with sensory handicaps such as blindness come to develop a sense of self efficacy within their parent–child interactions (Als, Tronick, & Brazelton, 1980; Bigelow, 1995; Fraiberg, 1977; Urwin, 1978). Blind infants have difficulty detecting the attentional focus of others and, therefore, what others are responding to. Their own social reactions are also more difficult for others to detect; there is little facial orienting, and smiles are fleeting. Yet through the efforts and patience of parents who provide sensitive tactile and vocal responses to their infants' actions, blind infants can become vibrantly interactive social partners. Parents and infants are amazingly resilient and ingenious in their ability to establish interaction patterns in which the infants sense their self-efficacy.

Nevertheless, there are concerns over long-term consequences for infants who experience persistent low levels of contingency in their most intimate social interactions. Children of depressed mothers are such a population. Depression is a relatively prevalent disorder, particularly in women with young infants. The reasons for this are complex and may be influenced as much by external factors, such as marital conflict, as by internal factors, such as physical or psychiatric illness (Downey & Coyne, 1990). The children of depressed mothers are a risk group also for complex reasons, one of which may be the parenting style to which they are exposed from an early age. The interaction patterns of depressed mothers and their infants show minimal contingent responsiveness and reduced synchronous behavior. Field (1987) found that although the infants may initially attempt to engage their relatively unresponsive mothers, by 3 months of age, the infants mirror their mothers' depressed activity and affect. When paired with nondepressed social partners, infants of depressed mothers continue to be relatively unresponsive (Field et al., 1988). Interestingly, these infants seem eventually to elicit depressive behavior from their nondepressed social partners. Perhaps such partners adopt lower levels of contingency, either with or without awareness, because it is at these levels that the infants can be most engaged. The infants may be sensitized to low levels of contingency in their maternal interactions, which they generalize to interactions with others regardless of the contingency pattern provided. Thus, the children's experience with low levels of social contingency may be easily perpetuated. Extended experience with minimal contingent responsiveness in social interactions can result in difficulties in the infants' ability to sense their self-efficacy, which in turn, may influence the development of functional impairments in cognitive, social, and emotional realms for which these children are at risk.

CONCLUSIONS

Infants' sensitivity to the imperfection in social contingency is important to their understanding of self and other. Research indicates that infants not only are sensitive to imperfect social contingency early in life, but they also are sensitive to particular levels of imperfect social contingency that correspond to levels found in their most intimate interactions. These findings have implications for the understanding of individual differences in the development of self-efficacy and in subsequent cognitive, social, and emotional development. Children's intimate relationships early in life may set the levels at which infants search for evidence of their effectiveness in the world. Although these levels can expand, particularly as infants enlarge their social networks, the ease with which new relationships are formed may be influenced by the similarity between others' interactive contingencies and the contingencies with which infants are most familiar. Infants whose parents respond to them at low levels of contingency may seek situations, both social and nonsocial, in which low levels of responsivity are present, and thus, they may have difficulty detecting the impact of their actions. Infants with highly contingent parents may seek high contingent responsiveness in others' behavior and in the environment. They may be more sensitive to, and interested in, people who are highly responsive to them, and they may spend more time in activities in the physical environment where their actions have predictable and noticeable consequences. In so doing, they are likely to learn readily about their own effectiveness. Thus, in the beginning of life, as well as throughout our lives, we can learn much about ourselves through our interactions with others.

ACKNOWLEDGMENTS

The research conducted by the author described in this chapter was aided by a grant from the Natural Sciences and Engineering Research Council of Canada. Gratitude is expressed to the infants and parents who participated in the studies, to Donna MacDonald and Barbara K. MacLean, who are coauthors of one of the studies; to Donna MacDonald (again), Jane Proctor, Erin Austen, and Alissa Pencer, who were research assistants; to Bonnie Quinn for her programming assistance; and to Gary Brooks, Tara Callaghan, Kim Chisholm, and Chris Tragakis for their helpful comments on earlier drafts of this chapter.

REFERENCES

Als, H., Tronick, E., & Brazelton, T. B. (1980). Affective reciprocity and the development of autonomy. *Journal of American Academy of Child Psychiatry, 19,* 22–40.

Amsterdam, B. (1972). Mirror self-image reactions before age two. *Developmental Psychobiology, 5,* 297–305.

Bahrick, L. E., & Watson, J. S. (1985). Detection of intermodal proprioceptive-visual contingency as a potential basis of self perception in infancy. *Developmental Psychology, 21*(6), 963–973.

Bell, S. M., & Ainsworth, M. D. S. (1972). Infant crying and maternal responsiveness. *Child Development, 43,* 1171–1190.

Bigelow, A. E. (1981). The correspondence between self and image movement as a cue to self recognition in young children. *Journal of Genetic Psychology, 139,* 11–36.

Bigelow, A. (1995). The effects of blindness on the early development of the self. In P. Rochat (Ed.), *The self in early infancy: Theory and research.* Advances in Psychology Book Series (pp. 327–347). Amsterdam: North Holland-Elsevier.

Bigelow, A. E. (1996). Infants memory for contingently responding persons. *Infant Behavior and Development, 19* (Special ICIS Issue), 334.

Bigelow, A. E. (1998). Infants' sensitivity to familiar imperfect contingencies in social interaction. *Infant Behavior and Development, 21,* 149–162.

Bigelow, A. E., MacLean, B. K., & MacDonald, D. (1996). Infants' response to live and replay interactions with self and mother. *Merrill-Palmer Quarterly, 42*(2), 596–611.

Blehar, M. C., Lieberman, A. F., & Ainsworth, M. D. S. (1977). Early face-to-face interaction and its relation to later mother-infant attachment. *Child Development, 48,* 182–194.

Bower, T. G. R. (1982). *Development in infancy* (2nd ed.). San Francisco: Freeman.

Carter, A. S., Mayes, L. C., & Pajer, K. A. (1990). The role of dyadic affect in play and infant sex in predicting infant response to the still-face situation. *Child Development, 61,* 764–773.

Cohn, J. F., & Elmore, M. (1988). Effect of contingent changes in mothers' affective expression on the organization of behavior in 3-month-old infants. *Infant Behavior and Development, 11,* 493–505.

Dixon, J. C. (1957). Development of self recognition. *Journal of Genetic Psychology, 91,* 251–256.

Downey, G., & Coyne, J. C. (1990). Children of depressed parents: An integrative review. *Psychological Bulletin, 108*(1), 50–76.

Dunham, P., & Dunham, F. (1990). Effects of mother-infant social interactions on infants' subsequent contingency task performance. *Child Development, 61,* 785–793.

Ellsworth, C. P., Muir, D. W., Hains, S. M. J. (1993). Social competence and person-object differentiation: An analysis of the still-face effect. *Developmental Psychology, 29,* 63–73.

Field, T. M. (1979). Differential behavioral and cardiac responses of 3-month-old-infants to a mirror and peer. *Infant Behavior and Development, 2,* 179–184.

Field, T. M. (1981). Infant gaze aversion and heart rate during face-to-face interaction. *Infant Behavior and Development, 4,* 307–315.

Field, T. (1987). Affective and interactive disturbances in infants. In J. D. Osofsky (Ed.), *Handbook of infant development* (2nd ed., pp. 972–1005). New York: Wiley-Interscience.

Field, T. M., Healy, B., Goldstein, S., Perry, S., Bendell, D., Schanberg, S., Zimmerman, E. A., & Kuhn, C. (1988). Infants of depressed mothers show "depressed" behavior even with nondepressed adults. *Child Development, 59,* 1569–1579.

Field, T. M., Yega-Lahr, N., Scafidi, F., & Goldstein, S. (1986). Effects of maternal unavailability on mother–infant interactions. *Infant Behavior and Development, 9,* 473–479.

Fogel, A., Diamond, G. R., Langhorst, B. H., Demos, V. (1982). Effective and cognitive aspects of two-month-old's participation in face-to-face interaction with its mother. In E. Tronick

(Ed.), *Social interchange in infancy: Affect, cognition and communication* (pp. 37–57). Baltimore: University Park Press.

Fraiberg, S. (1977). *Insights from the blind: Comparative studies of blind and sighted infants.* New York: Basic Books.

Gallup, G. G. Jr., & McClure, M. K. (1971). Preference for mirror-image stimulation in differentially reared rhesus monkeys. *Journal of Comparative and Physiological Psychology, 75,* 403–407.

Gergely, G., & Watson, J. (1996). The social biofeedback theory of parental affect-mirroring: The development of emotional self-awareness and self-control in infancy. *International Journal of Psycho-Analysis, 77,* 1181–1212.

Gesell, A., & Ames, L. (1947). The infant's reaction to his mirror image. *Journal of Genetic Psychology, 70,* 141–154.

Gusella, J. L., Muir, D. W., & Tronick, E. Z. (1988). The effect of manipulating maternal behavior during an interaction on 3- and 6-month-olds' affect and attention. *Child Development, 59,* 1111–1124.

Hains, S. M. J., & Muir, D. W. (1996). Effects of stimulus contingency in infant-adult interactions. *Infant Behavior and Development, 19,* 49–61.

Kaye, K. (1982). *The mental and social life of babies: How parents create persons.* Chicago: University of Chicago Press.

Lamb, M. E., & Easterbrooks, M. A. (1981). Individual differences in parental sensitivity: Origins, components, and consequences. In M. E. Lamb & L. R. Sherrod (Eds.), *Infant social cognition: Empirical and theoretical considerations* (pp. 127–153). Hillsdale, NJ: Lawrence Erlbaum Associates.

Lewis, M., & Brooks-Gunn, J. (1979). *Social cognition and the acquisition of self.* New York: Plenum.

Mandler, J. M. (1992). How to build a baby: II. Conceptual primitives. *Psychological Review, 99,* 587–604.

Mayes, L. C., & Carter, A. S. (1990). Emerging social regulatory capacities as seen in the still-face situation. *Child Development, 61,* 754–763.

Meltzoff, A. N. (1990). Foundations for developing a concept of self: The role of imitation in relating self to other, and the value of social mirroring, social modeling, and self-practice in infancy. In D. Cicchetti & M. Beeghley (Eds.), *The self in transition: Infancy to childhood* (pp. 139–164). Chicago: University of Chicago Press.

Meltzoff, A. N., & Moore, M. K. (1977). Imitation of facial and manual gestures by human neonates. *Science, 198,* 75–78.

Meltzoff, A. N., & Moore, M. K. (1983). Newborn infants imitate adult facial gestures. *Child Development, 54,* 702–709.

Meltzoff, A. N., & Moore, M. K. (1989). Imitation in newborn infants: Exploring the range of gestures imitated and the underlying mechanisms. *Developmental Psychology, 25,* 954–962.

Meltzoff, A. N., & Moore, M. K. (1994). Imitation, memory, and the representation of persons. *Infant Behavior and Development, 17,* 83–99.

Muir, D. W., & Hains, S. M. J. (1993). Infant sensitivity to perturbations in adult facial, vocal, tactile, and contingent stimulation during face-to-face interactions. In B. de Boysson-Bardies, S. de Schoenen, P. Jusczyk, P. McNeilage, & J. Morton, (Eds.), *Developmental neurocognition: Speech and face processing in the first year of life* (pp. 171–185). Netherlands: Kluwer.

Muir, D., Hains, S., Cao, Y., & D'Entremont, B. (1996). Three-to six-month olds' sensitivity to adult intentionality: The role of adult contingency and eye direction in dyadic interactions. *Infant Behavior and Development, 19* (Special ICIS Issue), 200.

Murray, L., & Trevarthen, C. (1985). Emotional regulation of interactions between two-month-olds and their mothers. In T. M. Field & N. A. Fox (Eds.), *Social perception in infants* (pp. 177–197). Norwood, NJ: Ablex.

Neisser, U. (1988). Five kinds of self-knowledge. *Philosophical Psychology, 1,* 35–59.

Neisser, U. (1991). Two perceptually given aspects of the self and their development. *Developmental Review, 11,* 197–209.

Neisser, U. (1993). The self perceived. In U. Neisser (Ed.), *The perceived self: Ecological and interpersonal sources of self-knowledge* (pp. 3–21). Cambridge, England: Cambridge University Press.

Papousek, H., & Papousek, M. (1974). Mirror-image and self-recognition in young human infants: I. A new method of experimental analysis. *Developmental Psychobiology, 7,* 149–157.

Piaget, J. (1963). *The origins of intelligence in children.* New York: W. W. Norton.

Rochat, P. (1995). Early objectification of the self. In P. Rochat (Ed.), *The self in early infancy: Theory and research.* Advances in Psychology Book Series (pp. 53–71). Amsterdam: North Holland-Elsevier.

Rochat, P., & Morgan, R. (1995). The function and determinants of early self exploration. In P. Rochat (Ed.), *The self in early infancy: Theory and research.* Advances in Psychology Book Series (pp. 395–415). Amsterdam: North Holland-Elsevier.

Rochat, P., Neisser, U., & Marian, V. (1998). Are young infants sensitive to interpersonal contingency? *Infant Behavior and Development, 21,* 355–366.

Schulman, A., & Kaplowitz, C. (1977). Mirror-image response during the first two years of life. *Developmental Psychobiology, 10,* 133–142.

Stern, D. N. (1985). *The interpersonal world of the infant: A view from psychoanalysis and developmental psychology.* New York: Basic Books.

Stern, D. N., Beebe, B., Jaffe, J., & Bennett, S. L. (1977). The infant's stimulus world during social interaction: A study of caregiver behaviors with particular reference to repetition and timing. In H. R. Schaffer (Ed.), *Studies in mother–infant interaction* (pp. 177–202). London: Academic Press.

Stern, D. N., Hofer, L., Haft, W., & Dore, J. (1985). Affect attunement: The sharing of feeling states between mother and infant by means of intermodal fluency. In T. M. Field & N. A. Fox (Eds.), *Social perception in infants* (pp. 249–268). Norwood, NJ: Ablex.

Stoller, S. A., & Field, T. (1982). Alternation of mother and infant behaviors and heart rate during a still-face perturbation of face-to-face interaction. In T. Field & A. Fogel (Eds.), *Emotion and early interactions* (pp. 57–82). Hillsdale, NJ: Lawrence Erlbaum Associates.

Trevarthen, C. (1979). Communication and cooperation in early infancy: A description of primary intersubjectivity. In M. Bullowa (Ed.), *Before speech: The beginning of interpersonal communication* (pp. 321–347). Cambridge, England: Cambridge University Press.

Tronick, E., Als, H., Adamson, L., Wise, S., & Brazelton, T. B. (1978). The infant's response to entrapment between contradictory messages in face-to-face interaction. *Journal of American Academy of Child Psychiatry, 17,* 1–13.

Urwin, C. (1978). The development of communication between blind infants and their parents. In A. Lock (Ed.), *Action, gesture, and symbol: The emergence of language* (pp. 79–108). New York: Academic Press.

Watson, J. S. (1979). Perception of contingency as a determinant of social responsiveness. In E. B. Thoman (Ed.), *Origins of the infant's social responsiveness* (pp. 33–64). Hillsdale, NJ: Lawrence Erlbaum Associates.

Watson, J. S. (1985). Contingency perception in early social development. In T. M. Field & N. A. Fox (Eds.), *Social perception in infants* (pp. 157–176). Norwood, NJ: Albex.

Chapter 7

Young Infants' Perception of Adult Intentionality: Adult Contingency and Eye Direction

Darwin Muir
Sylvia Hains
Queen's University

Behavioral contingency is a central construct in many theories of early development (e.g., Lewis & Goldberg, 1969; Schaffer, 1984; Symons & Moran, 1994). For example, Spelke, Phillips, and Woodward (1995) suggest that contingency (humans reacting to one another), reciprocity (humans responding in kind to one another's actions), and communication (humans supplying one another with information) are important to young infants. Dunham, Dunham, Hurshman, and Alexander (1989) point out that in most theories of infant development, contingent adult responsiveness is considered to have positive effects on the infant. Noncontingent stimulation is considered to have negative consequences by reducing the infant's motivation to participate in contingency relationships and impairing the infant's ability to detect contingent relationships.

Recently, Baron-Cohen (1994) proposed a model of the development of the child's theory of mind that emphasizes the importance of both adult contingent stimulation and eye contact (see Fig. 7.1). He postulates the existence of two primitive, possibly inborn, mechanisms: an intentionality detector (ID), which interprets stimuli as being volitional, and an eye direction detector (EDD), which detects another person's deflection of eye gaze relative to the self or to another object. The operation of these two mechanisms leads to the development of a shared attention mechanism (SAM), which emerges around 9 to 12 months of age. SAM permits an infant to infer another person's attitude about a third object—the object of their joint attention. Finally, the theory of mind mechanism (ToMM)

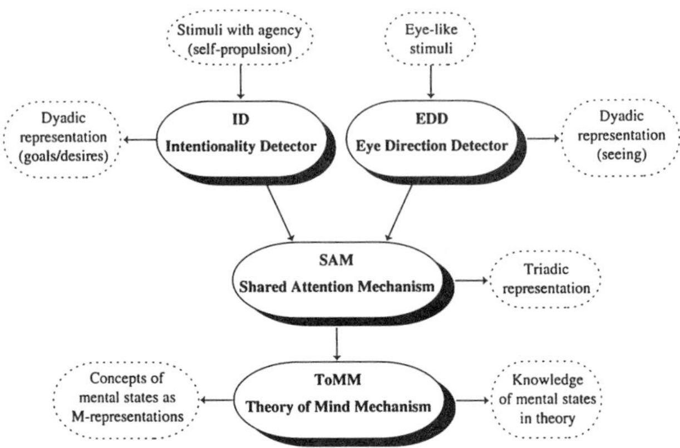

FIG. 7.1. A modified version of Baron-Cohen's (1994) model of the four cognitive mechanisms that make up the human "mind-reading" system (see text for details).

begins to operate around 1.5 to 2 years of age, when children begin to characterize mental state concepts in other people, using eye direction information to make inferences about another person's thoughts, desires, and goals. Baron-Cohen's core concept is the ID, which infants use to "read mental states of goal and desire into a wide range of stimuli" (p. 517) having inherent direction or self-propulsion. This ID builds dyadic representations of person–person relationships, which are bidirectional, contrasting with self–object relationships, which are unidirectional. This conceptualization seems to reflect the difference between infant's engagement with people and objects, but Baron-Cohen presented little evidence to support his case for the operation of the ID or EDD early in infancy. The research he reviewed mainly involved infants' response to static, noncontingent faces (e.g., pictures). However, Muir, Hains, & Symons (1994) noted that SAM and ToMM are purely social attributes and argued that Baron-Cohen (1994) needed to take into account the results from contingent interaction studies, such as those reviewed in this chapter, to determine when his various mechanisms begin to operate.

Given the purported importance of contingent stimulation, the adult behaviors that cue infants to regulate their social behavior during face-to-face interactions need to be identified. In this chapter, after reviewing our earlier work on these cues, we focus on young infants' sensitivity to adult contingency (representing Baron-Cohen's ID), breaks in adult eye contact (an aspect of Baron-Cohen's EDD), and the influence of the adult's direction of gaze on the infant's attention—referred to as joint attention (an aspect of Baron-Cohen's SAM).

Our first series of studies performed in the 1980s relates primarily to Baron-Cohen's ID. It is clear that infants rapidly learn to expect that their behavior has consequences, and when the rules change they become upset. For example, Blass, Ganchrow, and Steiner (1984) illustrated newborn sensitivity to contingent stimulation using a modified classical conditioning procedure. They established the neonates' expectancy for food by preceding its delivery to one side of the mouth with a stroke on their foreheads. Infants began to anticipate the reward by turning and making sucking responses when they were touched, demonstrating associative learning. Moreover, almost all infants cried when the food reward was withheld during extinction—their response to a violation of expectancy. Whereas crying is easy to generate during the first few weeks of life, other reciprocal responses are not. For example, social smiling, defined as selective smiling generated by the social behavior of people over other forms of stimulation, does not begin until the second month of life (e.g., Wolff, 1987).

Our own research derived originally from social expectancy theory (e.g., Lewis & Goldberg, 1969; Stern, 1977; Trevarthen, 1974; Tronick, 1989) and was based on the still-face effect that was first described by Tronick, Als, Adamson, Wise, and Brazelton (1978). Tronick et al. had mothers present a frozen neutral expression to their 3-month-olds for 2 minutes interposed between two periods of normal face-to-face interactions that included the mothers making eye contact, smiling, vocalizing, and touching their infants. The infants' reaction was striking; their level of visual fixation and smiling directed toward their mothers during the first normal period declined dramatically during the still-face period and recovered in the third normal period. Based on this and similar work, Tronick (1989) proposed that both adult and infant are active partners in face-to-face interactions; during the still-face period, infants were responding to a violation of their expectation of reciprocal positive maternal behavior.

In our work, beginning with Gusella, Muir, and Tronick (1988), we stressed the importance of two procedural aspects that have since been highlighted by Spelke et al. (1995): the experimental context and the use of multiple response measures. The context is the infant's version of experimental instructions and thus must be skillfully manipulated by the experimenter. Contextual factors, including preliminary interactions among the infant, the caretakers, and experimenters, are critical to activate the social response system of infants. The setting provides the scaffolding necessary to engage maximum infant performance. Toward that end, we usually begin our experiments on infant social perception by having the adult engage in a natural, contingent, face-to-face interaction for 1 to 2 minutes before manipulating some aspect of her behavior (hereafter referred to as the ABA design). If the infants' behavior changes, we have identified a cue used by infants to regulate their social behavior. We also follow the perturbation period by a final period of normal interaction to examine possible aftereffects of the manipulation and to "debrief" the infants. In this ABA design, infants serve as their own control, but young infants tire or become bored rather quickly. For this reason we also include a comparison (control) group of infants who have a normal interaction with the adult for the same length of time, allowing us to tease apart the effects of time and the perturbation in the adult's behavior.

A second critical point is the use of multiple response measures. Traditional studies of infant social perception used visual preference or habituation procedures, which relied on visual fixation measures. Although infant attention is an important aspect of their social response system, their interest in a display can reflect the operation of either cognitive or social processes. In fact, infant social responses are much more complex and include affective displays, vocalizations, and body movements. For example, infants may remain interested in a novel object but not smile at it; indeed, even adults find it hard to analyze a visual display and smile at the same time. The appreciation of adult intentionality may be indicated by a number of infant responses, but we will focus primarily on the duration of infant visual fixation and smiling in the studies reported here, since these can be defined easily and require no value judgments on the part of the coder.

CUES USED BY THE INFANT

The observation that adults are able to engage infants in dyadic interactions and that infants reduce or stop smiling when the adult's behavior violates their expectancies may reflect the infants' ability to infer adult intentionality. However, because the still-face involves the cessation of all contingent behaviors, it does not allow us to isolate possible cues used by infants to regulate their behavior. As well as the obvious shift from dynamic to static stimulation in the still-face period, there are also changes in adult behavior, such as the interruption of touch, facial and vocal expression, and contingency. The results of several studies conducted in our laboratory to find possible cues used by the infant are summarized in Fig. 7.2. An example of the still-face effect is shown at *a* in the top and bottom panels. The top panel of the figure gives (in percentage of total time per period) the duration of gaze, and the bottom panel gives the duration of smiling at the adult for the first two normal periods (control) compared with that of a normal period followed by a still-face period. Clearly, the still-face procedure produces a substantially greater drop in both infant gaze and smiling, relative to controls.

1. *Maternal touch.* In the traditional still-face procedure, mothers are allowed to touch their infants during the normal periods but must desist

Live Face-to-Face Interaction

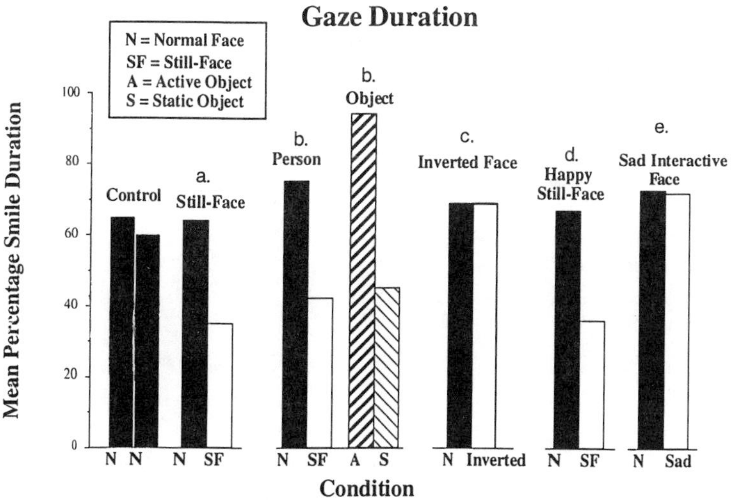

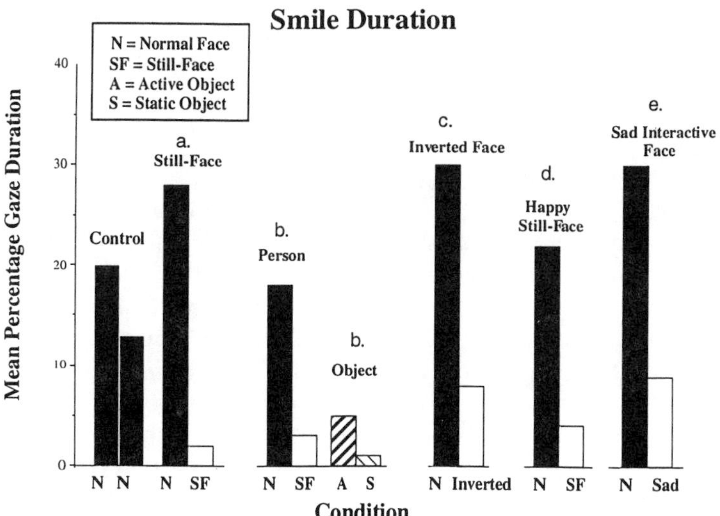

FIG. 7.2. A composite figure comparing gaze (top graph) and smile (bottom graph) duration recorded during normal periods of face-to-face (no touch) interaction with 5- to 6-month-olds (all black bars) with the same behavior recorded during various perturbations in adult behavior (all white bars), including (a and b—person) still-face, (c) inverted face, (d) happy still-face, and (e) sad interactive face. The (b) condition also compares the still-face response to a person (b—person) with that to an interactive and static object (b—object, hatched bars). The object was a nonhuman looking hand puppet that an adult moved in time with a melodic synthesized sound contingent on the infant's interactive behavior during the active condition.

during the still-face period. The role of touch was addressed first by Gusella et al. (1988), who had mothers interact either with or without touching their infants during the normal interaction periods in the still-face procedure. They reported that 6-month-olds showed a strong still-face effect regardless of whether maternal touch was present or absent but for 3-month-olds, a stronger still-face effect was generated when maternal touch was included. In subsequent studies, we found that adult touch was not necessary to elicit a still-face response from 3-month-olds (see Ellsworth, Muir, & Hains, 1993). However, it should be noted that touch can contribute to the modulation of the still-face effect for young infants (see Stack & Muir, 1990, 1992).

2. *Dynamic people versus objects.* We verified that the infant's behavior in the SF paradigm is a social response to changes in the behavior of a person rather than a response to variations in any type of contingent, dynamic, auditory–visual stimulation by comparing infants' responses to mothers, strangers, and nonhuman looking hand puppets. Infant responses to people and objects had been compared previously (e.g., Brazelton, Koslowski, & Main, 1974; Klin & Jennings, 1979; Legerstee, Pomerleau, Malcuit, & Feider, 1987) but the behavior of the two types of stimuli had not been equated, thus making the results difficult to interpret. Ellsworth, Muir, and Hains (1993) used an object which approximated the adult's social stimulation in terms of auditory and visual properties, movement, and contingency and distance. They constructed a hand puppet with abstract internal features that could be moved in various directions, accompanied by synthesized tones, contingent on the infant's behavior. The interactive puppet replaced the person's facial and vocal stimulation during the Normal periods in the SF paradigm. During the SF period, the puppet was silent and stationary. Each of Ellsworth et al.'s infants (3- and 6-month-olds) went through the SF procedure twice, once with the person and once with the object. The results are summarized in Fig. 7.2 (columns labeled *b*). Infants looked slightly longer at the novel object (puppet) than the person during the interaction periods, and about the same amount of time when the object and person were static. By contrast, substantial smiling was directed toward the interacting person, but was almost nonexistent in the presence of the interacting object and during the static periods for both the person and object; clearly in a social context infants differentiate between people and objects by 3 months of age. Also, it should be noted that despite a lack of adult touch during normal periods, an equally strong still-face effect was obtained for 3- and 6-month-olds, and no mother-stranger differences were found; thus, both of these variables were collapsed in Fig. 7.2 (columns labeled *b*). These latter findings allowed us to use practiced strangers in studies requiring more difficult perturbations in adult behavior and to eliminate touch from the procedure.

3. *Facial expression.* The contribution of the adult's facial expression to the regulation of the infant's behavior was examined in two ways. First, we inverted the adult's face while maintaining all other aspects of the interaction to see if infants, like adults (e.g., Thompson, 1980), would have difficulty responding to the adult's emotional expressions in an inverted face. Watson, Hayes, Vietze, and Becker (1979) had already reported that 3-month-olds but not 2- or 5-month-olds smiled more to upright than inverted faces. However, they used a complex, within-subject design in which infants were exposed to several different brief displays including stationary and dynamic (*noncontingent*) talking and silent mothers' and strangers' faces. This design may have contributed to the relatively small effect of face orientation and inconsistent age effects they found. In a series of experiments, Muir and Rach-Longman (1989) had mothers and strangers interact with 3- and 6-month-olds with their face upright and inverted. A summary of Rach-Longman's results are given in Fig. 7.2; at all ages, infants invariably looked at the upright and inverted faces for about the same amount of time (*c* column, upper panel) but almost never smiled (Fig. 7.2, *c* column, lower panel) when the adult's face was inverted. This large inversion effect on infant smiling and the failure to replicate Watson's age differences may be due to procedural differences, in particular our use of a contingent interaction procedure.

A second set of experiments was designed to test infant sensitivity to adult facial expressions directly. In previous still-face studies, the adult posed a neutral still-face expression, confounding the change in emotional facial expression with other factors. D'Entremont (1995; D'Entremont & Muir, 1997) separated these two factors using the ABA design described earlier by having a stranger display either a happy, sad, or neutral expression during the still-face period (B). D'Entremont obtained a large still-face effect for each facial expression (the three expressions are collapsed in Fig. 7.2; see *d* columns) for gaze and smile duration. However, the infants smiled slightly but reliably more to the smiling still-face (6%) than to either the neutral or sad still-faces (2% to 3%). Thus, although a static smiling face can elicit a few smiles from infants, contingent interactions appear to be necessary to elicit sustained infant social behavior. Next, D'Entremont used the ABA design but this time the adult stranger continued to interact contingently during B while displaying either happy or sad facial and vocal expressions. During B, infants were equally attentive to both happy and sad emotional displays, but their smiling dropped substantially (by about 50%, compared to controls) when the adult expressed sadness (see Fig. 7.2, *e* columns).

4. *Vocal expressions.* Gusella and Muir (1985; Gusella et al., 1988) developed a TV interaction procedure in an attempt to isolate the role of the adult's voice in the regulation of infant smiling and visual attention

(Note: Murray & Trevarthen, 1985, developed a similar TV-interaction procedure to test contingency—see further on). They had mothers and infants engage in face-to-face interactions while viewing each other on TV monitors as illustrated in Fig. 7.3. Using the standard ABA design, they replicated the still-face effect obtained during live interactions, as shown in Fig. 7.4 (*a* columns). They then replaced the traditional still-face with the mother's interactive face (she continued to interact with her infant) but eliminated the voice by turning off the sound on the TV monitor (no voice, contingent face condition). In the third condition, they presented a prerecording of the mother's still-face while she continued to talk to the infant during the still-face period (still-face, contingent voice condition). As shown in Fig. 7.4 (*c* columns), when the voice was eliminated from the interaction, the decline in infant visual attention and smiling was similar to that of no-change controls shown in the figure. By contrast, when the mother's voice remained contingent but she was still-faced (*b* columns), infants performed like the still-face group (*a* columns). Thus, loss of adult vocal stimulation is not responsible for the still-face effect.

In a number of studies, we found that live and TV-interaction procedures can be used relatively interchangeably to study various phenomena. For example, Roman (1986) and Muir and Rach-Longman (1989) also used Gusella and Muir's (1985) TV-interaction procedure to demonstrate a strong inverted-face effect (see Fig. 7.4, *d* columns), similar to that produced by live interactions, described previously. However, it should be noted that when TV and live interactions were compared directly both Rach-Longman (1988) and Hains and Muir (1996a; see Fig. 7.7, this chapter) found that infants clearly differentiated between the two procedures. They smiled less during TV than during live interactions.

CONTINGENCY DURING MOTHER–INFANT INTERACTIONS

The final aspect of the still-face effect to be examined was the role of maternal contingency during face-to-face interactions. Given the imputed effects of noncontingency, we expected that the infants would show fewer positive responses during noncontingent maternal behavior. Gusella (1986, reported in Hains & Muir, 1996a) examined this by having mothers interact with their 5-month-olds in the TV-interaction procedure, using the ABA design. This time the still-face period was replaced by a replay of the mothers' contingent behavior recorded during the first period. To our dismay, not only did the infants not respond negatively to her noncontingency in the replay period—they did not even seem to notice! When the

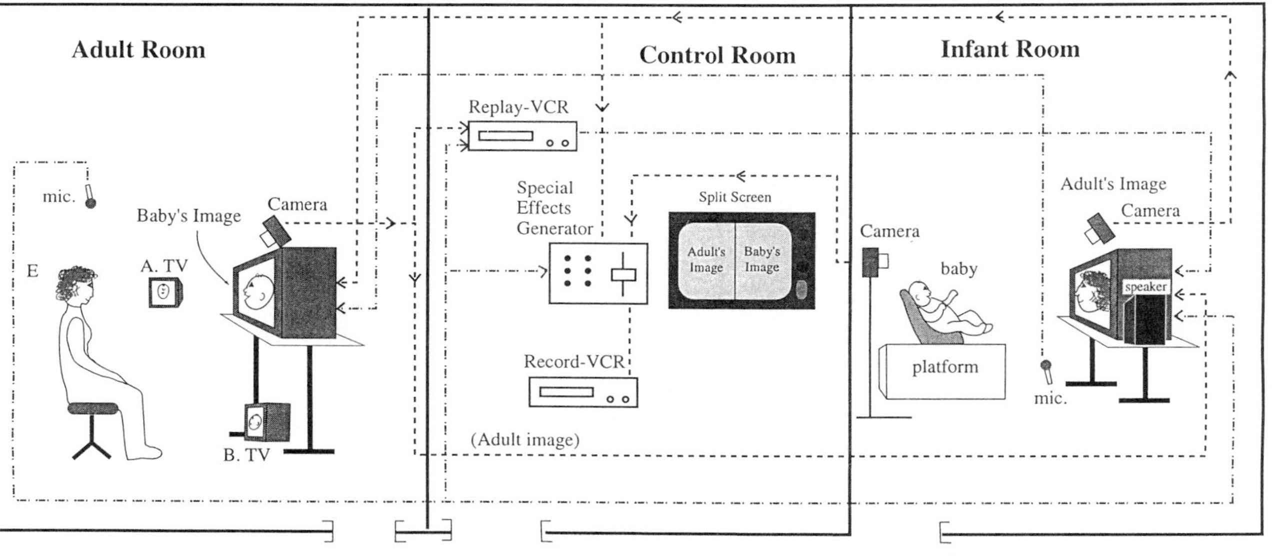

FIG. 7.3. A schematic design of the TV-interaction apparatus described in Gusella et al. (1988). It should be noted that the camera in the adult's room, recording the adult's behavior, was placed on top of the TV monitor (which displayed the infant's behavior) at a distance of 2 meters from the adult. This minimized the vertical displacement of the adult's eyes from straight ahead on the infant's TV monitor. In fact, Hains and Symons (reported in Hains & Muir, 1996b) found that from the infant's perspective, the adult was seen as making eye contact when she looked at the infant's face in the center of the TV monitor; when she looked at the camera she was seen to be looking up. The images from the infant camera and from the camera in the infant room focused on the TV monitor displaying the adult's face were fed to a split-screen generator and recorded for later behavioral analysis. Finally, in the Adult Room at A is the TV monitor that the adult looked at to avert her eyes to the left or right (not shown) by 40 degrees during the eye direction studies. B is the position of the monitor for eyes down.

TV Interaction

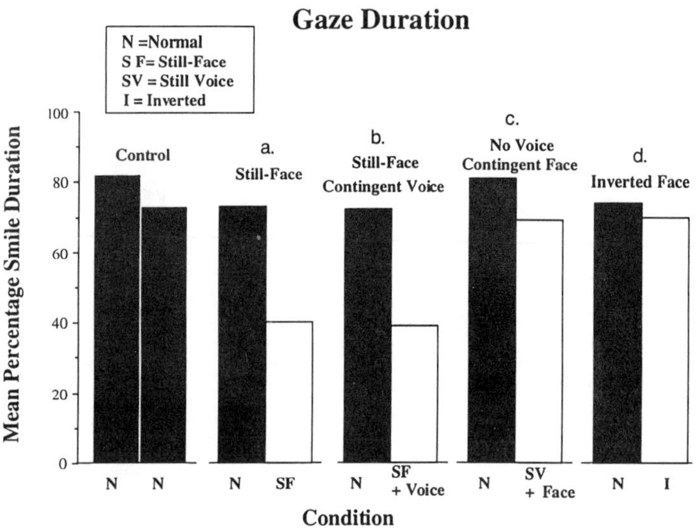

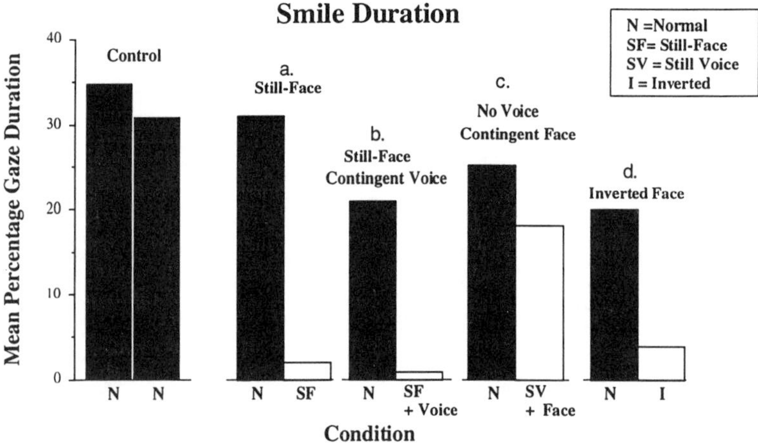

FIG. 7.4. A composite figure comparing the visual attention (top panel) and smiling (bottom panel) recorded during normal periods of televised face-to-face interactions between adults and 5- to 6-month-olds (all black bars) with the same behavior recorded when the infants were presented with various perturbations in adult behavior (all white bars) including (a) still-face, (b) still-face with contingent voice, (c) no voice with contingent face, and (d) inverted face.

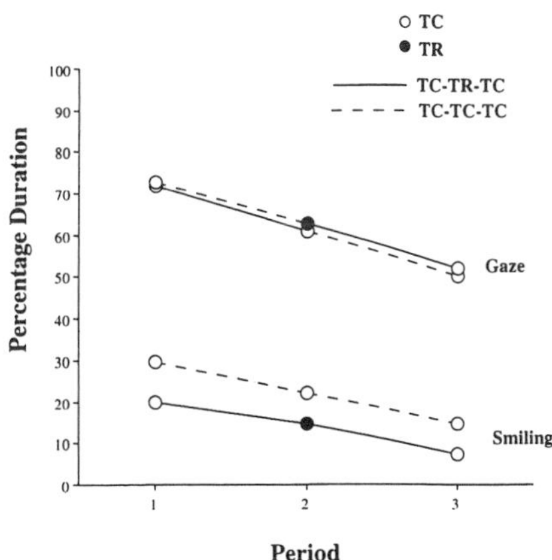

FIG. 7.5. Percentage of 5-month-olds' gazing and smiling at their mothers during TV-contingent (TC) interactions and TV replays of the preceding period (TR) as a function of period from Hains and Muir (1996a, Fig. 1). The TC-TC-TC is the control group. (Reprinted with permission from Ablex Publishing Corporation.)

instant replay group was compared with a control group who interacted contingently over TV for three periods, the two sets of data appeared to be interchangeable, as shown in Fig. 7.5. After an initial period of interacting—looking and smiling at the mothers—the infants usually found other things (mostly their feet) more interesting and only looked up at mothers now and again as if to check that they were still there. These brief looks were usually accompanied by a smile that became less frequent with time. Our suspicion that infants may not distinguish between contingent and noncontingent interactions of this sort was reinforced by Mann (1986, reported in Hains & Muir, 1996a), who replicated Gusella's (1986) results.

Murray and Trevarthen (1985) used a similar TV interaction and instant replay procedure to manipulate maternal contingency with four infants ranging in age from 6 to 12 weeks. These young infants displayed diminished positive affect and increased distress, including frowning and grimacing during the replay period, compared to the preceding contingent TV-interaction period. Unfortunately, Murray and Trevarthen did not include a control group or a third, normal interaction in their study, so their results might have been caused by the increase in fussiness we have observed over time (Gusella et al., 1988), especially given their observations that TV interactions were not as effective at engaging their young infants in positive interactions as live ones (i.e., smiling only occurred 5% of the time during TV interactions versus 32% of the time during live interactions).

CONTINGENCY IN REINFORCEMENT PROCEDURES

Despite the failure to find an effect of noncontingency in our experiments, it is clear that adult noncontingency during face-to-face interactions can have a negative impact on infant behavior. For example, in their seminal paper, Dunham et al. (1989) demonstrated that a stranger's lack of contingent social stimulation of 3-month-olds disrupted their performance on a subsequent visual habituation task. First, they had a female experimenter stand at the base of a crib for 6 minutes and maintain eye contact with the supine infant. In the contingent group, each time the infants vocalized, they were socially reinforced by the experimenter, who briefly smiled, touched the infant, and said "Hi (baby's name)." In the noncontingent group, the experimenter's social stimulation was independent of the infants responses; they received the same adult social stimulation pattern as was given to a previously tested infant in the contingent group (yoked control). Next, infants were tested in an infant-controlled visual habituation task. A trial began each time the infant looked at a steady orange target light, which began to pulse in synchrony with a tone during infant fixation. When the infant looked away, the light became steady again until the infant re-fixated on it, starting the next trial. Over 10 trials, the contingent group showed the usual pattern of an initial increased interest in the light–tone display, followed by a reliable decline in fixation of the target. The noncontingent group showed much less initial interest in the stimulus and a slow decline on subsequent trials; they also showed greater inter fixation times (gaze aversion) relative to the contingent group.

Studies based on Dunham and colleagues' (1989) work were conducted in our laboratory by Sapp, Stevens, Muir, and Hains (1993). They followed Dunham's general procedure, with some modifications. In the first study, they tested older infants (4- to 6-month-olds) who were assigned to either 5 minutes of contingent or noncontingent stimulation. The social reinforcement was the same as Dunham and colleagues', but in an attempt to closer approximate a normal social interaction between adults and infants, Sapp et al. reinforced any positive infant social signal, such as smiles, vocalizations, body movements, and initiation of eye contacts. The adult wore a Sony Walkman so that during the noncontingent period, she could present a social reinforcement each time she heard a beep on the prerecorded tape that indicated when another infant had received contingent stimulation. The habituation stimulus was similar to Dunham's; it was either a red light plus high tone or a yellow light plus low tone, pulsed at 200 msec on and 200 msec off during infant fixations. Each trial ended when the infant looked away; the target light stopped pulsing and sounding until the infant looked back at it, thus initiating the next trial.

As summarized in Fig. 7.6 (Sapp's data), no group differences in duration of gaze and positive vocalizations were found, but infants tended to smile more during the contingent stimulation, and there were significantly more negative vocalizations by infants receiving noncontingent stimulation. Also, Sapp et al. found no differences in visual fixation during habituation, but the noncontingent infants had longer look-away times (gaze aversion)

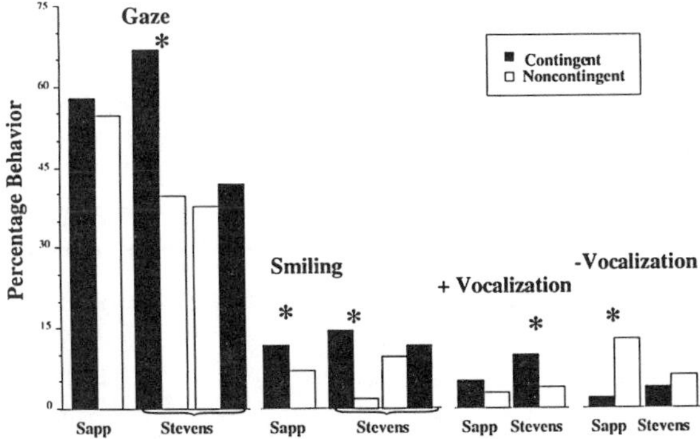

FIG. 7.6. Percentage of infant gaze, smiling, positive vocalization, and negative vocalization displayed by 5-month-olds in contingent (filled bars) and noncontingent (open bars) conditions in studies by Sapp (1993) and Stevens (1991). Note that Sapp used a between-groups (contingent versus noncontingent social stimulation groups) design, whereas Stevens used a mixed design, with one group receiving contingent stimulation first and noncontingent stimulation second and the other group the opposite order. Stevens's gaze and smiling data are shown for each group separately to illustrate the order by condition interaction—the noncontingency effect was larger when the stranger responded contingently in the first period (see text for details). * = significant differences between pairs.

between successive fixations of the visual target (6.8 sec. vs. 3.0 sec., respectively), partially replicating Dunham et al. (1989).

In a second experiment Sapp et al. (1993) presented each infant with two 3-minute periods of the same types of social stimulation, but this time the social stimulation was contingent in Period 1 and noncontingent (yoked) in Period 2, or vice versa. The two experimental groups were compared with a control group, which received contingent adult social stimulation in both periods. The social stimulation was followed by the infant-controlled habituation task (although this time the stimulus was a red target light flashing in synchrony with a 5-tone scale beginning on middle C). When the infants' behavior during the two periods was examined, there were contingency effects for gaze and positive affect and an order effect. As shown in Fig. 7.6 (Steven's, 1991, data), infants who received *contingent stimulation* first showed a significant decline in gaze during the noncontingent stimulation period (67% declined to 42%), whereas those receiving *noncontingent stimulation* first maintained a lower level of fixation during both periods (about 40%). A similar effect was found for smiling; infants who received contingent social stimulation first smiled 15 percent during Period 1 and only 1.5 percent of the time during the second, noncontingent period. By contrast infants receiving noncontingent stimulation first smiled about 10 percent of the time during both periods. The analysis of a positive behavior summary score (the total proportion of infant gazing, smiling, vocalizing, and moving) revealed that infants spent proportionately more time engaged in positive social behaviors ($M = .23\%$ vs. $M = .17\%$) during contingent than noncontingent periods. Finally, there were no differences in crying and grimacing between conditions.

The habituation results did not match those of Dunham et al. or the first experiment—none of the groups habituated to the abstract sound–light stimulus over the 10 trials, but there was a significant group difference. Infants receiving noncontingent stimulation first displayed much longer average fixation times per habituation trial ($M = 17$ sec) than either the control group or the infants receiving contingent stimulation in the first period (combined $M = 6$ sec). It appears that these infants were sensitive to the adult's contingent stimulation when they were introduced to it during the first period and continued to play an interactive game with the sound–light stimulus, turning it on and off with either their eye or head movements. The infants receiving noncontingent social stimulation in the first period appeared to be "turned off" to future social behavior by the adult. They also appeared to treat the subsequent, contingent sound–light stimulation as an interesting task and failed to participate in the "turn-on, turn-off" contingency game played by the other two groups or to show a typical habituation function. Procedural differences (e.g., age differences, contingent reinforcement rules, order effects) may have contributed to the failure to obtain the same results in the three studies. However, when it had an effect, the noncontingent social stimulation by adult strangers led consistently to a reduction in infant social behavior which, in turn, had a significant impact on subsequent cognitive processing.

CONTINGENCY DURING STRANGER–INFANT INTERACTIONS

Following Sapp and colleagues' demonstration that the lack of contingency on the part of the adult has a fairly long lasting effect on later behavior, Hains and Muir (1996a) reexamined the contingency effect using our TV-interaction procedure. Tronick, Als, and Brazelton (1980) and others (e.g., Kaye & Fogel, 1980) suggested that repeated interactions with the mother may result in an infant's becoming entrained on her behavior. This familiarity may lead the infant to expect a particular content and style of maternal interactive behavior that is the same during both normal and replay periods. On this basis, we reasoned that our 5-month-olds may not have shown any noncontingency effect because their mothers' behavior was highly familiar to them (shown by their relatively rapid loss of interest in her during the TV interaction). Murray and Trevarthen's (1985) young infants would just be learning about their mothers' behavior, and the unexpected noncontingent maternal behavior may have led to their distress. We speculated that we might be able to replicate Murray and Trevarthen's findings with older infants by using a stranger to whom they have not become entrained.

Given that Murray and Trevarthen did not assess the infants' response during a recovery period following their replay, other factors could have influenced the infants' behavior, such as either fatigue or memory or both. Such young infants may have become tired or have developed a memory trace of the previous interaction and responded to the repetition with disinterest (habituation). We decided to eliminate memory as a factor in the effect of noncontingency by presenting the noncontingent adult first, which required us to abandon our usual ABA procedure in favor of a quasi-factorial design. We presented TV-contingent, TV-replay, and live (face-to-face) conditions in different orders to four groups of infants (see Fig. 7.7 for presentation order). When the TV replay was presented in Period 1 or 2, it was a recording of the same adult interacting with a different infant. When the TV replay was presented in the third period, it was a replay of the adult's behavior during a preceding TV-contingent interaction period. These different conditions and orders allowed us to interpret possible effects of noncontingency more easily. Fatigue could be ruled out as a factor for the group receiving the noncontingent stimulation in Period 1, and stimulus repetition (habituation) could be ruled out as

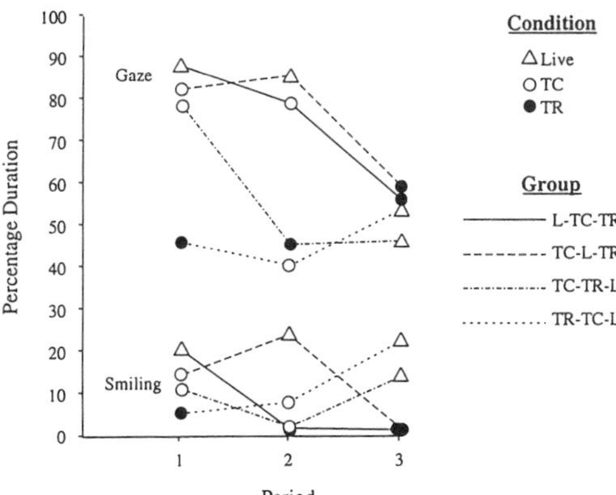

FIG. 7.7. Percentage of 4- to 6-month-olds' gaze and smiling at a stranger during three conditions of face-to-face interaction as a function of period from Hains and Muir (1996a, Fig. 3). The open symbols indicate the stranger interacted contingently, with circles representing TV and triangles representing live interactions. The filled circles indicate noncontingent TV-replay social stimulation. Each group (order) is identified by different connecting lines. (Reprinted with permission from Ablex Publishing Corporation.)

a factor if the same replay effect was obtained in all periods. Also, the equivalence of the live and TV-contingent displays could be examined as both a within- and a between-subject effect to examine possible differences between live and TV procedures.

We thought that this study would be of theoretical value: There should be no difference in the infant's smiling during the three periods if the adult's behavior is merely acting as a social releaser of infant behavior (see Caron, Caron, Mustelin, & Roberts, 1992; Meltzoff, 1981), because the quantity of adult smiling and vocalizing would be comparable in all conditions (i.e., contingency should be irrelevant). However, Gibson (1979) predicted that infants distinguish between two- and three-dimensional stimuli at an early age; thus, infants should be more responsive to the live adult but not necessarily more attentive. The expectancy model, on the other hand, suggested that the infants' behavior in subsequent periods should depend on the type of interaction they experienced earlier. Their behavior should become less positive during a noncontingent period that follows a contingent one; when a noncontingent period comes first, infants may become predisposed to simply ignore the adult during a subsequent contingent period, and their looking and smiling may remain depressed. Hence, evidence of both condition and order effects are necessary to support the expectancy model and to eliminate a social releaser as the controlling factor in infant–adult interaction.

The results shown in Fig. 7.7 appears to be complicated because of order effects; but, actually, they are simple and conform with the predictions of the expectancy hypothesis. First, infants smiled more during live-contingent interactions than during any other condition; and, smiling, but not attention, was reduced in all subsequent TV periods. Second, TV-contingent was preferred over TV-noncontingent stimulation; the infants looked and usually smiled more to the TV-contingent than the TV-noncontingent adult. The only exception was when the TV-contingent followed a live interaction. In this case, smiling dropped considerably (to $M = 3\%$). Last, once noncontingent stimulation was experienced, infant visual attention was reduced during subsequent contingent periods. Infant smiling, on the other hand, was very low during the TV-replay periods, but the infants smiled again during subsequent periods to both the live and televised-contingent adult.

The results of this study showed clearly that infants do not like noncontingent social stimulation from a stranger. That is not to say that they showed the upset described by Murray and Trevarthen (1985); in fact the infants who interacted with the noncontingent adult in Period 1 did not grimace or show any upset at all! The effect seemed to be a reduction in all behaviors rather than an increase in negative affect. Even in Period 1, when the infants had no expectation of how the adults would behave, smiling was at a low level ($M = 5\%$) during the TV replay, and when it occurred later, smiling disappeared completely for most infants ($M = 0.3\%$). Looking was also affected and dropped significantly, from about M equals 78 percent to about M equals 59 percent during the noncontingent period. Furthermore, smiling returned following the noncontingent TV-replay period, but attention did not recover.

The results showed that the memory of prior adult stimulation cannot account for the TV-replay effect. Similarly, the effect of noncontingent social stimulation does not appear to be caused by fatigue; it was similar irrespective of which period the TV replay occurred in. In fact, the impact of noncontingent stimulation by strangers on infant behavior was immediate. When they received a stranger's noncontingent behavior during the first period, infants lost interest and looked away within the first 20 seconds, and displayed little positive affect. Finally, only those infants who received the live interaction first showed a significant amount of negative behavior in this study. It seems that these infants set up an expectancy for a rich interaction and reacted negatively to subsequent televised interactions, even the contingent one.

These results contrast with those of Gusella (1986) and Mann (1986) described earlier. Inconsistencies reported in the literature regarding mother–stranger differences are probably paradigm specific. For example, Roe (1991) reported mother–stranger differences in vocal exchanges. Masi and Scott (1983) found infants looked more at mothers than strangers, but Sherrod (1979) and Kurzweil (1988) found the opposite. However, Ellsworth et al. (1993) found no mother–stranger differences. The discrepancy between infant responses to noncontingency of mothers and strangers also could be due to learned social expectancies of maternal behavior (after Lewis & Goldberg, 1969). By 5 months of age, infants have experienced a wide variety of maternal behaviors so that the mothers' behavior during a brief, TV-replay period may not have constituted a major violation in the infants' expectations. By contrast, infants had no previous experience interacting with the stranger. Presumably, the first experience with the stranger established the infant's expectancy for later interactions and led to the infant's sensitivity to the experimental manipulations.

The carryover effect found by Hains and Muir (1996a) was remarkably similar to the one found by Sapp et al. (1993). When their infants received live noncontingent social stimulation from a stranger in the first period, these infants appeared to remain disengaged when the stranger became contingent during the second period. Thus, the control of visual attention may depend on expectations set up in previous social interactions. Although we have only studied short-term effects, our findings are in line with Suomi's (1981) suggestion that giving infants noncontingent stimulation will disrupt their future ability to perceive contingency.

NONCONTINGENCY EFFECT IN PREFERENTIAL LOOKING

We have argued that the face-to-face interaction procedure may be the optimal method for studying infant social perception; however, we decided to test the generality of our noncontingency findings using a preferential looking task commonly used to test infant social perception (see Walker-Andrews, 1997). In our laboratory, Cao (1996; Muir, Hains, Cao, & D'Entremont, 1996) presented 4- and 5-month-olds with the simultaneous display of the same female stranger on two adjacent TV monitors. The design of Cao's apparatus is shown in Fig. 7.8. One monitor showed the stranger interacting contingently, whereas the other monitor displayed a replay of her interaction with a different infant. The adult's voice was eliminated, because it would have been coordinated with only one of the TV images, leading to a major confound in the study.

Cao discovered that her 4- and 5-month-olds looked significantly longer (about 70% of the time) at the silent contingent face than the noncontingent face (see Fig. 7.9). Also, in contrast to our dyadic interaction studies,

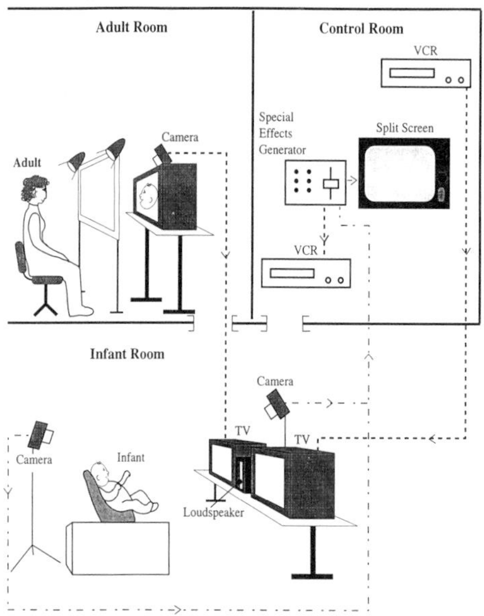

FIG. 7.8. A schematic diagram of the TV-preferential looking apparatus used by Cao (1996). The infant was presented with the adult's face on two TV monitors in the Infant Room; on one, the adult interacted contingently with the infant, and on the other, her image was the replay of a TV interaction with another infant. The sound was turned off.

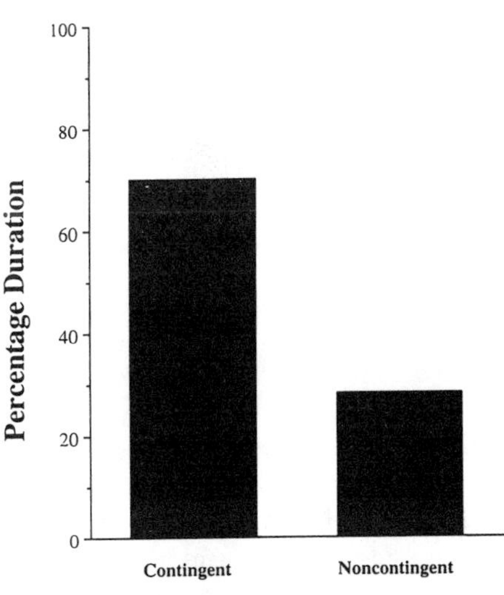

FIG. 7.9. The percentage of time, out of the total period, 4- and 5-month-olds looked at the contingent and the noncontingent TV displays of the same female stranger on adjacent TV monitors (shown schematically in Fig. 7.8) derived from Cao (1996).

Cao found that infant smiling was relatively infrequent at all ages and was not directed toward one face over the other during the study. Perhaps this is not surprising, given the unnatural simultaneous presentation of two identical faces doing different things. However, the main point is that social reinforcement, dyadic interaction, and preferential looking procedures all provide strong evidence that very young infants are highly sensitive to contingency in adult behavior. Such evidence may indicate that they use contingency as a cue for making inferences about the adult's intention to engage in social interactions.

INFANT SENSITIVITY TO ADULT EYE CONTACT

An important aspect of contingent stimulation is how infants determine when another person's social behavior is meant for them. Adults use eye contact as one cue to make this judgment, and its significance in adult communication has a long history of research (see review by Kleinke, 1986). Wolff (1987) also emphasized the importance of eye contact in infant social development. He reported that adult eye contact generated smiles at the end of the second month of life and tried to determine how sensitive infants were to small shifts in adult eye direction. Wolff used his subjective impressions to evaluate changes in infant motor activity when he broke eye contact and looked at the infant's ears or hair line (pp. 213–214). He found that his own direction of gaze had no effect on 2- and 5-week-olds, but when he made eye contact with 8- and 12-week-olds there was a brief drop in their motor activity. However, infant research on this topic is relatively sparse, particularly research on the role of eye contact during social interactions. Despite this, as noted in the introduction, Baron-Cohen (1994) postulated an eye detection detector (EDD) and argued that an appreciation of the meaning of an adult's averted gaze is the first step in developing an understanding of other people's mental state. However, the action of this EDD module was derived primarily from studies of non-human behavior. The few studies he referenced on young infants involved the use of static, noncontingent stimuli (e.g., studies by Haith, Bergman, & Moore, 1977; Maurer, 1985; Samuels, 1985; Vecera & Johnson, 1995) and produced mixed results. For example, Samuels (1985) reported that eye direction in schematic faces did not affect visual attention in 3-month-olds. Vecera and Johnson (1995) found that 4-month-olds, but not 2-month-olds, distinguished between line drawings of a face with frontal versus averted gaze in a preferential looking task, but only three of the eleven 4-month-olds preferred the frontal eyes.

Caron et al. (1992) presented a prerecorded video display of a female adult displaying positive interactive behavior under five conditions: normal, eyes forward; eyes averted; head and eyes averted; head averted, eyes forward; and eyes closed. They measured both visual attention and smiling. Caron et al.'s 3-month-olds smiled and gazed less when the adult's head was averted or her eyes appeared to be closed but did not differentiate between adult eye directions (i.e., forward or averted); their 5-month-olds looked at all adult displays equally but smiled somewhat more during the adult frontal eye gaze condition; and their 7-month-olds failed to show any discriminative behavior.

Only a few studies have used an interactive procedure. Bloom (1974) reinforced 3-month-olds' vocalization with adult social stimulation and varied the adult's eye direction. She found that although the adult's eyes had to be visible for infants to learn the contingency, eye direction per se was not necessary. Of course, Bloom's reinforcement procedure was not comparable to a natural, spontaneous social interaction. Lasky and Klein (1979) tested 5-month-olds' responses during face-to-face interactions when the adult stranger made eye contact versus when she looked above the infant's head at a picture. They reported that infants looked at the adult longer when she made eye contact, and the few infants who smiled did so in that condition. However, when the adult looked at the picture, presumably they were unable to maintain *contingent* interactions.

Hains and Muir (1996b) designed an experimental procedure that allowed an adult to maintain a contingent interaction while averting her eyes. They ensured that the interaction would be contingent by using the closed-circuit TV apparatus shown in Fig. 7.3 with a second TV monitor positioned at 40 degrees from center for the two eyes-away conditions. A third monitor was placed on the floor below the central monitor so that the adult's eyes appeared to be closed while viewing this monitor (eyes-closed condition). We reverted to our original design except that we had four periods of interaction instead of three so that each infant would receive two of the three manipulations (ABAC). We deliberately chose to use complete periods of looking away rather than to have the adult avert her eyes during an ongoing interaction, because in the latter case, the infant may have been responding to the movement of the adult's eyes or head rather than to the eye position per se.

We also were interested in a more subtle question: Is it eye contact that is important—implying that any deviation from "looking at me" would give the same signal to the infant—or is it eyes directed away that is important—looking at something else, which is the topic of shared attention? For this reason we used the same three manipulations as Caron et al. (1992): eyes averted with head directed toward the infant, head and eyes averted, and eyes down (which appear closed to the infant). If eye direction is irrelevant but the eyes need to be present, as Bloom's work suggests, then infants should look and smile at the contingently interacting adult equally during all conditions except when the eyes are closed. If the infant expects the person whose head is oriented toward them to interact provided the eyes are visible, then similar smiling and attention should be elicited by the eyes toward and eyes averted conditions and less interactive behavior should occur during the averted head and eyes closed conditions. However, if eye direction is a cue to interaction, then interactive behavior should decrease whenever the eyes are averted.

We included infants from 3 to 6 months of age in this study so that we could examine the behavior of infants both younger and older than Baron-Cohen's (1994) hypothesized emergence of the EDD at around 4 months of age. We also replicated this study using live rather than televised interactions with the adult's eyes being averted only 20 degrees. For the live study, the adult's eyes-away TV monitor was placed out of the infant's field of view, to one side of and behind the infant. We included two control groups of infants (one televised, one live), who received four periods of normal interaction.

As seen in the top panel (A) of Fig. 7.10, the control groups in both experiments showed little reduction in gaze or smiling at the adult across the periods. The experimental groups from the two studies did not differ from one another and showed a linear decrease in gaze across the four periods. By contrast, infant smiling was modulated by the direction of adult eye gaze, declining significantly each time the adult looked away during the interaction. We could find no differences in the infant responses to the three averted eye conditions and no interaction with age. The only

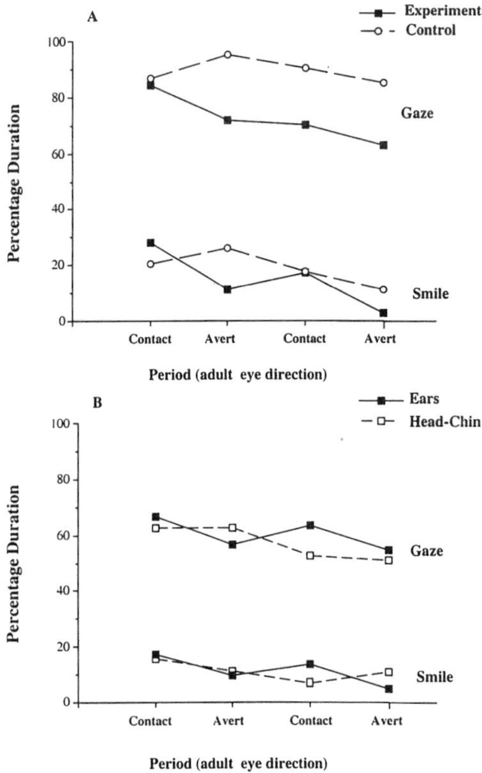

FIG. 7.10. Percentage of time infants looked and smiled at the contingently interacting adult as a function of period: (a) The adult in the experimental group shifted her eyes from making contact during Periods 1 and 3 (contact) by 40 degrees away from eye-contact during Periods 2 and 4 (avert), derived from Hains and Muir (1996b). (b) The adult continued to respond to infants contingently during Periods 2 and 4 (avert) while shifting her eyes horizontally approximately 5 degrees either to one of the infant's ears (filled squares) or vertically to the infant's chin or forehead (open squares), derived from Symons et al. (in press).

difference between 3- and 6-month-olds was that the younger infants looked longer at the adult.

Having thus demonstrated that infants are sensitive to eye contact, Symons, Hains, & Muir (in press) decided to explore the limits of this perceptual ability. They considered using one of the traditional psychophysical methods but found it difficult to incorporate these methodologies into a person-to-person interaction. Instead, they used the ABAC design and had the adult avert her eyes to look at one of the infant's ears during the averted eye periods. Note that when Wolff (1987) used a static version of this manipulation, he found no effects of eye aversion on the young infant's behavior. The idea was to increase the distance of the adult's eye direction from eye contact in the experimental periods until a point was reached where the majority of the infants reduced their smiling during the eyes away period and increased it again with the reinstatement of the adult's eye contact. This proved to be unnecessary because, as shown in the bottom panel (B) of Fig. 7.10, both smiling and gaze dropped significantly each time the adult's gaze shifted from making eye contact to looking the infants' ears (*filled* squares in Periods 1 vs. 2 and Periods 3 vs. 4; also compare the *filled* squares in panels A and B in Fig. 7.10 to see the difference in the effects for gaze and smiling). In order to complete the story, Symons et al. (in press) determined whether or not this ability was symmetrical on the other major axis by having the adult look at the infant's head and chin (the other condition used by Wolff, 1987) rather than the infant's ears. The results of this study were somewhat unexpected. When the adult looked at the head and chin, the infant did not appear to notice the deviation as shown by the open squares in Fig. 7.10, panel B. The infant's attention and smiling to vertical shifts in adult eye direction were very similar to those of the control groups in the previous study. Perhaps Wolff missed the effect because he did not differentiate between eyes away in the horizontal and vertical planes. The difference in sensitivity to vertical and horizontal shifts in adult eye direction may be related to a general orientation difference in the development of space perception, given that infants between 3 and 6 months of age also are more accurate in localizing invisible sounds along the horizontal than the vertical plane (see Muir & Clifton, 1985).

The results of this set of studies demonstrate that very young infants are sensitive to slight horizontal deviations in an adult's eye direction from "looking at me." The effect is substantial and contrasts with the mixed results, and generally small effects, of the studies that used noninteractive (nonsocial) stimuli cited by Baron-Cohen (1994).

PRECURSORS OF JOINT ATTENTION BEFORE 6 MONTHS OF AGE

It has been suggested that infants progress from dyadic eye-to-eye interactions with a partner to focusing attention on some object of common interest at around 6 months of age (see Bruner, 1983). Later, infants develop the ability to participate in triadic interactions in which each participant attends to an object while simultaneously monitoring the attention of the other: The partners are said to engage in joint visual attention. The usual procedure is for an adult to engage an infant in a face-to-face interaction and then to stop talking and turn to face an object out of the infant's field of view. Butterworth and Grover (1990) found that infants as young as 6 months of age will turn to look in the same direction as their mothers. Corkum and Moore (1994; Moore, this volume) reported a later age of onset. Their infants could not be conditioned to turn their heads toward a visible target before 8 to 9 months of age, and infants younger than 10 to 12 months of age did not spontaneously follow the adult's direction of gaze when the targets were not visible. One report by Scaife and Bruner (1975) suggested that infants as young as 2 month of age will turn their heads to follow an adult's line of visual regard; however, Scaife and Bruner's youngest infants may have been responding at chance level (see discussion by D'Entremont, Hains, & Muir, 1997; Moore, this volume), and no one else has shown that this ability exists in such young infants.

Having found that Baron-Cohen's EDD, if it indeed exists, is obviously operating to some extent by 3 months of age, at least to signal the presence of eye contact, possibly his shared attention mechanism (SAM) also is operating at an earlier age than he suggested. The key to prompting the operation of these mechanisms may be in giving the infant the proper instructions for the task at hand. As we emphasized in the introduction, particular care is needed to construct a context that optimizes the young infant's performance. We hoped to optimize conditions for demonstrating joint attention by modifying the standard procedure in the following way. The young infant's binocular visual field expands from 20 to 30 degrees around the midline at birth to almost adult levels by 6 months of age (Maurer & Lewis, 1991). We hypothesized that infants less than 6 months of age may require both the adult and the object to be present in the infants' visual field to show joint visual attention. Thus, D'Entremont et al. (1997) had an adult interact with the infant and then turn to interact with an object within 30 degrees of the infant's center of gaze. This guaranteed that both the adult and the objects of her attention remained within the infant's effective visual field throughout the procedure. There were eight infants in each of three groups: 3-month-olds (range 11 to 14 weeks), 4- to 5-month-olds (15 to 21 weeks), and 6-month-olds (range 22 to 26 weeks). The adult sat behind a frame between two hand puppets (lion heads) held within the frame on either side with her arms not visible to the infant. She interacted with the infant, smiling and talking in infant-directed speech, until the infant became fully engaged in the interaction; she then turned her head to look at one of the puppets while continuing to talk. After talking to the puppet for about 10 seconds, she turned back and reengaged the infant in an interaction. She did this at least four times (range 2 to 4 per side) during the 4-minute procedure.

D'Entremont et al. (1997) measured eye turning rather than the traditional head turning, because head turning is not required when the puppets were so close to the adult. The videotape was viewed twice. First, the direction of each eye movement (or head turn) by the infant was recorded together with the time (in 100ths of a second) of occurrence. The tape was viewed a second time, and the time of onset of each adult head turn was recorded. The two records were compared to determine the direction of the first infant head turn that occurred after an adult head turn. The direction was coded as correct when the infant looked at the appropriate puppet, no change when the infant continued to look at the adult, or incorrect when the infant looked elsewhere.

The first thing we noticed was that the adult could not hold the infants' attention as she could during standard face-to-face interaction studies: Infants glanced back and forth between the puppets and the adult's face, looking elsewhere infrequently. The total number of changes in infant eye direction ranged from 23 to 180 ($M = 79$, $SD = 39$) but did not differ across age groups. This contrasts with what happens in a normal interaction in which infants normally break eye contact fewer than five times per minute.

The proportion of eye turns in each category for each age group is shown in Fig. 7.11. Across all infants, the adult made a total of 175 head turns; infants made 159 eye or head turns of which 116 (72%) were in the correct direction. Only one 3-month-old turned more often in the wrong direction, and four infants (one at 3 months, one at 5 months, two at 6 months of age) looked equally at the correct and incorrect puppet. Some infants smiled a great deal in this study, but many did not smile at all (M duration = 28.00 sec, $SD = 29.1$ sec), and there were no age differences. Almost all the episodes of infant smiling began during an interaction with the adult; smiling was rare when the infant looked at the puppet.

These results demonstrate that infants as young as 3 months of age can follow adult head turns when the object of the adult's attention is within the infant's visual field and the adult head turning is part of an ongoing social interaction. The relatively long latency for eye turns (over 2 sec)

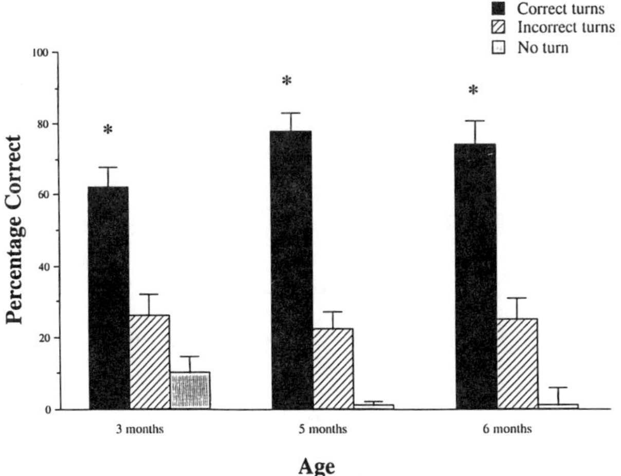

FIG. 7.11. The percentage of infant eye or head turns in the same direction as the adult (correct), the direction opposite to the adult (incorrect), or no turns as a function of infant age (from D'Entremont et al., 1997). The age ranges for the three age groups were: 3 months = 11 to 14 weeks; 4 to 5 months = 15 to 21 weeks; and 6 months = 22 to 26 weeks. Vertical lines indicate standard errors. (Reprinted with permission from Ablex Publishing Corporation.) * = significant difference between correct and incorrect turns.

compared with the latency for a head turn to an off-centered sound of about 1 second (Muir, Humphrey, & Humphrey, 1994) suggests that the infants are not simply tracking the eyes or nose. Our eye-contact studies show that infants are aware of whether or not an adult is making eye contact during contingent interactions, whereas this study demonstrates that infants also have some appreciation of where an adult is looking when she looks away. Thus, by 3 months of age, infants appear to have some appreciation of both dyadic and triadic adult attention.

SUMMARY AND CONCLUSIONS

Our work over the years has been directed primarily toward trying to understand what an infant knows about the world. By using variations in the still-face procedure, we showed that by 3 months of age, infants are sensitive to many perturbations in an adult's behavior during face-to-face interaction. The still-face effect involves a reduction in both looking and smiling by the infant during the perturbation followed by a recovery when normal adult behavior resumes. However, as shown in Table 7.1, none of the manipulations of the adult interaction that we thought could be the major cues for regulating infants' social behavior resulted in a similar loss of visual attention, whereas infant smiling was reduced by all the perturbations. It appears that young infants can use each of our manipulations as cues to a change in the adult's behavior, but none alone could account for the still-face effect. What stands out is that infant sensitivity was revealed only by a change in their affective behavior (i.e., smiling), because their visual attention seems to be captured by any of the novel adult behaviors. We emphasized in the introduction and elsewhere (e.g., Muir & Hains, 1993) that the key to revealing infant social perception is to use a method

TABLE 7.1
Summary of Adult Perturbation Effects on Infant Affect and Attention During Contingent Interactions Compared to Noncontingency Effects

Perturbation	*Visual Attention*	*Smiling*
1. Still-face (mom or stranger)	Large drop (~50%)	Almost disappears
2. Person to object	Maintained	Almost disappears
3. Inverted face	Maintained	Large drop (~80%)
4. Happy to sad face	Maintained	Moderate drop (~60%)
5. Breaking eye contact	Maintained or Slight drop	Moderate drop (~50%)
Noncontingency Effects:		
6. Noncontingent mother	Maintained	Maintained
7. Noncontingent stranger	Large drop (~50%)	Almost disappears

Note. All comparisons are with normal interaction periods.

that allows the infant to exhibit a range of social behaviors. Although cognitive tasks such as habituation and preferential looking procedures are valuable in telling us what infants can discriminate, they may underestimate the infants capacity to process information because they fail to fully engage the infant's response system (this concept is not new—e.g., see Lewis, Alessandri, & Sullivan, 1990).

Using an adult–infant interaction procedure allows adults to respond to infants' individual differences by adjusting the intensity and duration of their social signals (e.g., more or less adult vocal and facial stimulation) during the introductory interaction to engage the infants. This method of engaging the infants in social interaction before introducing perturbations, and measuring at least both infant affect and visual attention, has served us well in exploring the use of more subtle cues (e.g., eye direction) as well as drastic changes in adult behavior (e.g., the still-face). It should be emphasized that the behavior of young infants is highly variable, so that the absolute amount of behavior may vary from one study to the next. Once the appropriate rhythm of engagement is discovered, however, almost every infant shows the same *pattern* of responding to the perturbation.

The Ellsworth et al. (1993) study, which compared infant responses to an interacting object with that to an interacting adult, showed that the infants smiled only at people. This indicates that there is more to adult interactions than the rhythm of the adult's stimulation. The adult interacts with the infant using a continuous stream of looking, smiling, talking, and facial gestures. Her response to infant signals is imbedded in this stream and can take many forms including a look of surprise, a change in vocal pitch, a brightening of her smile among others. We attempted to demonstrate the effect of this maternal contingency on the behavior of 5-month-olds by using a televised replay of the mother's behavior and failed. Watson (1985), in his learning studies using social reinforcement, showed that young infants are most responsive to moderate levels of imperfect contingencies. They like an intermittent rather than a continuous reinforcement schedule and some social reinforcement that occurs independently from their own behavior. This would appear to describe the nature of normal maternal behavior, implying that the infants should not be able to distinguish maternal contingent and noncontingent behavior.

Very recently, there have been two attempts to replicate Murray and Trevarthen's TV-replay noncontingency effect that produced contradictory results. Both groups considered the possibility that Murray and Trevarthen's (1985) results may have been due to a failure to control for order effects. Nadel et al. (1997, this volume) tested *9-week-olds* using Murray and Trevarthen's double video-replay procedure, and their results were very similar to Murray and Trevarthen's. They found a significant drop in gaze and smiling and an increase in frowning and mouth closing during the brief replay period. They concluded that Murray and Trevarthen's results could not be due to a failure to control for order because 70 percent of their 9-week-olds stopped fussing and recovered both looking and smiling when their mothers became contingent again after the replay. Rochat, Neisser, and Marian (in press; Rochat & Striano, this volume) also used Murray and Trevarthen's (1985) double video-replay technique to present two groups of *3-month-olds* with three periods of TV maternal stimulation. Both groups received contingent TV interactions during Period 1, followed by a TV-replay and TV-contingent stimulation in Periods 2 and 3, with the order counterbalanced to control for changes over time. When the two groups' replay and live sequences were compared, no differences in the duration of infant attention or frowning were found, and slightly more smiling occurred during the replay period, matching the results of Hains and Muir (1996b) described earlier for *5-month-olds.* These two conflicting sets of results may reflect an important age effect—very young infants (e.g., 9-week-olds) may became upset by brief noncontingent maternal stimulation, whereas older infants (e.g., 3-month-olds) may not. A proper longitudinal study is needed to settle the issue.

By contrast, evidence that young infants do not respond well to noncontingent social stimulation by strangers is strong. In our preferential looking task, 4- to 5-month-olds' attention was captured more by the stranger interacting contingently over TV than the TV-replay of the same stranger interacting with another infant (Cao, Hains, & Muir, 1996). In live interaction studies, noncontingent social stimulation by strangers had an impact on infant visual attention in subsequent habituation tasks (Dunham et al., 1989; Sapp et al., 1993). When the dyadic TV-interaction procedure was used, the TV replay had a negative impact on infants, substantially reducing their positive affect and visual attention. As shown in Table 7.1, this was the only manipulation we used that matched the reduction in gaze and positive affect produced by the adult's still-face. Furthermore, the results of our interaction studies point to a long-lasting effect of noncontingency on infant visual attention. In both our TV-interaction (Muir & Hains, 1996a) and live interaction (Sapp et al., 1993) studies, following the TV-replay condition there was no recovery of attention during subsequent contingent social interaction periods. Thus, at least for adult strangers, the still-face may not be seen as negatively by the infants as the adults' noncontingent social stimulation.

Finally, we showed that adult eye contact appears to regulate the infant's social responses during dyadic interactions (Hains & Muir, 1996b; Symons et al., in press). Furthermore, by 3 months of age, infants will turn their eyes toward the object of an adult's attention, suggesting that they have an appreciation of both the adults' maintenance of eye contact and direction of adults' shift in focus of attention (D'Entremont et al., in press). It should be noted that D'Entremont and colleagues' adults shifted both their head and eyes; thus, the ability of the very young infant to follow the direction of the adult's eye gaze per se during joint attention studies has yet to be established. Recently, Willen, Hood, and Driver (1997) reported that infants as young as 10 weeks of age are capable of processing a shift in eye direction. They presented infants with a picture of a face with animated, blinking eyes that appeared to be staring straight ahead. Suddenly the pupils in the eyes shifted, appearing to look either left or right. This was followed by the appearance of a peripheral target on either the same side or the opposite side of the eye direction. Infants looked faster and more frequently toward the peripheral target when the eye gaze shifted to the same side. This does not prove that young infants use adult eye direction to infer intentionality (i.e., infant direction of gaze might be influenced by shifting the direction of any abstract stimulus), but they do appear to have the perceptual capacity to do so. These data are inconsistent with theories that have triadic interactions developing from dyadic interactions after 6 months of age (e.g., Adamson, 1995) and Baron-Cohen's (1994) theory of mind model that has a dyadic attention mechanism predating the triadic mechanism (SAM) that develops around 8 months of age.

Baron-Cohen's (1994) linear model of the development of the child's theory of mind appears to radically underestimate the infant's appreciation of adult intentionality as reflected by their sensitivity to adult contingency and eye contact during dyadic interactions. So far we have shown that infants as young as 3 months of age—the age when they first begin to smile socially to adults—already have a sophisticated knowledge of many aspects of adult behavior. We have moved beyond merely citing expectation as the controlling mechanism for infant social behavior to the identification of several important factors that appear to build infant expectancies. First, we found a surprising lack of a negative responding to brief episodes of *maternal* noncontingent social stimulation by 5-month-olds, which contrasted with their immediate drop in positive affect and attention when strangers were noncontingent. This suggests that familiarity with the social partner is a primary element in the regulation of infant social behavior. Contingency obviously is an important component of an adult's behavior if the infant is to develop an internal working model (using an attachment concept) for how to react to people. Conversely, noncontingency is important as an inhibitor of social learning and takes precedence over more minor perturbations such as a change in facial expression. Second, eye contact is one component of contingent interactions that infants may be using as an indicator of adult intention to engage in social interactions, and adult eye direction information is used as an indicator of where to look if the adult looks away. All these adult social signals appear to be processed at some level by infants very early in life. It appears that we have to look at even younger infants to uncover the possible origins of their responsiveness, and our methodology, dependent as it is on measuring affective behavior, is not useful for infants younger than 3 months of age. Perhaps contingency effects on other behaviors that young infants exhibit, such as modifications in infant motor behavior (activity levels) studied by Wolff (1987), need to be considered.

ACKNOWLEDGMENTS

Portions of this chapter were presented at the biennial International Conference on Infant Studies in Providence, RI, April, 1996. We gratefully acknowledge the contributions of Yan Cao, Barbara D'Entremont, Cathy Mann, Larry Symons, and Elizabeth Stevens to some of the research presented in this chapter and to Christine Hains, Monica Hurt, and Larry Symons for their editorial assistance. The research was supported by a grant to D. Muir from the Natural Sciences and Engineering Research Council of Canada.

REFERENCES

Adamson, L. B. (1995). *Communication development during infancy.* Madison, WI: Brown & Benchmark.

Baron-Cohen, S. (1994). How to build a baby that can read minds: Cognitive mechanisms in mindreading. *Cahiers de Psychologie Cognitive: Current Psychology of Cognition, 13,* 513–552.

Blass, E. M., Ganchrow, J. R., & Steiner, J. E. (1984). Classical conditioning in newborn humans 2–48 hours of age. *Infant Behavior and Development, 7,* 223–235.

Bloom, K. (1974). Eye contact as a setting even for infant learning. *Journal of Experimental Child Psychology, 17,* 250–263.

Brazelton, T. B., Koslowski, B., & Main, W. (1974). The origins of reciprocity: The early mother-infant interaction. In M. Lewis & L. A. Rosenblum (Eds.), *The effect of the infant on its caregiver* (pp. 49–76). New York: Wiley.

Bruner, J. G. (1983). *Child's talk: Learning to use language.* New York: Norton.

Butterworth, G., & Grover, L. (1990). Joint visual attention, manual pointing, and preverbal communication in human infancy. In M. Jeannerod (Eds.), *Attention and performance XIII* (pp. 605–624). Hillsdale, NJ: Lawrence Erlbaum Associates.

Cao, Y. (1996). *Infant responses to perturbations of adult face-voice coordination during face-to-face interactions.* Doctoral dissertation, Queen's University, Kingston, Canada.

Cao, Y., Hains, S. M. J., & Muir, D. W. (1996). Infant preferential looking: Face-voice synchrony vs. affect [Special ICIS issue]. *Infant Behavior and Development, 19,* 371.

Caron, A., Caron, R., Mustelin, C., & Roberts, J. (1992). Infant responding to aberrant social stimuli. [Special ICIS issue] *Infant Behavior and Development, 19,* 335.

Corkum, V., & Moore, L. (1994). Development of joint visual attention in infants. In C. Moore & P. J. Dunham (Eds.), *Joint attention: Its origins and role in development* (pp. 61–83). Hillsdale, NJ: Lawrence Erlbaum Associates.

D'Entremont, B. (1995). *One- to six-month-olds' attention and affective responding to adults' happy and sad expressions: The role of face and voice.* Doctoral dissertation, Queen's University, Kingston, Canada.

D'Entremont, B., Hains, S. M. J., & Muir, D. W. (1997). A demonstration of gaze following in 3- to 6-month-olds. *Infant Behavior and Development, 20,* 569–572.

D'Entremont, B., & Muir, D. (1997). Five-month-olds' attention and affective responses to still-faced emotional expressions. *Infant Behavior and Development, 20,* 563–568.

Dunham, P., Dunham, F., Hurshman, A., & Alexander, T. (1989). Social contingency effects on subsequent perceptual cognitive tasks in young infants. *Child Development, 60,* 1486–1496.

Ellsworth, C. P., Muir, D. W., & Hains, S. M. J. (1993). Social competence and person-object differentiation: An analysis of the still-face effect. *Developmental Psychology, 29,* 63–73.

Gibson, J. J. (1979). *The ecological approach to visual perception.* New York: Houghton Mifflin.

Gusella, J. (1986). *The effect of manipulating maternal behavior on infant affect and attention during an interaction.* Unpublished doctoral dissertation, Queen's University, Kingston, Canada.

Gusella, J., & Muir, D. (1985). Experimental manipulations of mother–infant interactions: Isolating affective components. Poster presented at the *17th Banff International Conference on Behavior Sciences.* Banff, Alberta Canada.

Gusella, J. L., Muir, D., & Tronick, E. A. (1988). The effect of manipulating maternal behavior during an interaction on three- and six-month-olds' affect and attention. *Child Development, 59,* 1111–1124.

Hains, S. M. J., & Muir, D. W. (1996a). Effects of stimulus contingency in infant–adult interactions. *Infant Behavior and Development, 19,* 49–61.

Hains, S. M. J., & Muir, D. W. (1996b). Infant sensitivity to adult eye direction. *Child Development, 67,* 1940–1951.

Haith, M., Bergman, T., & Moore, M. (1977). Eye contact and face scanning in early infancy. *Science, 198,* 853–855.

Kaye, K., & Fogel, A. (1980). The temporal structure of face-to-face communication between mothers and infants. *Developmental Psychology, 16,* 454–464.

Kleinke, C. L. (1986). Gaze and eye contact: A research review. *Psychological Bulletin, 100,* 78–100.

Klin, R. P., & Jennings, K. D. (1979). Responses to social and inanimate stimuli in early infancy. *The Journal of Genetic Psychology, 135,* 3–9.

Kurzweil, S. R. (1988). Recognition of mother from multisensory interactions in early infacy. *Infant Behavior and Development, 11,* 235–243.

Laskey, R. E., & Klein, R. E. (1979). The reactions of five-month-olds to eye contact of the mother and of stranger. *Merrill-Palmer Quarterly, 25,* 163–170.

Legerstee, M., Pomerleau, A., Malcuit, G., & Feider, H. (1987). The development of infants' responses to people and a doll: Implications for research in communication. *Infant Behavior and Development, 10,* 81–95.

Lewis, M., Alessandri, S. M., & Sullivan, M. W. (1990). Violation of expectancy, loss of control, and anger expressions in young infants. *Developmental Psychology, 26,* 745–751.

Lewis, M., & Goldberg, S. (1969). Perceptual-cognitive development in infancy: A generalized expectancy model as a function of mother–infant interaction. *Merrill-Palmer Quarterly, 15,* 745–751.

Mann, C. (1986). *Infants' responses to perturbations of mothers' behavior in mother–infant interactions.* Unpublished honors thesis, Queen's University, Kingston, Canada.

Masi, W. S., & Scott, K. G. (1983). Preterm and full-term infants' visual responses to mothers and strangers' faces. In T. Field & A. Sostek (Eds.), *Infants born at risk: Physiological perceptual and cognitive processes* (pp. 173–179). New York: Grune & Stratton.

Maurer, D. (1985). Infants' perception of facedness. In T. M. Field & N. Fox (Eds.), *Social perception in infants* (pp. 218–255). Norwood, NJ: Ablex.

Maurer, D., & Lewis, T. L. (1991). The development of peripheral vision and its physiological underpinnings. In M. J. Salomon-Weiss & P. R. Zelazo (Eds.), *Newborn attention: Biological constraints and the influence of experience* (pp. 218–255). Norwood, NJ: Ablex.

Meltzoff, A. N. (1981). Imitation, intermodal coordination, and representation in early infancy. In G. Butterworth (Ed.), *Infancy and epistomology: An evaluation of Piaget's theory* (pp. 85–114). Brighton, Sussex, England: Harvester Press.

Muir, D., & Clifton, R. K. (1985). Infants' orientation to the location of sound sources. In G. Gottlieb & N. A. Krasnegor (Eds.), *Measurement of audition and vision in the first year of postnatal life: A methodological overview* (pp. 167–222). Bethesda, MD: Ablex.

Muir, D., Hains, S. M. J., Cao, Y., & D'Entremont, B. (1996). 3- to 6-month-olds' sensitivity to adult intentionality: The role of adult contingency and eye direction in dyadic interactions [Special ICIS issue]. *Infant Behavior and Development, 19,* 200.

Muir, D. W., & Hains, S. M. J. (1993). Infant sensitivity to perturbations in adult facial, vocal, tactile, and contingent stimulation during face-to-face interactions. In B. de Boysson-Bardies et al. (Eds.), *Developmental neurocognition: Speech and face processing in the first year of life* (pp. 171–185). Netherlands: Kluwer.

Muir, D. W., Hains, S. M. J., & Symons, L. A. (1994). Baby and me: Infants need minds to read. *Cahiers de Psychologie Cognitive: Current Psychology of Cognition, 13,* 669–682.

Muir, D. W., Humphrey, D. E., & Humphrey, G. K. (1994). Pattern and space perception in young infants. Special issue: Invariance, recognition, and perception: In honor of Peter C. Dodwell. *Spatial Vision, 8,* 141–165.

Muir, D. W., & Rach-Longman, K. (1989). Once more with expression: On de Schonen and Mathivet's (1989) model for the development of face perception in human infants. *Cahiers de Psychologie Cognitive, 9,* 103–109.

Murray, L., & Trevarthen, C. (1985). Emotional regulation of interaction between two-month-olds and their mothers. In T. M. Field & N. A. Fox (Eds.), *Social perception in infants* (pp. 101–125). Norwood, NJ: Ablex.

Nadel, J., Marcelli, D., Pezé, A., Kervella, C., & Reserbat-Plantey, D. (1997, April). *Contingent interaction in French 2-month-olds with their mother.* Paper presented at the Biannual Meeting of the Society for Research in Child Development, Washington, DC.

Rach-Longman, K. (1988). *The effects of familiarity, orientation, and mode of transmission of interactive face presentations on infants' responses.* Unpublished master's thesis, Queen's University, Kingston, Canada.

Rochat, P., Neisser, U., & Marian, V. (in press). Are young infants sensitive to social contingency? *Infant Behavior and Development.*

Roe, K. V. (1991). Short-term stability of three-month-old infants' vocal responses to mother vs stranger. *Perceptual & Motor Skills, 73,* 419–424.

Roman, J. (1986). *Six-month-olds' responses to an inverted image of their mother's face during social interactions.* Unpublished honors thesis, Queen's University, Kingston, Canada.

Samuels, C. A. (1985). Attention to eye contact opportunity and facial motion by three-month-old infants. *Journal of Experimental Child Psychology, 40,* 141–166.

Sapp, F., Stevens, E., Muir, D., & Hains, S. M. J. (1993, March). *The effects of social contingency on infants affect and subsequent learning.* Poster presented at the biannual meeting of the Society for Research and Development, New Orleans, LA.

Scaife, M., & Bruner, J. S. (1975). The capacity for joint attention in the infant. *Nature, 253,* 265–266.

Schaffer, R. (1984). *The child's entry into a social world.* New York: Academic Press.

Sherrod, L. R. (1979). Social cognition in infants: Attention to the human face. *Infant Behavior and Development, 2,* 279–294.

Spelke, E. S., Phillips, A., & Woodward, A. L. (1995). Infants' knowledge of object motion and human action. In D. Sperber, D. Premack, & A. J. Premack (Eds.), *Causal cognition: A multidisciplinary debate* (pp. 45–78). Oxford, England: Clarendon.

Stack, D. M., & Muir, D. W. (1990). Tactile stimulation as a component of social interchange: New interpretations for the still-face effect. *British Journal of Developmental Psychology, 8,* 131–145.

Stack, D. M., & Muir, D. W. (1992). Adult tactile stimulation during face-to-face interactions modulates 5-month-olds' affect and attention. *Child Development, 63,* 1509–1525.

Stern, D. (1977). *The first relationship: Infant and mother.* Cambridge, MA: Harvard University Press.

Stevens, E. (1991). *The effect of contingent versus noncontingent social interactions on infant behavior and subsequent perceptual-cognitive task performance.* Unpublished honors thesis, Queen's University, Kingston, Canada.

Suomi, S. (1981). The perception of contingency and social development. In M. E. Lamb & L. E. Sherrold (Eds.), *Infant social cognition: Empirical and theoretical considerations* (pp. 177–203). Hillsdale, NJ: Lawrence Erlbaum Associates.

Symons, D., & Moran, G. (1994). Responsiveness and dependancy are different aspects of social contingencies: An example from mother and infant smiles. *Infant Behavior and Development, 17,* 209–214.

Symons, L., Hains, S. M. J., & Muir, D. W. (in press). Look at me: Five-month-old infants' sensitivity to very small deviations in eye-gaze during social interactions. *Infant Behavior and Development.*

Thompson, P. (1980). Margaret Thatcher: A new illusion. *Perception, 9,* 483–484.

Trevarthen, C. (1974, May). Conversations with a 2-month-old. *New Scientist,* 230–235.

Tronick, E., Als, H., Adamson, L., Wise, S., & Brazelton, T. B. (1978). The infants' response to entrapment between contradictory messages in face-to-face interactions. *Journal of the American Academy of Child Psychiatry, 17,* 1–13.

Tronick, E., Als, H., & Brazelton, T. B. (1980). Monadic phases: A structural descriptive analysis of infant-mother face-to-face interaction. *Merrill-Palmer Quarterly, 26,* 3–24.

Tronick, E. Z. (1989). Emotions and emotional communication in infants. Special issue: Children and their development: Knowledge base, research agenda, and social policy application. *American Psychologist, 44,* 112–119.

Vecera, S. P., & Johnson, M. H. (1995). Gaze detection and the cortical processing of faces: Evidence from infants and adults. *Visual Cognition, 2,* 59–87.

Walker-Andrews, A. S. (1997). Infants' perception of expressive behaviors: Differentiation of multimodal information. *Psychological Bulletin, 121,* 437–456.

Watson, J. S. (1985). Contingency perception in early social development. In T. M. Field & N. A. Fox (Eds.), *Social perception in infants* (pp. 156–176). Norwood, NJ: Ablex.

Watson, J. S., Hayes, L. A., Vietze, P., & Becker, J. (1979). Discriminating infant smiling to orientations of talking faces of mother and stranger. *Journal of Child Psychology, 28,* 92–99.

Willen, J. D., Hood, B. M., & Driver, J. R. (1997). An eye direction detector triggers shifts of visual attention in human infants. *Investigative Opthamology & Visual Science, 38,* 313.

Wolff, P. H. (1987). *The development of behavioral states and the expression of emotions in early infancy: New proposals for investigation.* Chicago: University of Chicago Press.

Chapter 8

Early Perception of Social Contingencies and Interpersonal Intentionality: Dyadic and Triadic Paradigms

Jacqueline Nadel
Ecole Pratique des Haute Etudes

Hélène Tremblay-Leveau
Université de Rouen

Studies of mother–infant interactions have come to a turning point. Rather than consisting mainly of anecdotal reports, they have started to produce data. Just as the creation of experimental paradigms such as habituation generated a shift in the study of early perception and physical cognition, the creation of experimental designs in the area of early social interactions is changing the landscape.

The first step was made 20 years ago when the face-to-face situation was designed. This allowed researchers to restrict the number of environmental variables in play in a social context and to control others. With the demonstration of regularities in infant and mother reciprocal patterns, it became obvious that some rules of interaction could account for these regularities. The idea followed of manipulating adult behavior to test the sensitivity of the infant to the violation of simple rules such as social responsiveness and contingent interaction. The still-face paradigm was the first design especially aimed at testing such hypotheses. New experimental possibilities were raised from the evidence that babies as young as 2 months can interact with their mothers through a televised system. Designs like the double closed-circuit TV system are now available to test predictions about infants' sensitivity to such parameters as synchrony, contingency, and agency.

However, attached to dyadic face-to-face paradigms is a significant handicap: The adult's behavior is the manipulated variable. Infants have no control over it and no power to change it. This cannot inform us much about infants' capacities to monitor others' behavior. We show in this chapter that multiparticipant designs allow experimenters to go a step further in the study of infants' awareness of their and others' social positions. The designs also provide experiments revealing early monitoring of others' attention and intention.

Based on dyadic and multiparticipant designs, the connection between the study of early interactive skills and the area of early cognition and reasoning is ready to be made. Indeed, some precursors of inferential capacities concerning human intentionality may well be found in the early detection of violations of social rules during face-to-face and triadic interactions. For instance, Premack (1990) put forward that very young infants are able to separate the category of self-propelled objects from the category of physical objects, and Spelke, Phillips, & Woodward (1995) demonstrated this point. They found that 9-week-olds react to violations of physical principles explaining physical movement. For instance, they were surprised when Object B started moving after Object A had stopped short of it (inconsistent with the principle of contact) but were not surprised if B started moving after A had hit it (consistent with the principle of contact). By contrast, 7-month-olds were not upset with violations of the principle of contact for human movement (see Poulin-Dubois, this volume, for a review). If babies already reason about human action according to principles different from those for physical action, this would mean that they might precociously infer goal-directed behavior, agency, and thus intentionality.

It is our contention that dyadic and more probably triadic interaction paradigms will fill the gap between physical and social cognition in the near future. The aim of this chapter is to examine to what extent the designs available, the parameters measured, and the data produced make such a contention reasonable.

EARLY PERCEPTION OF SOCIAL CONTINGENCIES: DYADIC PARADIGMS

More than 20 years ago, Brazelton and colleagues (Brazelton, Koslowski, & Main, 1974) ananyzed the recordings of a 3-week-old baby and demonstrated that this infant displayed a different and predictable pattern of attention and behavior when facing an object rather than a person: A smooth and rythmical pattern of attention and disengagement was consistently observed when the infant interacted with a person in contrast to a pattern of long attention to the object and abrupt turning away. This was one of the first attempts to demonstrate the early ability of infants to differentiate animate from inanimate entities. The different behavioral patterns displayed toward object and person were taken as the index of an early discriminative capacity. The hypothesis was that an object affords exploration, but a person is precociously seen as offering affective synchrony. According to the authors, the cyclical on–off pattern shown by the baby's interacting with a person accounts for cognitive and affective exchanges in the attention phase followed by a withdrawal phase of recovery. Further studies with experimental methods confirmed that the infants display different hand movements when facing a human partner or an object (Legerstee, Corter, & Kienapple, 1990).

After this basic experiment, the authors and other colleagues, such as Trevarthen (1977) and Stern (1977), started to use systematically the face-to-face play situation as a research design and to record different conditions: a mother with an infant, an infant alone with an object, a father with an infant, and so forth. Analyses of these interactions showed regularities in rythmic reciprocities. After 3 months of age, babies consistently reacted differently to their mothers than to their fathers, as if they expected different reactions from the two parents (Als, Tronick, & Brazelton, 1978).

To what extent do very young babies expect special behavior from a partner and behave according to expectancies? Tronick (1982) proposed that elementary rules govern joint regulation. The principal rule was hypothesized to be that a partner would display behaviors appropriate to the context. If joint regulation actually requires that partners follow this rule, then it can be predicted that when a partner violates this rule, the baby will first try to change the partner's display, and if unsucessful, will react negatively, indicating a disturbance in expectancies. To test this hypothesis, the original face-to-face method was modified to include rule violations. This led researchers to test with clinical dyads the influence of such rule violations as concurrent display of contradictory expressions; for instance, Massie (1977) observed mothers avoiding their baby's approach but then turning to an affectionate response when their babies turned away. Stern (1977) observed a very similar sequential-contingent violation that occurs when an adult expresses a message contingent on the infant's response to the preceding violation. These observations emphasize the clinical consequences of such contingent violations. The decisive demonstration, however, was an experiment based on the still-face paradigm, which was conducted among a nonclinical population by Tronick, Als, Adamson,Wise, and Brazelton (1978).

The Still-Face Paradigm

In a seminal experiment, Tronick and colleagues (1978) asked mothers to interact with their infants in a normal way for 3 minutes, then in a still-faced fashion, and finally to return to normal interaction. It was hypothesized that if the baby was expecting a reciprocal interaction, then the baby would react negatively when the mother presented the still face. They found that 3-month-old babies became wary, displayed protest cues, and alternately tried to reengage the mother and then withdraw. In contrast, they engaged in long periods of positive behavior during the normal interaction period. The rule-violation hypothesis was considered to be validated, since 3-month-olds showed significant changes in behavior under the different conditions (Tronick et al., 1978).

In one of several other experiments, Cohn and Tronick (1982) emphasized that when the mother displayed depressionlike behaviors, the baby exhibited different structures in behavioral organization, confirming the rule-violation hypothesis rather than the discrepancy or the understimulation hypothesis. Sequential analyses of the data also revealed that the behavioral perturbations generated by the still-face (depressionlike) condition persisted well after the end of the still period and could not be explained by these alternative hypotheses. Two-month-olds (Lamb, Morisson, & Malkin, 1987) and even 6-week-olds (Murray & Trevarthen, 1985), were shown to be sensitive to the still-face condition.

However, three main methodological problems are raised by the still-face procedure. One is the possible effect of tiredness over time, which could explain the increase of negative displays during the still-face period. The second possibility is that the infant is disturbed simply by the contrast between interaction (during the first period) and noninteraction (during the still-face period). A third possibility is that the infant is less attentive to a still face, since it is well known that babies are more attentive to moving than to static stimuli.

In an elegant set of experiments, Muir and colleagues investigated some aspects of these possibilities. For instance, Ellsworth, Muir, and Hains (1993) conducted the still-face experiment with both mothers and dolls and distinguished the part of the effect that is due to the infant's interest in moving stimuli from that which is due to the infant's expectancies about interaction. Smiling turned out to be a discriminative measure, because infants smiled only to reattract the attention of humans, not dolls, whereas their gaze decreased in the still-face period toward the mothers as well as toward the dolls.

To test the effect of tiredness on the infants' reactions to the still-face period, Guisella, Muir, and Tronick (1988) added a control group to the initial procedure. In the experimental group, mothers were instructed to interact normally with the face, voice, and hands; then to stop touching, speaking, and displaying emotional expressions; and finally to interact normally again. In the control group, mothers were instructed to interact normally during all three periods. Each period lasted 2 minutes and was followed by a 15-second interval during which the mother turned away. Results show that gaze was similar throughout the three periods for control babies and decreased significantly during the still face for experimental babies. Smile decreased regularly throughout the three periods for controls, but it showed the same U-shape pattern as gaze did in the experimental group. These results support the rule-violation hypothesis but not the hypothesis that infants simply became tired and fussy.

However, when the still-face procedure was modified by having the mother maintain touch during the still period, no difference was found between experimental and control groups of 3-month-olds. These results may lead to the conclusion that touch supports very young babies' attention and that when touch is suppressed, babies' attention to the mothers decreases, regardless of the visual and auditory displays of the mothers. In this case, the still-face design would not test sensitivity to rule violation but rather the links between attention and touch. Some other studies, however, indicate that reactions to the still-face procedure discriminate different clinical groups of 3-month-olds (Field, 1984). For instance, Field (1984) found a different pattern of heart rythm in 4-month-old babies of control mothers than for babies of depressed mothers. The differences in heart rate between interactive and still-face periods were significantly less for babies of depressed mothers, thus showing that they were less upset by a still face than were babies of control mothers. This finding demonstrates the discriminative power of the still-face design, but it does not inform us about the relevant parameters in play.

An experiment conducted by Nadel, Hudelot, and Lécuyer (in progress), also shows the discriminative power of the still-face procedure in children with autism. The children reacted differently to a still-face period experienced before they interacted with the experimenter (Still-Face1) than to a still-face period after having an interaction with her (Still-Face2).

The still-face design was used with a group of eight low-functioning, mute children with autism. They were all diagnosed according to DSM3r and CARS, and their mental ages according to PEPr scores ranged from 18 to 48 months (mean mental age = 36 months). Their chronological ages ranged from 5 to 13 years. There were six boys and two girls (the younger and the older of the group). The experimenter was a female adult whom they had never seen before. The first still-face period started as soon as the child entered a familiar room of their school, alone. The experimenter was sitting on a sofa, exhibiting a still face and still body. The room contained two identical sets of 10 objects, which proved to be attractive to these children. These were cowboy hats, sunglasses, plastic dolphins, strings, ringing mills, and balloons, among other objects. The still-face period lasted 3 minutes, then the experimenter stood up, and during the 3 following minutes, she imitated the child. She held a similar object(s), manipulated the similar object(s) in the same way, displayed similar facial expressions, made the same sounds, and replicated the child's motor behaviors (including stereotypies). During the 3 minutes following, she again sat on the sofa and displayed a still face, then ended with an interactive period.

The eight children stayed in the room, showing no interest in the unfamiliar experimenter on the sofa (except the youngest child who sat for 5 seconds near the adult without looking at her). All the children spent the 3 minutes exploring objects (except the 13-year-old girl, who walked around performing stereotyped gestures and vocalizations). They all responded positively with gaze and smile to the experimenter's imitative interaction (except two boys who systematically tried to take the two similar objects in order to escape being imitated). During the second still face, the children behaved uncharacteristically. All the children went close to the experimenter, gazed at her, and tried to initiate interactions by caressing, smiling, and offering objects to her, as Fig. 8.1 indicates. After about a minute or two of trying to make contact, they all withdrew except one who kept trying throughout the 3 minutes. This boy sat next to the experimenter and alternatedly glanced longingly at her while smiling and then withdrew while frowning. At times he touched the experimenter as if commanding her attention, then withdrew again. This resembled Cohn and Tronick's descriptions of 3-month-olds' behavior during a still face (Cohn & Tronick, 1982).

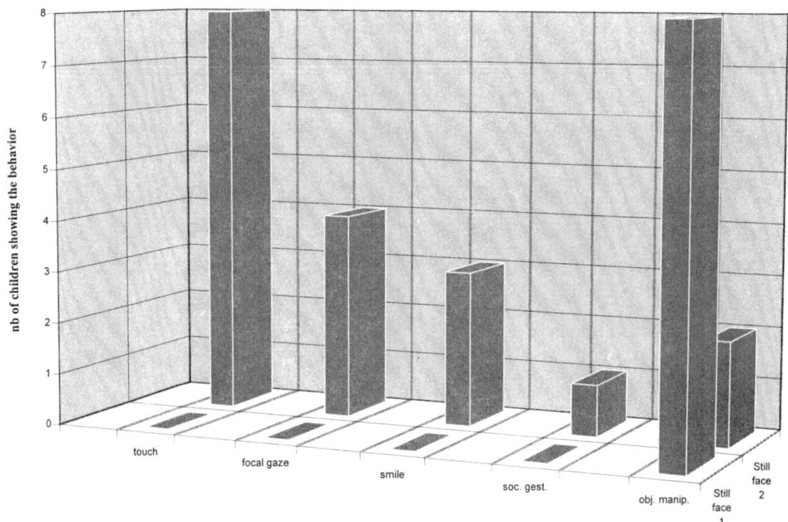

FIG. 8.1. Reactions of eight children with autism to a still face under two conditions.
During still-face1, the children were focused on the objects. By contrast, they were focused on the person during still-face2.

The study demonstrates that low-functioning mute children with autism are sensitive to a partner's display and have ontological expectancies concerning human social behavior. These results were obtained by using the still-face paradigm, which reversed the normal tendency of adults to approach autistic children. The children clearly tried to provoke a change in the adult's behavior, to get the adult's attention back. This indicates they are able to predict and to try to control a partner's behavior. Again, the rule-violation hypothesis is supported by these findings.

In summary, the still-face design opened a new methodological approach in infancy research in which adult behavior is systematically manipulated in order to test an infant's sensitivity to violations of interaction rules and to examine the infant's expectancies about human social behavior. This methodological tool can also be used to explore social expectancies in older socially impaired children. However the still-face design does not allow us to determine which rule violations babies are sensitive to. As mentioned by Cohn and Tronick (1982), it is important to vary the still-face design and manipulate adult behavior in other ways. The double video TV paradigm is one of these new manipulations.

The Double Video TV Paradigm

Trevarthen (1993) suggested that healthy 2-month-olds are able not only to respond to face-to-face communication with their mothers and to react to the still face but also to interact with a "live" televised image of their mothers talking to them. This early capacity to react to heard and seen televised signals was used by Murray and Trevarthen (1985) who extended the face-to-face design to a televised face-to-face image. It was shown that the still-face effect persisted in a televised face-to-face situation, indicating that infants react to televised partners in the same way they do to live, direct face-to-face encounters (Muir & Hains, 1993), and that televised face-to-face encounters can be used to standardize stimuli presentation. The televised face-to-face design allows researchers to manipulate communicative signals in a more natural way than the live or still test. Murray and Trevarthen created a new experimental paradigm based on a televised face-to-face interaction between mother and infant, the double closed-circuit TV paradigm. With this design, a segment of maternal behavior previously recorded can be presented to a baby out of synchrony, hence noncontingent with the baby's acts. It is thus possible to separate the effect of the violation of sequential contingency from other violations of interaction rules.

In their pionneer work, Murray and Trevarthen (1985) filmed babies and mothers interacting for 1 minute over closed-circuit video monitors. Thirty seconds later, they replayed to the babies a sample of good positive communication from their mother. In this replay condition, the mother coregulated her social actions to respond to behaviors that the baby no longer displayed. Was there any change in the babies' behavior? Did the babies react to these unexpected events? Did the babies act as if they recognize that their mother was noncontingent in their interaction? Murray and Trevarthen's reported that 2-month-olds behaved in dramatically different ways in the live and replay conditions. For instance, positive indexes, such as gaze to mother and communicative efforts (tonguing, mouth open), fell significantly during the replay session; whereas indexes of disturbance, such as gaze away, mouth closed, and frowning, increased significantly. However, these impressive results were obtained from a very small sample of babies (only four) of different ages (from 6 to 12 weeks old) and with repeated measures on the same infants. They needed confirmation. Moreover the procedure was critiziced for not having a control group (Rochat, Marian, & Neisser, in press). The possibility was raised that the negative responses displayed by the baby during the replay session reflected increased fussiness over time (Hains & Muir, 1996). Alternately, it was suggested that these could result from the break between the live and replay sessions, generating change in social context (Nadel, 1996).

Several replications took place. Hains and Muir (1996) used the same procedure with older infants and included a control group that received three periods of contingent interaction. They showed that 5-month-olds did not react negatively to the mother's replay but displayed a strong negative reaction to a stranger's replay. The differences between these results and Murray and Trevarthen's may be due to an effect of age. The 5-month-olds behaved as if the brief TV-replay period did not constitute a major violation of their well-established social relationships with their mother but did constitute a major violation of their expectancies for later interactions with a new partner.

More puzzling are the results by Rochat, Marian, and Neisser (1998), since they were obtained with 3-month-olds, the older age in Murray and Trevarthen's study. Using the same procedure and adding a control group to match for order, Rochat and colleagues failed to find differences between the experimental group, which experienced deferred maternal interaction, and the control group, which did not (see Rochat & Striano, this volume). Analyzing Rochat and colleagues' results, it appears that smiling increased significantly during replay. This is a counterintuitive result. If babies are not sensitive to noncontingent behavior during replay, this will result in no difference in smiling between the two conditions, or more probably, in a decrease during replay due to tiredness. But how can we explain an increase of smiling in the replay condition? A possible explanation is that the interactive condition is not as positive as expected. The authors conducted a rigorous experiment in which the sessions' timing was precisely scheduled. The live session lasted 30 seconds, and so far as we understand, it was defined as a face-to-face situation, whatever the content. Suppose the interaction was slow to become established; the two partners would hardly start interacting positively at the end of the 30 seconds. Then the break would come, and at the beginning of the replay the child would feel more at ease with the televised design and smile when recognizing the partner. In this case, the findings would result from comparing a sequence of preliminary contact to a replay sequence. Of course, we are ready to reconsider our explanation if we misinterpreted the procedure (see Rochat & Striano, this volume).

Nadel and colleagues modified the procedure so that the infants could continuously see their mothers rather than experience a break in the televised contact before the replay (Nadel, 1996; Nadel, Marcelli, Pezé, Kervella, & Reserbat-Plantey, 1997). This new procedure assured that the same social context would be maintained across the three conditions: Live1/ Replay/ Live2.

Live1 is the first live contingent sequence. From this, a sample of joyful face-to-face interaction was recorded for later replay, while the contingent live monitoring continued. The joyful communicative sample was then played to the infant without a break (Replay). This was immediately followed by a second contingent-live sequence (Live2). This second live session is a decisive piece to test the hypothesis of an early sensitivity to violations of contingency. Indeed, if the baby displayed negative behaviors during the replay session and then returned to exhibiting positive behaviors during Live2 session, this would indicate that the upset behavior observed during the replay was not simply due to tiredness. The whole session of three sequences lasted only 3 to 5 minutes (depending on when the mother succeeded in getting the baby's attention and when the dyad performed an alert face-to-face interaction). The replay lasted around 30 seconds. Figure 8.2 shows the experimental setup. In previous procedures, two video recorders were used: one for the baby and one for the mother. Our set up involved three video recorders: one for the baby and two for the mother, since two simultaneous records of the mother are needed (one for live and one for replay) in order to assure the continuity of the mother's televised image offered to the baby.

A video computer interfacing software allowed us to very accurately analyze the mother's and infant's synchronized behaviors, which were both presented on the screen, together with the coding grid. Every tenth frame was analyzed for each sequence condition (i.e., 75 frames for 30 seconds, since there are 25 frames per second).

The coding system consisted of categories such as *glance* (looks at the mother, turns away, eye closed, looks at something else . . .), *emotional display* (smiles, frowns, grimaces, neutral . . .), *mouth* (open, tonguing, closed, relaxed . . .), which were used in previous research by Murray and Trevarthen (1985). Two independant coders were blind to the conditions

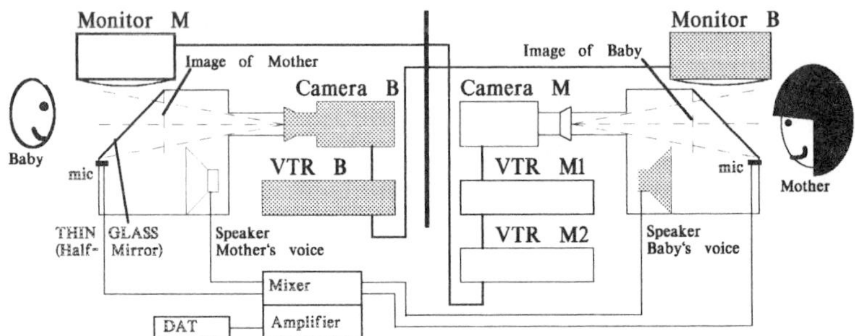

FIG. 8.2. Experimental device used for recording mother–infant interaction in contingent and noncontingent conditions. (Reprinted from Muir, D., & Nadel, J., 1998. Infant social perception. In A. Slater, Ed., *Perceptual development*, pp. 247–285.) Hove, East Sussex: Psychology Press.
Two videosystems filmed the mother, one for replay and the other for continuous televised presentation of the mother to the baby.

(live or replay), and one was blind to the aim of the study as well. The intercoder correlations were above 90 percent. Ten volunteer dyads of mothers and their 9-week-olds participated in the study.

As presented in Fig. 8.3, two positive and independent indexes decreased during the replay sequence: *gaze to mother* and *smiling*, and two negative and independent indexes increased during replay: *frowning* and *mouth closed.*

Our results mostly replicate Murray and Trevarthen's (1995) data. Nine-week-olds behave differently in the two conditions. However, although we found an increase of mouth closed during the replay, no significant change

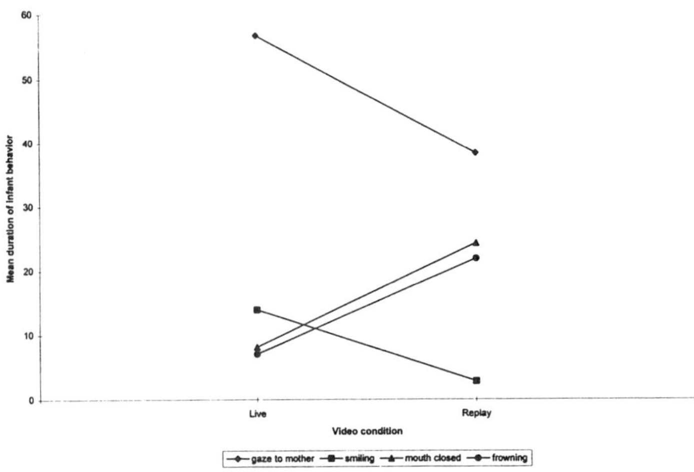

FIG. 8.3. Mean duration of infant behaviors across live and replay video conditions.

was observed in mouth opening or tonguing. This may be due to the age of the group. All our babies were 9 weeks old, whereas in Murray and Trevarthen's study, babies ranged in age from 6 to 12 weeks. Some of their infants were older than ours, and this could explain their higher scores for prespeech and hence the differences across conditions.

It is worth noticing that for the same reason, we should also expect higher scores for smiling in Murray and Trevarthen's (1995) study. On the contrary, our babies smiled more. On average, 14 percent of the time in Live1 versus only 5 percent for Murray and Trevarthen's babies. As it is improbable that French babies smile more than Scottish babies, this difference may account for different criteria defining our wait of an alert face-to-face interaction.

Nevertheless, Nadel and colleagues' results are mostly in agreement with Murray and Trevarthen's. Moreover, when the Live2 session was examined, Nadel and colleagues found that only three out of the ten babies did not recover during the second live televised interaction. Those three babies were particularly upset with the replay session: Two were crying and the third one displayed an avoidant behavior, with eyes and head turned away. The seven other babies quickly showed an increase of positive signals in the second live interaction. In particular, gaze to mother increased significantly and was even significantly higher for all seven babies than during the first live session, as if the infants were scrutinizing their mothers. Figure 8.4 gives the mean duration of gaze in the three conditions for these seven infants.

This finding indicates that we must take into account two aspects of the increase of gaze to mother. First, the disturbance observed during the replay session cannot be considered a function of fussiness over time, since babies recovered during the second live interaction. Second, we can consider that there is a renewal of attention toward the contingent partner, since the mean duration of gaze was higher in the second live interaction than in the first live one.

Another alternative explanation could be that the decrease of positive indexes during replay could be an effect of memory of the previous maternal behavior (already heard and seen). This appears to be very improbable, since the maternal facial expressions and speech are very repetitive during the televised face-to-face (and also in usual face-to-face). In addition, Hains and Muir (1996) found no difference between a replay of the adult's interaction with another infant and the replay of an earlier interaction with the focal infant. For these reasons, the decrease of attention and positive signals during the replay session cannot be explained by an effect of recall. Rather, all the results quoted account for an early sensitivity to the violation of sequential contingency during interaction. This leads us to propose that 2-month-olds apply some basic knowledge about human responsiveness to

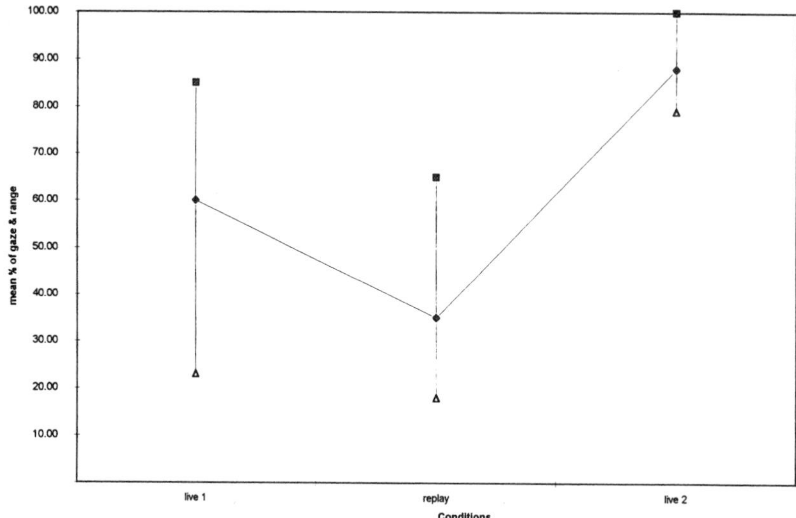

FIG. 8.4. Infant gaze to mother across conditions.

process social informations. They are sensitive to the violation of such principle of interaction as sequential contingency in their social partner.

Conclusion of the First Section

Face-to-face paradigms allow us to document babies' early capacity to discriminate between animate and still human stimuli—between neutral and expressive displays of the face—through the change in emotional expressions, heart rate variations, and other dependent changes. They permit us to infer babies' expectancies when facing a human partner and early capacity to predict maternal responses through their displayed positive attempts to get attention. They give evidence that the infants withdraw as a reaction to the unusual. They provide evidence that 2- to 3-month-olds expect agency from the intelligent self-propelled objects that are their human partners (Premack, 1990).

In conclusion, dyadic paradigms are powerful tools to test social perception. However, they do not provide evidence regarding an infant's capacity to initiate relevant social changes or to generate efficient reorganizations of the communicative system. Indeed, in a dyadic system, if one partner follows an experimental protocol, such as pausing a still face, or if the communicative behavior of one partner is manipulated, such as in a replay sequence, the system looses its flexibility, because it is not reciprocal anymore. Whatever the infant effort to make the mother smile or speak or look at her, the mother will remain either still or noncontingent. These are the limits of the dyadic paradigms presented so far.

Are babies able to exploit their perception of agency in others? Does this capacity lead to premisses of intentional monitoring of others' agency? Certainly other paradigms are necessary to go further with this question.

INTENTIONAL MONITORING OF OTHERS: TRIADIC PARADIGMS

If we are to examine children's intentional monitoring of others' agency, triadic paradigms appear to be a good option by allowing us to test the effects of the violation of other interaction rules. What do infants and toddlers do, for instance, when the adult turns her attention to another person and becomes engaged with that person rather than themselves? Murray and Trevarthen (1985) were the first to use this situation as an experimental paradigm, the *interruption paradigm.* They showed that under these conditions, 2- to 3-month-old infants decreased their communicative efforts (they performed fewer mouthing and tonguing movements) and decreased signs of positive affect toward their mothers. No distress was observed, however, unlike in the still-face or the double live–replay conditions. Such a description adopts a dyadic analysis of the situation. Let us now take another perspective and look precisely at infants' attempts to enter into a three-person interaction involving the mother and another adult. Are young infants capable to engage in such triadic exchanges? Are they able to respond to the initiations of two partners? Are they able to initiate a communicative system that includes two partners?

Understanding Two Others' Relatedness

Few studies have explored children's interest in interacting simultaneously with two persons during the first year of life. Murray and Trevarthen (1985) suggested that the reason why 6- to 12-week-old infants showed no distress when their mothers talked to an experimenter was because the baby's attention was caught by the experimenter's entrance. Infants spent 14 percent of the interruption sequence looking at the adult, they distributed short glances to the mother, and they maintained a relaxed expression. These data indicate a sensivity to the new social configuration that included a third person.

Scaife and Bruner (1975) reported that 4- to 5-month-old infants alternated looking first at the mother and then at the experimenter during pauses in the "joint attention" session. In a more systematic study of triadic play in 28 families, 2- to 9-month-old infants expressed positive affect while watching their parents interact, provided the adults engaged in lively interaction as opposed to conflictual interactions (Fivaz-Depeursinge, 1994). The babies also continued to self-regulate and succeeded in reengaging with their parents, now within a triad. These studies indicate that when very young infants watch two adults interact, they seem to be attentive to how adults alternate their actions and initiate interaction contingent on the adults' actions.

Molina, Spelke, and King (1996) further investigated whether 6-month-olds infer a person-to-person relationship, using an infant-controlled habituation paradigm. Infants were familiarized with both a person's face and a ball, each wearing a sharp-pointed hat. Both were moving, with self-propelled movements for the person and mechanical movements for the ball. After watching this sequence, the infant was shown a display presenting the person but hiding the supposed "interlocutor," another hat and its movements being the only visible information of this interlocutor's presence. When the experimental trials were over, two possible full scenes were presented. The interlocutor was either another person or a ball. In the first experimental condition, the person talked, then stopped, and the hat began to move as if talking. When the hat stopped moving, the person talked again to the hat, and so on. In the second condition, the person reached the hat and made it disappear. The results showed that in the first condition, infants looked longer at the scene presenting the person talking to another person than at the person talking to the ball. In the second condition, infants looked longer at the scene presenting the person pushing down the ball than at the person pushing another person. According to the authors, these findings indicate that the capacities to reason about a person-to-person relation develop at an early age, parallel to capacities to represent and reason about the physical world.

All these data bring to the foreground the possibility that very young children can understand how two people relate to each other in circumstances in which the child is not directly interacting with a partner. Indeed, such understanding is an important skill for participating in triadic interactions, since it enables children to predict how people will act in relation to one another based on their contingent movements, expressive signals, and conversational behaviors. It also enables enfants to know when and how to enter effectively into interaction with more than one partner at a time.

Understanding Self-Relatedness With Two Other Persons

Can an infant easily engage with two other people at the same time? Two-person comparison tasks have been designed to investigate young children's knowledge of others.

In a *simultaneous* comparison situation, infants will actively explore two other persons facing them and will look more systematically at the person they know. The preferential search pattern may therefore be considered a cognitive and selective engagement toward one of the two persons. Buschnell, Sai, and Mullin (1989) showed that 5-day-olds when presented with their mother's face and the face of another woman looked preferentially at their mother (61% of the session) even though both women had hair the same color and length.

Spelke and Owsley (1979) examined auditory and visual search for the mother and the father by infants who were 3.5, 5.5, and 7.5 months of age. First, the infants sat with the two parents in view and heard each parent speaking in turn. Then, during an experimental episode, the parents remained motionless but their tape-recorded voices were successively played over a speaker that was centered between them. Infants as young as 3.5 months looked systematically at the parent with matching voice. This pattern was especially pronounced when the parents actually spoke to their infants, but it was also observed when their speech was tape-recorded. Spelke and Owsley concluded that looking at the speaking parent could only have been guided by the baby's knowledge that specific voices come from specific people. Other studies presented separate films of two adults articulating sentences (Spelke & Corteyou, 1981) or expressing sad or happy faces (Walker, 1982) while a central speaker produced the specific sound of one of them. In such comparison tasks, it is clear that children extract the most relevant information to identify each of the two people.

However, being able to understand the coherence of each person in a triadic setting may not be equivalent to being able to make connections between self and others in a multiperson world. Recently, in order to understand how very young children make sense of a world in which people come and go and appear and disappear in front of them, Meltzoff and Moore (1992) presented to very young children a *successive* comparison of two different adults who each produced a different facial gesture from the same location in space. For example, first the mother showed the tongue-protusion gesture and left. Then a male stranger entered and demonstrated the mouth-opening gesture. When 6-week-old infants could visually track each adult as he or she entered and left the room, a significant number of these infants imitated the first person's gesture and then the second person's gesture in turn, apparently without confusion. On the other hand, when infants did not follow the adult's entrance and exit, as in the pilot experiment, they stared at the new person and then slowly and deliberately produced the previous person's gesture as if they were asking, "Are you the one who does the X gesture?" Meltzoff and Moore (1995) emphasized that by 6 weeks of age, infants recognize distinct human behaviors as gestural signatures of specific peoples. This helps infants differentiate *individuals* within the general class of *people* and construct representation of a person's identity from previous encounters maintained in memory.

Findings from both simultaneous and successive comparison tasks provide precious information on what young children's know about individuals in a multiperson situation, but neither of the experimental designs can assure us that infants go beyond person identification or animacy in order to understand the relations between two other people interacting and to enter into that interaction themselves. A next question is whether young children can understand not only others as "subjects," but also others as "subjects among other subjects."

The Exclusion Paradigm

So far, we have seen that infants process faces, voices, movements, and gestures in multiperson situations to explore others, to discover consistencies, and to recognize others as specific individuals in the environment. The challenge children face when they enter into a triadic communicative situation may help them develop the knowledge that they are also subjects among subjects. A person-person-person (P-P-P) interaction is special in the sense that there are only two communicative roles—agent and recipient—for three participants. This means that each participant in turn experiences exclusion as the other two interact. As adults, inasmuch as we intend to take part in the multiperson situation, we attend to the ongoing conversation, predict others' receptiveness, and time our initiation in order to continue or complete the topic. By the end of the second year, children actively paticipate in multiperson interactions, take a stand for one or another of the participants, remain on the topic others are actively engaged in, and share feelings, emotions, and social rules (Barton & Tomasello, 1991; Bretherton & Beegly, 1982; Cummings, Zahn-Waxler, & Radke-Yarrow, 1981; Dunn, 1991; Dunn & Shatz, 1989). But how do multiperson engagement develop in early infancy?

To study the development of multiperson engagement, we systematically explored how young children deal with momentary exclusion in a three person interaction. We created the *exclusion paradigm*, assuming that exclusion will challenge children's understanding of their own intentionality and how that relates to the intentionality of others.

The exclusion paradigm replicates ecological situations in which a child has to cope with a busy mother who is attending a baby sibling (Kendrick & Dunn, 1980) or a friend (Rubenstein, Howes, & Pedersen, 1982). Two main differences were introduced into these everyday situations. First, instead of studying family triads, we observed triads composed of a familiar adult experimenter and two familiar same-age infants. Second, instead of having a mother overwhelmed and trying to be careful not to ignore one child—reorienting the momentarily excluded child's attention to the ongoing interaction or adressing both children simultaneously—the adult experimenter in the exclusion paradigm followed an experimental protocol. She was trained to focus her attention solely on one child until the other child commanded attention.

Our general hypothesis was that momentary exclusion would enhance children's sense of relatedness to others and would confront children with momentary relational problems such as how to get another's attention and cooperation, how to understand others' intentions, and how to monitor effectively the response of others in relation to the self.

Sixty toddlers 11, 16, and 23 months of age were observed in the exclusion paradigm (see Tremblay-Leveau & Nadel, 1995, for more details). This research yielded two main findings. The first was that when children as young as 11 months were excluded from an ongoing dyadic interaction in a social triad, they produced three types of socially directed behaviors: those directed to the peer, those directed to the adult and also—this was the novelty—social behaviors directed to both the adult and the peer (see Table 8.1).

These double oriented acts increased significantly with age, and after 16 months, they outnumbered those directed to the peer alone or to the adult alone. These behaviors reflect solutions to the stuctural difference between dyadic and triadic interactions. The children regularly talked, smiled, or offered an object while looking at the two participants, directing their actions to both participants. Our interpretation is that children try to coordinate with both individuals and to introduce themselves in a triadic interaction in this way. These results do not support the hypothesis that children of the second year seek only exclusive dyadic attention within triads (Kendrick & Dunn, 1980; Rubenstein, Howes, & Pedersen, 1985).

The second main finding concerned how the excluded children successfully joined the ongoing adult–child interaction. Their social initiatives were oriented toward either the two partners (*triadic intrusions*) or only one partner (*dyadic intrusions*). Their intrusions could be mediated in three ways: joining the dyad's focus of attention, introducing a new topic with other available objects, or initiating a new topic without an object mediation. Eighty-six percent of all social intrusions referred to an object, thus indicating that objects facilitated children's entrance into the ongoing interaction. Table 8.2 shows the mean proportion of successful triadic and dyadic intrusions.

Both dyadic and triadic successful intrusions mainly referred to the dyad's ongoing focus of interest. However, changes over the second year

TABLE 8.1
Mean Frequency of Socially Oriented Intrusions per Child

Social Orientation of Intrusions	*Age (Months)*		
	11	*16*	*23*
Directed to peer	3.4	4.8	5.3
Directed to adult	5.5	5.7	8.5
Directed to both partners	5.2	8.4	14.3

TABLE 8.2
Mean Proportion of Intrusions by Object Used in Social Intrusions

Category of Use of Object	*Age (Months)*		
	11	*16*	*23*
Focal Object			
Dyadic	.46	.64	.52
Triadic	.57	.64	.40
New Object			
Dyadic	.25	.29	.17
Triadic	.17	.29	.36

were found exclusively for the triadic intrusions. Those mediated by the dyad's focal object decreased with age whereas those introducing a new object increased significantly across the three ages. Furthermore, at 23 months, a significant difference was found between the proportion of successful dyadic and triadic intrusions introducing a new topic.

This suggest that escaping social exclusion during the second year sharpens children's attention to others' attention and encourages them to seize their chance in renewing an interactive topic. The capacity for sharing and actively monitoring two other persons' attention appeared at an earlier age in our study than in Bakeman and Adamson's work (1984) on joint attention in adult–child dyads. The momentary exclusion might well account for this precocity, as if social exclusion strengthened social attention, and thus, attention to others' attention.

A more specific hypothesis was tested with forty 11- and 23-month-old children concerning the use and effects of these social skills in triadic situations (Tremblay-Leveau & Nadel, 1996). Comparing each child's participation in dyadic (child–peer or child–adult) and triadic (child–peer–adult) interactions within a 15-minute session, we found that 11-month-olds were engaged in adult–child dyadic interactions as often as in triadic interactions and that 23-month-olds were more frequently engaged in triadic interactions than in dyadic ones. Furthermore, at 23 months, the number of turns taken by each child in triadic interactions was twice as high as the number of turns in dyadic exchanges. This highlighted the toddlers' preference for triadic interactions within social triads and pointed out their early capacity to take turns in a complex social situation, even outside the family triads studied by Barton and Tomasello (1991). The striking result lies in the capacity of children as young as 11 months to participate actively and to take turns appropriately in triadic interactions.

Another finding was that even at 11 months of age, children became clearly aware of the social position they held in a triadic interaction. When we compared the communicative behaviors of the same child in the two distinct social positions, included and excluded, we found two different behavioral patterns. When included in an interaction with an adult, children initiated very few signals of interest toward the peer, but they, nevertheless, answered the peer's initiatives despite the fact that they were socially engaged with the adult. An interesting context comparison shows that the mean percentage of answers given by children in peer–peer dyads during the second year (the mean percentage is 40, according to Bronson, 1975; Lee, 1975; Maudry & Nekula, 1939) is equivalent to the mean percentage of answers given by children to peers in a triad (43% at 11 months and 50% at 23 months). This result showed that 11- and 23-month-olds social performance was not altered by their engagement with the adult and that they were not ignoring the peer's presence.

On the other hand, when excluded from the ongoing adult–child interaction, toddlers responded immediately to nearly all, even though few, peer initiatives (72 mean percentage at 11 months and 89% at 23 months). This high percentage of response can only be explained by an exceptional level of attention to the other's behaviors (checking whom he or she is looking at, following the topic of interest) and by an ability to reason about observables, to infer the other's target of attention, and to infer the other's goals (adressing to you, to him or her, to both, interested in the toy).

Based on these findings, we reasoned that information on intentionality in others must have been acquired much earlier in the first year of life and may well be derived from the situation experienced by a child when he or she watched the ongoing interaction. More precisely, if children as young as 11 months are so keen in joining ongoing interactions and excel in using varied patterns of gaze initiation and joint attention, then it is plausible that younger infants, in an adapted exclusion paradigm, may well demonstrate some form of awareness of self and others' agency.

To assess this question, a pilot experiment was conducted with three 3-month-olds and six 6-month-olds. Two adult experimenters alternately interacted with a child and then looked at each other, starting a reciprocal conversation and leaving the child momentarily excluded. We coded, second by second, the gaze direction and the facial expressions of the infant and examined in detail the last minute of the dyadic Adult1–Child and Adult2–Child interactions and the first minute of the Adult1–Adult2 condition. As Table 8.3 shows, in each dyadic interaction, the 3-month-olds as well as the 6-month-olds, while looking at the focal adult, also turned to glance at the other adult.

During the exclusion period, infants of both ages, and most strikingly at 3 months, increased the number of looks to the two adults talking. At both ages, they looked at Adult1, then Adult2, then back again to Adult1 an average of three times per minute. Another important feature of the exclusion period was that infants of both ages produced a mean of two

TABLE 8.3
Mean Number of Looks per Minute to the Social Setting as a Function of Age and Condition

	Looks Toward		
Conditions	*Adult₁*	*Adult₂*	*Elsewhere*
$Adult_1$–Child			
3 months	4.5	1.2	2.8
6 months	4	2.6	0.6
$Adult_2$–Child			
3 months	0.6	3.8	2
6 months	2.6	4	0.2
$Adult_1$–$Adult_2$			
3 months	7	6	7
6 months	5.5	4.4	4

social behaviors per minute (smile, vocalization, or groan) oriented toward the two adults. The results can be accounted for by postulating that a P-P-P communicative situation is a privileged structure for the develoment of infants' understanding of how to be a social entity among other social entities.

Conclusion of the Second Section

From the moment of birth, a child is embedded more frequently in multiparticipant contexts than in strict dyadic situations (Collis, 1982; Dunn, 1991; Hinde, 1976; Lewis & Rosenblum, 1984; Schaffer, 1984). As we argued earlier, infants very quicky develop featural discrimination of different persons. However, such knowledge provides no guarantee that self's and others' intentions are understood as being connected. Becoming effective in interacting with more than one person may be a precursor of an understanding of self and others as intelligent agents, in other words, entities behaving according to goals.

Interestingly, the P-P-P communicative system requires very early in life three of the four components of Baron-Cohen's *mindreading system* (1995). Our observation indicates that infants as young as 3 months detect when gazing is oriented toward them (*eye direction detector*). This is true not only when the focal adult looked at them but also when the other adult looked at them. Infants also understand that when the focal adult looks and talks to another adult, the former is intentionally oriented toward the other (*intentional detector*). In a social triad, this interaction took place between two agents independent of the self. That babies understood this was suggested by the to-and-fro visual pattern observed in all infants during the exclusion periods. The most stunning observation was that when the focal adult turned to look at the other adult, not only did most infants follow her line of regard but they also looked back at the focal adult, to confirm that they shared the same visual target. This can be understood as an early use of the *sharing attention mechanism* postulated by Baron-Cohen based on information about the perceptual state of another person in order to form triadic representations.

Triadic representations correspond to the relations between an agent, the self, and an object as proposed by Baron-Cohen. The object can be another agent as well. Evidence from the exclusion paradigm leads us to propose that a baby can share attention toward a third person more precociously than toward an object. Classically, joint attention is found around 9 months of age with the active monitoring of the other person's gaze toward the object (Butterworth, 1991; Scaife & Bruner, 1975) and pointing toward the object (Bates, Benigni, Bretherton, Camaioni, & Volterra, 1979). In our P-P-P design, infants younger than 6 months showed the classical organization of shared attention: They gazed in the same direction as the focal adult and alternated looks at the target (the other person).

If communicating with others about people in the P-P-P system is the first experience requiring sophisticated triadic interactive skills, then triadic representations of self and agent looking at, or attenting to, the same object may well be effective earlier in a person-person-person interactive system than in a person-object-person system. Like Dunn (1988, 1991), Perner, Ruffman, and Leekam (1994), and Jenkins and Astington (1996), we propose that opportunities for social experience with siblings may accelerate children's understanding of mental states in others.

General Conclusion

Reviewing dyadic and triadic experimental paradigms show that early on, infants demonstrate ontological expectancies concerning human social behaviors.

Dyadic interaction paradigms allow us to explore the direct consequences of violation of such social rules as "responsiveness" and "social contingency." They provide invaluable information about the early capacities of infants to detect changes in social behavior, to establish expectancies about facial expressions, to relate initiations and responses, to perceive noncontingency between initiations and responses, and to infer agency. The 2-month-old angry infant who never turned his head or his eyes toward his mother, although she called her pathetically during the Live2 session, ressembled an avoidant 9-month-old after a "strange situation." He behaved as if he were designating her as a deceptive objective and were trying to entrap her at her turn. Such capacities can only be revealed by experimental designs. And this is just a beginning. Dyadic designs and particularly televised designs are good candidates for generating other innovative paradigms. They will contribute further to enrich the body of data about the conditions and parameters of early social perception.

Triadic paradigms are new. They have not yet been fully exploited. They are an appropriate means through which to manipulate an adult's social behavior without breaking the communicative flow, since in a triadic system there are two roles (initiator and responder) for three persons. They allow us to study infants as initiators, not only as responders.

Dyadic as well as triadic paradigms can reveal early competencies in reasoning about, predicting, controlling, and monitoring social behavior. They can also reveal early abilities to monitor overt mental states, such as states of attention (look at, think, etc.). As Hobson (1991) put it, "The observable directedness of behaviour might complement the observed expressiveness of bodies in providing a child with pointers towards the mind's meaning-conferring rather than reality reflecting characteristics" (p. 47). We could add to Hobson's proposal that the monitoring of observable directedness provides other powerful pointers to the young apprentice mindreader. Exploring these mindreading pointers is a promising program based on promising new experimental paradigms.

REFERENCES

Als, H., Tronick, E., & Brazelton, T. (1978). Analysis of face-to-face interaction in infant–adult dyads. In M. Lamb, S. Suomi, & G. Stephenson (Eds.), *The study of social interaction: Methodological problems.* Madison: University of Wisconsin Press.

Bakeman, R., & Adamson, L. B. (1984). Coordinating attention to people and objects in mother–infant and peer–infant interaction. *Child Development, 55,* 1278–1289.

Baron-Cohen, S. (1995). *Mindblindness: An essay on autism and Theory of Mind.* Cambridge, MA: MIT Press.

Barton, M. E., & Tomasello, M. (1991). Joint attention and conversation in mother–infant–sibling triads. *Child Development, 62,* 517–529.

Bates, E., Benigni, L., Bretherton, I., Camaioni, L., & Volterra, V. (1979). Cognition and communication from 9–13 months: Correlational findings. In E. Bates (Ed.), *The emergence of symbols* (pp. 69–140). New York: Academic Press.

Brazelton, T. B., Koslowski, B., & Main, W. (1974). The origins of reciprocity: The early mother–infant interaction. In M. Lewis & L. Rosenblum (Eds.), *The effect of the infant on its caregiver.* New York: Wiley.

Bretherton, I., & Beegly, M. (1982). Talking about internal states: The acquisition of an explicit theory of mind. *Developmental Psychology, 18,* 906–921.

Bronson, W. C. (1975). Development in behavior with agemates during the second year of life. In M. Lewis & L. A. Rosenblum (Eds.), *Friendship and peer relations.* New York: Wiley.

Bushnell, I. W. R., Sai, F., & Mullin, J. T. (1989). Neonatal recognition of the mother's face. *British Journal of Developmental Psychology, 7,* 3–15.

Butterworth, G. (1991). The ontogeny and phylogeny of joint visual attention. In A. Whithen (Ed.), *Natural theories of mind.* London: Blackwell.

Cohn, J. F., & Tronick, E. Z. (1982). Communicative rules and sequential structure of infant behaviour during normal and depressed interaction. In E. Tronick (Ed.), *Social interchange in infancy: Affect, cognition, and communication* (pp. 59–77). Baltimore: University Park Press.

Collis, G. M. (1982). Beyond the dyadic interaction. *Bulletin of the British Psychological Society, 35*, A87.

Cummings, E. M., Zahn-Waxler, C., & Radke-Yarrow, M. (1981). Young children's responses to expressions of anger and affection by others in the family. *Child Development, 52*, 1274–1282.

Dunn, J. (1988). *The beginnings of social understanding*. Oxford: Blackwell.

Dunn, J. (1991). Young children's understanding of other people: Evidence from observations within the family. In D. Frye & C. Moore (Eds.), *Children's theories of mind* (pp. 97–114). Hillsdale, NJ: Lawrence Erlbaum Associates.

Dunn, J., & Shatz, M. (1989). Becoming a conversationalist despite (or because of) having a sibling. *Child Development, 60*, 399–410.

Ellsworth, C., Muir, D., & Hains, S. (1993). Social competence and person–object differentiation: An analysis of the still-face effect. *Developmental Psychology, 29*, 3–73.

Field, T. M. (1984). Early interactions between infants and their postpartum depressed mothers. *Infant Behavior and Development, 7*, 527–532.

Fivaz-Depeursinge, E. (1994). Triadic interactions as anchors for the conceptualization of interactive representations [Special ICIS issue]. *Infant Behavior and Development, 17*, 307.

Gusella, J., Muir, D., & Tronick, E. (1988). The effect of manipulating maternal behavior during an interaction on three- and six-month-olds' affect and attention. *Child Development, 59*(4), 1111–1124.

Hains, S., & Muir, D. (1996). Effects of stimulus contingency in infant–adult interactions. *Infant Behavior and Development, 19*(1), 49–61.

Hinde, R. (1976). On describing relationships. *Journal of Child Psychology and Psychiatry, 17*, 1–19.

Hobson, P. (1991). Against the theory of Theory of Mind. *British Journal of Developmental Psychology, 9*, 33–51.

Jenkins, J. M., & Astington, J. W. (1996). Cognitive factors and family structure associated with the Theory of Mind development in young children. *Developmental Psychology, 32*, 70–78.

Kendrick, C., & Dunn, J. (1980). Caring for a second baby: Effects on interaction between mother and firstborn. *Developmental Psychology, 16*, 303–311.

Lamb, M. E., Morrison, D. C., & Malkin, C. M. (1987). The development of infant social expectations in face-to-face interactions: A longitudinal study. *Merrill-Palmer Quarterly, 33*, 241–254.

Legerstee, M., Corter, C., & Kienapple, K. (1990). Hand, arm and facial actions of young infants to a social and nonsocial stimulus. *Child Development, 61*, 774–784.

Lee, L. (1975). Toward a cognitive theory of interpersonal development: Importance of peers. In M. Lewis & L. Rosenblum (Eds.), *Friendship and peer relations*. New York: Wiley.

Lewis, M., & Rosenblum, L. A. (1984). *Beyond the dyad*. New York: Plenum Press.

Massie, H. (1977). Patterns of mother–infant behavior and subsequent childhood psychosis. *Child Psychiatry and Human Development, 7*, 211–230.

Maudry, M., & Nekula, M. (1939). Social relations between children of the same age during the first two years of life. *Journal of Genetic Psychology, 54*, 192–215.

Meltzoff, A., & Moore, M. (1992). Early imitation within a functional framework: The importance of person identity, movement, and development. *Infant Behavior and Development, 15*(4), 479–505.

Meltzoff, A., & Moore, M. (1995). Infants' understanding of people and things: From body imitation to folk psychology. In J. Bermudez, A. Marcel, & N. Eilan (Eds.), *The body and the self* (pp. 43–69). London: MIT Press.

Molina, M., Spelke, E., & King, D. (1996). Animate and inanimate distinction in infancy [Special ICIS issue]. *Infant Behavior and Development, 19*, 625.

Muir, D. W., & Hains, S. M. J. (1993). Infant sensitivity to perturbations in adult facial, vocal, tactile, and contingent stimulation during face-to-face interactions. In B. de Boysson-Bardies, S. de Schönen et al. (Eds.), *Developmental neurocognition: Speech and face processing in the first year of life* (pp. 171–185). Netherlands: Kluwer.

Murray, L., & Trevarthen, C. (1985). Emotional regulation of interaction between two-month-olds and their mothers. In T. Field & N. Fox (Eds.), *Social perception in infants* (pp. 177–197). Norwood, NJ: Ablex.

Nadel, J. (1996, April). Early interpersonal timing and the perception of social contingencies [Special ICIS issue]. *Infant Behavior and Development, 19,* 202.

Nadel, J., Marcelli, D., Pezé, A., Kervella, C., & Reserbat-Plantey, D. (1997). *Contingent interaction in French 2-month-olds with their mother.* Paper presented at the *Society for Research in Child Development,* Washington, DC.

Perner, J., Ruffman, T., & Leekam, S. R. (1994). Theory of Mind is contagious: You catch it from your sibs. *Child Development, 65,* 1228–1238.

Premack, D. (1990). The infant's theory of self-propelled objects. *Cognition, 36,* 1–16.

Rochat, P., Neisser, U., & Marian, V. (1998). Are young children sensitive to interpersonal contingency? *Infant Behavior and Development,* 355–366.

Rubenstein, J. L., Howes, C., & Pedersen, F. A. (1982). Second order effects of peers on mother–toddler interaction. *Infant Behavior and Development, 5,* 185–194.

Scaife, M., & Bruner, J. S. (1975). The capacity for joint attention in the infant. *Nature, 253,* 265–266.

Schaffer, R. (1984). *The child's entry into a social world.* New York: Basic Books.

Spelke, E., & Cortelyou, A. (1981). Perceptual aspects of social knowing: Looking and listening in infancy. In M. E. Lamb & L. R. Sherros (Eds.), *Infant social cognition.* Hillsdale, NJ: Lawrence Erlbaum Associates.

Spelke, E., & Owsley, C. J. (1979). Intermodal exploration and knowledge in infancy. *Infant Behavior and Development, 2,* 13–27.

Spelke, E., Phillips, A., & Woodward, A. (1995). Infants' knowledge of object motion and human action. In D. Sperber, D. Premack, & A. James Premack (Eds.), *Causal cognition* (pp. 44–78). Oxford: Clarendon Press.

Stern, D. (1977). *The first relationship: Infant and mother.* Cambridge, MA: Harvard University Press.

Tremblay-Leveau, H., & Nadel, J. (1995). Young children's communicative skills in triads. *International Journal of Behavioral Development, 18,* 227–242.

Tremblay-Leveau, H., & Nadel, J. (1996). Exclusion in triads: Can it serve "meta-communicative" knowledge in 11- and 23-month-old children? *British Journal of Developmental Psychology, 14,* 145–158.

Trevarthen, C. (1977). Descriptive analyses of infant communicative behaviour. In R. Schaffer (Ed.), *Studies in mother–infant interaction* (pp. 227–269). London: Academic Press.

Trevarthen, C. (1993). The function of emotions in early infant communication and development. In J. Nadel & L. Camaioni (Eds.), *New perspectives in early communicative development* (pp. 48–82). London: Routledge.

Tronick, E. (1982). Affectivity and sharing. In E. Tronick (Ed.), *Social interchange in infancy: Affect, cognition, and communication* (pp. 1–6). Baltimore: University Park Press.

Tronick, E., Als, H., Adamson, L., Wise, S., & Brazelton, T. (1978). The infant's response to entrapment between contradictory messages in face-to-face interaction. *Journal of American Academy of Child Psychiatry, 17,* 1–13.

Walker, A. S. (1982). Intermodal perception of expressive behaviors by human infants. *Journal of Experimental Child Psychology, 33,* 514–535.

Part III

EARLY MONITORING OF OTHERS

Chapter 9

Action Analysis: A Gateway to Intentional Inference

Dare A. Baldwin
Jodie A. Baird
University of Oregon

> *To naïve thought, nothing is less problematic than that we grasp the actions of others, but it is precisely the task of psychology to remove the veil of self-evidence from these momentous processes.*
>
> —Solomon E. Asch (1952)

Humans in action present a complex picture: When in motion, we travel hither and thither, twisting and turning, appendages aflutter. As well, our action often makes contact in diverse ways and in rapid succession with an enormous array of different objects. Despite this complexity, we are able to achieve an orderly, coherent understanding of what others are doing. How do we do this? Although an answer to this question remains elusive, at least one thing is clear: The structure we as adults derive from observing others' actions seems typically framed in terms of ideas about their goals and intentions. Taking this as our starting point, we plan two things for this chapter. First, we examine some of the skills that enable adults to derive ideas about others' intentions from observing them in action. New here will be a focus on the central role of basic action analysis skills in supporting adults' inferences about intentions. Second, we present some suggestions regarding the ontogeny of intentional understanding, with an emphasis on action analysis skills as a crucial driving force for development in this arena. In particular, we propose that intentional understanding can begin early and progress rapidly, because even young infants possess some skills for organizing action into units commensurate with an intentional analysis, though they are not yet capable of conceptualizing action in adultlike intentional terms.

INTENTIONAL ANALYSIS, GENERATIVITY, AND THE ROLE OF ACTION PROCESSING

Especially striking about our adult-level skills for processing action is that novelty presents little interpretive impediment. For example, those of us addicted to sci-fi drama frequently encounter novel actions via the magic of modern special-effects technology. Relevant here are actions such as stepping into position on a pad and then vanishing (transporting), hurtling into the air only to be thrown back (attempting to penetrate an invisible forcefield), passing hands through others' bodies (attempting to injure a holographic image), and the like. Each of these action sequences was, at one time, quite novel to each of us, yet despite the novelty we easily process the actions, derive relevant intentions, and organize these into a larger appreciation of the overall goals. These examples illustrate that we each possess a system for analyzing others' action that is generative in kind. Actions that are new might leave us stymied and confused, but they do not. We can readily derive inferences about novel kinds of underlying intentions, and these intentional inferences are likely to show considerable consistency among different observers.

Some kind of basic, bottom-up skill at analyzing human action must be at least one important part of what we are doing in such cases. Preset expectancies about action–intention relations aren't enough to yield any sensible interpretation for novel action sequences; we are forced to derive new action–intention relations. Doing this requires the ability to process the action itself and to use it as a base for inferences about intentions.

A basic capacity for action analysis,[1] then, is implied by the generative nature of our system of intentional understanding. It is also implied by the fact that actions and our analysis of the intentions underlying them

---

[1]In the philosophical literature, it is common to distinguish between *action* (intentional movement) and *movement* (motion of the body, regardless of intentional status) (e.g., Searle, 1983). Were we to maintain this distinction, we would later be discussing how infants' *movement analysis* abilities enable them to construct an understanding of others' action, rather than how *action analysis* makes possible inferences about others' intentions. We have chosen to depart from the standard philosophical terminology, largely because we feel the term *movement* is misleading with regard to the data infants are actually capable of processing. In particular, as we argue in later sections, we believe that infants process more than just movement or motion: They process others' movements with respect to the objects acted on. For want of a better term, *action* seems the best descriptor of such data. Thus by attributing action analysis abilities to infants, we grant them skills for processing human movement patterns with respect to the objects involved.

are to some degree dissociable. Consider the action of poking a needle into someone's arm. This action could arise from an intent to heal (e.g., doctor) or an intent to harm (e.g., sadist). Likewise, one and the same intention, let's say to heal, can give rise to any number of different possible actions, ranging from mere talk to invasive surgery. To be at all successful in interpreting others' actions in appropriate intentional terms, one must appreciate this kind of dissociability between action and intention but at the same time be skilled at using action as a rich and complex source of information about intentions. This, in turn, requires a set of skills for analyzing action in its own right.

Interestingly, level of analysis seems to influence the dissociability of action and intention. Intentions such as "to heal" are at a relatively general level of analysis, and can give rise to a diversity of appropriate action, whereas intentions at a somewhat less general level are much more tightly linked to specific action. For example, the intention to poke (as when inserting a syringe into a patient's arm), if enacted, necessarily gives rise to some kind of poking action; there really is no other action that could fulfill a poking intention. The relative convergence of action and intention at this more "basic" level may be significant from a developmental perspective. This seems to be the level at which an analysis of action most directly informs inferences about intentions, and thus, developmentally, may be the jumping-off point for intentional inference.

To this point, we have suggested that adult interpretation of others' behavior requires two distinguishable kinds of abilities: an ability to process others' actions—their movement patterns in the world—as well as an ability to use such action analysis as a base for inferences at the level of others' goals and intentions. Several things are noteworthy about the framework we are attempting to articulate. First, in conceptualizing intentions as inferentially derived from an action analysis base (see Dittrich & Lea, 1994, for a similar view), we are departing from a "direct perception" account of intentional understanding, in which intentions are thought to be accessed directly in others' motion (e.g., Asch, 1952; Newtson, 1973, 1976, 1993; Premack, 1990). Second, we view analysis of actions and intentions as distinguishable in the adult-level system of intentional understanding, yet nevertheless deeply intertwined. In other words, we believe that intentional inferences can and in most ordinary, everyday circumstances do feed back to influence our processing of others' action. This kind of framework is akin to interactive models proposed to account for processing in other cognitive domains, such as word recognition (e.g., McClelland, 1985) and language comprehension (e.g., Gernsbacher, 1990; Marslen-Wilson & Tyler, 1980). Third, although we are focusing on the link between action analysis and inferences about intentions, action analysis abilities surely serve as a base for drawing inferences of other kinds as well. As Schult &

Wellman (1997) pointed out, for example, adults (and, as it turns out, even 3-year-olds) can reliably focus on distinctly different causes for varying kinds of action sequences. For example, a man's fall off a cliff may be interpreted in psychological terms as the result of an intention to jump, which implicates intentional inference, or as the result of basic physical forces. On any given occasion, we seek cues in action to aid in deciding whether an explanation in psychological terms is even warranted. As yet, little is actually known about the inferential processes operating here, although several researchers are beginning to redress this gap in discovering cues that adults (e.g., Bloom & Veres, 1996; Dittrich & Lea, 1994; Malle & Knobe, 1997), preschoolers (e.g., Dasser, Ulbaek, & Premack, 1989; Schult & Wellman, 1997), and even infants (e.g., Rochat, Morgan, & Carpenter, 1997) use in judgments of intentionality.

Recent evidence suggests that infants as young as 12 to 18 months already are skilled at using others' action as a base for drawing inferences regarding their intentions. We turn now to review this new body of evidence about early intentional understanding, with an eye to what such abilities suggest about preexisting skills for processing action.

EARLY ABILITY IN THE INTENTIONAL ARENA

By 18 months of age, infants already demonstrate remarkable social skill, ranging from language and gesture to social play, social referencing, assistance seeking, and the like. The richness of their functioning in the social realm suggests that they already possess real skills for interpreting others' intentions. Recent research investigating early intentional understanding confirms this suspicion. To illustrate this body of research, we focus on studies investigating imitation and language learning. In each of these two domains, infants' intentional skills appear to rest on a striking ability to organize complex action information and utilize it as a base for intentional inference.

Imitation

Meltzoff (1995) gave 18-month-old infants the opportunity to watch an adult repeatedly fail to complete an action on a novel object. For example, the adult failed successively in three somewhat different attempts to hang a flexible loop on a metal prong. When subsequently given the object to play with, infants immediately produced the intended action despite having never before seen that particular action sequence. In fact, infants were just as likely to accurately perform the intended action in response to viewing the adult's failed attempts as they were in response to a full and successful demonstration of the target action. These results powerfully suggest that infants 18 months of age are using action to drive inferences about intentions. On witnessing an interesting action sequence, infants reenacted not the action sequence per se but the actions that followed from what they deemed to be the underlying intention. At an even more basic level, these results indicate a superior skill at analyzing others' action. Faced with three distinct variants of each failed novel action sequence, infants readily achieved a unified conception of this complex action information, a conception obviously organized in such a way as to support inferences about intentions.

In another study of early imitation (Carpenter, Akhtar, & Tomasello, in press), infants watched an adult performing a sequence of two actions (e.g., pulling a handle and spinning a wheel) on a novel object with both actions producing a salient result (e.g., a toy appears). The adult's actions were marked vocally as intentional ("There!") in one case and accidental ("Whoops!") in the other. Following the modeled actions, the experimenter gave infants the object and asked them to "make it work." Infants across the 14- to 18-month age span produced the action marked as intentional far more often than the action marked as accidental. Thus, infants not only discriminated between the experimenter's two actions (implicating basic skills for analyzing action) but also distinguished them specifically with respect to their intentional status (implicating intentional understanding as well). Moreover, infants apparently viewed intentional actions as more noteworthy, or perhaps as more worthy of reenactment, than accidental actions, further implicating intentional understanding.

Together, the Meltzoff (1995) and Carpenter et al. (in press) studies converge to suggest that infants 14 months of age and older can spontaneously process new action sequences in ways that yield organized action percepts amenable to generating inferences about the intentions underlying such action. Infants' skills for analyzing others' action thus seem already powerful enough to support a germinal version of the open system for intentional inference that we as adults possess.

Language

Recent evidence from research in language acquisition provides another window into young children's abilities in the domain of intentional inference. In any face-to-face conversation, and especially in adult speech to children, speakers provide a host of action clues regarding their communicative intentions. Others' actions thus potentially provide a powerful scaffold for language learning, but only if infants and young children have the conceptual wherewithal to appreciate and properly utilize the relevant action information. A phenomenon we have termed *discrepant labeling* provides a case in point. Discrepant labeling occurs any time a speaker utters an object label when the addressee is focused on an altogether different object from the one to which the speaker is actually referring. This is the case for as many as 30 percent to 50 percent of labeling utterances that Western, middle-class infants hear (e.g., Collis, 1977). Discrepant labeling poses a risk for language learning: Infants might mistakenly link the label with the object of their own focus, engendering a mapping error and thus impeding language learning. However, if infants appreciate that speakers tend to supply action clues regarding their referential intentions—clues such as line-of-regard, gestures (e.g., pointing, showing), voice direction and body posture—they might note the discrepancy between their own and the speaker's focus and utilize the action clues to locate the correct referent of the label. Hence skill at analyzing others' action with respect to inferences about intentions would enable infants to avoid the potential pitfalls of discrepant labeling.

Our research indicates that this is well within the powers of infants as young as 18 to 19 months (Baldwin, 1991, 1993). In two separate studies, infants heard novel labels for novel objects in two situations: follow-in labeling, during which the speaker looked at and labeled the toy of the infant's focus, and discrepant labeling, during which the speaker looked at and labeled a toy other than that of the infant's focus. In the situation of discrepant labeling, infants actively sought clues to the speaker's referential intent by first checking and then following the speaker's line of regard to the other toy. Their responses to subsequent comprehension questions revealed that they avoided incorrectly associating the novel label to the toy of their own focus and instead linked the new label with its correct referent. This suggests that by 18 months of age, infants actively seek and successfully use clues in action to support inferences about a speaker's referential intentions. As well, infants rely on such intentional inferences in preference to purely associative information, such as temporal contiguity, when establishing new word–object mappings. A recent study suggests that infants as young as 12 months possess comparable abilities (Baldwin, Bill, & Ontai, 1996). As well, these findings are bolstered by a host of additional language-learning studies that are reviewed elsewhere (e.g., Baldwin & Tomasello, 1998; Tomasello, in press). Together, this body of evidence strongly suggests that language development is the beneficiary of a truly powerful system for intentional inference on infants' part.[2] Especially striking within this literature is the range and complexity of

[2]In some of the studies in this literature, alternatives to an intentional understanding account—explanations invoking salience or novelty effects, for example (see Samuelson & Smith, 1998)—remain untested. However, in studies rigorously designed to rule out such low-level alternatives (e.g., Baldwin, Bill, & Ontai, 1996), even infants as young as 12 months perform in sophisticated ways.

action scenarios from which infants can reliably glean clues to others' intentions.

Summary of Early Intentional Understanding

The research we have just reviewed indicates that infants engage in genuine intentional inference from as early as 12 months of age. They seem decidedly skilled at analyzing others' actions to generate inferences about underlying intentions—even when those actions are quite novel in kind or unfold in complex ways over time (e.g., Carpenter, Akhtar, & Tomasello, in press; Meltzoff, 1995; Tomasello & Akhtar, 1995). Moreover, they recruit such intentional understanding for language learning, relying on inferences about others' intentions to guide their establishment of new word–object mappings (e.g., Baldwin, 1991, 1993; Tomasello & Barton, 1994). Other recent research regarding infants' ability to interpret others' emotional messages (e.g., Baldwin & Moses, 1994; Mumme & Fernald, in press) and their playful intentions (e.g., Carpenter, Nagell, & Tomasello, in press; Phillips, Baron-Cohen, & Rutter, 1992; Reddy, 1991) points to the same general conclusion. All in all, current evidence indicates that infants possess a powerful ability to process action information and to generate intentional inferences based on such an action analysis.

Limitations of Early Intentional Understanding

Although it seems that even 12-month-old infants successfully "tune in" to others' intentions, it is also clear that 12-month-olds do not understand others' behavior in the same intentional terms that we as adults do. Their understanding remains limited in important ways. For one, as we mentioned earlier, infants are relatively deficient with respect to a vast array of world knowledge that helps to inform our own analysis of others' intentions. As well, infants lack an adultlike theory of mind, in which representational notions such as belief and knowledge underlie reasoning about others' motivations and intentions (e.g., Moses, 1993; Perner, 1991; Wellman, 1990). This means there are certain kinds of intentions adults entertain that infants cannot yet conceive of, such as intentions resting on false beliefs and intentions to acquire more knowledge or to test a belief. For this reason, a certain amount of others' behavior—such as checking an encyclopedia for desired information, for example—must at some level remain inscrutable to them.

Infants probably also lack an appreciation for other important subtleties regarding mental life that play an important role in adult-level intentional understanding. For example, infants' fledgling notion of intention may be undifferentiated from a notion of desire, whereas these represent distinct constructs within adult folk psychology (i.e., adults appreciate that one can want something but at the same time have no intention to pursue satisfaction of that desire). As well, infants may be skilled at inferring at least certain kinds of "intentions-in-action" (see Anscombe, 1963; Bratman, 1987; Meltzoff, 1995; Searle, 1983), but imputing "prior intentions"—intentions characterizing the mind that are formed before the actual performance of an action—may well be beyond their scope. Likewise, initially infants may depend heavily on concrete, physical, movement-based cues to drive inferences about others' intentions—cues such as direction of motion, line of regard, body posture, the presence versus absence of contact with an object, gestures such as pointing and showing, and the like. When such cues are absent or degraded, infants' ability to draw appropriate intentional inferences may be drastically undercut.

MECHANISMS UNDERLYING THE DEVELOPMENT OF INTENTIONAL UNDERSTANDING: AN INDISPUTABLE ROLE FOR ACTION ANALYSIS

The evidence we have reviewed suggests that intentional understanding is operative early—probably as early as the end of the first year or so—but nevertheless undergoes protracted development. But the mechanisms accounting for the early emergence and development of intentional understanding is another matter; one about which there is currently no consensus. One set of theorists has suggested that some kind of essential kernel of intentional understanding—say a diffuse and global sense that there is a "thrustiness" or purposiveness to others' action—is available from the very outset of infants' conceptual life (e.g., Premack, 1990; Reddy, 1991; Trevarthen, 1979). If so, infants would be interpreting others' actions as intentional right from the start. But this is not to say that intentional understanding is thought to be fully operative at birth on this kind of nativist account. Rather, attributions of intentionality are thought to be initially relatively undifferentiated, with experience enabling infants to construct increasingly refined and appropriate inferences regarding actors' specific intentions in varying contexts. A tiny infant viewing someone cleaning the kitchen, for example, might appreciate the basic purposiveness of the actor's movements, without yet being capable of inferring specific intentions to wash a dish, hang a towel, and the like.

Other theorists (e.g., Baron-Cohen, 1995; Barresi & Moore, 1996; Leslie, 1993; Piaget, 1932; Poulin-Dubois & Shultz, 1988; Tomasello, 1995) offer a contrasting account—that infants experience a relatively protracted period during which they observe and interact with others yet are not capable of drawing inferences regarding the intentions underlying others' actions.

The basic ability to understand others' actions as intentional or purposive is thus itself viewed as a developmental achievement. There is disagreement among this group, however, regarding the timing of this achievement and the mechanisms responsible for it. On the one hand, Leslie (1993) and Baron-Cohen (1995) suggest that the human brain is innately endowed with several autonomous "modules" specifically designed for interpreting others' behavior. These modules are thought to become functional according to a predictable, biologically based timetable in children's development, with the module responsible for a basic appreciation of others' purposiveness becoming active at about 6 months of age.

On the other hand, within this group are others who propose a more constructivist account for the emergence and development of intentional understanding. Tomasello and colleagues (e.g., Tomasello, 1995; Carpenter, Nagell, et al., in press), for example, argue that understanding others as intentional agents does not appear until the end of the first year of life. These researchers point to infants' experiences enacting their own intentions and the development of means–ends understanding as perhaps central in the emergence of such basic intentional understanding. In contrast, Moore and colleagues suggest that the advent of genuine intentional understanding must wait until roughly 18 months (e.g., Barresi & Moore, 1996; Moore & Corkum, 1994). They argue that this achievement hinges on infants gaining a "shared representational format" for action; in effect, coming to encode their own and others' actions in equivalent terms.

Amid these disparate positions concerning the development of intentional understanding there lurks a hidden source of agreement: All accounts presuppose that infants possess skills for action analysis. Even the nativist position—crediting infants with recognizing the purposiveness of action right from the start—takes seriously that important refinements in intentional understanding occur with development. A core ability for processing action would have to be involved to make such refinements possible. Gaining a sense of distinct intentions underlying different kinds of action would require that infants have some way of processing the action stream. And on the constructivist analysis, a basic capacity for analyzing action is logically necessary in enabling infants to construct a notion of others as intentional agents in the first place. That is, action information would be a primary supplier of raw materials from which infants could build intentional constructs and must therefore be analyzed and organized by infants in some fashion amenable to such an ambitious project.

In sum, then, precisely how and when infants begin to register others' actions as motivated by intentions remains controversial. It is clear, however, on any account that a basic ability to process action in intention-relevant ways must play a central role in making possible the ultimate acquisition of adultlike inferences about intentions.

We turn now to consider in more detail the kinds of core abilities for processing action needed to support both the early emergence of intentional inference and subsequent developments in this arena. In particular, we suggest that infants are sensitive to important sources of covariation in movement patterns that in turn enables them to parse human action into constituents amenable to an analysis of intentions. Their ability to parse action appropriately makes possible the rapid acquisition of action concepts that are likewise relevant to intentional inferences. As well, we suspect that infants have a propensity to relate their growing knowledge about objects and object functions to their analysis of action and that this propensity facilitates their ultimate achievement of refinements in intentional understanding.

ACTION ANALYSIS

In everyday action, no transparent demarcation of intentions seems to be available within the ebb and flow of motion. Pauses, for example, often fail to occur between actions driven by different intentions: One action tends to flow seamlessly into the next, probably because much of our everyday action is highly routinized and automatic. In many cases, actions deriving from distinct intentions actually overlap in time, as when one begins writing up tomorrow's shopping list with one hand while stirring the spaghetti sauce with the other. Infants, then, are supplied with no transparent "prepackaging" of the motion sequence that might serve as a base for organizing action and drawing inferences about the actor's goals and intentions. To get started, they need some method of breaking down or *parsing* action to achieve relevant units that can be represented.

Parsing

When parsing others' action, not just any units will do; in particular, infants need to pick out action units that are generalizable across different action sequences and thus can assist in processing novel actions encountered in the future. They must also locate action units that coincide in at least some number of cases with the units that are appropriate for driving inferences about others' intentions. To illustrate these points, imagine a kitchen clean-up scenario in which an orderly protagonist moves to the sink, picks up a dish, turns on the water, passes the dish beneath the water while scrubbing vigorously, turns off the water, places the dish aside in the dish drainer, turns and looks at a towel on the floor, moves toward the towel, and so forth. This all occurs in one continuous flow, with the actions described here separately actually overlapping to greater or lesser degree. In principle, there are an infinite number of possible ways that one could divide this flow of action, and a large number of the possibilities from this very large set would yield units of action that are incommensurate with inferences about intentions. For example, one could parse the action into vanishingly small components, but the overwhelming number of resultant units would surely swamp any possibility of generating relevant intentional inferences. Or one could divide the action according to a strict temporal rhythm—one unit for every 1.2 seconds, for example—yielding orderly but obviously meaningless action fragments. Or one could establish a new unit anytime something salient occurred, such as the onset of a rapid or large movement, an interesting sound, or an intriguing pattern of motion. This strategy might sometimes yield units of action relevant to drawing inferences about intentions (e.g., movement to the sink heralds a whole new unit of dishwashing action) but even more frequently would give rise to units inconsistent with intentional analysis (e.g., in the midst of dishwashing, the sound of water rushing might inappropriately suggest the opening of a new unit, which might then be inappropriately closed off, in the midst of dishwashing, as the interesting motion of swirling the brush inside the dish commenced).

We doubt that infants, at any point in development, mistakenly pursue such flawed parsing strategies. Such misguided parsing is simply inconsistent with their ability to interact with others and with their rapid acquisition of intentional understanding. We propose an alternative. One way that infants might achieve a parsing relevant to intentions would be to detect predictable clusters or sequences of features within the action stream that also happen to coincide with the movements linking the actor's initiation and completion of goals. Sequence learning of certain kinds is known to be within the capability of even 4-month-old infants (e.g., Haith, Hazan, & Goodman, 1988; Clohessy, Posner & Rothbart, 1992). Imagine, for example, that infants come to note that, as a rule, an actor's release of contact with an object predicts a change in gaze direction, which in turn predicts both subsequent direction of movement and contact with a new object targeted by gaze. In many cases, this swath of action—from the point at which gaze direction changes to target a new object to the point at which contact with the targeted object ceases—encompasses an intention-relevant unit. It is this kind of unit that adults readily interpret as intentional. Infants might note the structural predictability, and thus extract the appropriate units, even though they may not yet be capable of thinking about the actions in intentional terms.

Of course, such a parsing strategy would be viable only if such correlations between these two levels of analysis—the level of the action stimulus array and the level of psychological intent—in fact exist. Are there identifiable features of action that indeed predictably coincide with the actor's initiation and completion of goals? A small body of adult research within the social psychology tradition hints at a positive answer to this question.

Adult Parsing of Everyday Action

In sequences depicting continuous everyday action, such as a man repairing a motorcycle or a woman cutting out a dress pattern, adults readily and reliably identify natural *break points*—meaningful junctures that break up the flow of action (e.g., Newtson, 1973, 1976). Some individuals report more break points than others for a given action sequence, but these represent systematic differences in attention to detail rather than unpredictable divergence in the perception of break points. That is, the break points of individuals reporting few such break points coincide with break points that are among those perceived by individuals reporting many. However, when given little in the way of biasing instructions, adults tend to spontaneously segment action into units somewhere intermediate between the fine and gross levels that they are capable of detecting. This hints at the possibility that there is a natural or "basic level" for construing action, perhaps analogous in certain ways to the basic level that has been demonstrated for adults' categorization of objects (e.g., Rosch, Mervis, Gray, Johnson, & Boyes-Braem, 1976). Finally, adults seem to selectively attend to break points, which appear to be information-rich portions of action relative to action segments not identified as break points. For example, Newtson and Engquist (1976) showed adults action sequences in which a varying number of frames was deleted from either break points or nonbreak points. Adults showed higher accuracy for detecting such deletions when they occurred in break points than nonbreak points. In a second study, these researchers showed adults correctly and incorrectly ordered sequences of three break points and three nonbreak points and found that break-point sequences were linked to more accurate descriptions (intention-level descriptions, that is) and were rated as more intelligible. Adults were also more successful at detecting the correctness of ordering for break-point than nonbreak-point sequences, and showed better recognition memory for the break-point sequences. All in all, this body of work suggests that there are predictable and readily identifiable portions of the dynamic stimulus array that adults are sensitive to in deriving coherent and meaningful units of action describable in intentional terms.

Of course, the precise implication of these findings for how infants might parse such everyday action sequences is unclear. Adults—who are already in possession of a good deal of knowledge about the particular intentions involved in actions such as motorcycle repair and dress-pattern cutting—may be looking specifically for those portions of action that supply information relevant to just these specific intentions and goals and for this reason are able to reliably hit on break points as the information-rich portions of the action stream. In other words, perhaps intentional understanding itself drives adults' detection of break points in the Newtson research. In contrast, the question of present interest is whether infants *lacking* an intention-level understanding of such sequences might nevertheless be able to parse them in roughly the same way as would be derived by such an intention-level analysis. If so, then break points may be detectable for infants as well as adults. A series of studies investigating this possibility with infants ranging between 4 and 12 months of age is currently underway in our research laboratory.

Although Newtson's findings leave ambiguous the degree to which prior intentional understanding influences the perception of break points, these results nevertheless make clear that predictable features of the action array indeed correlate with an intention-level assessment of the transition from one goal to the next. That such correlations exist is surely no accident. Everything we know about human goal-directed action hints at the existence of such action–intention correlations. A number of powerful constraining factors produce such structure in our action as we pursue our goals in the world. First, our goal-directed movements comprise an organized sequence of action routines executed in a coordinated fashion (e.g., Gallistel, 1980; Miller, Galanter, & Pribram, 1960). Even seemingly simple actions like brushing our teeth, for example, involve such sequencing. We need to locate the brush and the paste in order to grasp them, the brush must be oriented the right way as toothpaste is extruded, and our mouths must be open before the pasty brush can be properly applied to the teeth. Intentional action thus inherently possesses a systematic sequencing of movements. Second, we all possess bodies that are much the same in overall conformation. We must use our sensory systems (such as eyes) in predictable ways to assist in locating relevant objects. This again engenders structure in the form of predictable sequencing; structure that is related to the intentions we enact in the world. Finally, there are strong constraints, both physical and physiological, governing the manner in which we move our bodies and the paths of motion we follow. All in all, acting intentionally from within a human body introduces many sources of intention-relevant structure into the flow of movement. Our hypothesis is that in the perception of action, infants may be sensitive to at least some elements of this inherent "structure-in-execution" enabling them to extract intention-relevant units even though they may lack a conceptual understanding of actors' intentions. Here we are in spirit echoing Bertenthal and Pinto's (1993) recent suggestion that complementary processes operate in both the perception and production of human movements.

Infant Parsing of Everyday Action

The plausibility of our action-parsing hypothesis is bolstered by recent findings concerning infants' ability to solve a different set of parsing problems; in particular, the problems associated with parsing the speech stream to identify relevant linguistic units such as words and clauses. Just as pauses are rarely available in everyday action to signal an actor's transition from the pursuit of one goal to another, pauses rarely occur at word or clause boundaries within fluent speech. For language acquisition to proceed, infants must somehow identify wordlike and clauselike units in the absence of the top-down lexical and grammatical knowledge that adults rely on to assist in this complex segmentation process. Recent evidence indicates that infants as young as 9 months are sensitive to intonational cues that correlate with phrasal units (e.g., Jusczyk, 1997; Jusczyk et al., 1992) and infants as young as 8 months can detect word boundaries based on the statistical properties of syllable transitions within the acoustic flow (Saffran, Aslin, & Newport, 1996).

Cognitive psychology has confirmed again and again that the adult human brain is exquisitely tuned to structure, and clearly, infant brains are no exception. Infants' ability to capitalize on the statistical properties of the perceptual array to assist in parsing within the language domain makes it seem possible that similar analytic abilities might play a role in assisting their parsing of dynamic human action.

Recent research by Wynn (1995, 1996) provides some initial evidence for our hypothesis that infants can detect intention-relevant structure in action. In one of a series of studies investigating early numerical reasoning, Wynn presented 6-month-olds with continuous action sequences in which a puppet jumped up and down either twice or three times. In the intervals between jumps, the puppet's head wagged jauntily from side to side. After becoming habituated to the two-jump sequence, infants looked significantly longer at the three-jump sequence than the two-jump sequence, and vice versa. These findings indicate that infants were sensitive to structure within the motion sequence and extracted units that could be recognized. Precisely what these units were is not clear, as Wynn herself points out. Infants may have extracted two different kinds of units—jumping versus head wagging—and counted them, or they may have parsed the event into several repetitions of a jumping-plus-head-wagging unit. In either case, the structure infants were sensitive to is potentially relevant to inferences about intentions. That is, the swath of action encompassed by the puppet's jumping movements is just the kind of unit adults readily interpret in intentional terms (e.g., jumping), as is the unit encompassed by the puppet's jumping-plus-head-wagging movements (e.g., dancing). Infants in Wynn's studies[3] thus seem to have identified structure within the action flow and extracted action units commensurate with units that would be relevant to an intentional analysis of that action.

Action Correlates of Intentional Break Points

Assuming for the moment that some such process of structure detection is indeed operative in infants' analysis of action, the next question is, which specific features of action might participate in the units that are detected? Once again, some recent and intriguing research findings embolden us to hazard a few tentative speculations. Our ideas here are in their early stages and are far from comprehensive; we hope only that they will illustrate how such structure detection might operate and serve some heuristic value for guiding research on these issues.

Three features of everyday action seem particularly likely to enter into structural links between action and intention. First, we suspect that marked changes in another's line-of-regard, especially changes linked to turns of the head, may be one feature of human action that tends to covary with transitions between intentions. Infants are especially attentive to others' eye region as early as 2 to 3 months of age (e.g., Haith, Bergman, & Moore, 1977; Maurer, 1985; Mendelsohn & Haith, 1976) and by 3 to 4 months, can detect at least some changes in gaze direction (e.g., Hains & Muir, 1996; Vecera & Johnson, 1995). By roughly 12 months of age, infants reliably follow changes in line-of-regard that are associated with head movements (e.g., Carpenter, Nagell, et al., in press; Corkum & Moore, 1995; Lempers, 1979), and by 15 to 18 months, infants rely on congruent head and eye orientation for determining another's gaze direction (Corkum & Moore, 1995). Typically, researchers have been interested in the emergence of infants' ability to follow gaze changes because of its importance to their participation in joint attention with others (e.g., Bruner, 1983; Tomasello, 1995). From the present vantage point, however, gaze-following ability may likewise be important, because sensitivity to others' gaze direction facilitates action analysis and ultimately promotes appropriate inferences about their goals and intentions.

---

[3]In Wynn and her colleague's research (1995, 1996; Sharon & Wynn, 1997), infants' looking times revealed a stronger tendency to enumerate distinct actions when actions were separated by motionless gaps relative to when motion flowed continuously from one action to the next. Their findings suggest, on the one hand, that infants' action parsing is aided by the presence of pauses between actions when these are available, and on the other hand, that their ability to parse action in the absence of such pauses may be fragile. However, these findings may underestimate infants' action-parsing abilities, because potentially important parsing cues, such as changes in gaze direction and initiation or cessation of object contact, were lacking in the actions shown to infants.

Second, rather abrupt changes in motion directionality of the body may also tend to be linked to boundaries between distinguishable intentions, as when one turns away from one place and moves off on a different trajectory to pursue a new goal. Consistent with this idea, Newtson, Engquist, and Bois (1977) found that periods within an action stream with relatively little in the way of position change are punctuated by short bursts of radical position change. These junctures of radical position change tend to coincide with adult judgments of break points. And of course, changes in path of body motion tend to result in such bursts of radical position change. Although we know of no evidence specifically confirming infants' sensitivity to such changes, it is of course well established that infants are very sensitive to motion (e.g., Bertenthal, 1993; Kellman, Spelke, & Short, 1986) and their ability to detect such changes seems in little doubt.

Third, changes in contact with an object—either the initiation or cessation of contact—may tend to be linked to intentional break points. Once again, little in the way of actual evidence is available to bolster this suggestion, but recent research by Woodward (in press, 1997a, 1997b) provides one relevant piece of information. Her research demonstrates that infants closely attend to an actor's initiation of contact with an object. She found, for example, that 9-month-olds, and possibly even infants as young as 3 to 5 months, note the difference between physically identical reaches toward two different objects (e.g., a teddy bear as opposed to a multicolored ball) but regard physically distinct reaches toward one and the same object (e.g., the teddy bear) in different locations as indistinguishable. This finding indicates that infants selectively encode contact with an object that is the focus of another's reaching action.

In addition to covarying with transitions between distinct intentions, the three features we target—change in gaze direction, change in path of motion, and initiation or cessation of object contact—tend to occur in predictable sequence: gaze direction changes, a change in path of motion commences, and a new object is contacted, manipulated, and ultimately released. This might well represent a sequence infants can detect and utilize to demarcate distinct action units. Adults, at least, can base their segmentation of continuous action displays on the presence of predictable sequences (e.g., Avrahami & Kareev, 1994).

Our proposals need substantiation. It will be important to discover the extent to which the three action features we target—changes in line-of-regard accompanied by changes in head direction, changes in path of motion, and changes in object contact—indeed cluster in everyday human action as well as covary with transitions between intentions. Clearly, these action elements do not appear and cluster in all human action, yet correlations among these elements may nevertheless emerge across a significant sample of everyday action. As well, likely there are additional features of action that play an important role in infants' parsing of action. For instance, infants are known to be sensitive to others' expression of emotion, both vocal (e.g., Mumme, Fernald, & Herrera, 1996) and facial (e.g., Nelson, 1987), and such emotion cues seem likely to participate in action–intention correlations. On the other hand, although abundant in the context of interaction, emotion cues seem relatively sparse in everyday action sequences of the kind we have focused on here (e.g., kitchen clean-up), which is why we have not pursued them at present. Finally, if it is the case that action–intention correlations in fact exist, whether infants are sensitive to those correlations nevertheless remains an open question. On this latter point, it is both interesting and promising that Spelke, Phillips, and Woodward (1995) recently reported that infants as young as 12 months, and perhaps somewhat younger, seem to be sensitive to a predictive relation between clusters of the action features we have identified. In particular, infants in their research seemed to appreciate that an actor's direction of focus (i.e., her gaze and head direction) predicted her subsequent path of motion and the object she acted on. In one study, for example, 12-month-olds looked for a significantly shorter period at a test event in which an actor contacted an object she had previously directed her head and eyes toward, accompanied by an expression of joy and interest, compared to a test event in which she contacted a different object than the one she had just looked at with pleasure and interest. Infants may be surprised when an actor looks toward one object but then reaches for and grasps another, suggesting that they have registered a correlation between these factors in everyday action and are struck when this correlation is violated.

Although there is much that is speculative in our proposal about infants' action parsing skills, there is strong reason for believing that something along these lines is part of infants' early perceptual or conceptual repertoire. Without an ability to derive units of action commensurate with those appropriate for driving intentional inferences, infants could not embark on developing intentional understanding. Parsing action appropriately is critical to establishing the action concepts necessary to support inferences about intentions.

Role of Parsing in Fostering the Establishment of Action Concepts

In 1978, Rosch and Lloyd pointed out that "the world consists of an infinite number of potentially different stimuli. Thus a basic task of all organisms (indeed, one mark of living things) is a segmentation of the environment into classifications by means of which nonidentical stimuli can be treated as equivalent" (p. 1). This statement is as true of the world of dynamic human action as it is of the world of concrete objects, the latter of which was, of course, Rosch's particular focus. More specifically, to be able to predict one another's actions and to interact with one another, we must achieve some way of conceptualizing and representing each other's actions that supports generalization across action instances.

Rosch (1978) also clarified that categories and concepts are of increasing benefit to the extent that they capture structure that is available in the world. She argued that structure-sensitive concepts supply maximal information while optimizing cognitive effort. On this principle, action concepts that capitalize on correlated structure present in action will maximize infants' ability to process action fruitfully and efficiently. Other researchers including Gelman and Markman (e.g., Carey, 1985; Gelman, 1988; Gelman & Coley, 1991; Gelman & Markman, 1986; Keil, 1989) have since elaborated on Rosch and colleagues' proposals to clarify that concepts capturing rich correlated structure in the world, such as natural kind categories, provide "rich inductive potential" (Gelman & Coley, 1991, p. 151). Put another way, concepts that group things sharing many commonalities can support inferences about additional nonobvious similarities. In this sense, action concepts that incorporate existing structure in action will better support inferences about nonobvious similarities, such as goals and intentions, common to actions grouped by those concepts.

To reiterate, then, an ability to extract richly structured units from action would greatly expedite infants' formation of advantageous action concepts with rich inductive potential. Such a parsing ability would assist by giving infants a productive starting foundation for action concept acquisition. A first requirement in establishing a concept such as *push*, for example, would seem to be the ability to identify the relevant sequence of actions—the pushing portion of stuff—as some kind of unit for analysis within the stream of action. Clearly, however, much else is still required to acquire an adultlike concept of *push*. Specific commonalities both obvious (e.g., person–object contact, muscle tension, ultimate movement of object away from the individual in contact, etc.) and nonobvious (e.g., exertion of pressure, intention to push regardless of whether movement occurs, etc.) must be noted or inferred, and relations to other related action concepts must be recognized (e.g., pull). How infants may solve these problems is little understood as yet, although Cohen and his colleagues (e.g., Cohen & Casasola, 1997) have recently begun an ambitious program of investigation targeting just this set of issues. Quite likely language learning and differences in semantic systems among languages influence this process of action concept formation in important ways. Exploring the full complexity of these issues would take us well beyond the scope of the present chapter, but we hope they become an increasing focus for investigation.

Thus far we have argued that infants' action analysis abilities recover structure from others' action, which aids in the establishment of action concepts. At least one other basic skill must also be operative to account for infants' documented success in processing others' action; in particular, an ability to readily integrate knowledge about objects with knowledge of action.

Integrating Knowledge of Actions and Objects

Intentions possess an inherent "aboutness"—they relate action to things in the world (e.g., Brentano, 1874/1970; Dennett, 1996). Drawing inferences about others' intentions requires some basic appreciation of this aboutness quality, and drawing *appropriate* inferences about others' intentions in turn requires careful analysis of others' actions with respect to characteristics of the specific objects toward which those actions may be directed. For adult observers, action–object relations impact inferences about intentions in complex ways. For example, consider the case in which we observe someone to approach an object with index finger extended, proceed to press the tip of the finger against that object, and then withdraw the digit forthwith. If the object involved is a TV, we are likely to infer that the intention was to turn the TV on by pressing the power button. If the object involved is a piece of paper hanging on the wall, we are more likely to infer that the intention was to leave a mark of some kind, perhaps a fingerprint. Other possibilities we might in other contexts entertain would include the intention to explore the object's surface, to push the object forward, or even to squash a bothersome bug. In other words, our knowledge about the specific objects involved in any given action influences the inferences we draw about the underlying intentions and goals.

At some point in development infants may be insensitive to the distinctly different intentions underlying these very similar finger-pressing movements; they simply may not know enough about paper, TVs, and other pressable things. As they learn more about these things, they can gain refinement in their intentional inferences, provided that they take the objects involved into account. However, what is their route to knowledge about TVs, paper, and the rest of the object world? People's actions on objects would seem to be the primary source of information. Making progress toward refinements in intentional inference thus must also require a complementary skill, the ability to update knowledge about objects based on the kinds of actions people undertake toward them. In this sense, an integrated processing of objects and actions would seem to lie at the heart of developments in intentional understanding.

As it turns out, integrating knowledge of actions and objects appears to be a characteristic of infants' action processing from quite early on. On the one hand, infants interpret action differently depending on the objects involved. Gergely, Nádasdy, Csibra, & Biró (1995) found that 10- to 15-month-olds who were habituated to an action sequence in which a little ball jumped over a barrier to reach a bigger ball on the far side then dishabituated to the same path of action when the barrier was removed. Infants seem to have interpreted the jumping action as unusual without the barrier present. In contrast, infants did not dishabituate to a new action in which the little ball moved along a straight trajectory to reach the bigger ball, indicating that they interpreted this new action as predictable given the absence of the barrier. These findings suggest that infants 10 to 15 months old can use information about the presence or absence of an object toward which action is directed (i.e., the barrier) to inform their interpretation of that action. Phillips (1997) obtained a similar pattern of results when a human hand carried out the action, indicating that infants use object information to inform their interpretation of human action as well.

Infants also seem to appreciate how the specific properties of an object are associated with action on that object. Using a paradigm similar to that of Gergely et al. (1995), Csibra and Gergely (1996) habituated 12-month-olds to an action sequence in which a large ball followed a smaller one. When the smaller ball passed through a narrow gap between two barriers, the larger ball was required to take a detour around the barriers to get to the other side. During the test events when the gap between the barriers was widened to accommodate the larger ball, infants dishabituated to the original circuitous path of action, suggesting that they interpreted this action pattern as unusual given the generous distance between the barriers. Infants did not dishabituate to a new sequence in which the larger ball followed the smaller ball through the widened gap, indicating that they interpreted this action sequence as appropriate given the change made to the position of the barriers. Among other things, these findings indicate that infants can use information about the specific properties of objects toward which action is directed (in this case, the placement of the barriers relative to one another) in their interpretation of that action.

Infants' interpretation of action is also influenced by the features of the object *enacting* the action. Woodward, Phillips, and Spelke (1993) found that 7-month-old infants reason about action differently depending on whether the object performing the action is a person or an inanimate. In particular, infants as young as 7 months expected contact to be required for transfer of motion to occur with inanimate objects, but they had no such expectation regarding contact for animates (humans). This in turn implies that by 7 months of age infants use information about the properties of an object in their interpretation of that object's action.

In addition to interpreting action in ways dependent on the objects acted on and enacting the action, recent evidence also documents the mirror-image ability on infants' part: Infants alter their intepretation of *objects* based on the way others act on them. For example, Meltzoff's (1995) imitation study revealed that 18-month-olds reenact an intention such as placing a loop on a prong after having viewed an adult repeatedly fail in his attempts at this action. From their analysis of the adult's action, then, infants noted something new about the loop and the prong. This basic skill at updating knowledge about objects based on observation of others' actions is one that infants much younger than 18 months display (see Gopnik & Meltzoff, 1994, and Meltzoff & Gopnik, 1993, for a similar point about implications of early imitation abilities). For example, Meltzoff (1988) has documented that 9-month-olds readily imitate an adult's action on a novel object.

This brief review of a small portion of potentially relevant evidence illustrates that action analysis on infants' part is not a simple processing of motion that occurs in a vacuum, isolated from their growing knowledge about the object world. On the contrary, infants readily use action to guide inferences about object properties and incorporate what knowledge they possess about relevant objects to assist in their interpretation of the actions they observe. Given that intentions themselves are rooted in the relation of action and object, this integrative quality to infants' processing of action should radically facilitate their ability to note the kind of information relevant to drawing appropriate inferences about others' intentions, once they become able to do so.

CONCLUSION

We have suggested that infants possess abilities for discovering structure in human action. This structure is present on the level of the dynamic perceptual properties of action itself, but it also coincides to some important degree with structure at the level of the actor's goals and intentions. Thus, infants' sensitivity to correlated structure in action enables them to parse action into units that ultimately are relevant to drawing specific inferences about the actor's intentions and goals. Along the way, extracting such intention-relevant units promotes infants' construction of action concepts—categories of dynamic movement patterns that are generalizable across different action sequences. These structure-capturing concepts in turn facilitate inferences about nonobvious commonalities, perhaps including inferences about goals and intentions. Finally, we suggest that infants have a propensity to process action with respect to the properties of the objects involved, which enhances their ultimate ability to achieve refinements in their inferences about the intentions motivating others' actions.

Others before us have likewise speculated that there is structure in action that observers can recover (e.g., Asch, 1952; Newtson, 1973, 1976,

1993). However, these theorists suspect that intentions themselves are accessed directly in such a recovery process. Our proposal is more complex but also potentially more powerful. In our view, it is possible to achieve a structured analysis of the action stream while nevertheless failing to recover the specific intentions motivating that structure. We have suggested that, in this sense, even tiny infants may possess some important foundational skills for analyzing action. At the same time, we have also proposed that infants are not capable of interpreting action in the same intentional terms that we as adults do. With development, children draw increasingly refined and appropriate inferences about the specific intentions underlying the action units they extract from the action stream. Their basic action analysis abilities play a core role in potentiating such developmental progress.

In our proposal, the ability to recover structure in action is something we as adults retain; it enables us to parse novel action sequences into units relevant to intentional inferences and therefore supports the generative nature of our system for intentional understanding. Thus our proposal helps to account for both the generativity and the ontogeny of intentional understanding.

ACKNOWLEDGMENTS

Sincere thanks to our research group (Leslie Ashburn, Marguerite Hoerger, Megan Houghton, Lenna Ontai, and Mark Sabbagh) for many lively discussions, and to Leslie Ashburn, Diego Fernandez-Duque, Bertram Malle, Lou Moses, Philippe Rochat, Mark Sabbagh, and Marjorie Taylor for helpful comments on previous drafts of this chapter. This work was supported by grants from the National Science Foundation to both authors and by a John Merck Scholars Award to the lead author.

REFERENCES

Anscombe, G. E. M. (1963). *Intention.* Ithaca, NY: Cornell University Press.

Asch, S. E. (1952). *Social psychology.* Englewood Cliffs, NJ: Prentice-Hall.

Avrahami, J., & Kareev, Y. (1994). The emergence of events. *Cognition, 53,* 239–261.

Baldwin, D. A. (1991). Infants' contribution to the achievement of joint reference. *Child Development, 62,* 875–890.

Baldwin, D. A. (1993). Infants' ability to consult the speaker for clues to word reference. *Journal of Child Language, 20,* 395–418.

Baldwin, D. A., Bill, B., & Ontai, L. L. (1996). *Infants' tendency to monitor others' gaze: Is it rooted in intentional understanding or a result of simple orienting?* Paper presented at the International Conference on Infant Studies, Providence, RI.

Baldwin, D. A., & Moses, L. J. (1994). Early understanding of referential intent and attentional focus: Evidence from language and emotion. In C. Lewis & P. Mitchell (Eds.), *Children's early understanding of mind: Origins and development* (pp. 133–156). Hove, UK: Lawrence Erlbaum Associates.

Baldwin, D. A., & Tomasello, M. (1998). *Word learning: A window on early pragmatic understanding.* In E. Clark (Ed.), *Proceedings of the Twenty-Ninth Annual Child Language Research Forum, 29* (pp. 3–23). Cambridge, UK: Cambridge University Press.

Baron-Cohen, S. (1995). *Mindblindness: An essay on autism and theory of mind.* Cambridge, MA: MIT Press.

Barresi, J., & Moore, C. (1996). Intentional relations and social understanding. *Behavioral and Brain Sciences, 19,* 107–154.

Bertenthal, B. I. (1993). *Emerging trends in perceptual development.* Paper presented at the Biennial Meetings of the Society for Research in Child Development, New Orleans.

Bertenthal, B. I., & Pinto, J. (1993). Complementary processes in the perception and production of human movements. In L. B. Smith & E. Thelen (Eds.), *A dynamic systems approach to development: Applications* (pp. 209–239). Cambridge, MA: Bradford Books/MIT Press.

Bloom, P., & Veres, C. (1996). *The perceived intentionality of groups.* Unpublished manuscript, University of Arizona, Tucson.

Bratman, M. E. (1987). *Intention, plans, and practical reason.* Cambridge, MA: Harvard University Press.

Brentano, F. von (1970). *Psychology from an empirical standpoint* (O. Kraus, Ed.; L. L. McAllister, Trans.). London: Routledge & Kegan Paul. (Original work published 1874)

Bruner, J. (1983). *Child's talk: Learning to use language.* New York: Norton.

Carey, S. (1985). *Conceptual change in childhood.* Cambridge, MA: MIT Press.

Carpenter, M., Akhtar, N., & Tomasello, M. (1998). Fourteen- through 18-month-old infants differentially imitate intentional and accidental actions. *Infant Behavior and Development, 21,* 315–330.

Carpenter, M., Nagell, K., & Tomasello, M. (in press). Social cognition, joint attention, and communicative competence from 9 to 15 months of age. *Monographs of the Society for Research in Child Development.*

Clohessy, A., Posner, M. I., & Rothbart, M. K. (1992). *Stability in anticipatory eye movement learning from four months to adulthood.* Paper presented at the International Conference on Infant Studies, Miami, FL.

Cohen, L. B., & Casasola, M. (1997). *Infants' learning of word-object versus word-action associations.* Paper presented at the Biennial Meetings of the Society for Research in Child Development, Washington, DC.

Collis, G. M. (1977). Visual co-orientation and maternal speech. In H. R. Schaffer (Ed.), *Studies in mother-infant interaction* (pp. 355–375). London: Academic Press.

Corkum, V., & Moore, C. (1995). Development of joint visual attention in infants. In C. Moore & P. J. Dunham (Eds.), *Joint attention: Its origins and role in development* (pp. 61–83). Hillsdale, NJ: Lawrence Erlbaum Associates.

Csibra, G., & Gergely, G. (1996). *Origins of naive psychology: Understanding rational actions in infancy.* Paper presented at the XIVth Biennial ISSBD Conference, Quebec City, Canada.

Dasser, V., Ulbaek, I., & Premack, D. (1989). The perception of intention. *Science, 243,* 365–367.

Dennett, D. C. (1996). *Kinds of minds: Toward an understanding of consciousness.* New York: Basic Books.

Dittrich, W. H., & Lea, S. E. G. (1994). Visual perception of intentional motion. *Perception, 23,* 253–268.

Fodor, J. A. (1983). *The modularity of mind.* Cambridge, MA: MIT Press.

Gallistel, C. R. (1980). *The organization of action: A new synthesis.* Hillsdale, NJ: Lawrence Erlbaum Associates.

Gelman, S. A. (1988). The development of induction within natural kind and artifact categories. *Cognitive Psychology, 20,* 65–95.

Gelman, S. A., & Coley, J. D. (1991). Language and categorization: The acquisition of natural kind terms. In S. A. Gelman & J. P. Byrnes (Eds.), *Perspectives on language and thought: Interrelations in development* (pp. 146–196). Cambridge, UK: Cambridge University Press.

Gelman, S. A., & Markman, E. M. (1986). Categories and induction in young children. *Cognition, 23,* 183–209.

Gergely, G., Nádasdy, Z., Csibra, G., & Biró, S. (1995). Taking the intentional stance at 12 months of age. *Cognition, 56,* 165–193.

Gernsbacher, M. A. (1990). *Language comprehension as structure building.* Hillsdale, NJ: Lawrence Erlbaum Associates.

Gopnik, A., & Meltzoff, A. N. (1994). Mind, bodies and persons: Young children's understanding of the self and others as reflected in imitation and "theory of mind" research. In S. T. Parker, R. W. Mitchell, & M. L. Boccia (Eds.), *Self-awareness in animals and humans* (pp. 166–186). New York: Cambridge University Press.

Gopnik, A., & Meltzoff, A. N. (1997). *Words, thoughts, and theories.* Cambridge, MA: MIT Press.

Hains, S. M. J., & Muir, D. W. (1996). Infant sensitivity to adult eye direction. *Child Development, 67,* 1940–1951.

Haith, M., Bergman, T., & Moore, M. (1977). Eye contact and face scanning in early infancy. *Science, 198,* 853–855.

Haith, M. M., Hazan, C., & Goodman, G. S. (1988). Expectation and anticipation of dynamic visual events by 3.5-month-old infants. *Child Development, 59,* 467–479.

Heider, F. (1958). *The psychology of interpersonal relations.* New York: Wiley.

Jusczyk, P. W. (1997). *The discovery of spoken language.* Cambridge, MA: MIT Press.

Jusczyk, P. W., Hirsh-Pasek, K., Kemler Nelson, D. G., Kennedy, L. J., Woodward, A., & Piwoz, J. (1992). Perception of acoustic correlates of major phrasal units by young infants. *Cognitive Psychology, 24,* 252–293.

Keil, F. C. (1989). *Concepts, kinds, and cognitive development.* Cambridge, MA: Bradford Books/MIT Press.

Kellman, P. J., Spelke, E. S., & Short, K. R. (1986). Infant perception of object unity from translatory motion in depth and vertical translation. *Child Development, 57,* 72–86.

Lempers, J. D. (1979). Young children's production and comprehension of nonverbal deictic behaviors. *The Journal of Genetic Psychology, 135,* 93–102.

Leslie, A. M. (1993). ToMM, ToBy and Agency: Core architecture and domain specificity. In L. A. Hirschfeld & S. A. Gelman (Eds.), *Mapping the mind: Domain specificity in cognition and culture* (pp. 119–148). Cambridge, UK: Cambridge University Press.

Malle, B. F., & Knobe, J. (1997). The folk concept of intentionality. *Journal of Experimental Social Psychology, 33,* 101–121.

Mandler, J. M. (1992). How to build a baby: II. Conceptual primitives. *Psychological Review, 99,* 587–604.

Marslen-Wilson, W. D., & Tyler, L. K. (1980). The temporal structure of spoken language understanding. *Cognition, 8,* 1–71.

Maurer, D. (1985). Infants' perception of facedness. In T. Field & M. Fox (Eds.), *Social perception in infants* (pp. 73–100). Norwood, NJ: Ablex.

McClelland, J. L. (1985). Putting knowledge in its place: A scheme for programming parallel processing structures on the fly. *Cognitive Science, 9,* 113–146.

Meltzoff, A. N. (1988). Infant imitation and memory: Nine-month-olds in immediate and deferred tests. *Child Development, 59,* 217–225.

Meltzoff, A. N. (1995). Understanding the intentions of others: Re-enactment of intended acts by 18-month-old children. *Developmental Psychology, 31,* 838–850.

Meltzoff, A. N., & Gopnik, A. (1993). The role of imitation in understanding persons and developing a theory of mind. In S. Baron-Cohen, H. Tager-Flusberg, & D. J. Cohen (Eds.), *Understanding other minds: Perspectives from autism* (pp. 335–366). Oxford, UK: Oxford University Press.

Mendelsohn, M. J., & Haith, M. M. (1976). The relation between audition and vision in the human newborn. *Monographs of the Society for Research in Child Development, 41*(4, Serial No. 167).

Miller, G. A., Galanter, E., & Pribram, K. H. (1960). *Plans and the structure of behavior.* New York: Henry Holt.

Moore, C., & Corkum, V. (1994). Social understanding at the end of the first year of life. *Developmental Review, 14,* 349–372.

Moses, L. J. (1993). Young children's understanding of belief constraints on intention. *Cognitive Development, 8,* 1–25.

Mumme, D. L., & Fernald, A. (in press). Infants' use of gaze in interpreting emotional signals. *Child Development.*

Mumme, D. L., Fernald, A., & Herrera, C. (1996). Infants' responses to facial and vocal emotional signals in a social referencing paradigm. *Child Development, 67,* 3219–3237.

Nelson, C. A. (1987). The recognition of facial expressions in the first two years of life: Mechanisms of development. *Child Development, 58,* 889–909.

Newtson, D. (1973). Attribution and the unit of perception of ongoing behavior. *Journal of Personality and Social Psychology, 28,* 28–38.

Newtson, D. (1976). Foundations of attribution: The perception of ongoing behavior. In J. Harvey, W. Ickes, & R. Kidd (Eds.), *New directions in attribution research.* Hillsdale, NJ: Lawrence Erlbaum Associates.

Newtson, D. (1993). The dynamics of action and interaction. In L. B. Smith & E. Thelen (Eds.), *A dynamic systems approach to development: Applications* (pp. 241–264). Cambridge, MA: Bradford Books/MIT Press.

Newtson, D., & Engquist, G. (1976). The perceptual organization of ongoing behavior. *Journal of Experimental Social Psychology, 12,* 436–450.

Newtson, D., Engquist, G., & Bois, J. (1977). The objective basis of behavior units. *Journal of Personality and Social Psychology, 35,* 847–862.

Newtson, D., Rindner, R., Miller, R., & LaCross, K. (1978). Effects of availability of feature changes on behavior segmentation. *Journal of Experimental Social Psychology, 14,* 379–388.

Perner, J. (1991). *Understanding the representational mind.* Cambridge, MA: Bradford Books/MIT Press.

Phillips, A. (1997). *Infant understanding of emotion and perception.* Paper presented at the Conference on Developmental Processes in Early Social Understanding, Ann Arbor, MI.

Phillips, W., Baron-Cohen, S., & Rutter, M. (1992). The role of eye contact in goal detection: Evidence from normal infants and children with autism or mental handicap. *Development and Psychopathology, 4,* 375–383.

Piaget, J. (1932). *The moral judgment of the child.* London: Kegan Paul.

Poulin-Dubois, D., & Shultz, T. R. (1988). The development of the understanding of human behavior: From agency to intentionality. In J. W. Astington, P. L. Harris, & D. L. Olson (Eds.), *Developing theories of mind* (pp. 109–125). Cambridge, UK: Cambridge University Press.

Premack, D. (1990). The infant's theory of self-propelled objects. *Cognition, 36,* 1–16.

Reddy, V. (1991). Playing with others' expectations: Teasing and mucking about in the first year. In A. Whiten (Ed.), *Natural theories of mind* (pp. 143–158). Oxford, UK: Basil Blackwell.

Rochat, P., Morgan, R., & Carpenter, M. (1997). Young infants' sensitivity to movement information specifying social causality. *Cognitive Development, 12,* 441–465.

Rosch, E. (1978). Principles of categorization. In E. Rosch & B. B. Lloyd (Eds.), *Cognition and categorization* (pp. 27–48). Hillsdale, NJ: Lawrence Erlbaum Associates.

Rosch, E., & Lloyd, B. B. (1978). *Cognition and categorization.* Hillsdale, NJ: Lawrence Erlbaum Associates.

Rosch, E., Mervis, C. B., Gray, W. D., Johnson, D., & Boyes-Braem, P. (1976). Basic objects in natural categories. *Cognitive Psychology, 8,* 382–439.

Saffran, J. R., Aslin, R. N., & Newport, E. L. (1996). Statistical learning by 8-month-old infants. *Science, 274*, 1926–1928.

Samuelson, L., & Smith, L. (1998). Memory and attention make smart word learning: An alternative account of Akhtar, Carpenter and Tomasello. *Child Development, 69*, 94–104.

Schult, C. A., & Wellman, H. M. (1997). Explaining human movements and actions: Children's understanding of the limits of psychological explanation. *Cognition, 62*, 291–324.

Searle, J. R. (1983). *Intentionality: An essay in the philosophy of mind.* New York: Cambridge University Press.

Sharon, T., & Wynn, K. (1997). *Individuation and categorization of actions in six-month-olds.* Unpublished manuscript, University of Arizona, Tucson, AZ.

Spelke, E. S., Phillips, A., & Woodward, A. L. (1995). Infants' knowledge of object motion and human action. In D. Sperber, D. Premack, & A. J. Premack (Eds.), *Causal cognition: A multidisciplinary debate* (pp. 44–78). Oxford, UK: Clarendon Press.

Talmy, L. (1988). Force dynamics in language and cognition. *Cognitive Science, 12*, 49–100.

Tomasello, M. (1995). Joint attention as social cognition. In C. Moore & P. J. Dunham (Eds.), *Joint attention: Its origins and role in development* (pp. 103–130). Hillsdale, NJ: Lawrence Erlbaum Associates.

Tomasello, M. (in press). Perceiving intentions and learning words in the second year of life. In M. Bowerman & S. Levinson (Eds.), *Language acquisition and conceptual development.* Cambridge, UK: Cambridge University Press.

Tomasello, M., & Akhtar, N. (1995). Two-year-olds use pragmatic cues to differentiate reference to objects and actions. *Cognitive Development, 10*, 201–224.

Tomasello, M., & Barton, M. (1994). Learning words in non-ostensive contexts. *Developmental Psychology, 30*, 639–650.

Tomasello, M., Kruger, A. C., & Ratner, H. H. (1993). Cultural learning. *Behavioral and Brain Sciences, 16*, 495–552.

Trevarthen, C. (1979). Instincts for human cooperation and for cultural cooperation: Their development in infancy. In M. von Cranach, K. Foppa, W. Lepenies, & D. Ploog (Eds.), *Human ethology: Claims and limits of a new discipline* (pp. 530–571). Cambridge, UK: Cambridge University Press.

Vecera, S. P., & Johnson, M. H. (1995). Gaze detection and the cortical processing of faces: Evidence from infants and adults. *Visual Cognition, 2*, 59–87.

Wellman, H. M. (1990). *The child's theory of mind.* Cambridge, MA: Bradford Books/MIT Press.

Woodward, A. L. (in press, April). *Infants selectively encode the goal object of an actor's reach.* Manuscript under review.

Woodward, A. L. (1997a). *Three-month-old infants' encoding of the path and goal-related properties of a reaching event.* Poster presented at the Biennial Meetings of the Society for Research in Child Development, Washington, DC.

Woodward, A. L. (1997b). *Selectivity and discrimination in infants' encoding of human behavior.* Manuscript submitted for publication.

Woodward, A. L., Phillips, A. T., & Spelke, E. S. (1993). Infants' expectations about the motion of animate versus inanimate objects. In *Proceedings of the Fifteenth Annual Conference of the Cognitive Science Society, Boulder, CO* (pp. 1087–1091). Hillsdale, NJ: Lawrence Erlbaum Associates.

Wynn, K. (1995). Infants possess a system of numerical knowledge. *Current Directions in Psychological Science, 4*, 172–177.

Wynn, K. (1996). Infants' individuation and enumeration of actions. *Psychological Science, 7*, 164–169.

Chapter 10

Gaze Following and the Control of Attention

Chris Moore
Dalhousie University

The ability to use another person to find out about the world is a profoundly important human characteristic. If a defining feature of human nature is its dependence on forms of cultural learning (Tomasello, Kruger, & Ratner, 1993), then it is evident that a necessary condition for such learning is the presence of capacities that allow a young child to make discoveries about the world by entering into situations in which attention to that world is shared with another. One of the simplest and most basic of such capacities is the ability to follow the gaze of another person so that the infant ends up attending to whatever it is that the adult finds of interest. Gaze following allows the child to pay attention to what adults are paying attention without requiring the adult to be constantly monitoring the child's focus. In this chapter, I review the research on gaze following and propose an account of its development that rests on changes in the way in which the infant's own attention is controlled.

Scaife & Bruner (1975) were the first to investigate gaze following in a laboratory experimental format and established the standard procedural core that most researchers have adopted and then modified. Infants were seated in face-to-face interaction with an experimenter, who delivered the cue. This format has been adopted in most of the studies that have been carried out subsequently, although a few (e.g., Butterworth & Jarrett, 1991, Exp. 3) used a different seating arrangement. Scaife and Bruner used two trials of adult head turn, one to each side. On each trial, the adult turned 90 degrees to fixate on a small light, concealed from the infant, for 7 seconds. They scored a positive response if an infant looked in the same direction within 7 seconds of the adult head turn and without an intervening look elsewhere. They reported that of 23 infants between 2 and 7 months of age, only 8 showed at least one positive response during the session. In contrast, 9 of 11 infants of 8 months or older showed at least one positive response. Scaife and Bruner did not report how many head turns were produced in the wrong direction, so it is difficult to know what to make of the small number of positive responses at the younger ages or even of the relatively good performance from 8 months onward.

Toward the end of their article, Scaife and Bruner (1975) made the following comments:

> In so far as mutual orientation implies a degree of knowledge in some form about another person's perspective then the child in its first year may be considered as less than completely egocentric. The source of such abilities (for example, imitation) remains to be investigated but utilization of another's gaze may be a very basic process. (p. 266)

In the more than 20 years since Scaife and Bruner's work, these joint issues of mechanism and perspective taking have continued to stimulate research on gaze following.

The most natural explanation of why one person would turn to look in the same direction as another person is that the former wants to see what the latter is looking at. In other words, the mechanism underlying gaze following is the interpretation of the other's behavior as a manifestation of his or her perspective coupled with the desire to share that perspective. Undoubtedly, this picture accurately represents the case for the adult. But, of course, just because something is true for adults does not mean that it has always been so throughout life, and a developmental account needs to examine carefully the origins of even those abilities that we take so much for granted. In the case of gaze following, its early origins make a mechanism of the perspective-taking kind particularly problematic (see Moore & Corkum, 1994) and a search for explanations consistent with what is known of infant cognition particularly warranted.

What follows examines in some detail the research on gaze following in three sections, corresponding to what are plausibly three phases in the infant's ability to follow gaze. First, there is evidence that the earliest signs of gaze following occur when there are targets already within the infant's visual field. Second, toward the end of the first year, infants will follow gaze even when there are no immediately obvious targets. Gaze following under these two conditions (targets present and absent) occurs in response to adult head turns. Third, I consider the evidence for when infants will start to use eye direction to follow gaze. Throughout these three sections,

I discuss the evidence on gaze following in association with what is known about the control of attention in infancy.

GAZE FOLLOWING TO VISIBLE TARGETS

Not long after Scaife & Bruner's (1975) original work, Butterworth and his colleagues started an extensive study of infants' gaze following in the presence of targets in a variety of locations. Butterworth and Cochran (1980) reported three experiments in which infant and mother (usually) sat face-to-face in the presence of pairs of targets placed one on each side of the room close to the walls. These targets were behind the mother in view of the infant, behind the infant in view of the mother, or in view of both. On different trials, the mother turned to fixate one or other of the targets. In the first experiment, Butterworth and Cochran tested 12-month-olds with two pairs of targets under three conditions. In one condition, one pair of targets was in the infant's visual field but not the mother's and one pair was in the mother's visual field but not the infant's. In a second condition, both pairs were in the baby's visual field, but only one pair was in the mother's visual field. Finally, in the third condition, both pairs were in the mother's visual field, but only one pair was in the infant's visual field. The results from this experiment showed that infants only turned reliably to fixate targets that were in their own visual field and did not turn behind them to look at targets when these were the focus of the mother's attention. Furthermore, the infants showed some tendency to fixate on the first target along their scan path even when the mother was in fact looking at another object that was also in the infant's visual field (Condition 2).

In their second experiment, Butterworth and Cochran (1980) presented only one pair of targets at a time but otherwise conducted the study in essentially the same way as the first experiment, again with 12-month-olds. Again they found good performance when the target was in the infants' own visual field but poor ability to locate the target when the mothers turned to fixate on targets behind the infants. They argued on the basis of these results that infants do not simply turn until they find a target to which to attend. Rather, they turn to scan the region of space that is within their own visual field but no further.

A third experiment examined infants of 6 and 18 months of age. On each of eight trials, there were two targets located in the baby's visual field but not in the mother's and two targets located in the mother's visual field but not the baby's. The mother turned to fixate on each target twice during the session. Infants at both ages performed very well for targets in their own field and showed some tendency to fixate on the same targets even when the mothers had turned toward the targets outside the infants' visual field. There was little evidence of developmental change in the infants' ability to locate targets outside their own visual field, although the authors did report that more of the older babies turned to look behind them on at least one trial.

In short, the Butterworth and Cochran (1980) experiments reveal that infants from 6 months old will follow gaze but only when there is a prospective target in peripheral vision. They speculate further that if the infant needs to have the mother and the potential target in view simultaneously, then such a mechanism might give the infant a range of gaze following equal to the angle given by the range of peripheral vision.

Butterworth and Jarrett (1991) reported further experiments using a similar setup. Their first experiment using 6-, 12-, and 18-month-olds essentially replicated the methodology of Butterworth and Cochran's (1980), except that the angle between the pairs of targets was held constant across conditions at 60 degrees of visual angle. For the most part, the results of the 12-months-olds were similar to those of Butterworth and Cochran. One notable exception is that there was some evidence that the 12-month-olds would ignore the first target on their scan path in order to fixate on the target that the mother was looking at, so long as both were in front of the infant. The 18-month-olds also showed this performance pattern, but the 6-month-olds did not. It is also noteworthy that in the condition in which both pairs of targets were in the mother's view but only one pair was in the infant's view and at nearly 90 degrees from the midline, the 6-month-olds failed to follow gaze on a large majority of trials. At no age did the infants reliably turn to look behind them in response to their mothers' looking at targets in this region.

A second experiment on 18-month-olds showed that at this age, infants looked behind them in response to a reorientation of mothers' gaze if there were no targets present within their visual fields. Furthermore, they did so in response to eye movements alone as well as to head turns, although the strength of the response was greater with the latter cue.

Butterworth and Jarrett (1991) also reported work involving a rearrangement of the testing setup such that mother and infant were in one corner of the room with targets presented either in pairs separated by 60 degrees of visual angle or singly along the walls of the opposite two sides of the room. These tests showed that although the infants looked toward targets presented alone at a spatial separation of up to 135 degrees from the position of the mother, when two targets were present, they tended to look at the first along their scan path.

Their work led Butterworth and colleagues to conclude that until the end of infancy, gaze following is essentially governed by the perceptual limits provided by the extent of peripheral vision such that infants from 6 months of age can turn to follow gaze so long as there is a target present and both mother and target are simultaneously within the visual field. Initially, the infant turns in the same direction but stops to fixate on the first attention-capturing target. From about 12 months of age, there is some ability to ignore a target in order to fixate on the target that the mother has turned toward. This ability improves over the next 6 months, and it is not until 18 months of age that infants will search in regions of space when this search will lead to the mother's going out of view.

While Butterworth and colleagues have conducted the most systematic series of studies on gaze following to visible targets, others also have contributed (D'Entremont, Hains, & Muir, 1997; Lempers, 1979; Morissette, Ricard, & Gouin-Decarie, 1995). At first glance, the results from Lempers (1979) on 9- to 14-months-olds seem inconsistent with those of Butterworth and colleagues. Even though there were targets present and these were located in front of the infants, Lempers failed to find reliable evidence of gaze following until 12 months of age. However, there are significant problems with Lempers' method and reporting that make his results difficult to interpret. First, Lempers used a head turn of only 4 seconds duration compared to Butterworth and colleagues' 6 seconds. Second, and probably more significantly, in order for a response to be counted as correct, Lempers required the infant's gaze reorientation to be either immediate or to last a few seconds or both, and it had to occur or continue to occur after the experimenter looked back at the infant's face. These stringent scoring criteria may well have masked some gaze following that occurred in the 9-month-old infants. Finally, Lempers did not report and apparently did not take into account infant head turns in the wrong direction. Consequently, there was no obvious control for random infant head turning.

Morissette, Ricard, and Gouin-Decarie (1995) also claimed that clear-cut gaze following does not occur until 12 months of age using targets within an infant's visual field. They studied a group of 24 infants longitudinally every 3 months from 6 to 18 months old. Again their scoring decisions differed somewhat from Butterworth and his collaborators. For Morissette et al., gaze following was only deemed to be present when infants turned to the correct side, although not necessarily toward the correct target, on significantly more trials than they did not, which included trials on which there was no response. Nevertheless, infants at both 6 and 9 months of age showed quite a number of head turns in the correct direction (31% of trials at 6 months and 47% of trials at 9 months). If the argument is accepted that the better criterion is to control for chance responding, by comparing head turns to the correct side with head turns to the opposite side (see Corkum & Moore, 1995), then it is possible that Morissette et al. (1995) do in fact have evidence for gaze following earlier than 12 months.

Recently, D'Entremont, Hains, and Muir (1997; Muir & Hains, this volume) showed that even younger infants can follow gaze at least when the targets are within a small visual angle from the adult. They had 3- to 6-month-olds interact face to face with an experimenter who was seated at a table in between two identical puppets. Periodically, the adult would turn to fixate on one of the puppets. D'Entremont et al. scored infant eye movements during each adult head turn and found significantly more reorientation of gaze at all ages toward the puppet to which the adult was attending than toward the other puppet.

The results from Butterworth and colleagues and D'Entremont and colleagues demonstrate that when there are targets in the infant's visual field, gaze following is possible in the first half of the first year of life, from at least 3 months of age. Butterworth's account of this early gaze following, the "ecological mechanism," is that the adult's head turn "triggers a search within the infant's field of vision, which terminates as a salient target is encountered in the periphery" (Butterworth & Jarrett, 1991, p. 69). Early gaze following depends, therefore, on a perceptual-attentional system. It is reasonable to suppose that the development of the ability to follow gaze under these conditions may depend in part on the maturation of the peripheral visual field, and it is possible that an extension of the D'Entremont et al. (1997) method, whereby the distance of the targets from the adult was varied, might allow any such developmental changes in gaze following to be mapped.

How does this account square with what is known about the development of visual attention? In the terminology of visual-attention research (e.g., Hood, 1995; Klein, Kingstone, & Pontefract, 1992), visual orienting away from a centrally presented cue can be classified in terms of 2 × 2 scheme. First, orienting can be either overt or covert depending on whether or not shifts in visual attention are accompanied by eye movements. Second, visual orienting can either be controlled *exogenously*, in the sense that the attentional shift is an obligatory or reflexive response to some sensory stimulation external to the observer, or *endogenously*, in the sense that the attentional shift depends on the observer's volition in relation to the meaning of the stimulation. Exogenous cueing has typically been assessed by measuring reaction times to the appearance of peripheral targets after the onset of a central cue. In the case of endogenous cueing, a central cue is presented, and it is the observer's understanding of the directional significance of the cue (which may or may not have been gained entirely within the experimental session) that controls orienting. Thus, for example, an arrow in a central location may lead an observer to shift attention, either overtly or covertly, to a peripheral location on the indicated side. It is important to note that the distinction between exogenously and endogenously controlled orienting is based on the characteristic and distinguishing experimental phenomena associated with each type of control. For example, exogenous shifts are generally faster than endogenous, and the phenomenon of inhibition of return, whereby attention is less likely or slower to return to a previously attended location, occurs with exogenous but not endogenous control (see Klein et al., 1992).

What is known of attention in infants? First, it is important to point out that it is difficult to study covert orienting in infants because of the inevitable reliance on the measurement of eye movements to the presentation of peripheral targets (see Johnson, 1997). Notwithstanding this limitation, there is good evidence for the development of exogenous control of orienting between 3 and 6 months of age. For example, Hood (1995) reported that 6-month-olds but not 3-month-olds react faster to targets appearing in cued peripheral locations than to targets appearing in uncued peripheral locations. In addition, Johnson, Posner, & Rothbart (1994) provided evidence for both endogenous and exogenous control of orienting with separable temporal characteristics. In their study, they were successful in training 4-month-old infants to orient to a target faster over a series of trials when it appeared 400 msec later in the opposite peripheral location to a cue (endogenous control). However, the infants were still significantly faster to orient to the target in later test trials when it appeared 100 msec later in the same peripheral location as the cue (exogenous orienting). It is also known that inhibition of return is present in visual orienting from at least 6 months but perhaps not as early as 3 months (Clohessy, Posner, Rothbart, & Vecera, 1991; Hood, 1993, 1995).

It is not unreasonable to consider the typical gaze-following procedure as analogous to visual orienting studies in that there is a central cue that is presented along with peripheral targets. There are, of course, some differences. First, in the gaze-following experiments described previously, the central cue (the head turn) occurs in the continued presence of peripheral targets. Second, peripheral targets are present on both sides. Third, the adult's head remains in view, albeit reoriented away from the infant. In visual orienting studies, the central cue is typically offset with the onset of the peripheral target on one side (although see Hood, 1995). Finally, in gaze following it is typical to record infant head turns, although eye turns are occasionally measured. In visual orienting studies, eye movements to peripheral targets serve as the response.

Notwithstanding these differences, my suggestion is that the earliest gaze following in the presence of peripheral targets can be conceived as relying predominantly on the operation of an exogenously controlled shift in visual orienting. The observation of the adult's head turn produces an obligatory or reflexive shift in visual orienting in the same direction, leading to a capture of attention by a target in the appropriate region of peripheral space. I make no claim here about whether this effect is achieved through control of covert attention or through control of the overt oculomotor system. In any case, attentional shifts lead to head movements in support of the eye movements. Again, it is important to be aware of a disparity between this proposal and standard thinking on exogenous control of attention. As noted, exogenous control of visual orienting is typically thought of in terms of an obligatory shift of attention toward a peripheral target rather than such a shift away from a central cue (but see Langton & Bruce, 1997, on exogenous control of attention in adults with centrally presented pictures of different head orientations). However, the proposal here is that the direction of the shift of visual orienting in the presence of two peripheral targets, one on each side, is controlled reflexively by characteristics of the central cue (the head turn). To put it another way, the choice of which of two peripheral targets captures attention is determined by characteristics of the central cue.

GAZE FOLLOWING IN THE ABSENCE OF VISIBLE TARGETS

If infants follow an adult head turn when targets are present in the periphery, what happens if there are no targets in the infant's visual field when the adult turns? The exclusion of targets in gaze-following studies allows inferences to be drawn on the decoupling of the gaze-following ability from the immediate perceptually given environment. After all, for adults gaze reorientation is understood to indicate the possibility of an object at the end of the line of sight, even if one is not obviously present.

Although, this was Scaife and Bruner's (1975) original strategy, fewer studies have examined infants' responses to adult gaze reorientation when there are no visible targets. What evidence there is points to the last quarter of the first year of life as the time at which infants will follow gaze even without visible targets. Scaife and Bruner, it will be remembered, found that four of six 8- to 10-month-olds and five of five 11- to 14-month-olds showed evidence of gaze following.

The only relevant evidence from Butterworth and colleagues' work comes from Butterworth & Cochran's (1980) Experiment 2. As noted before, in this experiment, there were some trials in which the only targets present were outside the infant's visual field. They found that 12-month-olds often turned to look to the correct side but rarely turned to look behind them. Nevertheless, these infants showed gaze following when there were no targets in the visual field.

Corkum and Moore (1995) also chose initially to exclude targets from the experimental setup. They presented infants from 6 to 19 months old with a variety of types of gaze reorientation, including a standard adult head turn, a head turn with eyes continuing to face forward, an eye turn without head turn, and a type of trial in which the head and eyes were turned simultaneously in opposite directions. Corkum and Moore also employed a scoring procedure that controlled for random infant head turning by using as the dependent variable a difference score calculated by subtracting infant head turns to the wrong side from head turns to the correct side. Their results showed no evidence of reliable gaze following, as measured by a difference score significantly greater than chance, until 12 months of age.

In subsequent research, Corkum, Moore, and colleagues (Corkum & Moore, 1998; Moore, Angelopoulos, & Bennett, 1997) modified the standard Scaife–Bruner (1975) paradigm in order to provide the contingent feedback of an interesting event at the location to which the adult turns. This feedback took the form of the activation of one of two remote-controlled toys. These toys were located one on each side of the room at about 90 degrees visual angle away from the midline. The toys were identical stuffed dogs and were placed on turntables in boxes behind Plexiglas windows. On activation, a house light in the box was illuminated, and the turntable rotated, creating an attractive sight. So, although there were targets present in these studies, the targets were located on the sides of the room between the participants and far enough away such that when the infant was facing forward they were not in the visual field.

In the standard Corkum–Moore (1998) procedure, the infant is first presented with four 7-second baseline trials of adult head turn, two to each side, during which the targets remain inactive. There are then four more trials, two to each side, in which the target is activated shortly after the adult makes a head turn. Finally, there is a period consisting of a maximum of 20 trials of adult head turn, during which the toy is activated only if the infant makes the appropriate response. The purpose of this procedure is to examine first whether the infants are showing gaze following spontaneously and then to provide them with experience of interesting sights to the side contingent on the adult turn in order to investigate the conditions under which gaze following might be acquired or modified. The relevance of this procedure to the preceding discussion is that here there is no perceptually available target when the infant observes the adult head turn. However, it is demonstrated to the infants in the experimental session that there is a "potential" target. The question is, under conditions in which infants know that something worth seeing is going to appear, when can they use an adult head turn to locate the interesting sight?

In their first experiment, Corkum & Moore (1998) tested children from 6 to 11 months old. They used a normal adult head turn with eye congruent in all phases of the experiment. The results showed that at 6 to 7 months, there was no evidence of spontaneous gaze following. Furthermore, on being shown the activated targets, the infants showed considerable head turning, but they were unable to use the adult head turn to predict accurately on which side the target would appear. Thus, they turned as often in the wrong direction as in the correct direction. Of infants aged 8 to 9 months, most did not follow the adult's head turn spontaneously in the baseline phase of the experiment, but about half did follow the adult's head turn reliably after having been shown that there were interesting sights to be seen at the side of the room. By 10 to 11 months old, about half of the infants needed no help to follow gaze—they did so spontaneously in the baseline phase. Most of those who did not follow gaze spontaneously did follow gaze once they had been shown the activation of the targets.

Subsequent studies (Corkum & Moore, 1998, Exp. 2; Moore et al., 1997) replicated and extended these findings. These follow-up experiments have shown that 9 months of age is typically the transition point between no spontaneous and spontaneous gaze following in the absence of visually available targets. Furthermore, they have partly elucidated the characteristics of the adult head turn that are important in infants' acquiring gaze following under these conditions. For example, it appears that the directional movement of the adult head is initially an important aspect of the cue (Corkum & Moore, 1998; Moore et al., 1997).

Thus, by about 9 to 10 months old, infants will follow adult head turns even when there is no obvious target in the peripheral visual field. From this finding, it appears that infant gaze following has moved beyond the purely exogenous attentional mechanism suggested previously to account for gaze following when peripheral targets are present. It is possible, however, that the mechanism is still attentional in that the adult head turn cues the infants to search in the direction indicated (Corkum & Moore, in press; Moore, 1994). The difference is that now it can be thought of as more endogenous in the sense that the infant has an expectation of encountering a target in the direction indicated by the adult head turn. The absence of a target in the visual field means that there is no stimulation of the peripheral visual field in association with the adult's head turn. In order to locate a target, the infant must produce a head movement in response to the adult's gaze shift. Where previously gaze following could be achieved through the central cue highlighting an already visible target, the head turn toward an invisible target is a more voluntary response based on the understanding that the central cue indicates the potential for a target in a particular location. From the results of Corkum, Moore, and colleagues, one might suggest that the developmental transition from an exogenous to an endogenous cueing mechanism is linked to the experience of a predictive relationship between adult head turns (and other referential behavior) and interesting sights at about 9 months of age. Whether this transition is a general change in infants' attentional processes or one that is particular to gaze remains to be determined.

It is worth mentioning that there is some evidence that even when the infant becomes capable of following gaze in the absence of targets, the presence of targets likely amplifies the response. The only study known to this author in which gaze-following performance in the presence and absence of targets was directly compared was reported in a conference paper by Caron, Krakowski, Liu, and Brooks (1996). Caron et al. tested 14-month-olds and found that although there was above-chance gaze following when there were no targets present, there was significantly more when there were targets in the infants' visual field. Notice that the target-absent condition here did not present the infants with the experience of potential targets as did the Corkum–Moore procedure. Therefore, it remains unknown whether gaze following in the presence of perceptually present targets is superior to that with potentially present targets equated for salience.

GAZE FOLLOWING AND SENSITIVITY TO EYE DIRECTION

By the end of the first year of life, therefore, infants are capable of following the gaze of another when that gaze is indicated by a head turn, even when there are no immediately obvious targets. I have argued that changes in the infant's attentional processes might account for the phenomena reviewed so far in this chapter. Notice that such an account does not attribute to the young infant any understanding of the other's attentional state as an intentional orientation to the target, and those who have investigated gaze following have been appropriately cautious in this regard (e.g., Butterworth & Jarrett, 1991; Corkum & Moore, 1998; Moore & Corkum, 1994). In contrast, other theorists commenting on the origins of social understanding or theory of mind have suggested that gaze following evidences the understanding of intentionality in infants (e.g., Baron-Cohen, 1995; Bretherton, 1991).

For gaze following to be evidence of the understanding of visual attention in others, it seems important that infants are sensitive to the visual activity that is manifested as changes in eye direction. There is no doubt that infants are sensitive to eyes from a very early age. In the first few months, infants scan the eye regions of faces more than other regions (e.g., Hainline, 1978; Haith, Bergman, & Moore, 1977) and smile more at facelike stimuli containing patterns of contrast in the eye region (e.g., Bower, 1982). More important, infants show sensitivity to eye direction within the first 6 months of life. Four-month-olds can discriminate photographs depicting direct gaze from averted gaze (Vecera & Johnson, 1995). Hains and Muir (1996) have reported that this sensitivity to eye direction impacts on the quality of dyadic interactions with others from 3 months of age. Muir and Hains have reviewed this work in their chapter in this volume, so I will not repeat it here.

Sensitivity to eye direction in early infancy, however, can be characterized as sensitivity to the disruption of normal face-to-face interaction involving eye contact. It does not indicate that an infant recognizes that when the eyes of a partner are averted they are looking at something else or even, on a more primitive level, that there is something to see in that direction. To address the issue of what infants might know of the significance of eye direction for objects in the world, information on gaze following is necessary.

A number of studies have investigated infants' sensitivity to eye direction in gaze-following situations by testing the tendency to follow gaze when the eyes and head are differentially oriented. The first to do so was Lempers (1979) in the study mentioned earlier. In addition to presenting infants with normal head reorientations, in which the eyes remained congruent with the head, Lempers also presented trials in which the adult reoriented the eyes but kept the head oriented toward the child. The results showed that no 9-month-olds and about 50 percent of 12- to 14-month-olds correctly followed the eye turns. This level of performance was worse than those for the head turn. As noted earlier, however, it is difficult to know what to make of Lempers' results, because no data are reported on the number of times successful infants also turned in the wrong direction.

In his work, Lempers (1979) had targets in full view of the infants. The only other studies to employ divergent head and eye cues have not had targets present in the infant's visual field. As noted earlier, Butterworth and Jarrett (1991, Exp. 2) found that 18-month-olds followed eye turns toward targets that were behind them when there were no targets in front. As in Lempers' study, performance was inferior to when the adult turned the head and eyes together.

Corkum & Moore (1995) presented, along with the normal convergent head and eye turn, three adult turn cues in which the eyes and head were divergent: a head turn with eyes focused on infant, an eye turn with head oriented toward infant, and a simultaneous head and eye reorientation but in opposite directions. There was no evidence for following the eyes-alone cue at any age in the study. Furthermore, it was not until 18 months of age that the congruent head and eyes cue was followed significantly more than the head turn with eyes focused on the infant. This study provides evidence that at 18 months old, infants recognize the significance of the eyes in gaze following in that they did not follow head turns when these were not accompanied by the eyes. The failure to find gaze following to eyes alone is inconsistent with the results of Butterworth and Jarrett (1991). It is likely, however, that the procedure employed by Corkum and Moore (1995) tended to deemphasize the significance of the eyes-alone cue in that they were presented in mixed blocks along with the other more salient cues.

In order to maximize the chances of finding gaze following to eye turns, Moore and Corkum (in press) used the training paradigm of Corkum and Moore (1998) substituting eye turns for head turns. The rationale here was that once the infants knew that there was an interesting event to see and were motivated to search for it, they used whatever cue they could in order to find it. Infants from 8 to 19 months old were tested, and as in their other work, a difference score of correct minus incorrect head turns was computed and used as the dependent variable. In this study, infants followed eye turns, but this only happened reliably in infants of 18 to 19 months of age. Thus, even though the infants were strongly motivated to try to find the interesting sight, they could not make use of eye direction until well after they are known to use head direction.

The few studies reviewed here that have assessed gaze following with eye direction cues do not provide as comprehensive a picture as those conducted on gaze following with head turns. It seems likely that when targets are not in the visual field, infants do not use eye direction for gaze following until around the middle of the second year, considerably later than when they use head turns. This finding implies that the meaning of eye direction for the endogenous control of attention develops well after the meaning of head direction.

Whether younger infants follow eye direction when there are targets in the visual field is unclear at present. There is some weak evidence from Lempers (1979), but as noted before his method differs in significant ways from most others in the field. There is no evidence as yet that infants younger than 12 months of age follow eye direction in standard gaze-following paradigms.

The only work that suggests an earlier ability to follow eye direction employed the kind of visual-orienting procedures described earlier. Using a computerized presentation with a 37-inch screen viewed at a distance of 22 inches, Hood, Willen, & Driver (1998) presented digitized photographs of shifts in eye orientation followed by peripheral targets. They reported that infants as young as 10 weeks showed significantly faster orientation to the target when it was presented on the side toward which the eyes had shifted than when it was presented on the opposite side, even though it was equally likely to appear on either side. If changes in eye direction are indeed able to exert exogenous control over the young infant's attention, then it is plausible to predict that infants will follow eye direction in gaze-following situations when there are targets within the visual field at relatively small degrees of visual angle.

CONCLUSIONS

A review of the evidence on gaze following to date seems consistent with the following developmental pattern. Infants from about 3 months of age will follow head turns when there are peripheral targets in the visual field. Until about 9 months of age, they will not follow gaze when there are no targets visible, but from this age they will turn in response to head turns of the interactive partner, indicating that they know there is potentially something interesting to see. From 9 months old through the first half of the second year, gaze following to absent targets appears limited to head-turn cues. Around 18 months of age, infants start to be able to use changes in eye direction of the interactive partner to achieve the same end.

Fitting these findings to the literature on attentional control, it appears likely that the earliest gaze following depends on exogenous control whereby the infant's attention is shifted toward peripheral targets by a central cue. Gaze following to absent targets is more consistent with endogenous control in that it implies some understanding of the meaning of the other's head-turning behavior. Over the next 9 months, the cues that can exert endogenous control over the infant's attention probably change from moving heads, through static head orientations, and finally to changes in eye direction at about 18 months old.

The association that I have outlined between gaze following and the control of attention is admittedly sketchy. I believe, however, that as an account of the development of gaze following, it has some attractive features. First, it links changes in social behavior during infancy with more general information-processing capacities and their development. This is not to say that the social changes depend on, or are paced by, these more general changes. Information-processing development almost certainly depends on the experiences the child encounters, and there are no more important experiences in the life of the infant than those encountered within the context of face-to-face social interaction. Second, it does not attribute to the infant an unwarranted sophistication of the understanding of the intentionality of others. Instead, because endogenous control of attention is internal or voluntary control of information processing based on meaning, an account of developing endogenous control has the potential to provide a continuous story of how increasingly more sophisticated forms of social meaning are realized within an infant's information-processing system.

ACKNOWLEDGMENTS

This chapter was prepared with support from Grant 410–95–1144 from the Social Sciences and Humanities Research Council of Canada. My thanks to Ray Klein for his comments on the manuscript.

REFERENCES

Baron-Cohen, S. (1994). How to build a baby that can read minds: Cognitive mechanisms in mindreading. *Cahiers de Psychologie Cognitive, 13*, 513–552.

Bower, T. (1982). *Development in infancy*. San Francisco: Freeman.

Bretherton, I. (1991). Intentional communication and the development of mind. In D. Frye & C. Moore (Eds.), *Children's theories of mind. Mental states and social understanding* (pp. 49–76). Hillsdale, NJ: Lawrence Erlbaum Associates.

Butterworth, G., & Cochran, E. (1980). Towards a mechanism of joint visual attention in human infancy. *International Journal of Behavioral Development, 3,* 253–272.

Butterworth, G., & Jarrett, N. (1991). What minds have in common is space: Spatial mechanisms serving joint visual attention in infancy. *British Journal of Developmental Psychology, 9,* 55–72.

Caron, A., Krakowski, O., Liu, A., & Brooks, R. (1996). *Infant joint attention: Cued orienting or implicit theory of mind.* Paper presented at the 10th International Conference of Infant Studies, Providence, RI.

Clohessy, A., Posner, M., Rothbart, M., & Vecera, S. (1991). The development of inhibition of return. *Journal of Cognitive Neuroscience, 3,* 345–356.

Corkum, V., & Moore, C. (1995). Development of joint visual attention in infants. In C. Moore & P. Dunham (Eds.), *Joint attention: Its origins and role in development* (pp. 61–84). Hillsdale, NJ: Lawrence Erlbaum Associates.

Corkum, V., & Moore, C. (1998). The origins of joint visual attention in infants. *Developmental Psychology, 34,* 28–38.

D'Entremont, B., Hains, S., & Muir, D. (1997). A demonstration of gaze following in 3- to 6-months-olds. *Infant Behavior and Development, 20,* 569–572.

Hainline, L. (1978). Developmental changes in visual scanning of face and nonface patterns by infants. *Journal of Experimental Child Psychology, 25,* 90–115.

Hains, S., & Muir, D. (1996). Infant sensitivity to adult eye direction. *Child Development, 67,* 1940–1950.

Haith, M., Bergman, T., & Moore, M. (1977). Eye contact and face scanning in early infancy. *Science, 198,* 853–855.

Hood, B. (1993). Inhibition of return produced by covert shifts of visual attention in 6-month-old infants. *Infant Behavior and Development, 16,* 245–254.

Hood, B. (1995). Shifts of visual attention in the human infant: A neuroscientific approach. In C. Rovee-Collier & L. Lipsitt (Eds.), *Advances in infancy research* (Vol. 9, pp. 163–216). Norwood, NJ: Ablex.

Hood, B. M., Willen, J. D., & Driver, J. (1998). Adult's eyes trigger shifts of visual attention in human infants. *Psychological Science, 9,* 53–56.

Johnson, M. (1997). *Developmental cognitive neuroscience.* Cambridge, MA: Blackwell.

Johnson, M., Posner, M., & Rothbart, M. (1994). Facilitation of saccades toward a covertly attended location in early infancy. *Psychological Science, 5,* 90–93.

Klein, R., Kingstone, A., & Pontefract, A. (1992). Orienting of visual attention. In K. Rayner (Ed.), *Eye movements and visual cognition* (pp. 46–65). New York: Springer-Verlag.

Langton, S., & Bruce, V. (1997). *Reflexive orienting in response to the social attention of others.* Unpublished manuscript, University of Stirling, Scotland.

Lempers, J. D. (1979). Young children's production and comprehension of nonverbal deictic behaviors. *The Journal of Genetic Psychology, 135,* 93–102.

Moore, C. (1994). Intentionality and self–other equivalence in early mindreading: The eyes do not have it. *Cahiers de Psychologie Cognitive, 13,* 661–668.

Moore, C., Angelopoulos, M., & Bennett, P. (1997). The role of movement in the development of joint visual attention. *Infant Behavior and Development, 20,* 83–92.

Moore, C., & Corkum, V. (1994). Social understanding at the end of the first year of life. *Developmental Review, 14,* 349–372.

Moore, C., & Corkum, V. (in press). Infant gaze following based on eye direction. *British Journal of Developmental Psychology.*

Morissette, P., Ricard, M., Gouin-Decarie, T. (1995). Joint visual attention and pointing in infancy: A longitudinal study of comprehension. *British Journal of Developmental Psychology, 13,* 163–175.

Scaife, M., & Bruner, J. S. (1975). The capacity for joint visual attention in the infant. *Nature, 253,* 265–266.

Tomasello, M., Kruger, A., & Ratner, H. (1993). Cultural learning. *Behavioral and Brain Sciences, 16,* 495–511.

Vecera, S., & Johnson, M. (1995). Eye gaze detection and the cortical processing of faces: Evidence from infants and adults. *Visual Cognition, 2,* 101–129.

Chapter 11

Infants' Distinction Between Animate and Inanimate Objects: The Origins of Naive Psychology

Diane Poulin-Dubois
Concordia University

The last 2 decades have witnessed an abundance of studies on infant cognition. There is now growing evidence that infants show precocious intuitions about several physical phenomena, such as support, collision, and occlusion (Baillargeon, 1995). Most of this research has focused on the content of infants' knowledge, although there has been recent interest in addressing the structural and developmental aspects of early physical reasoning (Baillargeon, 1995; Spelke, Breilinger, Macomber, & Jacobson, 1992). One current issue is whether infants' understanding of physical objects constitutes an early theory of objects or a simple perceptual organization of sensory experiences. Another issue is whether infants are born with substantive beliefs about objects or with constrained mechanisms that guide their acquisition of knowledge about objects (Baillargeon, Kotovsky, & Needham, 1995).

Research on infant's developing social cognition has also mushroomed in the last 10 to 15 years. Being a precocious physicist will certainly help infants to understand some aspects of human beings such as the occlusion and collision of their bodies; however, physical principles will clearly be inadequate to understand human behavior. Although people and inanimate objects share many properties, they differ in important ways. Only people and other animate objects can move autonomously, grow and reproduce, possess mental states, and have specific features (Gelman & Spelke, 1981). Aside from possessing unique morphological features such as faces and hands, people engage in interactive behaviors that involve contingency, reciprocity, and communication. They are also capable of self-propelled and goal-directed movements and, unlike most physical objects, their actions can be caused at a distance. In this chapter, I review the empirical evidence demonstrating that infants have acquired some understanding of the most basic properties that distinguish people, and other animates, from physical objects by the end of their second year. I further argue that this precocious knowledge provides the foundation for an implicit theory of mind in infancy. This foundation is based on the existence of principles such as a capacity for self-generated and goal-directed action that make possible the construction of basic ontological categories.

I propose three steps in the development of the concept of person: the person as a distinctive object, the person as an intentional agent, and the person as a mental agent. During the first phase, from birth to about 9 months of age, infants already treat people as different from physical objects. This discrimination is evident in the differential repertoire of behaviors infants display when facing objects or people. In the second phase, from 9 to 18 months, infants begin to treat people as purposive entities who are goal directed and self-propelled. In the third phase, starting at 18 months, people are conceived by the infants as sentient agents who plan their actions. This last phase marks a milestone in the development of a naive psychology. As support for each of these stages, I review recent empirical evidence, including data from my own laboratory. Some unresolved issues and contradictory findings are highlighted.

PEOPLE AS DISTINCTIVE OBJECTS

The main issue to be investigated when addressing the people versus inanimate object distinction is whether infants perceive and respond differently to the two types of objects. This issue has been explored through the comparison of infants' behaviors when imitating, exploring, categorizing, and interacting with people versus inanimate objects. Young infants' abilities to discriminate between people and inanimate objects was first investigated in the context of face-to-face interactions more than 20 years ago. Differential responding to people and objects was found when a caregiver was compared to a slowly moving object (Brazelton, Koslowski, & Main, 1974; Trevarthen, 1977). In these studies, infants as young as 2 months old were reported to produce expressive facial movements, to make prespeech sounds when facing their mother, and to make reach-and-grasp movements with neutral facial expressions when faced with graspable objects. Unfortunately, the results of these studies were inconclusive, because confounding variables such as visual features of the stimuli, type of movement, familiarity, and contingency were not properly controlled in these experiments.

Recently, the data from a number of carefully controlled studies seem to confirm that, from very early on, infants treat people differently from objects. In the context of face-to-face interactions, infants as young as 2 or 3 months of age are more likely to display a repertoire of social behaviors (e.g., smiling, vocalizing) toward responsive people than toward interactive objects (see Legerstee, 1992, for a review). Different responses are found when responsive and passive people (mother and female stranger) are presented in alternation with objects such as dolls (with or without facial features) (Ellsworth, Muir, & Hains, 1993; Legerstee, Corter, & Kineapple, 1990; Legerstee, Pomerleau, Malcuit, & Feider, 1987). These different responses are also found when the objects remain immobile. To my knowledge, only one study has been carried out on social responsiveness to people and objects in infants younger than 2 or 3 months. Ronnqvist and von Hofsten (1994) found that newborns produce different arm and hand movements when interacting with people relative to objects.

Another context in which differential responding to people and inanimate objects has been reported is during the exploration of a novel object. Typically, researchers have observed that infants old enough to crawl exhibit differential exploratory behavior when exposed to a human stranger and a novel nonsocial object designed to respond contingently on their actions (Eckerman & Rheingold, 1974; Ricard & Gouin-Décarie, 1989). In a recent study conducted in our laboratory, 9- and 12-month-old infants were exposed to a small robot and a female stranger in the presence of the mother. Infants as young as 9 months were found to approach and manipulate the robot. In contrast, in the presence of a stranger, infants took longer to approach, if they approached at all, but vocalized and smiled more often in the presence of the stranger (Poulin-Dubois, Lepage, & Ferland, 1996). A similar study compared the behaviors of infants of about the same age when they were exposed to an unfamiliar animal (a rabbit), a novel toy, and a stranger. Although the unfamiliar animal was not treated as an inanimate object (e.g., sustained attention), the findings confirmed that social behaviors such as smiling are reserved for people (Ricard & Allard, 1993).

Early facial imitation is another paradigm that provides evidence for an early differentiation between animate and inanimate objects. Two decades ago, Meltzoff and Moore (1977) challenged, after Zazzo (1957) 20 years earlier, the Piagetian view that facial imitation cannot be elicited until 8 to 12 months of age by reporting that newborns could imitate tongue protrusion, mouth opening, and lip protrusion. Since this study, this precocious matching effect has been replicated and extended in new directions by investigators around the world. The most current literature on early matching behavior focuses on the nature and functional significance of early imitation. It is worth noting that one prevalent interpretation of the early matching behavior is that it is indicative of early social cognition, not simple reflexive motor movements (Meltzoff, 1995; Meltzoff & Moore, 1992). If this is the case, we should not expect infants to imitate the movements of inanimate objects. The first experiment conducted to test this hypothesis yielded data suggesting that tongue protrusion could be elicited in babies by a person modeling this gesture but also by a white ball and a pen moving toward and away from the infant's mouth, thereby creating a similar motion (Jacobson, 1979). Recent studies have, however, reported that imitation is specific to people, with inanimate objects failing to elicit matching responses (Abravanel & deYong, 1991; Legerstee, 1991).

Another set of studies addressing indirectly the people–inanimate objects distinction comes from the literature on early categorization skills. Recent research in this area indicates that as early as 7 months infants begin to categorize animals as different from vehicles, although at first, they make few conceptual distinctions within the animal domain (Mandler & McDonough, 1993). This ability is achieved despite the great perceptual variability in the exemplars within that domain (e.g., fish, bird, mammals). What about the categorization of people? Surprisingly, there have been few studies addressing this issue directly, although some interesting findings can be drawn from available published reports on early categorization. To my knowledge, there has only been two studies that examined the people versus other animal (or artifacts) distinction (Oakes, Plumert, Lansink, & Merryman, 1996; Ross, 1980). In Ross' study, 12-, 18-, and 24-month-old children were familiarized with three different categories. For example, the category *men* was composed of small replicas of men that varied in color and texture (Ross, 1980). After familiarization, the infants saw a test pair composed of a new member of the category (e.g., another man) paired with a member of a novel category (e.g., an animal). Infants as young as 12 months old habituated to the men but also showed a preference for the animal during the test, suggesting that they perceive a distinction between people and animals. Other paradigms, such as the procedure recently developed to test object identity, have been adapted to test the person–inanimate distinction in 10-month-olds but have thus far yielded no significant results (Sorrentino, Xu, & Carey, 1996).

The research reviewed in the preceding section suggests that infants display different behaviors toward people and inanimate objects even at the youngest ages tested to date. The repertoire of behaviors that indicate an early person–inanimate distinction evolves as a function of age. During the first few months, infants display some gestures and facial expressions only in the presence of people. They already hold expectations about the behavior of a social partner, as shown in the increase in negative affect generated by the still-face procedure (Muir, this volume; Rochat & Striano, this volume). A few months later, they explore a novel object or a stranger in different ways, as shown in their vocalizations and displacements. It seems that an early concept of person has started to be formed, based on infants' detection and utilization of social affordances (Adolph, Eppler, & Gibson, 1993).

PEOPLE AS PURPOSIVE AGENTS

Toward the end of the first year, infants undergo a kind of revolution in their understanding of persons. Beginning around the age of 9 months, infants engage in a variety of behaviors such as joint visual attention, social referencing, imitative learning, and intentional communication (Tomasello, 1995). For example, infants of this age use deictic gestures, such as pointing, to request adult help in obtaining an object, a kind of social tool use (Bates, Benigni, Bretherton, Camaioni, & Volterra, 1979; Camaioni, 1992). Pointing is typically accompanied by gaze alternation that seems to indicate that the child expects the adult to behave autonomously after seeing the child's signals. Deictic gestures used around the end of the first year are aimed at influencing an agent psychologically, not mechanically. This unique pattern of gestural communication, involving triadic distal gestures, differs remarkably from the dyadic contact gestures used by nonhuman primates (Tomasello & Camaioni, 1997). This qualitative shift suggests that infants are beginning to understand other persons as intentional agents; that is, that people behave as independent and autonomous actors.

A rich interpretation of the emergence of intentional communication has been proposed that suggests that it may serve as a marker for emergence of an implicit theory of mind (Bretherton, McNew, & Beeghly-Smith, 1981). An alternative, and leaner, interpretation is that the child considers people, and not inanimate objects, as autonomous agents (Poulin-Dubois & Shultz, 1988). I would like to propose that infants construct a concept of people as agents by abstracting different types of motion characteristics. I argue, along with some others (Leslie, 1994; Mandler, 1992) that by the end of the first year, infants discriminate two broad types of onset of motion (self-motion vs. caused motion), two types of trajectories (goal directed vs. random) and two types of contingency of motion (at a distance vs. direct physical contact). I further argue that infants have also started to associate each type of motion with one category of objects; that is, people (and possibly animals) are self-propelled, goal-directed organisms whose movements can be caused at a distance. In contrast, inanimate objects like rocks and chairs are set into motion by an external agent through direct physical contact and do not pursue goals.

From birth, infants are highly responsive to motion as shown by their preference for moving over stationary objects (Slater, 1989) and by the fact that objects are detected and attended to at distances at which stationary objects are not (Burnham, 1987). When and how infants discriminate between different types of motion has received some attention recently. From an early age, infants are sensitive to the difference between caused and noncaused motion (Leslie, 1982, 1988; Oakes & Cohen, 1995; Premack, 1990). In a series of experiments, Leslie (1982) and Leslie and Kebble (1987) showed that infants as young as 6 months are sensitive to the well-known ball launching effect. One group of infants was habituated to a film of a direct launching event. A second group was habituated to a noncausal sequence in which either a short time delay or a spatial gap was inserted between the impact of the first object and the movement of the second object. When both groups of infants had been habituated to their respective events, they were each tested on exactly the same respective event, but reversed. The causal group recovered attention more than the noncausal group even though the spatiotemporal changes and the contingency properties were equated in the events presented to the two groups. It should be pointed out, however, that causal perception is not an all-or-none phenomenon since causal events are distinguished from noncausal events somewhat later during the first year when complex real objects (as opposed to simple blocks) are used (Oakes & Cohen, 1995).

Researchers have also been able to demonstrate that infants are sensitive to goal-directedness by the end of the first year. Rochat, Morgan, & Carpenter (1997) tested 3- to 6-month-olds' relative visual preference for two different dynamic events: a pair of discs moving around the screen independently or the same pair chasing each other. Infants discriminated between the two displays by the age of 3 months, as shown by their preference for one of the displays. The authors concluded that infants as young as 3 months are sensitive to information specifying social contingencies and intentionality.

In a recent study, Gergely and his colleagues (1995) habituated 12-month-old infants to the movements of a small computer-animated circle that repeatedly approached a large circle by jumping over a rectangular figure separating them. This event could be interpreted as a rational action (avoiding the obstacle) of the small circle toward a goal (reaching the large circle). In the posthabituation trials, the obstacle was removed, and the infants either saw a novel action that consisted of the small circle moving directly toward the large circle or the old jumping action, which was no longer justified in the new context. Infants showed more recovery of attention when they saw the familiar, nonrational action than the new but rational action. A recent experiment testing this hypothesis with younger infants revealed that this discrimination develops between the age of 6 and 9 months (Csibra, Gergely, Biro, & Koos, 1996).

Evidence of such discriminations indicates that early on (by 6 months) infants develop sensitivity to some of the properties of animate motion, such as action at a distance and self-propulsion. However, a critical issue is whether infants have also started to associate each type of motion with a specific object kind. Babies as young as 3 months prefer to look at a display of moving dots specifying a walking motion than one in which the same dots move randomly (Berthental, 1993). Unfortunately, we do not know if infants of that age can discriminate biological from mechanical motion nor do we know if they associate animates with biomechanical motion and inanimates with mechanical motion. However, some evidence indicates that for infants less than a year old, goal-directedness is associated with animates, particularly people. In a recent study, Woodward (1996) asked whether 5- and 9-month-old infants would attend to the goal-related properties of a reach act or merely to its spatiotemporal properties. She also assessed whether babies would encode as equivalent a reach act by an inanimate object or a human actor. The infants saw an actor reaching from one side of a stage to grasp one of two toys that rested side by side. A second group of babies at each age saw events in which a rod moved in and touched one of the two toys. Following habituation, the positions of the toys were switched and the infants either saw the actor's arm or the rod follow the same path of motion but grasp a different toy, or a different path of motion but grasp the same toy. Infants in both age groups looked longer to a change in goal object than to a change in path of reach in the person condition, not showing this pattern in the rod condition. These findings suggest that by the age of 5 months infants encode differently human action and object motion, attributing goal-directedness to human action only.

As previously mentioned, one notion that contributes to the distinction between inanimate and animate motion is the contingency of motion between objects, especially when contingency entails action at a distance rather than direct physical contact (Mandler, 1992). It was shown that it is the principle of contact that guides infants' reasoning about inanimate objects; that is, objects act on each other if and only if they get in physical contact (Leslie, 1988; Oakes & Cohen, 1995). Will infants suspend the contact principle in reasoning about human action? Spelke, Phillips, and Woodward (1995) attempted to answer this question by conducting a habituation study comparing 7-month-olds' reasoning about simple causal sequences involving either people or inanimate objects. Infants were first habituated to objects or people disappearing at one end of a large screen while a second object or person appeared at the other end. After babies were habituated to these events, test trials were presented in which the occluder was removed and one of the objects or people was shown moving toward the other, who started moving after either a collision or no collision. In the inanimate object condition, the majority of infants looked longer at the test films with no collision. Infants did not show this preference in the person condition despite a slight tendency for infants to look longer at the collision film. These findings provide preliminary evidence that, by the age of 7 months, infants assume that inanimate objects require contact to cause the other to move whereas people do not.

Infants' understanding of the role of contact in the motion of animate and inanimate objects was also tested by Leslie (1984), who habituated infants to a hand picking up a doll. They were then tested on a sequence showing the hand picking up the doll again but with a small gap between hand and object. Infants as young as 7 months recovered attention to this change yet not to a similar change when there was no hand but only another object making the same movements. These results suggest that early on, infants consider the human hand as agent of functional actions. However, as pointed out by Mandler (1992), the infants may have found the sight of a block of wood picking up an object difficult to interpret independently of any knowledge about the differential causal power of a hand and a block.

Another study that suggests a precocious understanding of the different type of causal power of animate and inanimate objects shows that infants as young as 6 months expect only inanimates to be contacted at a distance (Molina, Spelke, & King, 1996). Babies were first habituated to one of two videotaped scenarios. In both scenarios, two entities were wearing very bright, salient hats with a bell attached at the top. One was a person who was fully visible. The second was hidden by a screen such that only the hat was visible, so the baby was unable to tell what kind of thing it was. In the Talk condition, the person spoke to the partially hidden entity and the hat shook back and forth in reply. The same scenario was repeated in the test events, except that the occluder was removed, revealing either a person wearing the hat or a bright blue nerf ball. In another condition, the Touch condition, infants were habituated to an event in which the person turned to the occluded entity, spoke, and then reached out and shook the hat back and forth. As in the other condition, the tests presented either a person or a bright ball wearing the hat and the same interaction took place without the occluder. The results indicated that the babies looked longer at the person wearing the hat in the Talk condition and at the nerf ball in the Touch condition. It appears that 6-month-olds were able to make an inference regarding the hidden entity, whether it was a person or a ball. This inference was based on the contact or absence of contact between the actor and that entity in the course of the habituation.

In one of the studies using real objects, Carlson-Luden (reported in Golinkoff, Harding, Carlson, & Sexton, 1984) compared the ability of 10-month-olds to learn to push a lever in order to set either an inanimate object (a picture) or a person in motion. Infants seemed to appreciate that physical contact is necessary to set inanimate objects in motion, whereas action at a distance is sufficient for animate objects (such as people), because they only learned the association between pushing the lever and object motion in the case of the inanimate object. In a recent study carried out in my laboratory, 9- and 12-month-olds were exposed to a self-propelled small robot and a female stranger, both moving according to the verbal commands of the infant's mother who was present in the room (Poulin-Dubois, Lepage, & Ferland, 1996, Exp. 3). Infants from both age groups stared longer at the robot acting at a distance than at the person doing the same. These findings suggest that infants as young as 9 months expect a novel inanimate object to be constrained by the principle of contact.

Few studies have examined when infants come to realize that only animate objects can move independently or act as agents. Golinkoff and Kerr (1978) presented 15- and 18-month-olds with films in which there was a role reversal between agents and recipients. In one of the films, the initiator of the action alternated between a man and a chair. The prediction that infants would notice the violation of the agency concept in the chair-pushes-the-man event was not borne out. The use of films might have underestimated infants' abilities, because 15-month-olds probably know already that violations of common expectations are frequent in films. In a follow-up study using real-life events, Golinkoff and Harding (1980; cited in Golinkoff et al., 1984) presented 16- and 24-month-old infants with a chair moving by itself across the room. The emotional and motor responses of the infants indicated that only the older infants showed some emotional response to this anomalous event. The researchers concluded that by the end of the second year, self-propulsion in inanimate objects is judged as anomalous. The results of a study by Poulin-Dubois and Shultz (1988, 1990) suggest that this type of knowledge might even be present by the end of the first year of life. Infants aged 8 and 13 months were exposed to novel events featuring a person (female stranger) or an inanimate object (ball or chair) moving without any forces acting on them. The 13-month-old infants showed a significant decrease in visual fixation time in the person-as-agent condition but not in the ball-as-agent condition. The younger infants showed the opposite pattern. All infants habituated to the chair and person moving on their own. Although interesting, the results from this first experiment provided only preliminary support for the hypothesis that infants of 13 months of age believe that inanimate objects are not capable of self-motion. The objects we used were familiar, so older infants could simply have had more experience with them, explaining their reaction to the novel motion of these objects.

In the same series of experiments reported above we showed 9- and 12-month-olds a stationary unfamiliar inanimate object followed by the same object moving around the room without any impetus (Poulin-Dubois et al., 1996). The unfamiliar object, a self-propelled robot, possessed some human features such as a face with eyes. A female stranger was presented in the same manner. The self-propelled robot was considered incongruous by infants of both age groups as indexed by an increase in negative affect when it moved in comparison to the stationary condition (see Fig. 11.1). In contrast, no increase in negative affect was observed when the stranger started to move. Because the infants were allowed to explore the person and the robot before being exposed to its motion, we hypothesized that their responses to the motion was based on the expectations that they had developed about the two stimuli during the stationary condition.

In my laboratory, we have recently begun to examine what infants can infer about the identity of an object only from the type of motion it displays. Specifically, we are investigating whether 12-month-old infants are able to categorize an object with an ambiguous appearance as animate or inanimate, based mainly on characteristics of the object's motion, such as self-propulsion or goal-directedness (Baker & Poulin-Dubois, 1998).

In conclusion, sometime between 6 and 9 months of age, infants acquire the ability to predict the type of motion characteristic of people and inanimate objects. This ability may stem from a primitive mechanism that interprets *any* goal-directed and self-propelled stimuli in terms of desires and goals (Baron-Cohen, 1994; Premack & Premack, 1995). According to such a view, an "intentionality detector" is hard-wired into the human infants' visual system so that they read mental states of goal and desire into a wide range of stimuli that manifest self-propulsion (Baron-Cohen, 1994, 1995). This ability is modular because it meets some of the requirements of a Fodorian module such as obligatory firing, characteristic pattern

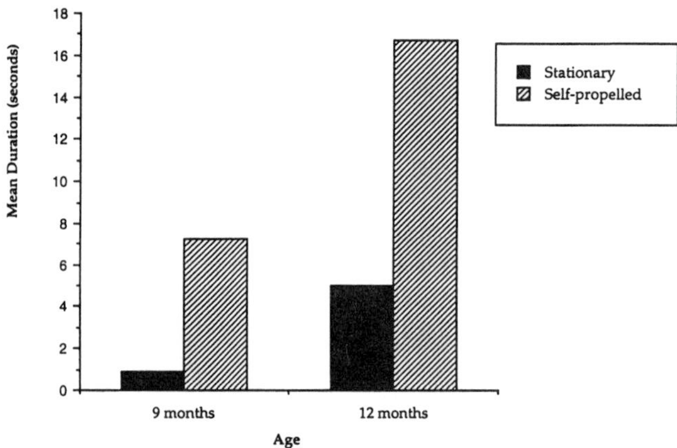

FIG. 11.1. Mean duration of negative affect displayed toward the robot by 9- and 12-month-olds in the stationary and self-propelled conditions.

of breakdown, and so on. Although the hypothesis of a domain-general, hard-wired sensitivity to animate-type motion remains to be more fully documented, the empirical evidence available so far suggests that by the time that infants engage in triadic interaction with people, they show an understanding that people are agents who pursue goals and that people can be set into motion at a distance or can start to act on their own. In other words, beginning sometime during the second half of the first year, infants understand that people not only move like inanimate objects but also *act* and *react*. There is no compelling evidence, however, that infants in this stage understand that people are intentional in the sense that they conceive human behavior as being the consequence of prior mental states, such as desires, but simply that people's *behavior* is goal directed (Bargh, 1990; Meltzoff, 1995; Zeedyk, 1996).

PEOPLE AS MENTAL AGENTS

In the past 10 years, there has been an explosion of research on the development of a naive psychology (Astington, Harris, & Olson, 1988; Frye & Moore, 1991; Lewis & Mitchell, 1994). This research has considered when and how children attribute to other people intentional mental states such as desires, beliefs, and intentions and predict their actions on the basis of these mental states. Most of this research has focused on the important transition that occurs between the ages of 3 and 5 years as demonstrated in age-related changes in young children's performance on tasks assessing false beliefs and the distinction between appearance and reality. One recent proposal is that children first develop a desire psychology sometime during their third year, before developing a belief-desire psychology around the age of 4 or 5 years (Wellman, 1990). Some progress has been made in tracing the developmental precursors to these achievements during the first 2 years of life. Leslie (1987) was among the first researchers to propose an early stage in theory of mind during the infancy period. Leslie suggested that pretend scenarios provide evidence for children's capacity for reasoning about people in terms of their attitudes toward pretend objects and actions, while keeping trace of the reality. Although the proposal that pretending requires some understanding of the mind is controversial (Harris, 1991; Perner, 1991), it has stimulated research geared toward the precursors of a full-fledged theory of mind. More recently, it has been proposed that the earliest mental states that infants are susceptible to grasp are the concepts of desires, perception, and emotion (Wellman, 1993). Understanding the mental state of attention is considered by many researchers an early precursor in the development of a theory of mind (Baron-Cohen, 1993; Gomez, 1991). For instance, the absence of declarative pointing, as opposed to instrumental pointing, in autistic children and nonhuman primates is contrasted with the behavior of human infants, who seem to be able to consider the interlocutor's mental state in their use of declarative pointing (Camaioni, 1992).

The production of the first mental terms has also been taken as evidence for the emergence of a naive psychology (Bretherton et al., 1981; Wellman & Bartsch, 1994). Shortly before their second birthday, children tend to show some rudimentary understanding of mental states by using such terms as *want, see,* and *sad.* Interestingly, terms referring to the child's own, as well as others', emotional states and desires are documented in the early lexicon earlier than terms referring to beliefs and knowledge (Wellman & Bartsch, 1994).

Researchers have made some progress in designing studies that could test the hypothesis of an early understanding of desires and intentions in preverbal infants. In one productive line of research, infants as young as 18 months were shown to be able to determine an adult's focus of attention on objects in order to determine the referential intent of a speaker (Baldwin, 1993, 1995; Tomasello & Barton, 1994; Tomasello, Strosberg, & Akhtar, 1996). In one example of this procedure, an adult and a child are visually focused on two different objects at the time that the adult utters a novel word. Children learn the label not for the object on which they are focused but for the object on which the adult is focused (Baldwin, 1995, this volume). Other studies showed that children as young as 18 months can learn novel labels in conditions requiring them to skip over visible, but unintended, referents (e.g., experimenter labels an object, then puts it into a bucket with a scowling face) in order to map the label to a perceptually absent referent (Tomasello, Strosberg, & Akhtar, 1996).

Recently, Baldwin and Moses (1994, 1996) tested 12- to 18-month-olds' ability to use information about focus of attention to disambiguate the referent of another's emotional message when at least two potential referents are available. Even in cases of discrepant attentional focus, infants as young as 12 months used the adult's attentional focus in determining which object was the target of the adult's vocal affect (pleasure or disgust) and subsequently behaved toward that object in accord with the affect. Similar results are reported by Repacholi and Gopnik (1997) who administered a food-request task to 14- and 18-month-old infants. Subjects observed an experimenter expressing disgust as she tested one type of food and happiness in response to another food. The experimenter then requested food by holding her hand between the two foods. Although 14-month-olds responded egocentrically by offering the food they themselves preferred, 18-month-old subjects correctly inferred that the experimenter wanted the food associated with her prior positive affect.

Meltzoff (1995) asked whether 18-month-olds who saw an actor fail in attempting to complete an action would infer what the intended action had been. For example, one of the target actions would be to place a peg in the hole of a box. For some children, the experimenter demonstrated the completed action (e.g., inserting the peg into the hole). For others, the experimenter acted out a failed attempt to complete the action (e.g., hit the box just above the hole). Infants re-enacted what the adult intended to do, whether or not they had seen the completed action. No such imitative behaviors were observed when the actions were modeled by a mechanical device. These findings suggest that 18-month-olds understand that goals (and possibly intentions) are connected to people and not to inanimate objects, such as mechanical devices.

In a recent study using a similar spontaneous imitation measure, Carpenter, Akhtar, & Tomasello (1996) explored 16-month-olds' understanding of others' intentions by investigating their ability to discriminate between accidental and intentional actions. Some modeled actions were marked vocally as intentional (e.g., "there"), whereas some were marked vocally as accidental ("whoops"). Infants imitated more intentional actions than accidental ones overall.

In my laboratory, Joanne Tilden, Julie Desroches, and I recently assessed infants' early understanding of the role of desires in human actions and emotional reactions (Tilden, Poulin-Dubois, & Desroches, 1997). Specifically, we tested the hypothesis that infants would expect a person who has expressed desire for an object (both verbally and gesturally) to reach for that object subsequently, as opposed to another object. We also predicted that infants as young as 18 months would predict that someone would be sad if she did not get what she wanted and happy if she did.

In order to test these hypotheses, we presented videotaped scenarios to 18- ($N = 29$) and 24-month-old infants ($N = 29$). A matching task was designed using the preferential looking paradigm. Infants faced two TV screens that displayed videotaped scenarios of an actor expressing a desire for an object and then reaching for the desired object or another object. Each videotape included two phases: an "information phase" and a "test phase." In the information phase, which was presented on a single screen, the actor expressed her desire for one of two objects on a table by pointing toward one of the objects while saying, "I want that one" (see Fig. 11.2). The information phase ended with the actor facing the camera, her hands under the table. In the test phase immediately following, two still frames representing two different actions were presented simultaneously on the two screens for 8 seconds. On one screen, the actor reached for the desired object (congruent frame) and on the other screen, she was shown reaching for the undesired object (incongruent frame).

Participants were administered a total of 4 trials, with a different set of objects used on each trial (flower–clock, apple–banana, shoe–hat, bottle–glasses). The amount of time (in seconds) infants looked at each screen

Information Phase

Screen 1

Screen 2

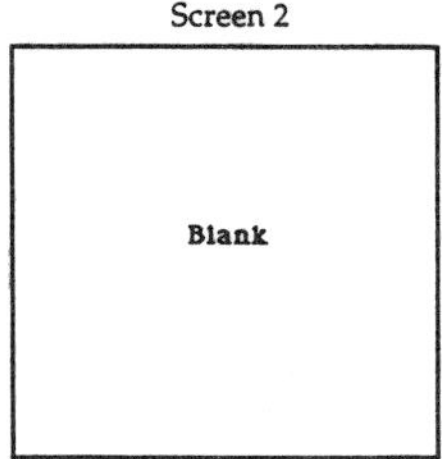

Test Phase

Screen 1

Screen 2

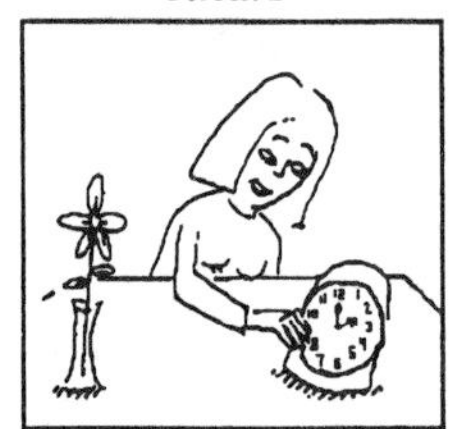

FIG. 11.2. Sample visual and auditory stimuli used in the desire-action experiment.

during the test phase was calculated. In order to ensure that only valid data were included in our analyses, we eliminated the trials for which the subject's visual fixation time to the screen was less than 80 percent of the time during the information phase. An analysis of variance revealed that across all trials, infants looked longer at the screen displaying the action that was incongruent with the actor's previously stated desire. As shown in Fig. 11.3, mean looking times were 3.69*s* and 3.17*s* at the incongruent screen and congruent screens, respectively, for the 18-month-olds ($t(28) = 3.01$, $p < .01$) and 3.62*s* and 3.29*s*, respectively for the 24-month-olds ($t(28) = 1.89$, $p < .07$). These raw looking times were then transformed into percentages by calculating looking time on the incongruent screen over total looking time on both screens combined. A comparison to chance (50%) analysis revealed that infants in both age groups looked more at the incongruent screens than what would be expected by chance ($M = 53.79\%$, $t(28) = 3.16$ $p < .01$ for 18-month-olds and $M = 52.24\%$, $t(28) = 1.85$, $p < .05$, for the 24-month-olds). The majority of infants in each group showed a preference for the incongruent screen (65% and 62% at 18 and 24 months, respectively).

These findings suggest that infants as young as 18 months expect people's actions to be congruent with their desires, expressed through visual, gestural, and verbal cues. Infants seemed surprised when a person reached for an object different from the one she wanted a few seconds earlier. Because the actor looked only at the object she desired in the first experiment, gaze direction was controlled for in the next experiment (Tilden,

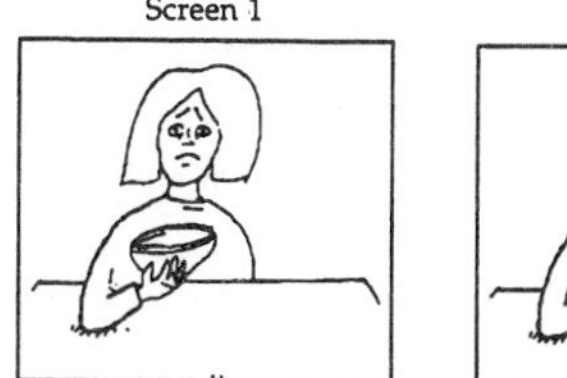

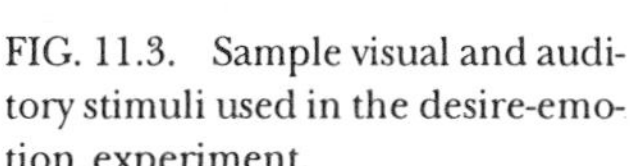
FIG. 11.3. Sample visual and auditory stimuli used in the desire-emotion experiment.

Poulin-Dubois, & Desroches, 1997). We introduced two changes in the design: The location of the two objects was switched between the information and test phase, and the actor also looked at and extended her arm toward the other, undesired, object during the information phase, saying, "Look at that one." We introduced these changes in order to ascertain whether the actor's attention (gaze, gesture) was the main cue used by infants to infer the desire of the actor. We expected that infants would look longer at the incongruent screen if gaze direction was not the single index of desire for these infants. Two groups of infants were tested: 18-month-olds ($N = 29$) and 24-month-olds ($N = 30$). The results indicate that infants in both age groups did not look at the incongruent screen more than would be expected by chance ($M = 48.8\%$, $t(28) = .85$, *ns*, and $M = 48.3\%$, $t(29) = 1.18$, *ns*, for 18- and 24-month-olds, respectively). Only about one third the subjects in each group showed a preference for the incongruent picture, with the rest of the groups showing a congruency effect or no preference. These data suggest that either gaze direction alone or both gaze and gestures toward a target object constitute more powerful indicators of desires than verbal expression for 18- and 24-month-olds.

When equal attention was given to two objects, infants likely expected the person to want both objects, so they were not surprised to see her reach for each of the two objects in the test phase.

In another experiment, we tested the hypothesis that infants would be able to associate facial expressions of sadness and happiness with the positive or negative outcomes of previously expressed desires. The same groups of infants as those tested in the desire-action follow-up participated in that experiment. The design was similar to the desire-action task, with videotaped scenarios showing actors expressing desires in the information phase, followed by different outcomes in the test phase. Each of the four trials included an information and a test phase. During the information phase, which lasted about 20 seconds, participants saw two female adults sitting at a table (see Fig. 11.4). A pair of objects was located in front of Actress 1. The scenario started with Actress 1 holding up each of the two objects in turn and labeling them for Actress 2 (e.g., "See what I have? I have a cup, and I have a bowl"). Actress 2 then expressed a desire for one of the two objects by looking and pointing at it while saying, "I want that one! I want that one!". Actress 1 then answered, "I will give it to you," holding her hand above and between the two objects. This information phase was immediately followed by a brief pause (about 500 ms) during which the two screens were blank. The child then saw two still frames showing Actress 2 holding the desired object (positive outcome) on one screen and holding the undesired object (negative outcome) on the other screen. The actress displayed a happy face on both screens for two trials and a sad face for the other two trials.

We expected infants to look differentially at the incongruent screens (sad face–positive outcome; happy face–negative outcome) and at the con-

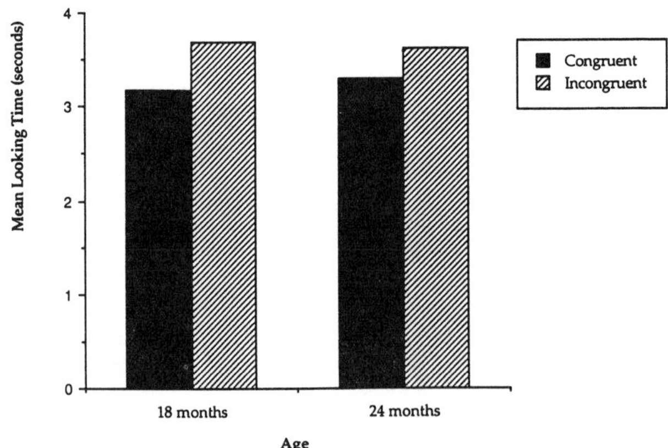

FIG. 11.4. Mean looking time at the congruent and incongruent screens by 18- and 24-month-olds in the desire-action experiment.

gruent screens (sad face–negative outcome; happy face–positive outcome) if they understood the relation between outcome of desire and emotional facial expressions. The results of the analysis of variance supported this hypothesis; infants in both age groups looked differentially at the two screens as a function of the emotional expression displayed, $F(1, 53) = 39.24$, $p < .001$ (see Fig. 11.5). On trials in which the actress displayed a happy expression, infants looked longer at the screen depicting the positive outcome ($M = 3.86$) than at the screen depicting the negative outcome ($M = 3.49$), $t(59) = 2.14$, $p < .05$. In the sad condition, infants looked longer at the screen with the negative outcome ($M = 4.36$) than at the screen with the positive outcome ($M = 3.12$), $t(56) = 5.40$, $p < .001$. When compared to chance (50%), the mean percentage looking time at the congruent screens was statistically higher than chance in both the happy ($M = 52.46\%$, $t(59) = 2.09$, $p < .05$) and the sad conditions ($M = 58.33\%$, $t(56) = 5.48$, $p < .001$).

Our findings suggest that infants as young as 18 months understand how people's emotional expressions are related to the fulfillment or lack of fulfillment of their desires. They expand to younger ages Wellman's (1990) proposal that 2-year-olds understand human behavior as being caused by internal states he calls *simple desires.* These simple desires reflect an attitude toward an actual (as opposed to represented) object or state of affairs. According to Wellman, "simple desires cause actors to engage in goal-directed actions, to persist in goal-directed actions, and to have certain emotional reactions" (p. 212). Our subjects seemed to understand that the actress had an internal experience of wanting, which made her look happy in the case of fulfilling her desire and sad in the opposite situation. They also understand that this internal state of wanting made a person reach for a desired object in the first experiment.

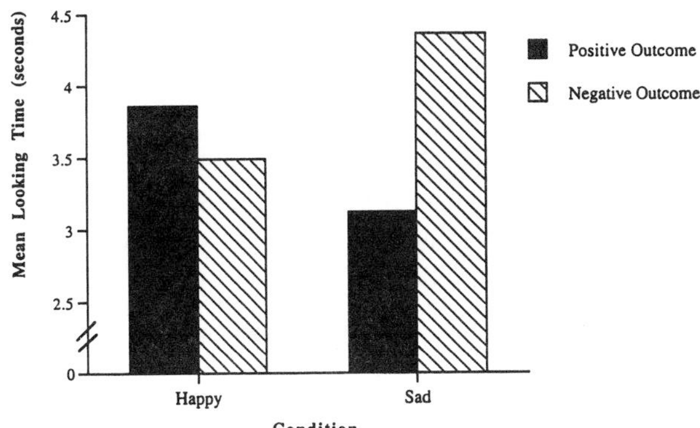

FIG. 11.5. Mean looking time at the screens with a positive and negative outcome in the sad and happy conditions of the desire-emotion experiment.

To sum up, the findings reviewed in this section support the proposal that by the age of 18 months, and possibly earlier, toddlers have acquired a rudimentary naive psychology in the sense that they understand that people are psychologically engaged with the external world. Specifically, they understand that people have internal experiences, wanting and requesting specific objects. Gestures and gaze are particularly salient perceptual cues from which infants appear to infer others' desires for specific objects. This was demonstrated by 18-month-olds' inference that two objects were equally desirable for a person when she gestured and looked at both objects, although she expressed desire verbally for only one of them (Tilden et al., 1997). These cues are remembered and used to make predictions about a person's future actions and emotional expressions. Although the data we have reviewed are not quite decisive enough to permit a mentalistic interpretation of human behavior by 18 months of age, they are more compelling than those reported for 9- to 12-month-olds. Older infants' attempts to comfort or hurt others and the mental terms that are part of their productive vocabulary also suggest that infants understand people's internal experiences toward the middle of the second year.

Despite these impressive achievements, understanding people as mental agents does not imply understanding people as representational agents. Specifically, toddlers' conception of desire does not require them to view people as representing a desired object in their heads. In other words, there is little available evidence that toddlers understand that desires and intentions are subjective states (but see Repacholi & Gopnik, 1997). Furthermore, there is no compelling evidence for toddlers' understanding of more complex internal states such as beliefs, although some grasp of how attention plays a role in the acquisition of knowledge has recently been documented in 18-month-olds (Poulin-Dubois, Tilden, & Levine, 1995). The results of this study showed that infants as young as 18 months were surprised when a person pointed at the incorrect location of a hidden object when she had witnessed where the object was being hidden a few seconds earlier.

CONCLUSIONS

In the first few months of life, and possibly at birth, infants display a repertoire of behaviors with specific social functions. This is first exhibited in the context of early face-to-face interactions. With the expansion of the infant's behavioral repertoire during the first year of life, other indexes of social discrimination appear, such as a different style of exploration for novel people (e.g., visual exploration) and novel objects (e.g., physical contact). Researchers' difficulty in obtaining evidence for this ability in the context of categorization tasks until the second year of life suggests that abstract representation of people develops later. Nevertheless, this precocious discrimination paves the way for perceiving people as goal directed and psychological organisms.

Around the time infants begin to show an ability to discriminate between people and objects, they start to display sensitivity to different types of motion, such as caused versus uncaused motion, biomechanical versus random motion. Whether these motion properties are associated with object kind is an issue that researchers have just started to tackle. From the few studies available, we can infer that by the middle of the first year, infants show some understanding that human action is goal directed whereas object motion is not. At that stage, a goal is conceptualized as the target of manual action or of gaze, but the concept of intention, as a mental state separable from the action, emerges a few months later. Around the same age, infants also show evidence of understanding that contingency resulting from action at a distance is typical of people but that inanimate objects need direct physical contact in order to be set in motion. Other studies testing the association between self-propulsion and ontological kind have reported that infants can infer that a person, but not an inanimate object, is capable of self-propulsion (Poulin-Dubois, Lepage, & Ferland, 1996). These other studies raise the interesting question of when infants are capable of making the opposite inference, that is, that a self-propelled ambiguous object is more likely to be animate than inanimate. The timing of this knowledge fits nicely with the emergence of communicative skills toward the end of the first year, such as pointing and gaze following. Although we have not considered the changes in sensitivity to gaze direction during the same period in the present review, it seems to be a powerful cue by which infants come to treat people as capable of attentional focus (Baron-Cohen, 1993). However, the relative importance of motion and facial cues in eliciting the type of behaviors found in communicative acts remains to be determined. There is some preliminary evidence for the equivalence of contingency and facial features, regardless of object kind (robot or person) as elicitors of gaze following in 12-month-olds (Johnson, Slaughter, Collins, Tyan, & Carey, 1996).

Around the middle of the second year, infants demonstrate that they conceive people as mental agents. Infants become *desire psychologists* (Wellman, 1990). Based on current evidence, infants as young as 18 months of age consult attentional cues when an adult produces an utterance or an emotional display in order to disambiguate the adult's referential intent (Baldwin & Moses, 1994). They also consider attentional cues in order to predict how a person will act or how she will react to others' actions (Tilden, Poulin-Dubois, & Desroches, 1997). The growing awareness of mental life during the first 2 years of life might be best characterized as a knowledge-desire psychology emerging before a belief-desire psychology.

For example, the skills displayed by infants in the middle of the second year of life may lay the groundwork for an early awareness of the seeing=knowing ability that develops sometime during the third year, and possibly earlier. Our own research, based on a matching paradigm similar to the one used by Tilden et al. (1997), suggests that 18-month-olds are surprised to see a person who has witnessed the hiding of an object point to an incorrect location when asked to locate it (Poulin-Dubois, Tilden, & Levine, 1995). They show, however, no differential looking when an ignorant person points to the correct location, an equally incongruous behavior. These findings provide preliminary evidence for an understanding of the relation between seeing and knowing in infants much younger than those tested so far. Paula Bennett and I have recently developed a hide-and-seek task that we hope will allow us to confirm this early awareness of the role of seeing in the knowledge–ignorance distinction.

This chapter attempted to demonstrate that the understanding of people within a psychological framework does not suddenly emerge around 3 years of age. Its roots can be found in an early responsiveness to people's actions, soon followed by an early sensitivity to what makes people's motions different from other objects' motion. These achievements prepare infants to account for the causes of human action. This account requires the detection of goals, which is evident by the end of the first year. The time lag observed between the acquisition of people-versus-object-motion distinction and an emerging theory of mind suggests that understanding how people's motions are different from object motions might be necessary but not sufficient for the understanding of people as mental agents. Evidence that autistic children, who fail theory of mind tasks yet are able to distinguish between animate and inanimate objects, supports this developmental sequence (Bowler & Thommen, 1996). By the middle of the second year, but possibly earlier, infants start to consider that people's actions are guided by intentions and desires. Children of that age still have a long way to go in order to fully grasp the intricacies of people's minds, but they, unlike some of their other primate relatives, already have grasped what sets people apart from the rest of the world. In that sense, they are as much budding psychologists as they are budding physicists.

ACKNOWLEDGMENTS

The research reported in this chapter was supported by grants from the Social Sciences and Humanities Research Council of Canada and the Natural Sciences and Engineering Research Council of Canada. I would like to thank Thérèse Gouin Décarie, Dale Stack, and Patricia Goldring-Zukow for their helpful comments on an earlier version of this chapter. I am also grateful for the editor's comments.

REFERENCES

Abravanel, E., & DeYong, N. (1991). Does object modeling elicit imitative-like gestures from young infants? *Journal of Experimental Child Psychology, 52,* 22–40.

Adolph, K. E., Eppler, M. A., & Gibson, E. J. (1993). Development of perception of affordances. In C. Rovee-Collier & L. P. Lipsitt (Eds.), *Advances in infancy research* (Vol. 8, pp. 51–98). Norwood, NJ: Ablex.

Astington, J. W., Harris, P. L., & Olson, D. R. (Eds.). (1988). *Developing theories of mind.* Cambridge, UK: Cambridge University Press.

Baillargeon, R. (1995). A model of physical reasoning in infancy. In C. Rovee-Collier & L. P. Lipsitt (Eds.), *Advances in infancy research* (Vol. 9, pp. 305–371). Norwood, NJ: Ablex.

Baillargeon, R., Kotovsky, L., & Needham, A. (1995). The acquisition of physical knowledge in infancy. In D. Sperber, D. Premack, & A. J. Premack (Eds.), *Causal cognition: A multidisciplinary debate* (pp. 79–116). Oxford: Clarendon.

Baker, R. K., & Poulin-Dubois, D. (1998). [Infants' sensitivity to the motion of animate and inanimate objects]. Unpublished raw data.

Baldwin, D. A. (1993). Early referential understanding: Infants' ability to recognize referential acts for what they are. *Developmental Psychology, 29,* 832–843.

Baldwin, D. A. (1995). Understanding the link between joint attention and language. In C. Moore & P. Dunham (Eds.), *Joint attention: Its origins and role in development* (pp. 131–158). Hillsdale, NJ: Lawrence Erlbaum Associates.

Baldwin, D. A., & Moses, L. J. (1994). Early understanding of referential intent and attentional focus: Evidence from language and emotion. In C. Lewis & P. Mitchell (Eds.), *Children's early understanding of mind: Origins and development* (pp. 133–156). Hove, UK: Lawrence Erlbaum Associates.

Baldwin, D. A., & Moses, L. J. (1996). The ontogeny of social information gathering. *Child Development, 67,* 1915–1939.

Bargh, J. A. (1990). Goal does not equal intent: Goal-directed thought and behavior are often unintentional. *Psychological Inquiry, 1,* 248–277.

Baron-Cohen, S. (1993). From attention-goal psychology to belief-desire psychology: The development of a theory of mind and its dysfunction. In S. Baron-Cohen, H. Tager-Flusberg, & D. J. Cohen (Eds.), *Understanding other minds: Perspectives from autism* (pp. 59–82). Oxford: Oxford University Press.

Baron-Cohen, S. (1994). How to build a baby that can read minds: Cognitive mechanisms in mindreading. *Cahiers de Psychologie Cognitive, 13,* 513–552.

Baron-Cohen, S. (1995). *Mindblindness: An essay on autism and theory of mind.* Cambridge, MA: MIT Press.

Bates, E., Benigni, L. Bretherton, I., Camaioni, L., & Volterra, V. (1979). *The emergence of symbols: Cognition and communication in infancy.* New York: Academic Press.

Berthental, B. I. (1993). Infants' perception of biochemical motions: Intrinsic image and knowledge-based constraints. In C. Granrud (Ed.), *Visual perception and cognition in infancy: Carnegie-Mellon symposia on cognition* (pp. 175–214). Hillsdale, NJ: Lawrence Erlbaum Associates.

Bowler, D. M., & Thommen, E. (1996, September). *Perception of physical and intentional causality in normal and high-functioning children with autism.* Paper presented at the conference The Evolving Mind, Geneva.

Brazelton, T. B., Koslowski, B., & Main, W. (1974). The origins of reciprocity: The early mother-infant interaction. In M. Lewis & L. A. Rosenblum (Eds.), *The effects of the infant on its caregiver* (pp. 49–76). New York: Wiley.

Bretherton, I., McNew, S., & Beeghly-Smith, M. (1981). Early person knowledge as expressed in gestural and verbal communication: When do infants acquire a 'theory of mind'? In M. E. Lamb & L. R. Sherrod (Eds.), *Infant social cognition* (pp. 333–373). Hillsdale, NJ: Lawrence Erlbaum Associates.

Burnham, D. K. (1987). The role of movement in object perception by infants. In B. E. McKenzie & R. H. Day (Eds.), *Perceptual development in early infancy: Problems and issues* (pp. 143–172). Hillsdale, NJ: Lawrence Erlbaum Associates.

Camaioni, L. (1992). Mind knowledge in infancy: The emergence of intentional communication. *Early Development and Parenting, 1,* 15–22.

Carpenter, M., Akhtar, N., & Tomasello, M. (1996, April). *Understanding of intentional versus accidental actions in 14- to 18-month-old infants.* Poster presented at the International Conference on Infant Studies, Providence, RI.

Csibra, G., Gergely, G., Bíró, S., & Koós, O. (1996). *The perception of "pure reason" in infancy.* Manuscript submitted for publication.

Eckerman, C. O., & Rheingold, H. L. (1974). Infants' exploratory responses to toys and people. *Developmental Psychology, 10,* 255–259.

Ellsworth, C. P., Muir, D. W., & Hains, S. M. (1993). Social competence and person-object differentiation: An analysis of the still-face effect. *Developmental Psychology, 29,* 63–73.

Frye, D., & Moore, C. (Eds.). (1991). *Children's theories of mind: Mental states and social understanding.* Hillsdale, NJ: Lawrence Erlbaum Associates.

Gelman, R., & Spelke, E. S. (1981). The development of thoughts about animate and inanimate objects: Implications for research on social cognition. In J. H. Flavell & L. Ross (Eds.), *Social cognition* (pp. 43–66). New York: Academic Press.

Gergely, G., Nádasdy, Z., Csibra, G., & Bíró, S. (1995). Taking the intentional stance at 12 months of age. *Cognition, 56,* 165–193.

Golinkoff, R., Harding, C., Carlson, V., & Sexton, M. E. (1984). The infant's perception of causal events: The distinction between animate and inanimate objects. In L. P. Lipsitt & C. Rovee-Collier (Eds.), *Advances in infancy research* (Vol. 3, pp. 145–151). Norwood, NJ: Ablex.

Golinkoff, R., & Kerr, J. (1978). Infants' perception of semantically defined action roles in filmed events. *Merrill-Palmer Quarterly, 24,* 53–61.

Gomez, J. C. (1991). Visual behaviour as a window for reading the mind of others in primates. In A. Whiten (Ed.), *Natural theories of mind* (pp. 195–207). Oxford: Basil Blackwell.

Harris, P. (1991). The work of the imagination. In A. Whiten (Ed.), *Natural theories of mind: Evolution, development, and simulation of everyday mindreading* (pp. 283–304). Oxford: Basil Blackwell.

Jacobson, S. W. (1979). Matching behavior in the young infant. *Child Development, 50,* 425–430.

Johnson, S., Slaughter, V., Collins, K., Tyan, J., & Carey, S. (1996, April). *Whose gaze will infants follow: Features that elicit gaze-following in 12-month-olds.* Poster session presented at the International Conference in Infant Studies, Providence, RI.

Legerstee, M. (1991). The role of person and object in eliciting early imitation. *Journal of Experimental Child Psychology, 51,* 423–433.

Legerstee, M. (1992). A review of the animate-inanimate distinction in infancy: Implications for models of social and cognitive knowing. *Early Development and Parenting, 1,* 59–67.

Legerstee, M., Corter, C., & Kineapple, K. (1990). Hand, arm, and facial actions of young infants to a social and nonsocial stimulus. *Child Development, 61,* 774–784.

Legerstee, M., Pomerleau, A., Malcuit, G., & Feider, H. (1987). The development of infants' responses to people and a doll: Implications for research in communication. *Infant Behavior and Development, 10,* 81–95.

Leslie, A. M. (1982). The perception of causality in infants. *Perception, 11*, 173–186.

Leslie, A. M. (1984). Infant perception of a manual pick-up event. *British Journal of Developmental Psychology, 2*, 19–32.

Leslie, A. (1987). Pretence and representation: The origins of 'theory of mind.' *Psychological Review, 94*, 412–426.

Leslie, A. (1988). The necessity of illusion: Perception and thought in infancy. In L. Weiskrantz (Ed.), *Thought without language* (pp. 185–210). Oxford: Clarendon.

Leslie, A. M. (1994). ToMM, ToBy, and Agency: Core architecture and domain specificity. In L. Hirschfeld & S. Gelman (Eds.), *Mapping the mind: Domain specificity in cognition and cultural* (pp. 119–48). Cambridge University Press, New York.

Leslie, A. M., & Keeble, S. (1987). Do six-month-old infants perceive causality? *Cognition, 25*, 265–288.

Lewis, C., & Mitchell, P. (Eds.). (1994). *Children's early understanding of mind: Origins and development.* Hove, UK: Lawrence Erlbaum Associates.

Mandler, J. M. (1992). How to build a baby: II. Conceptual primitives. *Psychological Review, 99*, 587–604.

Mandler, J. M., & McDonough, L. (1993). Concept formation in infancy. *Cognitive Development, 8*, 291–318.

Meltzoff, A. N. (1995). Understanding the intentions of others: Re-enactment of intended acts by 18-month-old children. *Developmental Psychology, 31*, 838–850.

Meltzoff, A. N., & Moore, M. K. (1977). Imitation of facial and manual gestures by human neonates. *Science, 198*, 75–78.

Meltzoff, A. N., & Moore, M. K. (1992). Early imitation within a functional framework: The importance of person identity, movement, and development. *Infant Behavior and Development, 15*, 479–505.

Molina, M., Spelke, E. S., & King, D. (1996, April). *The animate-inanimate distinction in infancy: Sensitivity to distinctions between social interactions and object manipulations.* Poster session presented at the International Conference on Infant Studies, Providence, RI.

Oakes, L. M., & Cohen, L. B. (1995). Infant causal perception. In C. Rovee-Collier & L. P. Lipsitt (Eds.), *Advances in infancy research* (Vol. 9, pp. 1–54). Norwood, NJ: Ablex.

Oakes, L. M., Plumert, J. M., Lansink, J. M., & Merryman, J. D. (1996). Evidence for task-dependent categorization in infancy. *Infant Behavior and Development, 19*, 425–440.

Perner, J. (1991). *Understanding the representational mind.* Cambridge, MA: MIT Press.

Poulin-Dubois, D., Lepage, A., & Ferland, D. (1996). Infants' concept of animacy. *Cognitive Development, 11*, 19–36.

Poulin-Dubois, D., & Shultz, T. R. (1988). The development of understanding of human behavior: From agency to intentionality. In J. W. Astington, P. L. Harris, & D. R. Olson (Eds.), *Developing theories of mind* (pp. 109–125). Cambridge, UK: Cambridge University Press.

Poulin-Dubois, D., & Shultz, T. R. (1990). The infant's concept of agency: The distinction between social and nonsocial objects. *The Journal of Genetic Psychology, 151*, 77–90.

Poulin-Dubois, D., Tilden, J., & Levine, B. (1995, June). *Infants' understanding of beliefs.* Paper presented at the Twenty-Fifth Annual Symposium of the Jean Piaget Society, Berkeley, CA.

Premack, D. (1990). The infant's theory of self-propelled objects. *Cognition, 36*, 1–16.

Premack, D., & Premack A. J. (1995). Intention as psychological cause. In D. Sperber, D. Premack, & A. J. Premack (Eds.), *Causal cognition: A multidisciplinary debate* (pp. 185–199). Oxford: Clarendon Press.

Repacholi, B. M., & Gopnik, A. (1997). Early reasoning of desires: Evidence from 14- and 18-month-olds. *Developmental Psychology, 33*, 12–21.

Ricard, M., & Allard, L. (1993). The reaction of 9- to 10-month-old infants to an unfamiliar animal. *The Journal of Genetic Psychology, 154*, 5–16.

Ricard, M., & Gouin-Décarie, T. (1989). Strategies of 9–10-month-old infants with a stranger and a novel object. *Revenue Internationale de Psychologie Sociale, 2,* 97–111.

Rochat, P., Morgan, R., & Carpenter, M. (1997). Young infants' sensitivity to movement information specifying social causality. *Cognitive Development, 12,* 441–465.

Ronnqvist, L., & von Hofsten, C. (1994). Neonatal finger and arm movements as determined by a social and an object context. *Early Development and Parenting, 3,* 81–93.

Ross, G. S. (1980). Categorization in 1- to 2-year-olds. *Developmental Psychology, 16,* 391–396.

Slater, A. (1989). Visual memory and perception in early infancy. In A. Slater & G. Bremner (Eds.), *Infant development* (pp. 43–72). Hove, UK: Lawrence Erlbaum Associates.

Sorrentino, C. M., Xu, F., & Carey, S. (1996, April). *Do 10-month-old infants individuate objects on the basis of the person/inanimate distinction?* Poster session presented at the International Conference on Infant Studies, Providence, RI.

Spelke, E. S., Breilinger, K., Macomber, J., & Jacobson, K. (1992). Origins of knowledge. *Psychological Review, 99,* 605–632.

Spelke, E. S., Phillips, A., & Woodward, A. L. (1995). Infants' knowledge of object motion and human action. In D. Sperber, A. J. Premack, D. Premack (Eds.), *Causal cognition: A multidisciplinary debate* (pp. 44–77). Oxford: Clarendon Press.

Tilden, J., Poulin-Dubois, D., & Desroches, J. (1997). *Young children's understanding of the role of desires in human actions and emotional reactions.* Unpublished raw data, Centre for Research in Human Development, Concordia University.

Tomasello, M. (1995). Joint attention as social cognition. In C. Moore & P. Dunham (Eds.), *Joint attention: Its origins and role in development* (pp. 103–130). Hillsdale, NJ: Lawrence Erlbaum Associates.

Tomasello, M., & Barton, M. (1994). Learning words in nonostensive contexts. *Developmental Psychology, 30,* 639–650.

Tomasello, M., & Camaioni, L. (1997). A comparison of the gestural communication of apes and human infants. *Human Development, 40,* 7–24.

Tomasello, M., Strosberg, R., & Akhtar, N. (1996). Eighteen-month-old children learn words in non-ostensive contexts. *Journal of Child Language, 23,* 157–176.

Trevarthen, C. (1977). Descriptive analyses of infant communicative behavior. In H. R. Schaffer (Ed.), *Studies in mother–infant interaction* (pp. 227–270). London: Academic Press.

Wellman, H. M. (1990). *The child's theory of mind.* Cambridge, MA: MIT Press.

Wellman, H. M. (1993). Early understanding of mind: The normal case. In S. Baron-Cohen, H. Tager-Flusberg, & D. J. Cohen (Eds.), *Understanding other minds: Perspectives from autism* (pp. 10–39). Oxford: Oxford University Press.

Wellman, H. M., & Bartsch, K. (1994). Before belief: Children's early psychological theory. In C. Lewis & P. Mitchell (Eds.), *Children's early understanding of mind* (pp. 331–354). Hove, UK: Lawrence Erlbaum Associates.

Woodward, A. L. (1996). *Infants selectively encode the goal object of an actor's reach.* Manuscript submitted for publication.

Zazzo, R. (1957). Le problème de l'imitation chez le nouveu-né. *Enfance, 10,* 135–142.

Zeedyk, M. S. (1996). Developmental accounts of intentionality: Toward integration. *Developmental Review, 16,* 416–461.

Chapter 12

Emotion Regulation and the Emergence of Joint Attention

Lauren B. Adamson
Connie L. Russell
Georgia State University

Developmentalists have studied the infant's changing relation to objects for decades, probing it to answer questions about the development of motor skills, cognition, communication, and attention. In our laboratory, we are trying to contribute to these efforts by focusing on how objects emerge as a topic of social interaction. We find that a central conceptual challenge is the selection of heuristic strands from the rich tapestry of communication between infants and their caregivers (Adamson, 1996). Our studies (Adamson & Bakeman, 1982; Bakeman & Adamson, 1984) have concentrated primarily on infant attention to describe patterns over time and across communicative contexts. Holding onto this thread, we have plotted the temporal succession of engagement, noting that the infant's turn toward objects occurs after they have mastered the rudiments of social interaction and that the integration of objects into communicative exchanges may begin well before the infant is able to modulate attention to both his social partners and events of shared concern (Adamson & Bakeman, 1991; Adamson & Chance, 1998). Furthermore, we have found that states of infant attention to objects and people provide a frame in which to view specific communicative acts such as gestures, words, and affective expressions (e.g., Adamson & Bakeman, 1985; Bakeman & Adamson, 1986).

This chapter attempts to follow a new thread—emotion regulation—through the period when infants initially discover objects. We know that this thread closely intertwines infant attention; indeed we conceive of this chapter as an attempt to highlight the affective aspects of joint attention.

We think that a fuller consideration of how infants come to regulate their emotions will help explain the initial timing and context of joint attention as well as its consolidation, by the end of infancy, both as a prevalent and stable organization for social interactions and as a context for the emergence of symbols.

We are not alone in the broad claim that emotion regulation is an important aspect of the development of object-focused social interactions. Historically, the development of emotion regulation during infancy captured the interest of several seminal developmental theorists. Wallon, for example, viewed infants as emotional beings whose contact with reality is socially mediated (Voyat, 1984). His perspective likely influenced Vygotsky (1978) who, in turn, has inspired many contemporary researchers to examine learning within the "zone of proximal development" created when a child and a more sophisticated social partner act together (van der Veer, 1996). Moreover, when researchers within the psychoanalytic tradition, such as Sander (1962), Spitz and Wolf (1946), and Wolff (1987), began to observe young infants, they stressed the importance of describing emotional expressions. Their arguments led several researchers (e.g., Brazelton, Koslowski, & Main, 1974; Stern, 1977; Tronick, Als, & Adamson, 1979) to focus on the modulation of affectivity and attention during early face-to-face caregiver–infant interactions. However, when the transition to joint attention is considered, emotion regulation has typically been relegated to, to use Piaget's famous phrase, "the other side of the coin." Although affect has not been ignored (see, e.g., Stern, 1985), it has been considered far less thoroughly than the more cognitive concerns of subjectivity and intentionality.

This chapter seeks to highlight emotional regulation during the transition to joint attention. Its first section abstracts three major orienting themes from current discussions of emotion regulation during infancy. It then keys these themes to the situation of typically developing 5- to 10-month-old infants and their caregivers as they negotiate a shared focus on objects. The last section concludes this exercise by suggesting promising strategies for future research on joint attention. Our aim throughout is to display the importance of taking note of affect as objects become integrated into periods of shared attention.

EMOTION REGULATION DURING INFANCY

To capture a phenomenon as complex as emotions, researchers often stake their lot on one of two perennial theoretical positions, structuralism or functionalism. Recently, several developmentalists have banded together (e.g., in a special section of *Developmental Psychology*, Dodge, 1989, and in an entire *Monograph of the Society for Research in Child Development*, Fox, 1994), to declare the advantages of moving from a structuralist to a functionalist position. This shift toward a more dynamic, process-oriented, relational treatment of emotions is a relative one; several scholars (e.g., Lewis, 1993) continue to refine descriptions of the infant's emotional repertoire. Nevertheless, those who advocate the shift have issued new definitions of emotion and new declarations of primary principles. Their basic thrust is that emotion regulation helps us adapt to our social and nonsocial world by serving both motivational and cue-producing functions that contribute to survival (Campos, Campos, & Barrett, 1989; Kopp, 1989; Thompson, 1994).

Although emotion regulation as a concept is rather elusive (Thompson, 1994), there appears to be broad consensus about its general qualities during infancy. Three interrelated themes have been sounded repeatedly in recent discussions. The first theme is that emotion regulation is a *dynamic process*. Although specific affective expressions play an important role in this process, it cannot be reduced to discrete emotive events. Rather, the stream of behavior should be described in terms of "emotion dynamics" (Thompson, 1994) so that the flow of affectivity, including its intensity, persistence, modulation, and lability, is characterized. Moreover, these descriptions should be of periods of sustained interest as well as of peaks of intense pleasure and upset (Wolff, 1987), and they should consider the full range of emotions, negative as well as positive (Kopp, 1989).

The second theme is that emotion regulation is fundamentally a *relational process*. Campos and colleagues emphasize this theme in their definition of emotions as "processes of establishing, maintaining, or disrupting the relations between the person and the internal or external environment, when such relations are significant to the individual" (Campos et al., 1989, p. 395). This definition leads them to argue that "to understand emotion, one must understand that the human being lives in a web of interrelationships with social and physical objects" (p. 397). This fundamental connection between emotion and relationships is elaborated in recent discussions about affective attunement between partners (Stern, 1985), about communication as a process critical to emotion regulation (Gianino & Tronick, 1988), and about the development of emotion management skills within social encounters (Thompson, 1994).

The final theme is that emotion regulation is a complex activity that entails *a multitude of component processes* that reside on different levels of analysis. Thus, to understand why and how regulation occurs, an appreciation of the relational aspects of emotion regulation must be supplemented with a consideration of many other processes, including those related to physiological arousal, cognitive appraisal, attention modulation, and goal-directed actions (Kopp, 1989; Thompson, 1994; Thompson, Flood, & Lundquist, 1995). Furthermore, an adequate understanding of how infants manage emotional arousal during a particular developmental moment must be far-reaching, drawing into view not only the developing capacities of the infant but also the intertwining contributions of the context, including other people (Campos et al., 1989; Stern, 1985).

EMOTION REGULATION AND THE EMERGENCE OF JOINT ATTENTION

We now turn to the core concern of this chapter: emotion regulation during the central months of the first year of life as typically developing infants begin to master the rudiments of joint attention with their supportive caregivers. Our aim is to draw on current research both to characterize major changes in the process of emotion regulation and to understand its role in the emergence of joint attention.

The general demands of this project are not very daunting. The portrait of early emotion regulation as a dynamic, relational, multifaceted process that appears in general discussions is well suited to the description of affect regulation during object-focused social interactions. Moreover, the key accomplishment of the development of joint attention, the coordination of attention to both a partner and a shared object, can be rephrased readily in terms of emotion regulation to focus on the accomplishment of integrating *engagement* with social partners with *interest* in objects. However, as with most broadly conceived objectives, difficulties arise as soon as we seek details. In short, the available data are disappointingly thin. Thus far, the literature on the development of shared attention provides only a sketchy outline of changes in emotion management during the critical period between the 6-month-old's avid turn toward objects and the 1-year-old's new facility at punctuating object-focused communication with affective expressions. In addition, explanations of developmental progress tend to overlook affect. Treatments of why joint attention emerges tend to search for indication of a new social-cognitive accomplishment between 9 and 15 months of age rather than to examine the period from 5 to 10 months of age for preludes to joint attention in new arrangements of affect and attention.

Theme 1: Emotion Dynamics During Early Moments of Joint Attention

Given the dearth of research focused specifically on the modulation of affect, it is too early to chart the integration of person engagement and object interest as joint attention emerges. But in our search of the literature for observations related to the themes of emotion regulation and objects, we found several descriptions that support the importance of attending to emotion dynamics during early moments of joint attention. Even a brief observation of early object sharing can reveal how emotions permeate the field of shared meaning that is established during periods of joint attention, providing definition to moments and direction to the exchange.

Consider, for example, Stern's (1985) observation of an early episode of joint attention:

> A nine-month-old girl becomes very excited about a toy and reaches for it. As she grabs it, she lets out an exuberant "aaah!" and looks at her mother. Her mother looks back, scrunches up her shoulders and performs a terrific shimmy with her upper body, like a go-go-dancer. The shimmy lasts only about as long as her daughter's "aaah!" but is equally excited, joyful, and intense. (p. 140)

In his discussion of this observation, Stern emphasized the process of affective attunement that "renders feelings" (p. 142) as the mother matches the intensity and timing of her infant's emotions. For our current purposes, it is also interesting to note that the infant integrates the height of arousal (an exuberant "aaah!") with a shift of gaze from toy to mother, so that attention then frames the mother's display. From this angle, a peak of infant emotion appears to occasion interpersonal attention as well as shared affect. This observation prompts the question of whether there are moments within the dynamic flow of emotion relative to objects that are especially likely to engender looks toward a social partner. One possibility is that the likelihood of glances toward a partner increases as the emotional charge of a situation heightens. Thus a rise in tension might lead to a look.

There are several hints in the literature that are consistent with this hypothesis. First, changes in the form and communicative function of infant affective expression from 6 to 18 months are consistent with the notion that peaks of affect may increasingly interweave with shifts of attention between an object and a social partner. Over time, infants' bursts of positive affect within a play session with their mothers become increasingly briefer, and they are increasingly likely to be expressed vocally rather than visually (Adamson & Bakeman, 1985). Moreover, they start to serve a fuller range of communicative functions. They may, for example, modulate social interactions by marking the beginning of an episode of joint attention (see Reddy, 1991, for amusing observations from the public sphere) and provide comment on shared objects and on the act of object sharing (e.g., a squeal of delight as a just-proffered object is teasingly retracted; Trevarthen, 1988). Negatively toned expressions have also been found to undergo a similar change in form and function during the end of the first year. For example, Gustafson and Green (1991) report that cries, like positive affective expressions, become briefer with age and become increasingly integrated into the attentional stream that includes the caregiver and objects.

In addition, there is much evidence that in months before and following the emergence of joint attention, peaks of affect augur shifts in attention. During the first months of life, gaze modulation toward and away from a partner is an important part of the infant's repertoire of emotion regulatory behavior (Tronick, 1989). By 1 year of age, uncertainty provoked by a novel or ambiguous object is a likely precursor to a glance toward an adult as part of the process of social referencing (Campos & Stenberg, 1981). Furthermore, there are indications that temporary disruption in an interaction that might frustrate or disappoint an infant may promote increased attention to a social partner. For example, when Ross and Lollis (1987) had adults temporarily interrupt their supportive actions during a turn-taking game, even 9-month-olds, their youngest subjects, increased the rate of gaze alternation, although they were less likely than older subjects to signal to an adult to maintain involvement.

These results provide support for the conclusion that interruptions in the patterned flow of interaction focused on a shared object may prompt attention to both partner and object that might otherwise not occur. It may well be, as Tronick (1989) and others (e.g., Biringen, Emde, & Pipp-Siegel, 1997) have suggested, that it is within moments when agenda do not smoothly mesh, when emotions flare, or when desires are not readily understood and fulfilled that we may most fully appreciate the importance of emotion regulation to the emergence of joint attention.

Theme 2: The Relational Balance of Person Engagement and Object Interest

By definition, during a period of joint attention a person relates to a web of sites that includes both a social partner and events beyond the boundary of their dyadic interaction. From the perspective of emotion regulation, if an infant is to achieve joint attention, he or she must integrate affective aspects of instrumental actions on objects and interaction with people.

A considerable amount is already known about the earliest periods along the path toward the integration of object interest and person engagement (see Adamson, 1996, for a review). It has often been noted that infants in the first half-year of life regulate emotion differently when they act toward objects and communicate with people (Brazelton et al., 1974; Trevarthen, 1979; Tronick, 1989). Engaging emotional expressions such as smiles are reserved for people (Ellsworth, Muir, & Hains, 1993; Legerstee, Corter, & Kienapple, 1990), and displays of interest and sustained attention are primarily directed toward objects (Ruff & Rothbart, 1996; Weinberg &

Tronick, 1994). It has also often been documented that the balance between engagement with people and objects shifts from the former to the latter in the months before the emergence of joint attention. During early infancy, infant–adult interactions that are characterized by the mutual regulation of attention and affect dominate (Brazelton et al., 1974; Stern, 1977). Then, as infants gain access to objects, first by hand and then by crawl and step, their attention is increasingly drawn to the exploration of objects and, concomitantly, away from engagement solely with a person (Kaye & Fogel, 1980; Lamb, Morrison, & Malkin 1987; Messer & Vietze 1984; Shinn, 1900). Once an infant turns primarily toward objects at about 6 months of age, there is a prolonged period of many weeks before joint attention is first evident and many months before an infant can sustain periods of communication in which his or her attention is coordinated to people and objects (Bakeman & Adamson, 1984).

During this period, whether or not an infant maintains joint attention depends on the partner's skillful support of the infant's emotions as well as attention. The partner may monitor and manage the child's emotions (Thompson, 1994) and interpret an infant's expression of interest as revealing a nascent intention (Adamson, Bakeman, Smith, & Walters, 1987). He or she may modulate an infant's attention to an object by lending it affect, as when, for example, a parent bounds a doll rapidly toward the infant while saying "I'm going to get you!" (Adamson & Bakeman, 1984). Furthermore, he or she may inform the infant about the emotional significance of an object, imbuing the inanimate with cultural and interpersonal definition.

In terms of emotion regulation, the long stretch between the surge of interest in objects and the integration of this interest with person engagement is filled with fluctuations in how infants react to different objects (Ruff & Rothbart, 1996). Tronick (1989) provides an excellent portrait of the vicissitudes of affect at the beginning of this period in the following description of a 6-month-old infant's reaction to the mundane challenge of obtaining a just-out-of-reach object:

> The . . . infant stretches his hands out toward the object. Because he cannot get hold of it, he becomes angry and distressed. He looks away for a moment and sucks on his thumb. Calmer, he looks back at the object and reaches for it once more. But this attempt fails too, and he gets angry again. The caretaker watches for a moment, then soothingly talks to him. The infant calms down and with a facial expression of interest gazes at the object and makes another attempt to reach for it. The caretaker brings the object just within the infant's reach. The infant successfully grasps the object, explores it, and smiles. (p. 113)

As Tronick suggests, this observation illustrates both the infant's capacity to self-regulate, using actions such as looking away and sucking, and the caretaker's assistance as he or she reads the infant's displays and then modulates the infant's affect using communicative acts that soothe upset and instrumental ones that eliminate a disturbing event. For our current purposes, it is also interesting to notice that this emotionally expressive infant is not engaged with the helpful caretaker. From this young infant's perspective, affectivity is primarily object related. Even the smile at the end of the episode of object seeking is an expression of object interest, not a display of gratitude acknowledged or pleasure shared. In short, the caretaker and infant are clearly focused on the same object but the infant does not achieve coordinated joint attention. Its absence is apparent not only by the absence of a glance toward the supportive partner but also by the lack of affect directed toward this person.

In terms of the relational aspect of emotion regulation, this illustration prompts us to ask about the developmental progress that must be made before person engagement will occur along with object interest. To address this question fully, it is important to recognize that the primary difference between the 6-month-old's hungry apprehension of a desired object and a 13-month-old's well-timed plea for and then happy acknowledgment of an adult's helpful actions on the object is internal neither to person engagement, which has been structured rudimentarily for months, nor to object interest per se. Rather, the developmental challenge is to achieve a new level of organization that integrates two separate organizations of emotion regulation.

This proposal that the emergence of joint attention is concomitant to a developmental transformation in the relation between object interest and person engagement finds anecdotal support in Gesell's classic depiction of normative development. During the middle of the first year, researchers at the Gesell Institute described how infants typically sustain both object interest and person engagement, and how during periods of each, their activity seems well organized. For example, Ilg and Ames (1955) report that the proverbial 28-week-old infant:

> gets on well, whatever the situation. For 28 weeks, like 16, represents an age of extremely good equilibrium. Behavior patterns and emotions (which actually are in themselves behavior patterns) are in good focus. (p. 18)

They report that this characterization suits both periods of object exploration ("The baby of this age not only likes to grasp and to finger objects, but he likes to shift them from one hand to the other. This behavior we call 'transfer,' and he can spend many happy minutes thus engaged"; p. 17) and of social interaction ("He likes to smile at onlookers and is usually enthusiastically friendly to both intimates and strangers"; p. 17). Yet, although Ilg and Ames recognize that the 7-month-old "alternates with ease between self-directed and socially referred activity" (p. 17), they add a provocative conceptual qualification:

> as Dr. Gesell has commented, this period of equilibrium, like all such, tends to be short-lived. For the growth complex never fully stabilizes. New thrusts, new tensions of development, soon upset any state of balance, producing unstableness, which is in turn resolved by further temporary stages of equilibrium. (p. 18)

Theme 3: Emotion Regulation as a Component Process in the Emergence of Joint Attention

One intriguing fact about the period of "unstableness" that precedes the integration of object interest and person engagement is that it is several months long. Although joint attention behavior, such as following a partner's referential point (Butterworth & Grover, 1990) or glancing toward a partner when a novel toy suddenly appears (Walden & Ogan, 1988), is evident in the last quarter of the first year, coordinated attention to people and objects is not a prevalent attentional organization until considerably later. Even when the infant is in interaction with a supportive caretaker, sustained periods of coordinated joint attention are not typical until the beginning of the second year (Bakeman & Adamson, 1984). When a partner lends little support either due to inability (e.g., peers; Bakeman & Adamson, 1984) or cultural inclination (e.g., the !Kung; Bakeman, Adamson, Konner, & Barr, 1990), sustained periods of joint attention may not occur until late in infancy.

Most often, explanations of the delay between interest in objects and the onset of joint object involvement focus on a cognitive factor. Advocates for the primacy of cognition abound. Traditional Piagetians have tended to search for an overarching new structure of actions (e.g., the coordination of secondary circular reactions) that might promote new accomplishments in all cognitive domains (see Demetriou, 1988, especially the chapter by Fischer & Farrar, 1988, for a discussion of this approach). Others have looked instead for what they call "local homologies" (Bates, Benigni, Bretherton, Camaioni, & Volterra, 1979), constellations of specific domains that undergo change simultaneously, presumably because they depend on the development of a common structure. Within this view, the specific link between the development of the concept of causality and intentionality has been considered of focal importance to the emergence of joint attention (see, e.g., Tomasello, 1995; Trevarthen, 1988).

Such a single-factor explanation has the benefit of mapping changes in shared attention to changes in the well-charted stream of cognitive development. But it fails to account for the fragility of early joint attention across a range of conditions. Cross-partner and cross-cultural observations suggest that a myriad of processes may be involved with the emergence of a stable organization of joint attention. Moreover, a consideration only of cognition fails to heed Vygotsky's (1978) wise warning that:

> if we ignore the child's needs, and the incentives which are effective in getting him to act, we will never be able to understand his advance from one developmental stage to the next, because every advance is connected with a marked change in motives, inclinations, and incentives. (p. 92)

Several factors related to emotion regulation are good candidates for variables that may act in concert with cognitive ones in the emergence of joint attention. The capacity to experience as well as to regulate both self-directed and other-directed emotions undergoes significant changes at the end of the first year of life (Gianino & Tronick, 1988). Desires, including those related to attachment and mastery motivation, also change markedly. Furthermore, by about 9 to 10 months of age, maturational changes in the central nervous system contribute to a growing ability to manage arousal and to cope with emotionally arousing events as well as to produce emotional blends and to use emotional expressions as means to achieve desired ends (Dawson, 1994; Thompson, Flood, & Lindquist, 1995).

Yet, it is one exercise to list emotion regulation as a factor that should be included in any complete explanation for the development of joint attention and quite another to accomplish the theoretical feat of fitting elements of this list together to explain the emergence of a new developmental form. To do this involves focusing on the orchestration between factors rather than on the characteristics of any single one. Fortunately, this challenge has been recognized by many contemporary developmentalists who have been elaborating classic notions of development (e.g., Werner, 1957) to articulate systemic understandings of change. In particular, the dynamic systems theory of development has provoked great interest lately, including that of researchers interested in early communication development (Eckerman, 1993; Fogel & Thelen, 1987).

From the perspective of dynamic systems theory, change results because of the self-organizing processes of continually active living systems. New patterns emerge as different heterochronic elements in an open system fluctuate, not because a prespecified plan unfolds or because a primary structural component takes control (Thelen & Smith, 1994). Although applying dynamic systems theory's formal mathematics to the emergence of joint attention is not yet feasible, the theory's metaphors for developmental change may help us place emotion regulation relative to a myriad of other factors, including endogenous ones related to voluntary attention, cognition, and motor behavior, and exogenous ones such as a partner's social skill, the infant's interactive history with a specific partner, the physical arrangement of the environment, and the culture's interpretation of specific objects. As Smith and Thelen (1993) suggest, dynamic systems:

> is a metaphor that turns empirical questions around by focusing attention on mechanism, the relation between stability and variability, and the process of change. It is a metaphor that asks us to shift our attention from the study of knowledge structures in development to a study of the developmental pathway itself. (p. 166)

In the terms of dynamic systems theory, a sustained state of joint attention may be considered an "attractor state." It may, in other words, be a stable organization of behavior "that the system prefers over all the possible modes" under certain conditions (Thelen & Smith, 1994, p. 56). Wolff (1993) has considered the states of very young infants in a similar light, proposing that they might best be conceptualized not as entities with distinct boundaries but rather as multiple points of stability within a single complex system. The regions between these points are unstable; individual states are themselves "deep attractors" (Smith & Thelen, 1993, p. 167).

The question then becomes, What factors control or limit the occurrence of joint attention? One element may often be the "rate limiting" factor whose mastery ushers in this new organization of attention. For example, an infant's apprehension of a partner as an intentional being may often play the decisive role in explaining socially directed acts during a period of shared object manipulation. But other elements may also serve this critical function under certain circumstances. For example, a sudden change in an infant's affective reaction to a person may serve as an "internal pertubation" that shifts attention from one phase (e.g., attention only to an object) to another (e.g., attention both to this object and to a partner who is sharing it). Or, an infant's heightened desire to obtain an object may tip the balance to prompt a shift of attention back and forth between the object and a potentially helpful partner.

FUTURE RESEARCH ON JOINT ATTENTION'S EMERGENCE

Throughout this chapter, we have lamented the lack of a picture of early episodes of shared object exploration that retains the varied colors of fluctuating affect. Nowhere does this lack seem more evident than when we begin to try to think dynamically in metaphoric terms. To test even the simplest hypotheses about whether or not changes in affect toward people and toward objects contribute to a shift in the organization of attention to both people and objects, we need more fine-grained information about the relation between the modulation of affect and the flow of attention. Therefore, in this closing section, we suggest research strategies that may produce the empirical details that will be needed to capture emotional dynamics during the early negotiation of joint attention.

Our first suggestion is that researchers complicate their codes. It is now common practice to employ parsimonious descriptive schemes that provide information about the timing of affective expressions and about the gaze direction of the infant. It is then an analytic challenge to put the streams together. An alternative worth trying is to formulate codes that are synthetic at the start. A good example of such a scheme is being developed by Tronick and his colleagues to track points of miscoordination during interactions (Gianino & Tronick, 1988) and to locate expressive constellations (Weinberg & Tronick, 1994).

A second promising methodological move is to systematically expand views of early social interactions that involve objects. This expansion can take two forms. First, "free play" observations may be supplemented with more targeted probes so that a fuller range of communicative functions, such as commenting about objects, object-focused social interacting, and object requesting, are observed (e.g., the communication play protocol; Adamson, Russell, & McArthur, 1997). Second, experimental manipulations may be formulated to produce a fuller range of affective response. So far, such manipulations have tended to target the organization of infant–adult interactions before the transition to joint attention (e.g., the still-face manipulation; Tronick, Als, Adamson, Wise, & Brazelton, 1978) or after it has begun to emerge in the last quarter of the first year (e.g., the affective social referencing situation; Klinnert, Campos, Sorce, Emde, & Svejda, 1983). What is called for is a paradigm that simultaneously challenges 5- to 10-month-old infants' interest in objects and engagement with people in a way that systematically varies each parameter. One example of this approach is provided by Parrinello and Ruff's (1988) experiment on the effect of adult intervention on infants' interest in objects in which an adult provided a low, a moderate, or a high level of support as an infant explored an object. Although their primary focus was on the effect of intervention on infant attention (they found that adults could subtly, but not brazenly, entice an initially reluctant infant to become more involved with objects), their conditions might also provide a window on how young infants balance reactions to people and shared objects.

One overarching strategy that also may help further an understanding of emotion regulation and the emergence of joint attention is to challenge notions of "typical" developmental order by observing natural variations (Adamson, 1997). There are several possible candidates that might help expand views of emotion regulation during the transition to joint attention. For example, we have found it informative to contrast the expression of affect when an infant interacts with peers and with a caregiver (Adamson & Bakeman, 1985) and to investigate processes of social referencing in human-reared infant chimpanzees (Russell, Bard, & Adamson, 1997). Another intriguing variation involves the observation of young children with autism and other pervasive developmental disorders who experience severe difficulty initiating and maintaining joint attention (Baron-Cohen, 1989; Loveland & Landry, 1986; Sigman & Kasari, 1995) and regulating emotion (Hobson, 1993; Rogers & Pennington, 1991; Sigman, Kasari, Kwon, & Yirmiya, 1992). We are particularly interested in observing emotional dynamics when a child with autism declines an adult's invitation of joint attention. Not only are these moments more likely to occur when adults interact with children with autism than with typically developing children or children with development language delay, they also appear to be interactive points at which a child with autism experiences difficulties modulating affectivity (McArthur & Adamson, 1996; Adamson, McArthur, & Markov, 1998).

Taken together, these various strategies will hopefully provide us with a clearer view of the arrangements of affect and attention that occur as infants come to integrate object interest and person engagement. We suspect that this new information will both supplement and challenge explanations of joint attention's emergence that do not take note of emotional expression and regulation during this important period of developmental change. Transformations in the organization of affect in relation to people and to objects are likely to be appreciated as an important aspect of the process of attentional transformation that pervades an infant's interactions with people and objects during the second half of the first year.

ACKNOWLEDGMENTS

Preparation of this chapter was supported by grants from the National Institutes of Health (HD 35612) and from Georgia State University.

REFERENCES

Adamson, L. B. (1996). *Communication development during infancy.* Boulder, CO: Westview Press.

Adamson, L. B. (1997). Order and disorder: Classical developmental theories and atypical communication development. In L. B. Adamson & M. A. Romski (Eds.), *Communication and language acquisition: Discoveries from atypical development* (pp. 2–23). Baltimore, MD: Brookes.

Adamson, L. B., & Bakeman, R. (1982). Affectivity and reference: Concepts, methods and techniques in the study of communication development of six to eighteen month old infants. In T. M. Field & A. Fogel (Eds.), *Emotion and interaction* (pp. 213–236). Hillsdale, NJ: Lawrence Erlbaum Associates.

Adamson, L. B., & Bakeman, R. (1984). Mothers' communicative actions: Changes during infancy. *Infant Behavior and Development, 7,* 467–478.

Adamson, L. B., & Bakeman, R. (1985). Affect and attention: Infants observed with mothers and peers. *Child Development, 56,* 582–593.

Adamson, L. B., & Bakeman, R. (1991). The development of shared attention during infancy. In R. Vasta (Ed.), *Annals of child development* (Vol. 8, pp. 1–41). London: Kingsley.

Adamson, L. B., Bakeman, R., Smith, C. B., & Walters, A. S. (1987). Adults' interpretation of infants' acts. *Developmental Psychology, 23,* 383–387.

Adamson, L. B., & Chance, S. (1998). Coordinating attention to people, objects, and symbols. In A. M. Wetherby, S. F. Warren, & J. Reichle (Eds.), *Transitions in prelinguistic communication: Preintentional to intentional and presymbolic to symbolic* (pp. 15–37). Baltimore, MD: Brookes.

Adamson, L. B., McArthur, D., & Markov, Y. (1998, April). *Autism and resisting joint attention.* Poster presented at the International Conference on Infant Studies, Atlanta, GA.

Adamson, L. B., Russell, C. L., & McArthur, D. (1997, April). *Joint attention and symbols at the end of infancy.* Poster presented at the Society for Research in Child Development, Washington, DC.

Bakeman, R., & Adamson, L. B. (1984). Coordinating attention to people and objects in mother-infant and peer-infant interaction. *Child Development, 55,* 1278–1289.

Bakeman, R., & Adamson, L. B. (1986). Infants' conventionalized acts: Gestures and words with mothers and peers. *Infant Behavior and Development, 9,* 215–230.

Bakeman, R., Adamson, L. B., Konner, M., & Barr, R. G. (1990). !Kung infancy: The social context of object exploration. *Child Development, 61,* 794–809.

Baron-Cohen, S. (1989). Joint-attention deficits in autism: Towards a cognitive analysis. *Development and Psychopathology, 1,* 185–189.

Bates, E., Benigni, L., Bretherton, I., Camaioni, L., & Volterra, V. (1979). *The emergence of symbols: Cognition and communication in infancy.* New York: Academic Press.

Biringen, Z., Emde, R. N., & Pipp-Siegel, S. (1997). Dissynchrony, conflict, and resolution: Positive contributions to infant development. *American Journal of Orthopsychiatry, 67,* 4–19.

Brazelton, T. B., Koslowski, B., & Main, M. (1974). The origins of reciprocity: The early mother-infant interaction. In M. Lewis & L. Rosenblum (Eds.), *The effect of the infant on its caregiver* (pp. 49–76). New York: Wiley.

Butterworth, G., & Grover, L. (1990). Joint visual attention, manual pointing, and preverbal communication in human infancy. In M. Jeannerod (Ed.), *Attention and performance XIII* (pp. 605–624). Hillsdale, NJ: Lawrence Erlbaum Associates.

Campos, J. J., Campos, R. G., & Barrett, K. C. (1989). Emergent themes in the study of emotional development and emotion regulation. *Developmental Psychology, 25,* 394–402.

Campos, J. J., & Stenberg, C. R. (1981). Perception, appraisal, and emotion: The onset of social referencing. In M. E. Lamb & L. R. Sherrod (Eds.), *Infant social cognition: Empirical and theoretical considerations* (pp. 273–314). Hillsdale, NJ: Lawrence Erlbaum Associates.

Dawson, G. (1994). Frontal electroencephalographic correlates of individual differences in emotion expression in infants: A brain systems perspective on emotion. In N. A. Fox (Ed.), The development of emotion regulation: Biological and behavioral considerations (pp. 135–151). *Monographs of the Society for Research in Child Development, 59* (2–3, Serial No. 240).

Demetriou, A. (Ed.). (1988). *The neo-Piagetian theories of cognitive development: Toward an integration.* Amsterdam: Elsevier Science.

Dodge, K. A. (Ed.). (1989). Development of emotion regulation [Special section]. *Developmental Psychology, 23,* 339–402.

Eckerman, C. (1993). Toddlers' achievement of coordinated action with conspecifics: A dynamic systems perspective. In L. B. Smith & E. Thelen (Eds.), *A dynamic systems approach to development: Applications* (pp. 333–357). Cambridge, MA: MIT Press.

Ellsworth, C. P., Muir, D. W., & Hains, S. M. J. (1993). Social competence and person-object differentiation: An analysis of the still-face effect. *Developmental Psychology, 29,* 63–73.

Fischer, K. W., & Farrar, M. J. (1988). Generalizations about generalization: How a theory of skill development explains both generality and specificity. In A. Demetriou (Ed.), *The neo-Piagetian theories of cognitive development: Toward an integration* (pp. 137–171). Amsterdam: Elsevier Science.

Fogel, A., & Thelen, E. (1987). Development of early expressive and communicative action: Reinterpreting the evidence from a dynamic systems perspective. *Developmental Psychology, 23,* 747–761.

Fox, N. A. (Ed.). (1994). The development of emotion regulation: Biological and behavioral considerations. *Monographs of the Society for Research in Child Development, 59* (2–3, Serial No. 240).

Gianino, A., & Tronick, E. Z. (1988). The mutual regulation model: The infant's self and interactive regulation and coping and defensive capacities. In T. M. Field, P. M. McCabe, & N. Schneiderman (Eds.), *Stress and coping across development* (pp. 47–68). Hillsdale, NJ: Lawrence Erlbaum Associates.

Gustafson, G. E., & Green, J. A. (1991). Developmental coordination of cry sounds with visual regard and gestures. *Infant Behavior and Development, 14,* 51–57.

Hobson, R. P. (1993). *Autism and the development of mind.* Hillsdale, NJ: Lawrence Erlbaum Associates.

Ilgs, F. L., & Ames, L. B. (1955). *Child behavior.* New York: Harper & Row.

Kaye, K., & Fogel, A. (1980). The temporal structure of face-to-face communication between mothers and infants. *Developmental Psychology, 16,* 454–464.

Klinnert, M. D., Campos, J. J., Sorce, J. F., Emde, R. N., & Svejda, M. (1983). The development of social referencing in infancy. In R. Plutchik & H. Kellerman (Eds.), *Emotion: Theory, research, and experience: Vol. 2. Emotion in early development* (pp. 57–86). New York: Academic Press.

Kopp, C. (1989). Regulation of distress and negative emotions: A developmental view. *Developmental Psychology, 25,* 343–354.

Lamb, M. E., Morrison, D. C., & Malkin, C. M. (1987). The development of infant social expectations in face-to-face interaction: A longitudinal study. *Merrill-Palmer Quarterly, 33,* 241–254.

Legerstee, M., Corter, C., & Kienapple, K. (1990). Hand, arm, and facial actions of young infants to a social and nonsocial stimulus. *Child Development, 61,* 774–784.

Lewis, M. (1993). The emergence of human emotions. In M. Lewis & J. M. Haviland (Eds.), *Handbook of emotions* (pp. 223–235). New York: Guilford.

Loveland, K. A., & Landry, S. H. (1986). Joint attention and language in autism and developmental language delay. *Journal of Autism and Developmental Disorders, 16,* 335–349.

McArthur, D., & Adamson, L. B. (1996). Joint attention in pre-verbal children: Autism and developmental language disorder. *Journal of Autism and Developmental Disorders, 26,* 481–496.

Messer, D. J., & Vietze, P. M. (1984). Timing and transitions in mother–infant gaze. *Infant Behavior and Development, 7,* 167–181.

Parrinello, R. M., & Ruff, H. A. (1988). The influence of adult intervention on infants' level of attention. *Child Development, 59,* 1125–1135.

Reddy, V. (1991). Playing with others' expectations: Teasing and mucking about in the first year. In A. Whiten (Ed.), *Natural theories of mind: Evolution, development and simulation of everyday mindreading* (pp. 143–158). Cambridge, MA: Basil Blackwell.

Rogers, S. J., & Pennington, B. F. (1991). A theoretical approach to the deficits in infantile autism. *Development and Psychopathology, 3,* 137–162.

Ross, H. S., & Lollis, S. P. (1987). Communication within infant social games. *Developmental Psychology, 23,* 241–248.

Ruff, H. A., & Rothbart, M. K. (1996). *Attention in early development: Themes and variations.* New York: Oxford University Press.

Russell, C. L., Bard, K. A., & Adamson, L. B. (1997). Social referencing by young chimpanzees (*Pan troglodytes*). *Journal of Comparative Psychology, 111,* 185–193.

Sander, L. W. (1962). Issues in early mother–child interaction. *Journal of the American Academy of Child Psychiatry, 1,* 141–166.

Shinn, M. W. (1900). *The biography of a baby.* Boston: Houghton-Mifflin.

Sigman, M., & Kasari, C. (1995). Joint attention across contexts in normal and autistic children. In C. Moore & P. Dunham (Eds.), *Joint attention: Its origin and role in development* (pp. 189–203). Hillsdale, NJ: Lawrence Erlbaum Associates.

Sigman, M. D., Kasari, C., Kwon, J.-H., & Yirmiya, N. (1992). Responses to the negative emotions of others by autistic, mentally retarded, and normal children. *Child Development, 63,* 796–807.

Smith, L. B., & Thelen, E. (1993). Can dynamic systems theory be usefully applied in areas other than motor development? In L. B. Smith & E. Thelen (Eds.), *A dynamic systems approach to development: Applications* (pp. 151–170). Cambridge, MA: MIT Press.

Spitz, R. A., & Wolf, K. M. (1946). The smiling response: A contribution to the ontogenesis of social relations. *Genetic Psychology Monographs, 34,* 57–125.

Stern, D. N. (1977). *The first relationship: Infant and mother.* Cambridge, MA: Harvard University Press.

Stern, D. N. (1985). *The interpersonal world of the infant: A view from psychoanalysis and developmental psychology.* New York: Basic Books.

Thelen, E., & Smith, L. B. (1994). *A dynamic systems approach to the development of cognition and action.* Cambridge, MA: MIT Press.

Thompson, R. A. (1994). Emotion regulation: A theme in search of definition. In N. A. Fox (Ed.), The development of emotion regulation: Biological and behavioral considerations (pp. 25–52). *Monographs of the Society for Research in Child Development, 59* (2–3, Serial No. 240).

Thompson, R. A., Flood, M. F., & Lundquist, L. (1995). Emotional regulation: Its relations to attachment and developmental psychopathology. In D. Cicchetti & S. L. Toth (Eds.), *Rochester Symposium on Developmental Psychopathology, Vol. 6: Emotion, cognition, and representation.* Rochester, NY: University of Rochester Press.

Tomasello, M. (1995). Joint attention as social cognition. In C. Moore & P. J. Dunham (Eds.), *Joint attention: Its origins and role in development* (pp. 103–130). Hillsdale, NJ: Lawrence Erlbaum Associates.

Trevarthen, C. (1979). Communication and cooperation in early infancy: A description of primary intersubjectivity. In M. Bullowa (Ed.), *Before speech: The beginning of interpersonal communication* (pp. 321–347). Cambridge, UK: Cambridge University Press.

Trevarthen, C. (1988). Universal co-operative motives: How infants begin to know the language and culture of their parents. In G. Jahoda & I. M. Lewis (Eds.), *Acquiring culture: Cross cultural studies in child development* (pp. 37–90). London: Croom Helm.

Tronick, E. Z. (1989). Emotions and emotional communication in infants. *American Psychologist, 44,* 112–119.

Tronick, E., Als, H., & Adamson, L. B. (1979). The communicative structure of early face to face interaction. In M. Bullowa (Ed.), *Before speech: The beginnings of interpersonal communication* (pp. 349–372). Cambridge, UK: Cambridge University Press.

Tronick, E., Als, H., Adamson, L. B., Wise, S., & Brazelton, T. B. (1978). The infant's response to entrapment between contradictory messages in face to face interaction. *Journal of the American Academy of Child Psychiatry, 17,* 1–13.

van der Veer, R. (1996). Henri Wallon's theory of early child development: The role of emotions. *Developmental Review, 16*, 364–390.

Voyat, G. (Ed.). (1984). *The world of Henri Wallon.* New York: Jason Aronson.

Vygotsky, L. S. (1978). *Mind in society: The development of higher psychological processes.* Cambridge, MA: Harvard University Press.

Walden, T. A., & Ogan, T. A. (1988). The development of social referencing. *Child Development, 59*, 1230–1240.

Weinberg, M. K., & Tronick E. Z. (1994). Beyond the face: An empirical study of infant affective configurations of facial, vocal, gestural, and regulatory behaviors. *Child Development, 65*, 1503–1515.

Werner, H. (1957). The concept of development from a comparative and organismic point of view. In D. Harris (Ed.), *The concept of development* (pp. 125–148). Minneapolis: University of Minnesota Press.

Wolff, P. H. (1987). *The development of behavioral states and the expression of emotions in early infancy.* Chicago: University of Chicago Press.

Wolff, P. H. (1993). Behavioral and emotional states in infancy: A dynamic perspective. In L. B. Smith & E. Thelen (Eds.), *A dynamic systems approach to development: Applications* (pp. 188–208). Cambridge, MA: MIT Press.

Part IV

COMMENTARY

Chapter **13**

Social Cognition Before the Revolution

Michael Tomasello
Emory University

Most mammals, and virtually all primates, are highly social beings. Mammalian and primate infants typically begin their lives clinging to their mothers and nursing, and they spend their next few months, or even years, still in close proximity to her. As adults, most mammals and primates live in close-knit social groups in which members individually recognize one another and form various types of social relationships (Tomasello & Call, 1997). Since they are primates, human beings follow this same pattern, of course, but they also have some unique forms of sociality that may be characterized as "ultra-social" (Boyd & Richerson, 1996) or, in more common parlance, cultural (Tomasello, Kruger, & Ratner, 1993).

The forms of sociality that are mostly clearly unique to human beings emerge in their ontogeny at around 9 months of age—what I have previously called the 9-month social–cognitive revolution (Tomasello, 1995). This is the age at which infants typically begin to engage in the kinds of joint attentional interactions in which they master the use of cultural artifacts, including tools and language, and become fully active participants in all types of cultural scripts, rituals, and games. The problem is that we know very little about the ontogenetic origins of these social-cognitive skills before 9 months of age. That is why the current volume is such a welcome addition to the literature. Although we are certainly left with more questions than answers, the chapters in this volume demonstrate dramatically how much more we know empirically about infant social cognition than just a decade ago, which of course makes for much more sophisticated and detailed theories as well.

In this commentary, I would like to do two things. First, I would like to characterize the 9-month revolution in human social cognition, arguing that it is indeed a unitary and coherent developmental phenomenon based on infants' newly emerging understanding of other persons as intentional agents. Second, I would like to provide a typology of currently available theoretical accounts for how infants come to this new understanding, that is, for infant social cognition before the revolution.

THE NINE-MONTH REVOLUTION

Six-month-old infants interact dyadically with objects, grasping and manipulating them, and they interact dyadically with other people, expressing emotions back-and-forth in a turn-taking sequence. But at around 9 to 12 months of age, infants begin to engage in interactions that are triadic in the sense that they involve the referential triangle of child, adult, and some outside entity to which they share attention. Thus, infants at this age begin to flexibly and reliably look where adults are looking (gaze following), use adults as social reference points (social referencing), and act on objects in the way adults are acting on them (imitative learning)—in short, to "tune in" to the attention and behavior of adults toward outside entities. At this same age, infants also begin to use communicative gestures to direct adult attention and behavior to outside entities in which they are interested (imperatives and declaratives)—in short, to get the adult to "tune in" to them. In many cases, several of these behaviors come together as the infant interacts with an adult in a relatively extended bout of joint engagement with an object (Bakeman & Adamson, 1984). Most often the term *joint attention* has been used to characterize this whole complex of triadic social skills and interactions (Moore & Dunham, 1995), and it represents something of a revolution in the way infants relate to their worlds.

My own view is that infants engage in joint attentional interactions when they begin to understand other persons as intentional agents (Tomasello, 1995). Intentional agents are animate beings with the power to control their spontaneous behavior, but they are more than that. Intentional agents have goals and make active choices among behavioral means for attaining those goals. Importantly, intentional agents also make active choices about what they pay attention to in pursuing those goals (see Gibson & Rader, 1979, for the argument that attention is intentional perception). The central theoretical point is that all the specific joint attentional behaviors in which infants follow, direct, or share adult attention and behavior are not separate activities or cognitive domains; they are simply different behavioral manifestations of this same underlying understanding of other persons as intentional agents.

Support for this view is provided by a recent study in which a group of 24 infants were followed longitudinally from 9 to 15 months of age (Carpenter, Nagell, & Tomasello, in press). At monthly intervals, these infants were assessed on nine different measures of joint attention: joint engagement, gaze following, point following, imitation of instrumental acts, imitation of arbitrary acts, reaction to social obstacles, use of imperative gestures, and use of declarative gestures (including proximal such as "show" and distal such as "point"). In each case, very stringent criteria were used to ensure that infants were attempting either to follow into or to direct the adult's attention or behavior (e.g., alternating attention between goal and adult), not just reacting to a discriminative stimulus. The findings of most importance in the current context were: (a) all nine of these triadic joint attentional skills emerged for most children by 12 months of age; (b) all these skills emerged in close developmental synchrony for individual children, with nearly 80 percent of the infants mastering all nine tasks within a 4-month window; and (c) age of emergence was intercorrelated for all the skills (although only moderately since near simultaneous emergence of the skills led to low individual variability).

Importantly, the decalage that was observed within individual children's development had a very clear explanation, since there was a very consistent ordering of tasks across children. Twenty of the 24 children first passed tasks that required sharing and checking of adult attention in close proximity (e.g., simply looking up to the adult during joint engagement); then tasks that required following into adult attention to more distal external entities (e.g., gaze following); and finally tasks that required directing adult attention to external entities (e.g., pointing to a distal entity). The explanation for this ordering is that the tasks of sharing and checking all required the child to simply look to the adult's face (e.g., spontaneously as they played with a toy or in response to the adult blocking their attempt to grasp an object); in this case the children only had to know that the adult was present and attending. On the other hand, the tasks in which infants either followed or directed adult attention required them to zero in on precisely what the adult was attending to, with comprehension (in the form of attention following) preceding production (in the form of attention directing). Quite clearly knowing what external entity an adult is focused on requires more precise joint attentional skills than simply knowing that an adult is attending to the interaction as a whole. The conclusion is thus that for virtually all infants, the whole panoply of joint attentional skills emerge in fairly close developmental synchrony, in moderately correlated fashion, with a highly consistent ordering pattern across children reflecting the different levels of specificity in joint attention required.

The question is thus: Where does this new understanding of other persons come from? How does it develop in the first 9 months of life? In surveying the available theoretical accounts, both in this volume and elsewhere, I am able to discern basically three classes of answer: those based on nativism of various types, those based on learning of various types, and those based on simulation.

ANSWER 1: NATIVISM

Some theorists believe that human infants have adultlike social cognition from birth and that the emergence of joint attentional behaviors at 9 to 12 months of age simply reflects the development of behavioral performance skills for manifesting this cognition in overt behavior (e.g., Trevarthen, 1979). Following Braten (1987), Trevarthen claimed that infants are born with a dialogic mind, with an innate sense of "the virtual other," and they only need to acquire the motoric skills necessary to express this knowledge behaviorally. Trevarthen's evidence for this view is infants' complex dyadic social interactions in the early months, what he has dubbed *primary intersubjectivity*. Most impressively, in the study of Murray and Trevarthen (1985), 2-month-olds seemed to display an exquisite sensitivity to the contingencies of social interactions with others. However, the three sets of authors in this volume who have attempted to replicate these results (with mixed success: Rochat & Striano, Muir & Hains, and Nadel & Tremblay-Leveau) do not believe that sensitivity to social contingencies reveals an innate sense of other persons but only that it provides a starting point from which infants may learn about other persons and how they work (see further on). From my own perspective, it seems clear that 5-month-old infants have all the motoric skills necessary to follow the gaze of others (they visually track moving objects) and to point for them (they both reach for objects and extend their index fingers quite often).

Some other nativist theorists believe that infants are preprogrammed with several independent social–cognitive modules, including an Eye Direction Detector, an Intention Detector, and a Shared Attention Mechanism (Baron-Cohen, 1995). In Baron-Cohen's view, each of these modules has its own predetermined developmental timetable that is affected neither by the ontogeny of the other modules nor by the organism's interactions with the social environment. Infants are not born knowing about other persons, but they do not have to learn about them either; the appropriate cognitive modules simply mature on their ineluctable timetables during the first months of life. The problem in this case is that the data simply are not consistent with this view. Evidence from the Carpenter et al. (in press) study, and indirect evidence from other studies, showed that the key skills in this account (gaze following, understanding intentional action, and joint engagement) emerge in close developmental synchrony and in a correlated fashion. These facts are dissonant with an independent modules account, nor is there any empirical support for the view that the emergence of these skills does not require some kind of social interaction with others (see also the critique of Baldwin & Moses, 1994).

In any case, none of the theorists in this volume opts for a strongly nativistic account of how human infants acquire their species-typical skills of social cognition. Although a number of theorists posit innate bases for such things as infants' attraction to faces (Blass) and emotions (Stern), they all believe that to get to the full-fledged form of adult social cognition, some serious ontogenetic work must be done.

ANSWER 2: PREPARED LEARNING

In modern approaches to learning, the organism is never viewed as a tabula rasa (Gallistel, 1990). Several of the theorists in this book focus on the different types of preparedness with which human infants come to the task of learning about other persons. These fall generally into three categories: the attraction to social stimuli, the sensitivity to emotion, and the detection of patterns of motion in behavior. These foundations, then, set the stage for infants' learning about other persons and how they work, mostly through an analysis of the contingencies of social interaction.

Blass enumerates and delineates the many ways in which human infants from birth, and even before birth, are attracted to social stimuli such as voices and faces. In Blass' account, infants' earliest learning is about what should be the target of their biologically prepared systems of behavior and learning, and these innate attractions give the infant an important leg-up on the process. Muir and Hains also focus on very early learning as prepared by attraction to the face (especially the eyes) of others, and Moore even claims that the very earliest gaze following of infants is "reflexive." Despite various nits that might be picked, overall, the data presented in these chapters demonstrate quite clearly that infants have an early attraction to various kinds of social stimuli, and so they do not need to learn about the social world from scratch; evolution has prepared them for the task.

Stern proposes a new way to analyze infants' dealings with emotions. He proposes that infants deal with temporally extended patterns of emotional expression and that these are not tied to specific modalities; they are overall *vitality contours.* He also points out that these vitality contours have predictable endpoints and that this might give the infant a headstart in understanding other persons as directed towards endpoints (i.e., as intentional). Adamson and Russell also focus on emotions, but in this case they describe the kinds of active emotion regulation that go on at a later point in development as infants engage in joint attention with others. They argue that joint attention is perhaps better characterized as joint interest, since this terminology includes the motivational component for infants as well. Together these two chapters provide a very strong argument that the emotional dimensions of infants' social interactions—which are clearly distinct from the emotional dimensions of their interactions with inanimate objects—also reflect infants' biological preparation for social interaction.

Baldwin and Baird make a very strong case that infants cannot understand intentional actions unless and until they can perceptually parse the continuous flow of behavior into at least somewhat discrete units. Poulin-Dubois makes a similar argument in characterizing young infants dealings with persons as "distinctive objects" that move in distinctive ways. Rochat and Striano focus on the directedness of human behavior, for example, as individuals pursue goals in the environment. These theorists focus on such things as self-generated movement, "clusters of action features," and directed motion as being aspects of the behavior of other persons that attract infants' interest and attention. Although none of these chapters attempts to explore in depth infants' possible biological preparedness for parsing and finding patterns in the behavior of animate beings, neither do they search for possible developmental precursors, suggesting that the perceptual analysis of biological motion is something that infants engage in quite early and quite readily without extended tuition (Bertenthal, 1996).

To reiterate, none of these theorists thinks that infants' biological preparedness for social interaction suggests an adultlike understanding of other persons. In one way or another their chapters all, along with virtually all the other chapters of the volume, focus on infants' awesome powers of contingency learning. Contingency learning is of course a biologically prepared skill as well, and so the predominant view in this volume is that infants begin with various kinds of preparedness in terms of content—for example, an attraction to social stimuli, a sensitivity to emotional exchanges, and an ability to parse and find patterns in animate motion—and then they use their powers of contingency analysis to learn more specifics about other persons and how they work. Thus, Muir and Hains; Bigelow; Nadel and Tremblay-Leveau; Gergely and Watson; and Rochat and Striano all place the greatest burden of their accounts on infants' analyses of social contingencies. And although he does not elaborate here, Moore (1996) also stresses the importance of infants' learning of various behavioral sequences and contingencies, especially those involving the infant behaving and the adult reacting in specific ways (e.g., the child looks to the adult, who then smiles). Bigelow even proposes that infants' interactions with primary caregivers leads them to develop a preferred style of social interaction (level of contingency) with other persons that can be detected as they interact with strangers, and Gergely and Watson speculate that social interaction leads typically developing infants (but not autistic infants) to prefer contingencies containing some degree of unpredictability. Whether infants are especially prepared for analyzing the contingencies of social interaction in particular, or whether social interaction is simply fertile ground for use of their general skills of contingency analysis, is not a question that can be answered at this time.

My own view is that these various proposals each have identified an important part of the picture. There is no doubt that infants are biologically prepared for social interaction and that the full development of human skills of social cognition depend on the infant's ability to analyze the contingencies that obtain when they interact with other persons. But even though these preparations and skills are all necessary, I do not believe they are sufficient. Indeed, all primate species are biologically prepared to interact socially with conspecifics (although there may be differences in the nature of this preparedness across species), and they are all very skillful at analyzing contingencies of all kinds. Why then do they not develop an understanding of conspecifics as intentional beings like themselves whose interest and attention to outside entities may be followed into, directed, and shared? Coming from the ontogenetically later phenomena of language acquisition and other forms of cultural learning and interaction, my view is that a satisfactory theory of infant social cognition simply must take account of the special way that human infants identify themselves with other persons. For what makes other persons such special interactive partners for infants, in my view, is not that they are especially contingent and unpredictable and emotional as compared with inanimate objects, although they are all these things. The most important characteristic of other persons—that allows me to understand them in a way I cannot understand inanimate objects—is that they are "like me."

ANSWER 3: SIMULATION

The majority of chapters in this book mention one or more phenomena in which infants do not just interact with other persons in a reciprocal fashion, but rather, they actually match, or align themselves, with their interactive partners. Most prominent in this context is the phenomenon of neonatal imitation, in which infants match their overt behavior to that of adults (e.g., Meltzoff & Moore, 1989). Also important, although still without experimental demonstration, is Stern's (1985) notion of *affect attunement* in which infants take on the affective states of their interactive partners. Affective attunement does not reduce to neonatal mimicking but rather is a distinct phenomenon since, for instance, an infant might match an adult's smile with a positive vocalization. Nevertheless, despite the fact that these phenomena are mentioned by many of the authors of this volume, with one major exception, they are not given the special treatment I think they deserve.

In my view, and the view of many social theorists from Vico and Dilthey to Cooley and Mead, our understanding of other persons rests on a special source of knowledge that is not available (at least not in the same way) when we attempt to understand the workings of inanimate objects: the analogy to the self. The crucial point is that we have sources of information about the self and its workings that are not available for external entities. As I act, I have available various forms of proprioception (correlated with my exteroception) and the internal experience of goals, and the striving for goals, and how these relate to behavioral expression. To the extent that I understand an external entity as "like me," and can therefore attribute to it the same kinds of internal workings as my own, to that extent can I gain extra knowledge of a special type about how it works. Presumably, the analogy is closest and most natural when it is applied to conspecifics, but human beings also extend it with some regularity to animals, machines, and even inanimate objects. We more or less simulate other persons' behavior and psychological functioning on analogy to our own.

In the various theories of infant social cognition, I find only three that elevate this important difference to its appropriate theoretical status—although none of them applies it in a clear way to the 9-month revolution. First, Meltzoff and Gopnik (1993) believed that infants understand that other persons are "like me" from birth. There is still much to learn about other persons, however, and so the view is dubbed "starting state nativism." But nowhere in their theory do Meltzoff and Gopnik show how the understanding of other persons as "like me" is linked in explicit ways to the learning process. In particular, they do not show how the "like me" stance is responsible for the emergence of the complex of joint attentional behaviors at 9 to 12 months of age. Indeed, as adherents of one version of the "theory theory," Gopnik and Meltzoff (1997) believed that infants come to understand other persons by using the same kind of protoscientific theorizing they use in other domains of cognition, with the "like me" stance playing no special role in this development beyond early infancy (and Gopnik, 1993, in fact argues that we know the intentional states of others as well as we know our own).

Second, Barresi and Moore (1996) were skeptical of neonatal imitation, and thus they believe that more interactive experiences with other individuals are required before the infant can understand that others are "like me." Of special importance are experiences in which the infant can simultaneously observe similar behaviors and reactions to outside entities on her own part—observed from her own first-person perspective—and on the part of others—observed from a third-person perspective. But Barresi and Moore (1996) also made no attempt to relate this "like me" understanding to the emergence of joint attentional behaviors at 9 to 12 months of age. Indeed, they do not believe that these behaviors reflect a social-cognitive revolution at all (see also Barressi & Moore, 1993). Rather, they believe that the various joint attentional behaviors at 9 to 12 months of age reflect independently learned behavioral contingencies (e.g., the use of the gaze direction of others as a discriminative cue) with their close developmental synchronies due to some as-yet-to-be-discovered change in information processing capacity.

Third, Gergely and Watson (this volume; see also Rochat & Striano) focus on a phenomenon they call *social mirroring*. Social mirroring does not involve the infant's matching the adult's behavior and emotional expression, but rather it involves the adult's matching the infant's, perhaps even reflecting it back in exaggerated form (thus "marking" it as not wholly genuine but done for the infant's benefit). From these experiences, given their great powers of contingency analysis, infants are able to discern that other persons are "like me." Although no one has yet demonstrated that infants are indeed sensitive to being imitated or matched affectively, it is possible that they are (Meltzoff, 1990, demonstrated this for 14-month-olds only). But even if infants are sensitive to being imitated in this way, it is very difficult to believe that a developmental function of such vital importance is dependent on such a special type of social interaction. Although the requisite cross-cultural work has not been done, there would seem to be some cultures in which infants do not experience the large amounts of face-to-face interaction of Western middle-class infants (even though they clearly do receive plenty of loving and contingent social interaction), and in which parents do not seem as motivated as Western middle-class parents to interpret and mirror their infants' behavior (Schieffelin & Ochs, 1986). If social mirroring is absent, would an infant not acquire its species-typical skills of social cognition? Gergely and Watson also do not make any special provisions for 9 months of age as a special developmental moment in infants' social interactions with others.

All these views clearly have much to recommend them. But I have a slightly different view of the problem that derives from the special importance I place on the the 9-month revolution as the ontogenetic expression of the human adaptation for culture. In agreement with Meltzoff and Gopnik, I believe that infants' early understanding of other persons as "like me" is the result of a uniquely human biological adaptation, although the precise age at which it emerges in ontogeny and the amount and types of personal experience necessary in the species-typical developmental pathway remain unclear. This understanding, which in any case is present within the first few months of life, is then a key element in infants' coming to understand others as intentional agents at 9 months of age. My disagreement with other theorists involves the role of another key factor. In my view, the other indispensable factor in this unique ontogenetic event, and the one that explains the specific age at which the understanding of other persons as intentional agents emerges, is infants' understanding of their own intentional actions. At about 8 or 9 months of age, infants come to understand the intentionality of their own actions in a new way, and since other persons are "like me," this leads immediately to a new understanding of these other persons.

Early in ontogeny, infants understand that their actions produce results in the world, but they understand very little of how this works. Six-month-old infants, for example, know how to produce interesting effects on objects and can reproduce those effects basically ad infinitum. But they only do so if the environmental circumstances remain relatively constant across encounters (Piaget, 1952, 1954). Starting at around 8 months of age, however, a new understanding of action–outcome relations seems to emerge. At around 8 months, infants begin systematically to use multiple behavioral means toward the same goal in novel circumstances and even to recognize and deal with behavioral intermediaries (obstacles and tools) in the pursuit of goals. For example, if an infant wants to reach a toy, and a pillow is inserted as an obstacle, before 8 months of age, infants either start interacting with the pillow, forgetting the original toy, or else they stay focused on the toy and become frustrated. But at 8 months of age, infants react to the intervention of the pillow by pausing, then removing the pillow or smashing it down, then proceeding deliberately to grasp the toy. It is also at this age that they begin to use intermediaries, mostly human intermediaries, to achieve ends. For example, when infants want to operate some toy but cannot, they often push an adult's hand toward it and wait for a result (and even sometimes attempt to use inanimate intermediaries, i.e., tools).

Although it is fair to say that before 8 months of age infants are acting intentionally in the general sense that they are acting toward a goal, the use of multiple means to the same end and the use of intermediaries indicates a new level of intentional functioning. A means that was useful toward a goal in one circumstance is replaced by another in another circumstance; the infant must choose different means toward the same end based on an evaluation of the situation. A behavior that on one occasion was an end in itself (e.g., smashing down a pillow) is now only a means to a greater end (e.g., grasping the toy); the infant must understand that the same means may be used toward different ends. The implication is thus that infants now have a new understanding of the different roles of ends and means in their own behavioral acts. They have come to differentiate the goal they are pursuing and the behavioral means they use to pursue that goal much more clearly than in their previous sensory-motor actions. The fact that an action can in different circumstances be either end or means, and the fact that some actions are in some cases definitely subordinated to others, suggests that we now have truly intentional behavior in the sense that infants have in mind a goal (presumably in the form of an imagined state of affairs in the world) that they clearly differentiate from the various behavioral means among which they must choose in order to attain that goal. This goal is the first mental entity that infants clearly differentiate from their overt sensory-motor actions.

The theory is thus that human infants identify with other human beings from very early in ontogeny; this is based on uniquely human biological inheritance. As long as infants understand themselves only as animate agents with the ability to make things happen in some generalized way, for the first 7 months or so, that is how they will also understand other persons. When they begin understanding themselves as intentional agents in the sense that they recognize that they have goals that are clearly separated from behavioral means, at 8 months of age or so, that is how they understand (simulate) other persons as well. This understanding also paves the way for understanding the perceptual choices that others make—their attention as distinct from their perception—though we currently have little understanding of this process. Although at this point we should not push the argument too far, it is also possible that infants make some of these same kinds of attributions or simulations, perhaps somewhat inappropriately, to inanimate objects and that this is the source of their understandings of how some physical events "force" others to happen: the first billiard ball is pushing the second with the same kind of force that I feel when I push it (Piaget, 1954). Perhaps this kind of simulation is weaker for infants than the simulation of other persons because the analogy between themselves and inanimate objects is not as good.

It is important that this account also provides a straightforward explanation for the fact that only humans understand others as intentional agents. Nonhuman primates interact with conspecifics socially and emotionally in many complex ways, some of which resemble the kinds of complex dyadic interactions of human adults and infants. They also understand something of the efficacy of their own actions on the environment, and indeed some species engage in sensory-motor actions in which they use different means toward the same end, remove obstacles, and use intermediaries such as tools. Many nonhuman primates are thus both social and intentional beings, and some individuals even receive special treatment by humans that resembles that received by human infants. The only remaining explanation for why they do not understand their social partners as intentional beings is that they do not understand that others are "like me," and so they cannot use their knowledge of self to simulate and help them to understand their conspecifics (Tomasello & Call, 1997).

CONCLUSION

I am very impressed with the wealth of knowledge we have accumulated, mostly within the last decade, on infants' skills of social interaction and cognition. We are not faced with the stark alternatives of nature and nurture typically invoked when little is known about a phenomenon. Instead, we now have the kind of detailed empirical work that is necessary to actually begin to map out the ontogenetic course of early social cognition, with appropriate roles for both biological preparedness of many diverse types and for different kinds of individual and social experiences at different points in the process. This volume is a testament to the rich fruits that careful scientific research may bear. In looking to the future of research on these most interesting and important questions, I have three recommendations.

First, it is of vital importance, in my view, to have a comparative perspective on human infancy and development. Obviously, if we are seeking to account for the species unique characteristics of human ontogeny, we need to specify the ways in which human ontogeny in a particular domain differs from that of other primates and animals. In explaining that difference, if we posit a special human competency we must be able to demonstrate that indeed it is unique to humans. If we posit a particular learning experience as responsible for some uniquely human competency, it must be one that other primates do not have. In the current case, my own belief is that nonhuman primates have many of the same social experiences as humans and that they have many of the same skills of contingency analysis as well. So we must look elsewhere if we are to find the species-unique sources of human social cognition, in my view, to something like simulation.

Second, it is also of vital importance to keep a cross-cultural perspective in mind as well. The main problem in this case is the lack of quantitative data. Although there are a number of ethnographic reports of cultures in which infants are not treated in the way they are in Western middle-class culture, these are almost always relatively informal, and in any case non-quantitative, descriptions. But the importance of such comparisons is obvious. If we are positing a certain trajectory for any developmental phenomenon during infancy, it is important to know the range of variation in the species in terms of the basic steps and their timing. This information is of special importance in the social domain, because we know that children growing up in different cultures end up interacting with groupmates socially in many diverse ways. And it is of even greater importance for theorists of social cognition who posit certain kinds of social experiences as critical for development—because some infant social experiences are common across cultures, and so could be a part of the species universal ontogenetic pathway, whereas others are culturally specific, and so could not play such a role.

Third, let me make the mundane but never trivial plea for more empirical research. From the point of view of my own particular theoretical account, we need to know much more about the nature of neonatal imitation and affect attunement as ways that human infants identify with conspecifics from a very early age (comparative and cross-cultural work on these issues would be very helpful as well). And to my knowledge, there has been basically no research on infants' comprehension of social mirroring in early infancy, a potentially very important developmental mechanism (with cross-cultural work being especially important here). And finally, the relationship between infants' understanding of their own actions as they relate to the actions of others is basically, as far as I know, unexplored territory. As will probably always be the case, we have come a long way, but there is still a long way to go.

ACKNOWLEDGMENT

Thanks to Philippe Rochat for comments on an earlier draft of this chapter.

REFERENCES

Baldwin, D., & Moses, L. (1994). The mindreading engine: Evaluating the evidence for modularity. *Cahiers de Psychologie, 13,* 553–560.

Bakeman, R., & Adamson, L. (1984). Coordinating attention to people and objects in mother–infant and peer–infant interactions. *Child Development, 55,* 1278–1289.

Baron-Cohen, S. (1995). *Mindblindness: An essay on autism and theory of mind.* Cambridge, MA: MIT Press.

Barresi, J., & Moore, C. (1993). Sharing a perspective precedes the understanding of that perspective. *Behavioral and Brain Sciences, 16,* 513–514.

Barresi, J., & Moore, C. (1996). Intentional relations and social undersanding. *Behavioral and Brain Sciences, 19,* 107–154.

Bertenthal, B. (1996). Origins and early development of perception, action, and representation. *Annual Review of Psychology, 47,* 431–459.

Boyd, R., & Richerson, P. (1996). Why culture is common but cultural evolution is rare. In W. Runciman (Ed.), *Evolution of social behavior patterns in primates and man* (pp. 251–274). London: British Academy.

Braten, S. (1987). Dialogic mind: The infant and adult in protoconversation. In M. Cavallo (Ed.), *Nature, cognition, and system* (pp. 1–32). Boston: Riedel.

Carpenter, M., Nagell, K., & Tomasello, M. (in press). Social cognition, joint attention, and communicative competence from 9 to 15 months of age. *Monographs of the Society for Research in Child Development.*

Gallistel, R. (1990). *The organization of learning.* Cambridge, MA: MIT Press.

Gibson, E., & Rader, N. (1979). Attention: The perceiver as performer. In G. A. Hale & M. Lewis (Eds.), *Attention and cognitive development* (pp. 1–21). New York: Plenum Press.

Gopnik, A. (1993). How we know our minds: The illusion of first-person knowledge of intentionality. *Behavioral and Brain Sciences, 16,* 1–15.

Gopnik, A., & Meltzoff, A. (1997). *Words, thought, and things.* Cambridge, MA: MIT Press.
Meltzoff, A. (1990). Foundations for developing a concept of self: The role of imitation in relating self to other and the role of social mirroring, social modelling, and self practice in infancy. In D. Cicchetti & M. Beegly (Eds.), *The self in transition: Infancy to childhood* (pp. 318–335). Chicago: University of Chicago Press.
Meltzoff, A. N., & Gopnik, A. (1993). The role of imitation in understanding persons and developing a theory of mind. In S. Baron-Cohen, H. Tager-Flusberg, & D. J. Cohen (Eds.), *Understanding other minds: Perspectives from autism* (pp. 335–366). New York: Oxford University Press.
Meltzoff, A. N., & Moore, M. K. (1989). Imitation in newborn infants: Exploring the range of gestures imitated and the underlying mechanisms. *Developmental Psychology, 25,* 954–962.
Moore, C. (1996). Theories of mind in infancy. *British Journal of Developmental Psychology, 14,* 19–40.
Moore, C., & Dunham, P. (1995). *Joint attention: Its origins and role in development.* Hillsdale, NJ: Lawrence Erlbaum Associates.
Murray, L., & Trevarthen, C. (1985). Emotion regulation of the interactions between two-month-olds and their mothers. In T. Field & N. Fox (Eds.), *Social perception in infants* (pp. 89–111). Norwood, NJ: Ablex.
Piaget, J. (1952). *Origins of intelligence in children.* New York: Norton.
Piaget, J. (1954). *The construction of reality in the child.* New York: Norton.
Schieffelin, B., & Ochs, E. (1986). *Language socialization across cultures.* Cambridge, UK: Cambridge University Press.
Stern, D. (1985). *The interpersonal world of the infant.* New York: Basic Books.
Tomasello, M. (1995). Joint attention as social cognition. In C. Moore & P. Dunham (Eds.), *Joint attention: Its origins and role in development* (pp. 103–130). Hillsdale, NJ: Lawrence Erlbaum Associates.
Tomasello, M., & Call, J. (1997). *Primate cognition.* New York: Oxford University Press.
Tomasello, M., Kruger, A. C., & Ratner, H. H. (1993). Cultural learning. *Behavioral and Brain Sciences, 16,* 495–552.
Trevarthen, C. (1979). Instincts for human understanding and for cultural cooperation: Their development in infancy. In M. von Cranach, K. Foppa, W. Lepenies, & D. Ploog (Eds.), *Human ethology: Claims and limits of a new discipline* (pp. 530–571). Cambridge, UK: Cambridge University Press.

Author Index

A

Abravanel, E., 15, 260
Adamson, L., 157
Adamson, L. B., 9, 13, 23, 112, 139, 142, 183, 191, 192, 206, 281, 282, 285, 286, 287, 289, 292, 293, 301, 305
Adolph, K.E., 261
Agnew, J., 86
Ainsworth, M. D. S., 138, 145
Akhtar, N., 219, 221, 268, 269
Alberts, J. R., 36, 37
Alessandri, S. M., 181
Alexander, T., 155, 166, 167, 168, 182
Allard, L., 259
Als, H., 23, 112, 139, 142, 150, 157, 168, 191, 192, 282, 292
Alson, D., 72
Ames, L., 141
Ames, L. B., 288
Amsterdam, B., 141
Angelopoulos, M., 249, 250
Anscombe, G. E. M., 222
Artola, A., 70
Asch, S. E., 86, 215, 217, 235
Aslin, R. N., 228
Astington, J. W., 209, 276
Atwater, J. D., 110
Avrahami, J., 230

B

Baddeley, A. D., 72
Bahrick, L. R., 106, 108, 114, 124, 127, 145
Baillargeon, R., 6, 257
Baird, 23, 306
Bakeman, R., 9, 13, 206, 281, 285, 287, 289, 293, 301
Baker, R., 266
Baldwin, D., 24, 111, 305, 306
Baldwin, D. A., 220, 221, 268, 275
Balzano, G. J., 67
Bandura, A., 101
Bannister, D., 86
Bard, K. A., 293
Bargh, J. A., 267
Barkovich, A. J., 94
Baron-Cohen, S., 9, 101, 126, 155, 156, 174, 175, 177, 178, 183, 208, 209, 221, 222, 223, 251, 266, 267, 275, 293, 304
Barton, M. E., 204, 206, 221, 268
Bartrip, J., 42
Barr, R. G., 13, 47, 289
Barrett, K. C., 283, 284
Barresi, J., 121, 222, 223
Bartsch, K., 268
Basili, J. N., 25
Bates, E., 9, 24, 72, 74, 120, 121, 209, 261, 289
Bauer, R., 70
Baumel, M. H., 83
Bean, N. J., 39
Beauchamp, G. K., 38
Beck, M., 37
Becker, J., 161
Beebe, B., 24, 72, 112, 150

Beegly, M., 203
Beeghly-Smith, M., 261, 268
Behbehani, M. M., 50
Bell, S. M., 145
Bendell, D., 113, 150
Benigni, L., 9, 209, 261, 289
Bennett, P., 249, 250, 276
Bennett, S. L., 72, 150
Benson, J. B., 113
Berger, J., 52, 58
Bergman, A., 10, 109, 112
Bergman, T., 52, 174, 229, 251
Barresi, J., 222, 223, 308, 309
Barton, M.,
Berthental, B. I., 227, 230, 263, 306
Bertonici, J., 72
Bettes, B. A., 113
Bigelow, A., 20, 150, 306
Bigelow, A. E., 140, 142, 145, 147
Bijeljac-Babic, R., 72
Bill, B., 220
Bion, W. R., 112
Birch, H. G., 110
Birch, L. L., 39
Biringen, Z., 286
Biró, S., 75, 121, 234, 262
Bjorklund, D. F., 15
Black, R., 13
Blass, E. M., 11, 18, 36, 38, 39, 40, 41, 43, 44, 45, 46, 47, 48, 49, 50, 51, 52, 53, 157, 305
Blatt, 23
Blehar, M. C., 138
Bloom, K., 46, 58, 103, 174, 175
Bloom, P., 218
Blumstein, S., 72
Bois, J., 230
Borton, R. W., 121
Bower, G. H., 85, 121
Bower, N. J. A., 42
Bower, T., 251
Bower, T. G. R., 42, 104, 110, 144
Bowlby, J., 101, 112
Bowler, D.M., 276
Boyd, R., 301
Boyes-Braem, P., 226, 232
Braten, S., 304
Bratman, M. E., 222
Brazelton, T. B., 6, 13, 23, 112, 139, 142, 150, 157, 160, 168, 190, 191, 192, 258, 282, 286, 287, 292
Breilinger, K., 6, 257
Brentano, F., von, 233
Bretherton, I., 9, 24, 120, 121, 204, 209, 251, 261, 268, 289
Brian, J. A., 47
Brignol, M. M., 46
Brody, L. B., 72
Bronson, W. C., 207
Brooks, J., 110
Brooks, R., 251
Brooks-Gunn. J., 88, 89, 93, 141, 144
Brosch, M., 70
Brown, E., 11
Brown, S., 126
Bruce, V., 248
Bruner, J. S., 9, 76, 82, 101, 102, 110, 112, , 122, 177, 178, 201, 209, 229, 241, 242, 243, 248, 249
Burke, K., 76
Burnham, D. K., 262
Bushnell, I. W. R., 14, 42, 203
Busnel, M. C., 12
Butterworth, G., 11, 92, 177, 209, 241, 243, 244, 245, 246, 248, 251, 252, 289

C

Call, J., 301, 311
Camaioni, L., 9, 24, 209, 261, 268, 289
Campos, J. J., 24, 71, 283, 284, 286, 292
Campos, R. G., 283, 284
Cao, Y., 140, 172, 173, 182
Carey, S., 56, 57, 232, 260, 275

Carlson, V., 264, 265
Caron, A., 170, 174, 175, 251
Caron, R., 170, 174, 175
Carpenter, G. C., 218, 219, 221, 223, 229
Carpenter, M., 24, 26, 58, 262, 269, 303, 304
Carter, A. S., 139
Casasola, M., 232
Chaika, H., 72
Chance, S., 281
Christensen, K. M., 36
Ciarimatero, V., 48
Clark, M. M., 38
Clarkson, M. G., 72
Clifton, R. K., 72, 177
Clohessy, A., 225, 247
Clynes, M., 70
Cochran, E., 243, 244, 248
Cohen, D., 42
Cohen, J. A., 56
Cohen, K., 72
Cohen, L. B., 232, 262, 263
Cohn, J. F., 112-3, 149, 192, 194, 195
Coldren, J. T., 110
Coley, J. D., 232
Collins, K., 275
Collis, G. M., 208, 220
Colombo, J., 110
Connell, D., 113
Cooley, C. H., 84, 111, 308
Cooper, J. R., 46
Cooper, P., 113
Corkum, V., 121, 177, 223, 229, 242, 245, 248, 249, 250, 251, 252
Cortelyou, A., 203
Corter, C., 191, 259, 286
Cottman, C., 43, 44
Courchesne, 126
Coyne, J. C., 150
Cramer, C. P., 37
Crick, F. H., 69
Crook, C. K., 11
Crown, C., 72
Csibra, G., 75, 101, 121, 234, 262
Culver, C., 109, 112, 113
Cummings, E. M., 204
Cunningham, C. C., 52, 58

D

Dailly, R., 11
Damasio, A. R., 69
Darwin, C. B., 7, 82, 90, 93
Dasser, V., 218
Davis, L. B., 36, 46
Dawson, G., 290
DeCasper, A. J., 12, 13, 17, 36, 104
de Haan, M., 46
Delaney, S., 48, 49, 52
Demos, V., 112, 139, 142
Demetriou, A., 289
Dennett, D., 69, 233
D'Entremont, B., 140, 161, 172, 178, 179, 182, 183, 245, 246
Deruelle, C., 45
de Schonen, S., 45
Desroches, J., 269, 270, 271, 274, 275, 276
de Vries, J. L. P., 12
de Waal, F., 6
DeYong, N., 260
Diamond, G. R., 139, 142
Diamond, R., 56
Dicara, L. V., 115
Dilthey, 308
Dittrich, W. H., 25, 217, 218
Dixon, J. C., 141
Dodge, K. A., 282
Dore, J., 70, 73, 119, 120, 138, 144, 148
Downey, G., 150
Driver, J. R., 183, 253
Dubner, R., 50
Dunn, J., 204, 205, 208, 209
Dunham, F., 138, 145, 155, 166, 167, 168, 182
Dunham, P., 138, 145, 155, 166, 167, 168, 182, 302

Duval, S., 88, 91
Dziurawiec, S., 14, 42

E

Easterbrooks, M. A., 138
Eckerman, C. O., 259, 290
Eckhorn, R., 70
Edelman, G. M., 70
Edward, M., 112
Eimas, P. D., 17
Ekman, P., 109
Ellis, H. D., 14, 42, 45
Ellsworth, C., 192
Ellsworth, C. P., 139, 160, 181, 259, 286
Ellsworth, P., 109, 171
Elmore, M., 149
Emde, R. N., 71, 286, 292
Engquist, G., 226, 230
Engel, A.K., 70
Ennis, M., 46, 50
Eppler, M.A., 261
Epstein, A. N., 38

F

Fabre-Grenet, M., 45
Fagen, J. W., 105
Fantz, R. L., 82, 83
Farrar, M. J., 289
Feider, H., 160, 259
Feldman, N. S., 86, 87
Feldstein, S., 72
Ferland, D., 259, 265, 266, 275
Fernald, A., 221, 231
Field, T., 112, 113, 127
Field, T. M., 42, 43, 139, 143, 150, 193
Fifer, W. P., 12, 13, 17
Fillion, T.J., 11, 46
Finnegan, L. P., 48
Fiori-Cowley, A., 113
Fischer, K. W., 93, 289
Fitzgerald, E., 45
Fivaz-Depeursinge, E., 201
Flood, M. F., 283, 290
Fodor, J. A.,
Fogel, A., 139, 142, 168, 287, 290
Fonagy, P., 112, 116, 118
Fox, N. A., 283
Fraiberg, S., 150
Fraisse, P., 72
Freud, S., 88, 101, 102, 109
Friesen, W. V., 109
Frith, U., 126
Frye, D., 267

G

Galanter, E., 227
Galef, B. G., Jr., 37, 38, 39
Gallistel, C. R., 227, 305
Gallup, G. G. Jr., 144
Ganchrow, J. R., 44, 157
Garcia, R., 42
Gazzaniga, M. S., 88, 91
Gianino, A., 283, 290, 292
Gelman, S. A., 232
Gelman, R., 257
Gergely, G., 19, 75, 101, 102, 103, 108, 109, 110, 114, 116, 117, 118, 119, 121, 125, 129, 130, 138, 234, 262, 306, 309
Gernsbacher, M. A., 217
Gesell, A., 141, 288, 289
Gewirtz, J. L., 121
Gholson, B., 110
Gibbs, J., 36,
Gibson, E. J., 261, 302
Gibson, J. J., 67, 170
Gilligan, S. G., 85
Glass, L., 46
Goldberg, S., 155, 157, 171
Goldstein, S., 113, 139, 150
Golinkoff, R., 264, 265
Gomez, J.C., 267
Goodman, G. S., 225
Gopnik, A., 19, 89, 101, 107, 109, 123, 124, 125, 126, 235, 268, 274, 308, 309
Goren, C. C., 11, 14, 42, 43, 44

Gottman, J. M., 112
Gouin-Decarie, T., 245, 259
Granier-Deferre, C., 12
Gravel, R.G., 47
Gray, W. D., 226, 232
Green, J. A., 285
Greenberg, R., 42
Greenfield, P. M., 110
Grover, L., 177, 289
Gusella, J. L., 139, 157, 160, 161, 162, 163, 165, 171, 192
Gustafson, G. E., 285
Guy, L., 113

H

Haft, W., 70, 73, 119, 120, 138, 144, 148
Hainline, L., 58, 251
Hains, S. M. J., 20, 23, 112, 139, 140, 142, 156, 160, 162, 163. 165, 166, 167, 168, 169, 171, 172, 174, 176, 177, 178, 180, 181, 182, 192, 195, 196, 199, 229, 245, 146, 251, 259, 286, 304, 205, 306
Haith, M. M., 52, 58, 174, 225, 229, 251
Halil, T., 13
Hall, W. G., 37, 41, 53
Hamlyn, D. W., 84
Harding, C., 264, 265
Harris, P., 267
Hayes, L. A., 161
Hayne, H., 54
Hazan, C., 225
Healy, B., 113, 150
Hegel, 111
Heiber, L., 37, 39
Heider, F., 25, 87
Henker, B., 83
Hen-Tov, A., 83
Herrera, C., 231
Hespos, S. J., 10, 11
Hesse, E., 116
Higley, J. D.,
Hind, H., 39
Hinde, R., 208
Hirsh-Pasek, K., 228
Hobson, P., 9, 210
Hobson, R. P., 112, 293
Hoebel, B. G., 45
Hofer, L., 70, 73, 119, 120, 138, 144, 148
Hoffman, M. L., 82
Hoffmeyer, L. B., 11, 47
Hogan, J. A., 36, 38
Holmes, W. G., 36, 40, 59
Hood, B. M., 183, 246, 247, 253
Hooper, R., 113
Hopkins, B., 7, 11
Howes, C., 204, 205
Hudelot, 193
Hubley, P., 75, 121
Humphrey, D. E., 180
Humphrey, G. K., 180
Hurshman, A., 155, 166, 167, 168, 182
Husserl, E., 77
Huttenlocker, J., 85
Hyde, T. S., 85

I

Ilg, F. L., 288
Irwin, F. W., 83
Itino, A., 11
Izard, C. E., 109, 112, 113

J

Jacobson, E., 112
Jacobson, K., 6, 257, 260
Jacobson, S. W., 15, 83
Jaffe, J., 72, 112, 150
James, W., 72, 110
Jarrett, N., 241, 244, 246, 250, 251, 252
Jasnow, M., 72
Jenkins, J. J., 85
Jenkins, J. M., 209
Jennings, K. D., 160

Johnson, D., 226, 232
Johnson, M. H., 6, 11, 14, 42, 44, 45, 47, 128, 174, 229, 247, 251
Johnson. S., 275
Jordan, W., 70
Jusczyk, P. W., 17, 228

K

Kagan, J., 7, 83, 110
Kaplan, B., 70
Kaplowitz, C., 141
Kareev, Y., 230
Karmiloff-Smith, A., 111, 123
Kasari, C., 293
Kaye, K., 148, 168, 287
Kaye, K. L., 18, 19, 72, 121
Kaye, S., 112
Keeble, S., 262
Kehoe, P., 45
Keil, F. C., 232
Kelley, H. H.,
Kellman, P. J., 230
Kemler Nelson, D. G., 228
Kendrick, C., 204, 205
Kennedy, L. J., 228
Kernberg, P. F., 112
Kerr, J., 265
Kervella, C., 181, 197, 199
Kienapple, K., 191, 259, 286
King, D., 202, 264
Kingstone, A., 246, 247
Kirker, W. S., 85
Klein, R., 246, 247
Klein, R. E., 174
Kleinke, C. L., 173
Klin, R.P., 160
Klinnert, M. D., 71, 292
Knobe, J., 218
Koch, C., 69
Koenig, P., 70
Kohut, H., 112
Konner, M., 13, 289
Koós, O., 262
Kopp, C., 283
Koslowski, B., 112, 160, 190, 258, 282, 286, 287
Kotovsky, L., 257
Koupernik, C., 11
Krakowski, O., 251
Kreiter, A. K., 70
Kruger, A. C., 241, 301
Kruper, J. C., 113
Kruse, W., 70
Kuhl, P. K., 41
Kuhn, C., 113, 150
Kuiper, N. A., 85
Kurzweil, S. R., 171
Kwon, J. H., 293

L

Labov, W., 76
Lachmann, F. M., 112
LaCross, K.,
Lamb, M. E., 138, 192, 287
Landry, S. H., 293
Lang, R. D., 94
Langer, S. K., 68, 70
Langhorst, B. H., 139, 142
Langton, S., 248
Laskey, R. E., 174
Lavelli, M., 52, 58
Lea, S. T. G., 25, 217, 218
Lecanuet, J. P., 12
Lécuyer, R., 3, 193
LeDoux, J., 91
Lee, L., 207
Leekam, S. R., 126, 209
Lefford, A., 110
Legerstee, M., 160, 191, 259, 260, 286
Lempers, J. D., 229, 245, 252, 253
Lennon, E., 43
Leon, M., 36, 39, 43, 44
Lepage, A., 259, 265, 266, 275, 265, 266
Leslie, A. M., 101, 117, 118, 126, 129, 222, 223, 261, 262, 263, 264, 267
Levenson, R. W., 109

Levine, B., 274, 276
Levine, J., 83,
Lewis, C., 267
Lewis, M., 81, 83, 88, 89, 90, 91, 92, 93, 94, 95, 110, 141, 144, 155, 157, 171, 181, 208, 283
Lewis, T. L., 178
Lewkowicz, D. J., 72
Lieberman, A. F., 138
Lipsitt, L. P., 11
Liu, A., 251
Lloyd, B. B., 231, 232
Lollis, S. P., 286
Lott, I., 43, 44
Loveland, K. A., 293
Lowel, S., 70
Lundquist, L., 283, 290

M

MacDonald, D., 140, 142
MacLean, B. K., 140, 142
MacFarlane, A. J., 11, 36
Macomber, J., 6, 257
Magyar, J., 125, 130
Mahler, M. S., 10, 109, 112
Main, M., 112, 116, 258, 282, 286, 287
Main, W., 160, 190
Makin, J. W., 36
Malatesta, C. Z., 109, 112, 113
Malcuit, G., 160, 259
Malkin, C. M., 192, 287
Malle, B. F., 218
Mandler, J. M., 143, 260, 261, 263, 264
Manilla, J. A., 38
Mann, C., 165, 171
Maratos, O., 11
Marcelli, D., 181, 197, 199
Marian, V., 20, 112, 140, 182, 196
Marino, L., 46
Mark, G. P., 45
Markman, E. M., 232
Markov, Y., 293
Marlin, D. W., 39
Marslen-Wilson, W. D., 217
Martins, T., 39
Mason, J. R., 39
Mathivet, E., 45
Masi, W. S., 171
Massie, H., 191
Matias, R., 113
Maudry, M., 207
Maugeais, R., 12
Maurer, D., 6, 174, 178, 229
Maurer, K., 14
May, B., 36
Mayes, L. C., 139
Mays, K., 72
McArthur, D., 292, 293
McCabe, A., 76
McCabe, V., 67
McClelland, J. L., 217
McClure, M. K., 144
McDevitt, J. B., 112
McDonough, L., 260
McNew, S., 261, 268
Mead, G. H., 84, 111, 112, 308
Mehler, J., 72
Meltzoff, A. N., 11, 15, 16, 19, 54, 75, 89, 101, 107, 109, 121, 123, 124, 125, 126, 138, 141, 170, 203, 218, 219, 221, 222, 235, 259, 260, 267, 268, 307, 308, 309
Mendelsohn, M. J., 229
Mendoza, R., 43, 44
Merleau-Ponty, M., 84
Mervis, C. B., 226, 232
Messer, D. J., 287
Metzger, M.A., 11
Michaelson, L., 92, 110
Michotte, A., 25
Milders, M., 126
Millar, W. S., 104
Miller, G. A., 227
Miller, N. E., 115
Mitchell, D. W., 110, 267
Molina, M., 202, 264

Moore, C., 24, 121, 177, 178, 222, 223, 229, 242, 245, 248, 249, 250, 251, 252, 302, 305, 306, 308, 309
Moore, L., 177
Moore, M., 174, 203, 229, 251
Moore, M. K., 11, 15, 16, 52, 54, 101, 109, 121, 138, 259, 260, 267, 307
Moran, G., 155
Morgan, R., 26, 27, 47, 106, 107, 108, 127, 144, 218, 262
Morissette, P., 245
Morrison, D. C., 192, 287
Morton, J., 6, 11, 14, 42, 45, 47, 128
Moses, L. J., 221, 268, 275, 305
Muir, D. W., 20, 23, 56, 58, 112, 139,140, 142, 156, 157, 160, 161, 162, 163, 169, 171, 172, 174, 176, 177 198, 180, 181, 182, 192, 195, 196 199, 229, 245, 246, 251, 259, 260, 286, 304, 305, 306
Mullin, J. T., 42, 203
Mumme, D. L., 221, 231
Munk, M., 70
Murphy, A., 50
Murray, L., 20, 21, 112, 113, 139, 140, 162, 165, 168, 170, 181, 182, 192, 195, 196, 197, 198, 199, 201, 304
Mustelin, C., 170, 174, 175

N

Nádasdy, Z., 75, 121, 234, 262
Nadel, J., 20, 21, 181, 193, 196, 197, 198, 199, 205, 206, 304, 306
Nagell, K., 24, 221, 223, 229, 303, 304
Needham, A., 257
Neisser, U., 20, 112, 137, 140, 182, 196
Nekula, M.,
Nelson, C. A., 46, 231
Newport, E. L., 228
Newtson, D., 217, 226, 227, 230, 235

O

Oakes, L. M., 262, 263
Oberlander, T. F., 47
Ochs, E., 309
Ogan, T. A., 289
Olson, D. R., 267
Olver, P. R., 110
Ontai, L. L., 220
Ourth, L. L., 103, 104,
Owsley, C. J., 203
Ozonoff, S., 126

P

Pajer, K. A., 139
Pantel, M. S., 47
Papousek, H., 9, 18, 72, 112, 127, 143
Papousek, M., 9, 18, 72, 112, 127, 143
Parrinello, R. M., 292
Pascalis, O., 45, 57
Payne, T., 43, 44
Pecheux, M-G., 37
Pedersen, F. A., 204, 205
Pedersen, P. E., 36, 38
Pelaez-Nogueras, M., 121
Pennington, B. F., 126, 293
Perner, J., 9, 29, 209, 221, 267
Perret, D., 126
Perry, S., 113, 150
Peterson, C., 76
Pezéé, A., 181, 197, 199
Phillips, A. T., 155, 157, 190, 231, 234, 263
Phillips, W., 221
Piaget, J., 10, 84, 85, 127, 139, 222, 282, 310, 311
Pickens, J., 113
Pine, F., 10, 109, 112

Pinto, J., 227
Pipp-Siegel, S., 286
Piwoz, J., 228
Poli, M., 52, 58
Polyani, M., 84
Pomerleau, A., 160, 259
Pontefract, A., 246, 247
Porter, R. H., 36
Posner, M. I., 225, 247
Poulin-Dubois, D., 190, 222, 259, 261, 265, 266, 269, 271, 274, 275, 276, 306
Prechtl, H. F. R., 12, 13,
Premack A. J., 266
Premack, D., 190, 200, 217, 218, 222, 262, 266
Prescott, P. A., 104
Preti, G., 39
Pribram, K. H., 92, 227

Q

Quek, V., 47
Querido, 21

R

Rach-Longman, K., 161, 162
Rada, P. V., 45
Rader, N., 302
Radke-Yarrow, M., 204
Ramey, C. T., 103, 104
Rao, M., 46, 51
Ratner, H. H., 241, 301
Rebelsky, F., 13
Reddy, V., 221, 222, 285
Reitboeck, H. J., 70
Ren, K., 50
Reserbat-Plantey, D., 181, 197, 199
Repacholi, B. M., 268, 274
Rheingold, H. L., 39, 259
Ricard, M., 245, 259
Richerson, P., 301
Ricks, M., 112
Rindner, R.,
Ringland, J. T., 112
Roberts, J., 170, 174, 175
Rochat, P., 10, 11, 12, 16, 20, 21, 23, 25, 26, 27, 28, 56, 58, 106, 107, 108, 112, 127, 137, 140, 144, 182, 196, 197, 218, 260, 262, 304, 306, 309
Roe, K. V., 171
Rogers, S. J., 126, 293
Rogers, T. B., 85
Roman, J., 162
Ronnqvist, L., 259
Rosenblum, L. A., 208
Rosch, E., 226, 231, 232
Ross, H. S., 286
Ross, G. S., 260
Roth, R. H., 46
Rothbart, M. K., 225, 247, 286, 287
Rotter, J., 39
Rovee-Collier, C., 54, 104, 105, 110
Rovee, D. T., 104, 105
Rubenstein, J. L., 204, 205
Ruff, H. A., 286, 287, 292
Ruffman, T., 209
Russell, C. L., 292, 293, 305
Russell, J., 126
Rutter, M., 221

S

Sai, F., 42, 204
Saffran, J. R., 228
Salapatek, P., 14
Samuels, C., 11
Samuels, C. A., 174
Samuelson, L., 220
Sander, L. W., 112, 282
Sapp, F., 16, 17, 18, 171, 182
Sarty, M., 11, 14, 42
Scafidi, F., 139
Scaife, M., 177, 178, 201, 209, 241, 242, 243, 248, 249
Schaal, B., 36, 44
Schaffer, R., 155, 208
Schanberg, S., 113, 150
Scheffelin, B., 309
Schellenberg, E. G., 74

Schillen, T. B., 70
Schmuckler, M. A., 107, 108, 127
Schneider, W., 111
Schulman, A., 141
Schult, C. A., 217, 218
Sclafani, A., 59
Scott, K. G., 171
Searle, J. R., 216, 222
Sexton, M. E., 264, 265
Shah, A., 48
Shantz, C. U., 82, 84
Sharon, T., 229
Shatz, M., 204
Shepard, B., 109, 112, 113
Sherrod, L. R., 171
Sherry, D. F., 38
Shide, D. J., 36, 40, 45
Shiffrin, R. M., 111
Shinn, M. W., 287
Shipley, M. T., 50
Short, K. R., 230
Shultz, T. R., 222, 261, 265, 266
Sigafoos, A.D., 15
Sigman, M., 293
Simmel, S., 25
Singer, W., 70
Skinner, B. F., 101
Slater, A., 11, 261
Slaughter, V., 275
Smith, B. A., 46, 47
Smith, C. B., 287
Smith, G. P., 36
Smith, L., 220
Smith, L. B., 290, 291
Smith, S. E., 45
Snidman, N., 7
Sorce, J. E., 71, 292
Sorrentino, C. M., 260
Spelke, E. S., 3, 6, 37, 155, 157, 190, 202, 203, 230, 231, 234, 257, 263, 264
Spence, M. J., 12, 36, 72
Spitz, R., A., 4, 13, 282
Sroufe, L. A., 112
Stack, D. M., 56, 160
Stenberg, C. R., 286
Stern, D. N., 6, 19, 22, 68, 70, 71, 72, 73, 76, 101, 102, 109, 112, 119, 120, 121, 122, 123, 138, 144, 148, 149, 150, 157, 191, 282, 283, 284, 285, 287, 305, 307
Sternberg, C., 24
Steiner, J. E., 7, 44, 157
Stevens, E., 166, 167, 168, 171, 182
St. James-Roberts, I., 13
Stoller, S. A., 139
Streri, A., 37
Striano, T., 16, 21, 23, 25, 28, 56, 58, 182, 196, 197, 262, 304, 306, 309
Strosberg, R., 268
Sullivan, M. W., 83, 181
Sullivan, R. M. 43, 44
Suomi, S. J., 171
Svejda, M., 71, 292
Swain, I. U., 72
Symons, D., 155
Symons, L., 176, 177
Symons, L. A., 156, 163

T

Taborsky-Barbar, S., 43, 44
Tagiuri, R., 82, 86
Talmy, L., 221
Target, M., 112, 116, 118
Teicher, M. H., 38
Tesman, R. J., 109, 112, 113
Thelen, E., 290, 291
Thommen, E., 276
Thompson, P., 161
Thompson, R. A., 283, 287, 290
Tilden, J., 269, 270, 271, 274, 275, 276
Tomasello, M., 24, 204, 206, 219, 220, 221, 222, 223, 229, 241, 261, 268, 269, 289, 301, 302, 303, 304, 311
Tomkins, S. S., 70

Tremblay-Leveau, H., 20, 21, 205, 206, 304, 306
Trevarthen, C., 19, 20, 21, 24, 75, 101, 112, 121, 138, 139, 140, 157, 162, 165, 168, 169, 170, 181, 191, 192, 195, 196, 197, 198, 199, 201, 222, 258, 285, 286, 289, 304
Tronick, E. Z., 23, 56, 73, 112, 113, 139, 142, 150, 157, 160, 161, 163, 165, 168, 191, 192,194, 195, 282, 283, 286, 287, 290, 292
Tulving, E., 82, 92
Tyler, L. K., 217

U

Ulbaek, I., 218
Umbel, V., 113
Urwin, C., 150
Uzgiris, I. C., 113

V

van der Veer, R., 282
van Palthe, W., 7,
Vasek, M. E., 113
Vasen, A., 83
Vecera, S. P., 174, 229, 247, 252
Veres, C., 218
Vico, 308
Vietze, P. M., 161, 287
Visser, G. H. A., 12
Volterra, V., 9, 24, 209, 261, 289
von Bartalanffy, L., 92
von der Schulenburg, C., 11
von Hofsten, C., 259
Voyat, G., 282
Vygotsky, L. S., 282, 290

W

Walden, T. A., 289
Wallon, H., 10, 282
Walker, A. S., 203
Walker-Andrews, A. S., 43, 172
Walters, A.S., 287
Walton, G. E., 42, 104
Watson, J. B., 102
Watson, J. S., 19, 89, 92, 102, 103, 104, 106, 107, 108, 109, 110, 114, 116, 11, 12, 13, 14, 15, 16, 17, 18, 119, 121, 124, 126, 127, 128, 129, 130, 138, 139, 143, 144, 145, 146, 148, 161, 180, 306, 309
Weinberg, K. M., 73, 286, 292
Weiskrantz, L., 90, 91
Weller, A., 36
Wellman, H. M., 218, 221, 267, 268, 273, 275
Werner, H., 70, 290
Whitehead, M. C., 40
Wicklund, R. A., 88, 91
Willatts, P., 3
Willen, J. D., 183, 253
Williams, C. L., 36
Wilson, C. D., 83
Winnicott, D. W., 112
Wise, S., 23, 112, 139, 142, 157, 191, 292
Wolf, K. M., 282
Wolff, P. H., 7, 13, 52, 58, 157, 173, 176, 177, 184, 282, 283, 291
Woo, C. C., 36
Woodward, A. L., 155, 158, 190, 228, 230, 231, 234, 263
Wright, J.H., 47
Wu, P. Y. K., 11, 14, 42
Wylie, R. C., 88
Wynn, K. 228, 229

X

Xu, F., 260

Y

Yega-Lahr, N., 139
Yirmiya, N., 293
Young, A. W.,

Young, S. N., 47
Youniss, J., 82, 84

Z

Zahn-Waxler, C., 204
Zazzo, R., 259
Zeedyk, M. S., 267
Zeifman, D., 48, 49, 52
Zelazo, P. R., 72
Zhou, Q., 50
Zimmerman, E. A., 113, 150
Zimmerman, S. I., 39

Subject Index

Symbols and acronyms
2-month revolution, 4, 12, 14
9-month revolution, 4, 24, 302
ABA design, 161
EDD eye direction detector, 155, 208
ID intentionality detector, 155, 208, 266
SAM shared attention mechanism, 155, 178, 209
ToMM theory of mind mechanism, 155

A

ABA design, 161
"aboutness", 233
account, constructivist, 223
acquisition of language, 85, 307
action
    analysis, 215, 222, 224
    concept, 231–232, 233
    concept formation, 232
    goal-directed, 258, 283
    -intention relation, 216
    intentional, 219, 310
    intentions-in-, 222
    parsing, 224
    -parsing hypothesis, 228
    processing, 216
    self-, 139, 145–146
    stream, 225, 227
    stream of, 232
    understanding intentional, 304
    unit, 230
adult
    contingency, 155
    eye contact, 173
    intentionality, 155, 158, 183
    parsing, 226
    social signal, 183
    TV-contingent, 170
affect, 71
    attunement, 119–120, 122, 307
    categorical, 109
    mirroring, 109, 113–118, 130
    positive, 149
    regulation, 284
affect-reflective mirroring, 111–113
affective
    aspects of joint attention, 281
    attunement, 285
    configuration, 73
    display, 158
    expression, 283
agent
    people as mental, 267
    people as purposive, 261
    self as self-regulating, 114
agency, 190
    concept, 265
    of others', 201, 207
    perception of, 201
    self-, 17
alert-awake state, 13
analysis,
    action, 215, 222, 224

constructivist, 223
contingency, 108
intention, 216
animacy, 204
appraisal, cognitive, 283
arousal
physiological, 283
to perfect contingency, 139
array, dynamic stimulus, 226
associative learning, 157
attachment, 148
security of, 113
attention
affective aspects of joint, 281
directing, 303
dyadic, 205
endogenous control of, 254
exogenous control of, 248
following, 303
joint, 156, 177, 207, 209, 281, 284–285, 289–293, 302
joint, affective aspects of, 281
mechanism, shared (SAM), 155, 178, 209
modulation, 283
shared, 209, 284
state of, 210
visual, 162
attentional skill, joint, 303
attunement
affect, 119–120, 122, 307
affective, 285
audition pattern, 37
auditory
feature, 43
-visual stimulation, 160
autism, 10, 126–130, 193
averted gaze, 174
avoidant behavior, 199
awake, state alert-, 13
awareness
emotional self-, 108
objective self-, 91–93
of others' agency, 207
of self, 207
self-, 90–93, 108
subjective self-, 91–93

B

back-and-forth contingency, 143
behavior
avoidant, 199
conversational, 202
goal-directed, 190
instrumental, 75
movement-testing, 141
noncontingent, 143
prosocial, 10
self-, 141
self-referential, 95
socially-directed, 205
behavioral contingency, 155
belief, 4
false, 267
task, false-, 29
belief-desire psychology, 267, 275–276
biofeedback
model, social, 101–102, 108, 114
social, 114
theory, social, 119, 124
training procedure, 115
biomechanical motion, 275
blind infant, 150
blindness, 150
blind-sighted, 91
bodily self, 108
body movement, 158
break points, 226–227, 229

C

calming
effect, 58
system, 46
categorical affect, 109

categorical emotion, 113
categorization
early, 260
skill, early, 260
causality
concept of, 289
social, 25–27
caused motion, 275
circular reaction
primary, 127
secondary, 139
classical conditioning, 43–44
coconstruction, 19
cognition
development levels of social, 94–95
nonsocial, 82
social, 81–82, 84–85, 87, 94–96, 301
cognitive
appraisal, 283
mastery, 138
module, social-, 304
scaffolding, 122
skills, social, 301
communication
intentional, 74, 261
communicative intention, 219
comparative perspective, 312
competency, triadic, 30
concept
action, 231–232, 233
agency, 265
formation, action, 232
of causality, 289
conditioning, 101
classical, 43–44
olfactory, 46
tactile, 46
conjugate reinforcement, 105
constructivist
account, 223
analysis, 223
contact
adult eye, 173
eye, 21, 155–156, 173, 176
eye-to-eye, 52, 57–58
physical, 274
contemplative stance, 4, 12, 16, 23, 29–30
contingency, 139, 162, 165, 168, 258
adult, 155
analysis, 108
arousal to perfect, 139
back-and-forth, 143
behavioral, 155
detection, 109, 114, 116, 126–127
detection module, 102, 107
imperfect, 137 138, 144, 148
imperfect social, 138, 144
learning, 306
levels, familiar, 149
maximizing, 116
one-way, 143
perception, 101–102
perfect 139, 143–145
relation 103, 117–118
sensory relational, 104–105
simultaneous, 143
social, 140–141
spatial, 107
task
nonsocial, 145
perfect, 145
temporal, 103–104, 107
contingent
adult, TV-, 170
imitative display, imperfectly, 125
responsiveness, 146, 148
stimulation, TV-, 170
control
endogenous, 247
exogenous, 247
of attention, endogenous, 254
of attention, exogenous, 248

conversational behavior, 202
coordination, hand-mouth, 10
coping strategy, 138
cross-cultural perspective, 312
crying, 13, 47, 49–51, 168, 199
cue
  exteroceptive, 110
  proprioceptive, 110
cultural
  learning, 241, 307
  perspective, cross-, 312

D

deception, self-, 88
declarative pointing, 267–268
deferred imitation, 75
depressed mother, 150, 193
depression, 150
design, ABA, 161
desire, 276
  simple, 273
desire psychology
  belief-, 267, 275–276
  knowledge-, 275–276
detection
  contingency, 109, 114, 116, 126–127
  module, contingency, 102, 107
  self-, 108
detector
  eye direction (EDD), 155, 208
  intentionality (ID), 155, 208, 266
development
  language, 220
  levels of social cognition, 94–95
differentiation of self-other, 90, 94
direct perception, 217
directed
  action, goal-, 258, 283
  behavior, socially-, 205
directedness, goal-, 263
directing, attention, 303
direction
  eye, 155, 173, 183–184, 242, 251, 253
  gaze, 207, 229
  head, 253
direction detector, eye (EDD), 155, 208
directionality, 74–75
discrepant labeling, 219
discrimination
  face, 47
  social, 83
discriminative measure, smiling as a, 192
display
  affective, 158
  emotional, 197
  imperfectly contingent imitative, 125
dispositional world (private world), 5
distinction, people-inanimate object, 260
double video TV paradigm, 195
duration
  gaze, 159, 164
  smile, 159, 164
dyadic
  attention, 205
  interaction, 173
  intrusion, 205
  paradigm, 189–191
  situation, 208
dynamic
  stimulus array, 226
  systems theory, 290
dynamics, emotion, 284

E

early
  categorization, 260
  skill, 260

development of intersubjectivity, 9
ecological mechanism, 246
effect
calming, 58
still-face, 157, 195
efficacy, self-, 145–146, 149–151
egocentrism, 84
emotion, 7–8, 14, 24, 204
categorical, 113
dynamic, 284
facial expression, 109
regulation, 281–282, 284, 289
emotional
display, 197
expression, 274, 286
impulsivity, 129
responsiveness, 138
self-awareness, 108
state, 82
stimulus, facial 83, 109
empathy, 10
endogenous control, 247
of attention, 254
engagement
joint, 303
person, 286
rhythm of, 181
envelope, proto-narrative, 76
exclusion paradigm, 204
execution, structure-in-, 227
executive function problem, 128
exogenous control, 247
of attention, 248
expectancy
model, 170
ontological, 209
social, 171
theory, social, 157
violation of, 157
expectation, 171
social, 18
violation of, 3
experience
"like me", 123
shared (primary intersubjectivity), 4–6, 9, 18, 20, 24
exploration
object, 288
visual, 274
expression
affective, 283
emotional, 274, 286
facial, 71, 161, 207, 209
facial emotion, 109
exteroception, 308
exteroceptive cue, 110
eye
contact, 21, 155–156, 173, 176
direction, 155, 173, 183–184, 242, 251, 253
direction detector (EDD), 155, 208
movement, 246
turning, 178
eye-to-eye contact, 52, 57–58

F

face, 6, 11–12, 14, 18, 42
discrimination, 47
effect, still-, 157, 195
familiarity, 55, 58–59
identification, 53
influences, 44
inverted, 161
processing, 45
-processing regions, 58
recognition, 35–36, 42, 47, 54–57, 59
recognition systems, 60
scanning, 44
schema, 83
still-, 23, 58, 112, 139, 162
effect, 157, 195
stimulus, 85

facelike stimulus, 83
face-to-face
interaction, 25, 241, 251
situation, 197
facial
emotional
expression, 109
stimulus, 83, 109
expression, 71, 161, 207, 209
familiarity, 55, 58
imitation, 259
orienting, 150
false-belief 267
task, 29
familiar contingency levels, 149
featural knowledge, 87
feature
auditory, 43
olfactory, 43
tactile, 43
visual, 43
feeling, 6–9, 14, 24, 67–68, 71, 75, 204
feeling flow pattern, 68–69, 73
See also: vitality contour
fetus, 36
flow
of feelings, 68, 75
of movement, 227
pattern, 78
pattern, feeling, 68–69, 73
pattern, stimulus, 69, 78
temporal, 75
See: vitality contour
folk psychology, 222
following
attention, 303
gaze, 241–244, 248, 251, 303
point, 303
formation, action concept, 232
frown, 197
frowning, 181, 198
fructose, 47
function problem, executive, 128
functionalist position, 283
fussiness, 196

G

game, turn taking, 286
gaze, 48, 149, 174, 181, 194
averted, 174
direction, 207, 229
duration, 159, 164
following, 241–244, 248, 251, 303
initiation, 207
reorientation, 248
to mother, 198
gazing, 168
gesture, 71, 194
imperative, 303
stereotyped, 194
glucose, 47
goal-directed
action, 258, 283
behavior, 190
goal-directedness, 263
grimace, 197
grimacing, 168

H

habituation, 3, 27, 189
handicaps, sensory, 150
hand-mouth coordination, 10
head
direction, 253
orientation, 254
turn, 178
turning, 178, 245, 254
heart rate, 49–50
human fetus, 36
hypothesis
action-parsing, 228
"like me", 123–125
rule-violation, 192–193, 195

I

idea of me, 82, 89–92, 94

identification
  maternal, 43
  person, 204
image, self-, 141–142
imitation, 10, 15, 83, 121,125, 138, 218, 303, 307
  deferred, 75
  facial, 259
  imperfectly contingent display, 125
  neonatal, 308
imperative gesture, 303
imperfect contingency, 137–138, 144, 148
imperfect social contingency, 137–138, 144
imperfectly contingent imitative display, 125
impulsivity, emotional, 129
inanimate, object distinction, people-, 260
infant
  blind, 150
  face processing, 45
  interaction, stranger-, 168
  parsing, 228
inference, intentional, 215, 217, 220, 224
initiation, gaze, 207
initiative, social, 205
innate mechanism, 101
instrumental
  behavior, 75
  pointing, 267
intention, 4, 276
  analysis, 216
  communicative, 219
  referential, 220
  relation, action-, 216
  -relevant structure, 227
intentional
  action, 219, 310
  action, understanding, 304
  analysis, 216
  break points, 229
  communication, 74, 261
  contemplative, 29
  detector, 208
  inference, 215, 217, 220, 224
  monitoring of others, 201
  orientation, 251
  skill, 218
  stance, 5, 18, 24–25, 27–29
  status, 219
  understanding, 215, 218–219, 221–222
  vitality contour, 75, 78
intentionality, 68, 75, 122, 155, 158, 183, 190, 289
  adult, 155, 158, 183
  detector, 155, 208, 266
  interpersonal, 189
  of others, 254
intentionality detector (ID), 155, 208, 266
intentions-in-action, 222
interaction
  dyadic, 173
  face-to-face, 25, 241, 251
  mirroring, 108
  procedure, TV 162
  stranger-infant, 168
  system, person-person-person, 209
  triadic, 183, 190
  TV, 164
interest
  joint, 306
  object, 286
interpersonal intentionality, 189
interruption paradigm, 201
intersubjectivity, 4–10, 18–20, 24, 29
  early development of, 9
  primary (shared experience), 4–6, 9, 18, 20, 24
  secondary, 24, 75
intrusion
  dyadic, 205

triadic, 205
inverted face, 161

J

joint
attention, 156, 177, 207, 209, 281, 284–285, 289–293, 302
attention affective aspects of, 281
attentional skill, 303
engagement, 303
interest, 306

K

knowledge
-desire psychology, 275–276
duality of, 86
featural, 87
self-, 82, 137
social, 86

L

labeling, discrepant, 219
lack of
pretense, 129
social responsivity, 128
social understanding, 128
language
ability, 96
acquisition, 85, 307
development, 220
learning, 218, 220, 232
learning
associative, 157
contingency, 306
cultural, 241, 307
language, 218, 220, 232
operant, 17
prepared, 305
levels
familiar contingency, 149
of social cognition, development, 94–95
"like me"
experience, 123
hypothesis, 123–125
stance, 5, 19
looking
preferential, 3, 27
procedure, preferential, 173
task, preferential, 172, 174

M

machinery of the self, 91–93, 95
mapping, word-object, 220
mastery, cognitive, 138
maternal
identification, 43
preference, 43
recognition, 41
maximizing, contingency, 116
me, idea of, 82, 89–92, 94
means-end understanding, 223
mechanism
ecological, 246
innate, 101
shared attention (SAM), 155, 178, 209
theory of mind (ToMM), 155
memory, 169
mental agent, people as, 267
mental state, 82, 89, 92–96, 156, 210, 257
in others, 209
mimicking, neonatal, 307
mind mechanism, theory of (ToMM), 155
mind
mechanism (ToMM), theory of, 155
task, theory of, 276
theory of, 9, 29–30, 267
mindblindness 9
mindreading system, 208
mirroring, 20, 138

affect, 109, 113–114, 116, 130
affect-reflective, 111–113
interactions, 108
social, 309
model
expectancy, 170
social-biofeedback, 101–102, 108
modulation, attention, 283
module, 223
contingency detection, 102, 107
social-cognitive, 304
monitoring of others, intentional, 201
mother
depressed, 150, 193
gaze to, 198
smiling to, 198
motherese, 21, 137, 140
motion
biomechanical, 275
caused, 275
random, 275
uncaused, 275
motivated vitality contour, 76, 78
movement
body, 158
eye, 246
flow of, 227
movement-testing behavior, 141

N

naive psychology, 257, 274
narrative, 69
proto- narrative envelope, 76
vitality contour, 78
nativism, 304
starting state, 308
neonatal
imitation, 308
mimicking, 307
newborn
face discrimination, 47
stage, 10
nine-month revolution, 4, 24, 302
noncontingency, 142
noncontingent
behavior, 143
social stimulation, 168
stimulation, 155
stimulation, TV- 170
nonface stimulus, 85
nonsocial cognition, 82
nonsocial contingency task, 145
nursing, 59

O

object
distinction, people-inanimate, 260
exploration, 288
interest, 286
self-propelled,190
objective self-awareness, 91–93
oculomotor system, 247
olfactory, 39, 43
conditioning, 46
features, 43
preference, 45
one-way contingency, 143
ontological expectancy, 209
operant learning, 17
opioid release, 45, 51
orientation
head, 254
intentional, 251
orienting
facial, 150
visual, 247
others'
agency, 201, 207
purposiveness, 225
others
differentiation of self-, 90, 94
intentionality of, 254
mental states in, 209

P

pain, 47
paradigm
  double video TV, 195
  dyadic, 189–191
  exclusion, 204
  interruption, 201
  still-face, 189, 191
  triadic, 189, 201, 210
parsing, 231
  action, 224
  adult, 226
  hypothesis, action-, 228
  infant, 228
pattern
  audition, 37
  feeling flow, 68–69, 73
  flow, 78
  stimulus flow, 69
  tactile, 36
  U-shaped, 193
  vision, 37
patterned flow, 78
people as mental agents, 267
people as purposive agents, 261
people-inanimate objects distinction, 260
perception
  contingency, 101–102
  direct, 217
  of agency, 201
  person, 86
perfect contingency, 139, 143–145
  arousal to, 139
perfect contingency task, 145
peripheral vision, 244
period, still-face, 158
person
  engagement, 286
  identification, 204
  -object-person system, 209
  perception, 86
  -person-person interactive
    system, 209
perspective
  comparative, 312
  cross-cultural, 312
physical
  contact, 274
  reasoning, 257
physiological arousal, 283
play, triadic, 201
point following, 303
pointing, 209
  declarative, 267–268
  instrumental, 267
position
  functionalist, 283
  social, 206
positive affect, 149
preference
  maternal, 43
  olfactory, 45
  social, 83
preferential looking, 3, 27
preferential looking task, 172, 174
preferential looking procedure, 173
prepared learning, 305
pretense, lack of, 129
primary circular reaction, 127
primary intersubjectivity (shared experience), 4–6, 9, 18, 20, 24
private experience, 7
private world (dispositional world), 5
problem, executive function, 128
procedure
  biofeedback training, 115
  preferential looking, 173
  still-face, 112, 192–193
  TV interaction, 162
processing
  action, 216
  infant face, 45
  regions, face-, 58
proprioception, 308
proprioceptive cues, 110

prosocial behaviors, 10
protention, 77
proto-narrative envelope, 76
psychoanalytic tradition, 282
psychology
  belief-desire, 267, 275–276
  knowledge-desire, 275–276
  folk, 222
  naive, 257, 274
purposive agents, people as, 261
purposiveness, others', 225

R

random motion, 275
reaction
  primary circular, 127
  secondary circular, 139
reasoning, physical, 257
reciprocal turn-taking, 142
reciprocity, 258
recognition
  face, 35–36, 42, 47, 54–57, 59
  maternal, 41
  self-, 94, 141, 144
  system, face, 60
  visual self-, 141
redescription, representational, 123
referencing, social, 286
referential
  intention, 220
  triangle, 302
reflective mirroring, affect-, 111–113
regions, face-processing, 58
regulating agent, self as self-, 114
regulation
  affect, 284
  emotion, 281–282, 284, 289
reinforcement
  conjugate, 105
  social, 173
relatedness, sense of, 205
relation
  action-intention, 216
  contingency, 103, 117–118
  sensory, 104
relational
  contingency, sensory, 105
  information, sensory, 105
release, opioid, 45, 51
releaser, social, 170
relevant structure, intention-, 227
reorientation, gaze, 248
representation, dyadic, 209
representational redescription, 123
responding, tactile, 148
responses
  rooting, 10
  tactile, 150
  vocal, 150
responsiveness
  contingent, 146, 148
  emotional, 138
  tactile, 148
responsivity, lack of social, 128
revolution
  nine-month, 4, 24, 302
  two-month, 4, 12, 14
rhythm, 73
  of engagement, 181
rooting, 11
  responses, 10
rule-violation hypothesis, 192–193, 195
rules, social, 204

S

safety, 31
scaffolding, 157
  cognitive, 122
scanning, 44
  face, 44
schema, 83
  face, 83
secondary
  circular reaction, 139
  intersubjectivity, 24, 75

security of attachment, 113
self, 18, 81–82, 84, 86–87, 89, 90–92, 94, 108, 114
  as self-regulating agent, 114
  bodily, 108
  machinery of the, 91–93, 95
  principles of the, 92–93
self-
  action, 139, 145–146
  agency, 17
  awareness, 90–93, 108
  emotional, 108
  objective, 91–93
  of, 207
  subjective, 91–93
  behavior, 141
  bodily, 108
  deception, 88
  detection, 108
  efficacy, 145–146, 149–151
  knowledge, 86, 137
  image, 141–142
  movement, 141
  other, differentiation of, 90, 94
  propelled object, 190
  recognition, 94, 141, 144
  visual, 141
  referential behavior, 95
  regulating agent, self as, 114
  state, 110, 117
  stimulation, 10, 12
  system, 92
sense of relatedness, 205
sensory handicaps, 150
sensory relation, 104
sensory relational
  contingency, 104–105
  information, 105
shared
  attention, 209, 284
  attention mechanism (SAM), 155, 178, 209
  empathetic feelings, 6
  experience (primary intersubjectivity), 4–6, 9, 18, 20, 24
  meaning, 95
signals, adult social, 183
simple desire, 273
simulation, 307
simultaneous contingency, 143
situation
  dyadic, 208
  face-to-face, 197
skills
  early categorization, 260
  intentional, 218
  join attentional, 303
  social-cognitive, 301
  triadic social, 302
smile, 12, 29, 146, 194, 197, 286
  duration, 159, 164
smiling, 19, 55, 148, 158, 160–162, 168, 170, 181, 259
  as a discriminative measure, 192
  social, 107, 157
  to mother, 198
social
  biofeedback, 101–130, 101, 114
  biofeedback model, 102, 108
  biofeedback theory, 119, 124
  causality, 26–27
  cognition, 81–82, 84–5, 87–88, 93–96, 301
  development levels of, 94–95
  -cognitive module, 304
  -cognitive skills, 301
  contingency, 140–141
  arousal to perfect, 139
  imperfect, 137–138, 144
  discrimination, 83
  expectancy, 171
  expectancy theory, 157
  expectation, 18
  initiatives, 205

knowledge, 86
mirroring, 309
position, 206
preference, 83
referencing, 286
reinforcement, 173
releaser, 170
responsivity, lack of, 128
rules, 204
signals, adult, 183
skills, triadic, 302
smiling, 107, 157
stimulation, noncontingent, 168
understanding, lack of, 128
socially-directed behavior, 205
spatial contingency, 107
stage, newborn, 10
stance
contemplative, 4, 12, 16, 23, 29–30
intentional, 5, 18, 24–25, 27–29
"like me", 5, 19
starting state nativism, 308
state
alert-awake, 13
emotional, 82
mental, 82, 89, 92–96, 156, 210, 257
mental, in others 209
of attention, 210
self-, 110, 117
starting state nativism, 308
status, intentional, 219
stereotyped
gesture, 194
vocalization, 194
stereotypy, 127, 193
still-face, 23, 58, 112, 139, 162
effect, 157, 195
paradigm 189, 191
period, 158
procedure, 112, 192–193
stimulus
array, dynamic, 226
external, 109
face, 85
facelike, 83
facial emotional, 83, 109
flow pattern, 69, 78
internal, 109
nonface, 85
stimulation
auditory-visual, 160
noncontingent, 155
noncontingent social, 168
olfactory, 36
self-, 10, 12
tactile,,36
TV-contingent, 170
TV-noncontingent, 170
stranger-infant interaction, 168
strategy, coping, 138
stream
action, 225, 227
of action, 232
structure
-in-execution, 227
intention relevant, 227
subjective self-awareness, 91–93
sucking, 11–13, 16–17, 44
suckling, 44, 46, 56
sucrose, 47–51, 55, 58–59
surprise, 181
system,
calming, 46
face recognition, 60
gustatory, 50
mindreading, 208
oculomotor, 247
person-object-person, 209
person-person-person interactive, 209
self-, 92
systems theory, dynamic, 290

T

tactile
conditioning, 46
features, 43
pattern, 36
responses, 150
responsiveness, 148
stimulation, 36
task
false-belief, 29
nonsocial contingency, 145
perfect contingency, 145
preferential looking, 172, 174
theory of mind, 276
temporal
contingency, 103–104, 107
flow, 75
testing, behavior movement-, 141
theory
dynamic systems, 290
of mind, 9, 29–30, 267
mechanism, 155
module, 101
task, 276
social biofeedback, 119, 124
social expectancy, 157
touch, 56, 137, 160
tradition, psychoanalytic, 282
training procedure, biofeedback, 115
triadic
competency, 30
interaction, 183, 190
intrusion, 205
paradigm, 189, 201, 210
play, 201
representation, 209
social skills, 302
triangle, referential, 302
turn
head,, 178
taking game, 286
taking vocal, 145
turning, head, 178, 245, 254
TV
-contingent adult, 170
-contingent stimulation, 170
interaction, 164
procedure, 162
-noncontingent, 170
-noncontingent stimulation, 170
paradigm, double video, 195
two-month revolution, 4, 12, 14

U

U-shape pattern, 193
uncaused motion, 275
understanding
intentional, 215, 218–219, 221–222
intentional action, 304
lack of social, 128
means-ends, 223
unit, action, 230

V

violation, hypothesis, rule-, 192–193, 195
violation of expectancy, 157
violation of expectation, 3
vision
pattern, 37
peripheral, 244
visual
attention, 162
exploration, 274
feature, 43
orienting, 247
self-recognition, 141
stimulation, auditory-, 160
vitality contour, 67–78, 305
intentional, 75, 78
motivated, 76, 78
narrative, 78
vocal

response, 150
turn taking, 145
vocalization, 103, 146, 158, 174
stereotyped, 194
vocalizing, 168

W

weaning, 37
word-object mapping, 220
world, dispositional or private, 5